T0355822

Get the eBook FREE!

(PDF, ePub, Kindle, and liveBook all included)

We believe that once you buy a book from us, you should be able to read it in any format we have available. To get electronic versions of this book at no additional cost to you, purchase and then register this book at the Manning website.

Go to https://www.manning.com/freebook and follow the instructions to complete your pBook registration.

That's it!
Thanks from Manning!

Writing for Developers

Writing for Developers

BLOGS THAT GET READ

PIOTR SARNA
CYNTHIA DUNLOP

FOREWORD BY BRYAN CANTRILL
AFTERWORD BY SCOTT HANSELMAN

MANNING
SHELTER ISLAND

Manning Publications Co.
20 Baldwin Road
PO Box 761
Shelter Island, NY 11964

Development editor:	Doug Rudder
Technical editor:	Eric Lippert
Review editor:	Radmila Ercegovac
Production editor:	Keri Hales
Copy editor:	Lana Todorovic-Arndt
Proofreader:	Olga Milanko
Typesetter:	Tamara Švelić Sabljić
Cover designer:	Marija Tudor

ISBN 9781633436282
Printed in the United States of America

To Wiktoria, Aurelia, and...
—Piotr

To David
—Cynthia

brief contents

contents

11 The "Lessons Learned" pattern 196

12 The "Thoughts on Trends" pattern 207

foreword

"You're not writing enough."

It was May 31, 2008, and I was at UC Berkeley, listening to Pat Helland eulogize database pioneer Jim Gray. (Fittingly, I wrote about attending the tribute: https://mng .bz/Dpln.) Over a year earlier, Gray had been tragically lost at sea and was presumed deceased; the computer science community had now gathered to pay tribute to him, and to the influence he had had on the domain and its practitioners.

I had known Gray only by his works, but with each passing speaker, the throughlines of his life emerged: not merely of an exceptional thinker and extraordinary researcher, but of an engaged mentor; a connector; a bridge. Of the recollections, it was Helland relaying being admonished by Gray that I found particularly resonant:

> *He always said, "write, write, write." He looked at me and said, "Pat, you're not writing enough." For twenty years, he told me "You're not writing enough." And he was right—and I still tell myself "You're not writing enough."*
>
> —Pat Helland, Tribute to Honor Jim Gray, May 31, 2008
> (https://mng.bz/NBvN)

Hearing Helland give voice to Gray's words was a revelation for me: while I had always viewed writing as personally important, Gray pointed me to its larger purpose of serving our collective craft. To write is not just to polish and sharpen our own thinking, but also to collaborate with our fellow practitioners and to bridge to future generations—to share our findings and perspectives so others can benefit from our experience and wisdom, just like we have learned from others. In short, while it is our work that gives us meaning, it is our writing that allows us to connect that meaning in an enduring way to our broader community of practitioners.

So, we can tell ourselves Gray's admonition—that we're all not writing enough—but where do we start? Writing begins with reading: if we are all not writing enough, we are also certainly not reading enough. If one is to read with an eye toward writing, you have an apt book in your (perhaps virtual!) hands: in this volume, Piotr and Cynthia give not merely guidance on how to write, but suggestions of *what* to write—of unearthing the narrative arcs that naturally occur within the work of software practitioners. Fittingly for a book on technical writing, they have also loaded the book with specific examples of writing in the wild that can serve as object lessons.

As you delve into this book, let it and its examples inspire you, but remember that reading is but a waystation to writing; as Jim Gray would remind you, you're not writing enough!

—BRYAN CANTRILL,
PIEDMONT, CALIFORNIA

preface

Engineering blogs feed and foster developers' insatiable curiosity. Think of all the times that a blog post

- Sparked an idea for a new approach or project
- Taught you about a new technology or tool that you ended up trying out
- Saved you from going down a disastrous path
- Led you to an *Aha!* moment in the depths of despair
- Gave your project an unexpected lift
- Pushed you to apply for a dream job

Engineering blogs clearly matter. And we're both obsessed with them, from two rather different angles (the engineering side and the writing side).

This book began as a crazy idea, a challenge to ourselves. If we collaborated, with our vastly different experiences and perspectives, could we come up with a resource that would bring more, and better, engineering blogs into the world? Could we help hesitant developers overcome the barriers preventing them from sharing their ideas in writing? Could we also help experienced engineering blog writers increase their reach and influence?

We didn't pretend to know all the secrets to creating amazing engineering blog posts (we still don't). But we wanted to think deeply about it, learn more, and share what we knew. So, we committed to writing a book on it—as a "weekend project" that sprawled into early mornings and evenings across different sides of the globe. And here we are.

While this book focuses on writing engineering blog posts, the strategies you learn will help you make *all* your technical communications clearer and more compelling. Software engineering involves a surprising amount of writing—commit messages, code comments, API docs, design docs, requests for comments [RFCs], progress reports, bug report threads, code review comments, async team messages, user interactions, and oh all the emails. Through these channels, strong writing skills will naturally increase your influence as an engineer. That leads to more interesting engineering experiences, which in turn leads to more interesting blog posts that further increase your influence. It's a "virtuous cycle."

We've had a ton of fun writing this book, and we truly hope you enjoy reading it and applying it to your writing. We look forward to reading what *you* write!

acknowledgments

If you've ever written an engineering blog post, we owe you—immensely! This book wouldn't exist if it weren't for the community of developers sharing their experiences through writing—educating and inspiring more people than they will ever know. Special thanks to all the authors whose work we have highlighted throughout this book.

Bryan Cantrill, thank you for the fantastic foreword, distinguished history of great blog posts...and talks...and innovations...and all that you do to foster a collaborative engineering community. What else can we say—except that YOU need to write more.

Scott Hanselman, thank you for sharing your blogging brilliance, offering killer suggestions, and providing the perfect sendoff!

We'd like to thank the entire team at Manning for supporting this project in more ways than we ever anticipated. Doug Rudder, our developmental editor, served as wise Obi-Wan throughout the various twists and turns of the process. Thank you for your steady hand and valuable guidance. Our technical editor Eric Lippert made this a much better book by calling out our blind spots and challenging our thinking with his keen insights. There are clearly many stories to share if our paths ever cross, and we'd love to hear them all. We're thrilled that we finally had the pleasure of working with Jonathan Gennick, our acquisitions editor. We deeply appreciate you taking a chance on our crazy idea and can't thank you enough for making this a reality. We also want to thank the many, many other professionals at Manning who work behind the scenes to get well-crafted books published, promoted, and sold: Ivan Martinović, Robin Campbell, Courtney Kimball, Aira Dučić, Keri Hales, Lana Todorovic-Arndt, Aleksandar Dragosavljević, Alisa Larson, Radmila Ercegovac, Olga Milanko, Tamara Švelić Sabljić, and the rest of the amazing Manning production crew.

Many people provided valuable feedback on various drafts of the book, and we appreciate their time and expertise: Abel Sen, Adam Koch, Adam Wendell, Alireza Aghamohammadi, Andres Damian Sacco, Aniket Wattamwar, Ariel Otilibili, Bill LeBorgne, Christopher Haupt, Eric Dickey, Felipe Provezano Coutinho, Fyodor Yarochkin, Gunjan Paliwal, Jared Duncan, Jason Content, Javid Asgarov, Jeremy Zeidner, Joel Luukka, Jose Alberto Reyes Quevedo, Juan José Durillo Barrionuevo, Juan Luis Barreda, Mario Pavlov, Mary Annc Thygesen, Matthew Greene, Monica Guimaraes, Nadir Doctor, Narayanan Jayaratchagan, Nicolantonio Vignola, Ofek Shilon, Oleg Kopychko, Oliver Korten, Owen Morris, Patrick Regan, Pradeep Chintale, Radhakrishna MV, Rick Bunnell, Roman Levchenko, Ruud Gijsen, Sachin Handiekar, Satish Prahalad Gururajan, Shiroshica Kulatilake, Simon Verhoeven, Victor Durán, Vidhya Vinay, and William Jamir Silva. Your suggestions helped make this a better book.

We'd especially like to thank Natalie Estrada (RISE Event Co) for reviewing chapter 16 and Brian Sletten (author of *WebAssembly: The Definitive Guide*) for reviewing chapter 17. It's quite a luxury to have domain experts like you just a text or Slack away!

From Piotr: I would like to thank Avi Kivity, Glauber Costa, and Pekka Enberg for making ScyllaDB such a good environment to start writing engineering blog posts ~~by incentivizing people with promises of glory (and death threats if they don't write regularly)~~.

From Cynthia: I would like to thank Jonathan Boswell for leading me into this field; Wayne Ariola for keeping me challenged (and sane) over the years, companies, and continents; and Dor Laor for unintentionally bringing me and Piotr together.

about this book

This book will guide you to write more compelling engineering blog posts—ones that get read, shared, discussed, and remembered. You benefit from two distinctly different perspectives: an engineer who learned to enjoy writing and a writer who spent decades collaborating with engineers. As long as you're interested in writing and have distinctive engineering experiences to write about, we can help!

We cover pragmatic strategies for optimizing all phases of the blogging process, from planning to promoting. Specifically, we explore

- Identifying and prioritizing topics that make intriguing posts
- Getting a draft written and reviewed as painlessly as possible
- Making your ideas clearer and more convincing to technical readers
- Tapping the strengths of AI for revision while avoiding misuses and abuses
- Squeezing more value out of each blog post that you publish
- Using your blogging success as a stepping stone to additional opportunities

One of the best ways to improve your craft is to learn from the masters. Early in the book, we discuss core characteristics shared across successful blog posts and show how they're applied in real-world examples. However, a captivating bug hunt article varies dramatically from an opinion piece roasting a highly hyped technology, or an article that shares how a team implemented an industry-changing algorithm. That's why the heart of the book involves in-depth analysis of these and other blog post "patterns"—exploring examples, characteristics, and dos and don'ts for each. By the time you're done reading, you'll start seeing these patterns everywhere and (we hope!) applying them to shape your own blog posts.

Who should read this book

This book is designed for developers, engineers, and technical leaders of all writing skill levels—even if you're not a native English speaker and never took a writing class in your life. It assumes that you're tackling intriguing engineering challenges and want to share your experiences, achievements, and lessons learned with the community. It is most likely to resonate with people who are

- Building the next big thing at a startup
- Working on intriguing projects at larger tech companies
- Spearheading open source projects
- Aspiring to any of the above

Note that this book does not focus on blogging for profit (e.g., writing freelance articles about what someone else developed). Also, it was not written with DevRel or Product Marketing professionals in mind. However, people in those roles might find many parts helpful—especially if they collaborate closely with engineers.

How this book is organized: A road map

This book includes 17 chapters divided into four parts, plus two appendixes.

Part 1: Fundamentals

- Chapter 1 explores the benefits of writing engineering blog posts and common excuses for *not* writing them.
- Chapter 2 helps you identify topics for compelling blog posts.
- Chapter 3 shares critical characteristics of compelling blog posts.

Part 2: Nailing the writing process

- Chapter 4 walks you through capturing your ideas and getting to a working draft.
- Chapter 5 helps you optimize the draft so it resonates with your target readers.
- Chapter 6 is all about getting the feedback you want/need before publication.
- Chapter 7 delineates what to check as you send the post off into the world.

Part 3: Applying blog post patterns

- Chapter 8 analyzes "Bug Hunt" blog posts that share the thrill of finding and fixing some elusive bug.
- Chapter 9 analyzes "Rewrote It in X" blog posts that are all about rewriting an app in a new programming language, library, or framework.
- Chapter 10 analyzes "How We Built It" blog posts that share your most impressive engineering achievements.
- Chapter 11 analyzes "Lessons Learned" blog posts that share lessons learned from technical challenges.
- Chapter 12 analyzes "Thoughts on Trends" blog posts that are highly opinionated takes on industry trends.

- Chapter 13 analyzes "Non-markety Product Perspectives" blog posts where the product is embedded into a genuinely intriguing and educational article.
- Chapter 14 analyzes "Benchmarks and Test Results" blog posts that share various flavors of benchmarks and tests.

Part 4: Promotion, adaptation, and expansion

- Chapter 15 presents options for squeezing more value from your blog post.
- Chapter 16 shares strategies for presenting conference talks based on your blog post.
- Chapter 17 provides an honest look at what to consider if you're intrigued with becoming a book author.

Appendixes

- Appendix A runs through publishing options and noteworthy writing/reviewing tools.
- Appendix B shares generative AI uses and abuses to consider.

liveBook discussion forum

Purchase of *Writing for Developers* includes free access to liveBook, Manning's online reading platform. Using liveBook's exclusive discussion features, you can attach comments to the book globally or to specific sections or paragraphs. It's a snap to make notes for yourself, ask and answer technical questions, and receive help from the author and other users. To access the forum, go to https://livebook.manning.com/book/writing-for-developers/discussion. You can also learn more about Manning's forums and the rules of conduct at https://livebook.manning.com/discussion.

Manning's commitment to our readers is to provide a venue where a meaningful dialogue between individual readers and between readers and the author can take place. It is not a commitment to any specific amount of participation on the part of the author, whose contribution to the forum remains voluntary (and unpaid). We suggest you try asking the author some challenging questions lest their interest stray! The forum and the archives of previous discussions will be accessible from the publisher's website as long as the book is in print.

Other online resources

As a not-so-subtle hint to our readers, we created https://writethat.blog. We'll be continuously updating this site with intriguing engineering blog posts, including Piotr's pundit commentary. It also points to a GitHub repo where we'll keep a living list of links to the examples referenced throughout this book as well as other resources that might be helpful as you write that blog.

about the authors

PIOTR SARNA is a fearless technologist who dives headfirst into fun engineering challenges such as forking SQLite for modern distributed apps, introducing Rust & Wasm into C++ projects, and contributing to the Linux kernel. He's an experienced book author, tech reviewer, speaker, and blog author. Piotr graduated from University of Warsaw with an MSc in computer science.

CYNTHIA DUNLOP has been writing for and with developers for 20+ years, covering topics across C/C++, Java, testing, DevOps, and back-end infrastructure. She's behind several technical books, hundreds of articles, and countless blog posts. Cynthia holds a BA from UCLA and an MA from Washington State University, where she taught writing once upon a time.

about the cover illustration

The figure on the cover of *Writing for Developers* is "Likanien," or "A man from Lika," taken from Balthasar Hacquet's *Images and Descriptions of Southwestern and Eastern Wenda, Illyrians, and Slavs,* published in 1815.

In those days, it was easy to identify where people lived and what their trade or station in life was just by their dress. Manning celebrates the inventiveness and initiative of the computer business with book covers based on the rich diversity of regional culture centuries ago, brought back to life by pictures from collections such as this one.

Part 1

Fundamentals

What factors help blog posts get read to the end, shared, and discussed? How can you find and prioritize promising blog post topics that complement your specific engineering experiences? And what kind of benefits might you gain once you translate your ideas into your own captivating blog posts? The first chapters of this book answer those questions:

- Chapter 1 explores the benefits of writing engineering blog posts, as well as common excuses for *not* writing them.
- Chapter 2 helps you identify topics for compelling blog posts.
- Chapter 3 shares critical characteristics of compelling blog posts.

Why write

This chapter covers

- The benefits of writing engineering blog posts
- Excuses for not writing
- A general book overview

Sharing technical experiences and expertise is an integral part of engineering culture. For developers interested in writing words as well as writing code, engineering blogs open up intriguing new possibilities. From startups to big tech, people write blog posts for a variety of reasons that we'll explore more deeply in a bit:

- Connecting with the community
- Advancing the state of the art
- Expanding career opportunities
- Gaining recognition as an expert in a particular niche
- Building interest in products and projects
- Simply collecting and clarifying their thoughts

Although some engineers already enjoy writing about their achievements, many are still flat-out terrified by the thought of publishing. That's fair. Most engineers never set out to become writers. And while writing code might seem distinctly different from writing words, there are actually many commonalities and your skill at coding can help you with writing.

Moreover, if you're already working on complex technical problems, seeing how far you can push your technology of choice, and/or building the next big whatever, you're already about 95% of the way to delivering an interesting engineering blog post. As long as you're building the deep technical experience that's fundamental, there are many tricks that can help you capture your insights in blog posts that get read and remembered. That's where this book comes in.

We're here to help you write technical blog posts that stand out, fast. You'll read about the core blog post patterns that are most common today (e.g., "The Bug Hunt," "How We Built It," "Lessons Learned," "We Rewrote It in X," "Thoughts on Trends"), dos and don'ts for each, and pragmatic ways to capture your ideas in a written piece that keeps readers engaged. In addition to detailed examples of what works and why, we'll share strategies for how to make the biggest impact with minimal revision time, how to thoroughly refine a critical work, and how to squeeze more value from your writing time and effort.

While this book focuses on engineering blogs, its strategies help you make *all* your technical communications clearer and more convincing. That includes various flavors of writing such as commit summaries, code review comments, docs, proposals, reports, requests for comments (RFCs), presentations, even videos if you're so inclined.

But first things first. Why write engineering blog posts at all? Some benefits are less obvious than others. Let's start with the many ways writing blog posts can help you and then zero in on a personal perspective (Piotr's).

1.1 Why write engineering blog posts

If you want to start writing but are desperately looking for a compelling motive to finally take action, you've come to the right place. And if you're an experienced writer who has fallen out of practice, perhaps a few moments reflecting on the benefits will inspire you to reprioritize writing.

1.1.1 Leaving your comfort zone

Enjoying small personal challenges is often "a thing" for programmers. It may manifest as

- Coding daily HackerRank challenges
- Participating in the Advent of Code
- Enduring personal all-night hackathons
- Finishing the 100 pushups program
- Catching up on those long-abandoned piano lessons

So, why not write a blog post or two, just to show yourself that you can do it? Getting started requires an act of willpower, and the outcome is just as satisfying as finally figuring out the asymptotically optimal solution for an algorithmic problem you've been trying to solve for hours.

1.1.2 Really understanding your code

Want to see if you really understand your code? Try explaining it to someone else. Writing a blog post can help you with that.

First of all, you need to articulate the problem and solution in natural language. That's proven to be a helpful debugging mechanism, which even earned an adorable name: rubber duck debugging. Instead of talking to a bathtub toy, you can write your thoughts down for other people to read and learn from.

Writing a blog post sometimes exposes that your code has a terrible logical fallacy, missed a corner case, or was designed incorrectly. Quite often, blogging becomes yet another part of the iterative programming technique. Describing the design and implementation becomes just a phase of development, followed by returning to the code to fix the mistakes and rethink incorrect assumptions.

All those blog posts also improve knowledge retention. If you can just redirect somebody to your blog post instead of explaining your design decisions over and over one-on-one, it saves everyone's time. And if you move on, it's nice to know that people who take over the code can onboard themselves with your articles describing how you found and fixed the problems. You also tend to get your work vetted by the community, as described in the next section.

1.1.3 Free peer review

Code review is a vital part of most successful programming projects. Very few people have the superhero brains capable of hacking a complicated system on their own and maintaining it later. The more people review the code, the better. A small number of reviewers can lead to bias, especially in small startup companies where like-minded people collaborate on a common problem.

Writing a public blog post is an implicit call for (unsolicited) help. One certain thing about the online community of programmers is that they love pointing out other people's mistakes and suggesting their own ideas as ultimate sources of truth.

Our dear colleague Pekka Enberg often jokingly says: "Don't read the comment sections on the orange site" (referring to the distinctive coloring theme of the Hacker News web page). Although the online commentary is negative more often than not, it's still just as valuable, maybe even more so. Comment sections on various web pages are accurately called "cesspits" and other derogatory terms. Yet, among all the vitriol, you can often find genuine suggestions on how to improve. It's quite common for authors to publish an errata for both the blog post and the corresponding code because somebody was kind enough to point out a mistake in the comment section.

1.1.4 Personal brand boost

Thousands of self-proclaimed life coaches infiltrating social media sites try to convince you that improving your personal brand is very important, especially if you want to earn tens of thousands of dollars a day, just like them. Writing blog posts isn't a direct line to wealth (see the "Writing ≠ riches" section), but it certainly is a good start for earning recognition and respect across the tech community.

Publishing a blog post is usually naturally followed by promoting it on social media. You'll want to share your own blog post in a non-cringey way (we'll talk more about this later), and the publisher (often your company) will most likely promote it, too. That's a prime opportunity to slowly build your audience and get noticed. A good blog post can earn you the label of "that person who wrote an interesting article on XYZ." This builds the foundation for a personal brand.

That seed audience helps expand your reach. If you write additional blog posts or comments on topics that resonate with this group, they're likely to share your posts across their own network. Rinse and repeat, and you'll be an influencer writing viral content in no time (or, in reality, you'll gain a reputation for writing blogs worth reading and sharing). Having a large group of regular readers also increases the chances of your blog post landing on the trending list of an article aggregator, like Hacker News or Reddit.

Once you've reached some critical mass of exposure, interesting people start approaching you, and leaders in that space begin to recognize you as an expert. Blogs are a prime hunting ground for publishers, conference organizers, and other talent scouts. It's not uncommon for a single successful blog post to spark invitations to meetups, conferences, discussion panels, podcasts, and similar. Others might just contact you with a congratulatory note. Regardless of the reason, each such contact is an opportunity to stay in touch with a community peer who cares about what you've been working on.

If you have a personal web page, a list of your published blog posts is a great addition to it. And if you don't have a personal web page, the fact that you can list your published blog posts is a great excuse to go and build one!

1.1.5 *Career development*

Once you've published at least one blog post, there's one thing you can be certain of: armies of LinkedIn talent sourcers have already found it and are ready to put the title in that first (and only) customized sentence of an otherwise templated message: "Hi <your slightly misspelled name here>, I read your article on <the blog post topic>, it was such a treat! I am also impressed beyond belief by your experience at (…)."

But the benefits of blogging go beyond slightly more customized poaching attempts. You're also standing out to CTOs and founders of startups that work in the same industry, who might have genuinely enjoyed that technical take of yours. When the people reaching out to you have taken the time to read your work and track you down, it's fair to expect that 1) the position will be well-aligned with your interests and 2) you'll skip to the front of the hiring line.

Even if your blog doesn't directly land you new job opportunities, listing compelling blog posts on your resume helps you stand out in a crowded applicant pool. And if one of those blogs links to a Hacker News discussion with an impressive amount of points or shows some nice engagement via Medium claps, social media reactions, and similar, it's even more prestigious. Put yourself in the hiring manager's shoes. Would you rather spend time on someone who has authored an intelligible blog post on a technology that the team uses or someone who simply tosses the technology name into a long laundry list of "competencies"?

Blogs are also helpful for internal advancement. Wish leaders who don't read code had some idea what you've accomplished and the challenges you faced? This is your chance. Moreover, publishing a compelling blog post could help make the case for a promotion. For example, completing and communicating a significant technical achievement is often a key factor for promotion to staff engineer. And remember the pain of completing the "what you did this year" section of the dreaded annual performance review forms? Having blog post URLs is quite handy when it's time to remember what you did and explain complex projects in n characters or less.

Moreover, the writing skills that you develop and refine while working on blogs help your career in other ways too. For example, if you want your design decisions to be adopted, you will need to communicate their merit in writing so your ideas can be reviewed asynchronously by multiple stakeholders. Being able to produce correct code is one thing. If you want to have a greater influence, you often need to convince others (and sometimes yourself as well) that your proposed specification, architecture, and design all make sense.

1.1.6 *Staying on top of the latest technologies*

Readers turn to tech blogs to learn about modern technology, bleeding-edge software, and the latest groundbreaking hardware. When a new CPU architecture gets released, you can expect to see a surge of articles describing how it works (or doesn't), whether it's a good fit for some specific use cases, whether it was a life-changing performance boost for somebody, or whether it was rather disappointing after running some real-life benchmarks.

Given that there's a sizable audience hungry for new content about new technologies, why not volunteer to learn and share something interesting? That's a very healthy environment for an engineer—staying up to date with modern technology quickly pays off. It not only helps you with your daily duties but also increases the chances you're still a valuable asset on the job market in case you ever want (or require) a career change. We all know firsthand that it's quite tempting to become lazy in a cushy programming job (please don't tell my boss that I typed that), and regular blogging about the latest technologies is a perfect solution for this.

Weekend programming projects also help—twofold. Of course, they help you stay up-to-date with the latest tech. But what's more important here, they're great material for a blog post. A fair number of popular technical blog posts are just descriptions of unusual (reverse-engineering a Christmas lights controller), nerdy (a new toy Raft implementation), melancholic (one about your good ol' gameboy™), or otherwise impressive weekend projects.

1.1.7   *Improving your skills*

Blog posts are a perfect training ground for all kinds of skills, not just technical ones. The process of putting your thoughts into words simultaneously boosts your writing, language, and engineering skills.

WRITING

Writing proficiency comes with practice. The more you write, the better you become at expressing ideas, structuring content, and crafting clear sentences. Consistent practice (and feedback—if you're lucky enough to have somebody review your work) contributes significantly to your writing skills. It also helps you find and polish your writing style.

 With each post you write, the next one becomes easier and more natural, like another entry in your diary. Every time you write, you're essentially considering and navigating countless decisions with every word, sentence, and revision. Each negotiation builds up a personal knowledge base that you can subconsciously tap the next time you're stuck. And confronting your own writing challenges prepares you to provide constructive feedback for other people's blog posts. That, in turn, creates a healthy writing culture among your colleagues and peers.

LANGUAGE

Regular writing sessions provide an opportunity to enhance language skills in the context of your work. This is especially valuable for nonnative English speakers. You'll be forced to think hard about vocabulary (both technical and nontechnical), grammar, and overall proficiency. It's a great exercise, especially in the age of automatic grammar-checking software and all kinds of tools for finding synonyms, antonyms, and all the other -nyms. Rather than mechanically accepting suggestions, you learn as you go!

ENGINEERING

Writing a blog post creates internal pressure to verify all the information you're about to publish under your name. It compels you to research the topic, double-check that the code snippets are sensible and correct, and browse the internet for similar articles. And that's great! It is motivation to learn in its purest form because if you don't do it, you may make a fool of yourself online. You usually won't, of course, but try to explain that to your impostor syndrome. In the rare event that you actually do make a fool of yourself, remember there's lots of educational value in feeling ashamed, followed by acknowledging the failure and correcting the problem.

1.1.8   *Attracting new hires*

Writing blog posts cuts both ways (in a positive sense)! Candidates are more likely to join your company if it maintains an interesting engineering blog. That's especially true for startups, which often work with bleeding-edge technology. People interested in one of the technical articles you or your teammates wrote are more likely to click on that Careers tab in your company's web page. And, conversely, when a candidate is debating whether to join, an interesting article on your site could be what tips the scales in your favor, while unimpressive or nonexistent technical blogs might drive a good candidate elsewhere.

1.1.9 *Attracting users for a developer-focused product*

If you're working on a developer-focused product and you want it to be broadly adopted, writing an engineering blog post about it is an effective way to reach and educate target users. Spending thousands of dollars on carefully crafted paid ads for a developer-focused product is typically like throwing money into the wind. Most ads are blocked, and those that evade defense mechanisms like pi-holes and whatnot are likely to breed contempt. An interesting blog, however, could actually meet the eyeballs of your target users.

To be clear, we're not suggesting you use a technical blog to try to sell the reader on why your product is the most amazing thing ever. That's actually worse than all the pretty ads because a markety blog is much easier to shame on Hacker News or other comment sections of choice. But if you write authentic blog posts that share how you engineered your differentiators or implemented critical architectural changes, there's a good chance they will earn some eyeballs. And that added exposure could let new users know that you exist or motivate on-the-fence users to finally take the plunge.

1.1.10 *Write once, share everywhere*

You have a limited amount of time on this planet. Why waste your precious minutes repeating the same thing over and over again? Capture it in a blog. Think about all the critical points that need to be covered, express them clearly in a written blog, and tada! You never need to do it again. Just link back to the blog post whenever appropriate, for example:

- Writing one-on-one emails and Slack messages to new hires, forgetful colleagues, or confused users
- Referencing the topic in user docs, commit summaries, code review comments, and problem reports
- Chiming in on relevant social media discussions or forum threads
- Providing context in a subsequent blog post you write

By blogging your thoughts, you're reaching more people with less typing (or talking). Scott Hanselman, a highly influential and prolific tech blogger, is a well-known champion of this idea. As he explains it in "Do they deserve the gift of your keystrokes?" (https://mng.bz/aVBj): "If you email someone one-on-one, you're reaching that one person. If you blog about it, you get the message out on the web itself, and your keystrokes travel farther and reach more people. Assuming you want your message to reach as many people as possible, blog it. You only have so many hours in the day."

If you later decide to extend or adjust your take on the topic, simply update the related post. You don't need to track down the 21 miscellaneous places you have already discussed this topic and try to get them all in sync—until the next update.

1.1.11 *Writing ≠ riches*

Note that we deliberately didn't mention all the money you'll make by writing blog posts. Some of the listed benefits, especially building your brand, could certainly have a financial benefit. And if you're a consultant, regular blogging is fundamental for showcasing your expertise. But reports of thriving paid newsletters and best-selling tech books are the exception, not the rule. The underlying economics are surprisingly discouraging.

For some insider insight on the economics of being a full-time content creator, see the candid blogs published by two of the most successful and well-known tech authors. Gergely Orosz, who runs *The Pragmatic Engineer* newsletter that has been the #1 paid tech Substack newsletter for a few years running, has shared specific income stats in several blog posts (start with "I removed all affiliate links from my blog: numbers" [https:// blog.pragmaticengineer.com/affiliates/]). Martin Kleppmann, the author of the best-selling (currently no. 1) O'Reilly book *Designing Data Intensive Applications*, reflects on the unexpected success of his book in light of the reality of book publishing in "Writing a book: is it worth it?" (https://mng.bz/gA5e).

1.2   *Why write: A personal perspective*

Next, here's a personal perspective on why writing engineering blogs is such a gratifying experience—once you've overcome that initial terror barrier, at least. Story time!

I (Piotr) was once the epitome of the stereotypical introverted programmer. I dreaded speaking in front of what I considered a crowd (more than two people), and authoring blog posts never crossed my mind. I thought that only well-recognized industry experts could publish articles, and I certainly didn't consider myself a member of that group. But then I was forced to do it, and I actually grew to enjoy it.

I've spent my professional career hacking open source projects, and one of the earlier ones happened to be ScyllaDB. That company had a great writing culture already established, ready to suck me in. Just as I was completing my first real coding assignment, my boss casually suggested that I should write a blog post on the new feature I added. Imagining myself putting together prose that would be published for anyone to read, my first reaction was an anaphylactic shock. But then an even more powerful irrational fear took over: my carefully cultured impostor syndrome. I hesitantly agreed. Also, I was pretty sure that refusing to write would get me fired on the spot (which probably wasn't the case at all).

I started writing a blog post based on that initial coding assignment, and within a few hours, I had somehow written six or seven pages. The result was a rather mediocre blog post that described the new feature, explained some examples, and recommended that everyone use it from that point forward. It certainly didn't lead to a spike in product usage, but I quoted it a few times when asked about the feature on our user mailing list (yes, we used this ancient technology, and I loved it). Was it worth it?

Yes, it was! I was pleasantly surprised that just a few hours of writing enabled me to collect my thoughts about the feature, convince myself that I understood it deeply enough to write about it, and gain confidence that it really worked. The blog post also made my boss happy and my impostor syndrome less severe. Finally, it made me realize that I didn't need to be some vaunted industry expert to write blog posts. Quite the opposite! I had the epiphany that writing blog posts could likely help me become recognized as an expert (shameless self-promoting spoiler alert: it did!).

Two months passed, and I delivered another feature. This time, I proactively volunteered to write another blog post, something that would have been unimaginable for the two-months-ago me. From then on, it was muscle memory to write a blog post draft after implementing anything even remotely interesting. Engineering leaders encouraged everyone to write, and impressive efforts received praise from the team as well as the company co-founders. Sometimes the posts even went viral in the programming world, bringing yet more validation and an occasional dopamine rush.

Looking back, I'm extremely grateful that I was gently forced to write that first blog post. The same company also had a very healthy public speaking culture, and I found that flipping blog posts into presentation decks and speaker notes was surprisingly simple. (More on this in chapter 16.)

I couldn't resist writing dozens more posts and speaking at various virtual and in-person conferences. Some of the blog posts landed on the front page of Hacker News, which provided surprising insight into how blogging can open the door to some interesting career opportunities. It seems that just a few 15-minute-ish bursts of Hacker News fame can almost instantly change recruitment outreach from spammy LinkedIn messages into personal outreach from well-known tech leaders offering senior positions.

Blogging also fit nicely into an internship program that the company ran for the students at the University of Warsaw. My blogging experience helped me mentor students through what was often the most daunting success criteria: writing a blog post describing the project, its design decisions, and results. Some of these interns' posts ended up trending on Hacker News, providing them with an early insight into the crazy world of the aforementioned Hacker News fame.

The connections I made along the way were also important—other people who write and read blog posts often work for interesting companies or start their own. And I got to know quite a few of them! I was invited to one of the design meetings working on standardizing WebAssembly and its WASI subproject, met a few co-founders from the generative AI world, casually chatted with authors of tech books I really admire, and was offered a tech reviewer gig. And this was just a start.

Totally hooked by this point, I convinced my colleagues to co-author a book on databases. That's how *Database Performance at Scale* came to life. And now, here I am, writing drafts for the first chapters of a new book, barely a month after the last one was released. Still worth it!

1.3 Excuses for not writing

Given all these great benefits, why isn't every engineer blogging? Let's take a look at a few of the most common reasons for not writing at all, or for not writing specific blog posts that a teammate might have suggested.

1.3.1 Not a writer

Maybe you're not an experienced writer. But you *are* an engineer working on really interesting projects with the potential to influence your global peers, building other amazing things. People read engineering blogs to discover what's possible, identify new ways of approaching their challenges, and prepare for what's next. The goal is to inform and maybe inspire—not entertain the reader with your eloquent prose.

To start, you just need something interesting to share. Since you're working as a developer, you're most likely covered in that respect (if you truly don't think you have anything worth writing about, see all the topic triggers in chapter 2).

> **NOTE**   Will Larson's blog post "Writers Who Operate" (https://lethain.com/writers-who-operate/) takes a detailed look at how technical professionals who remain deep in the trenches are best positioned to write the valuable content that advances the industry.

People (especially engineers) are sometimes intimidated by the thought of writing. If they've endured an unnecessarily painful blog-writing process that dragged on for weeks or months, it's easy to understand how they might be reluctant to start another. Other times they're trapped in analysis paralysis, staring at a blinking cursor without a clear idea of how to translate the tangle of thoughts in their head into an article that some unknown reader will understand. Or maybe they're still haunted by a time when an academic paper returned bloody with redlined grammatical nitpicks.

It doesn't have to be that hard. We'll show you how to focus your efforts on what matters most (getting your point across clearly and convincingly) while delegating time drains such as checking punctuation usage to automation and AI.

> **NOTE**   To be clear, we are absolutely *not* going to recommend that you use AI to actually generate any text for your blog posts. We'll even provide specific examples of what happens when you attempt to do so (spoiler: it ranges from banality to hilarity). But there are ways that AI can assist with reviewing and revising what has already come out of your brain. That's what we'll cover in this book.

1.3.2   *Not even a native English speaker*

It's no secret that many engineers are not native English speakers, and that can add an additional layer of intricacy to the writing process. But if you're one of them and you've reached this point, you're clearly not scared off by challenges. And if you start looking into the people behind many of the blog posts and technical books you've read, you'll likely find an impressively high concentration of nonnative English speakers.

With all of the decent-quality grammar checkers and translation programs now at your fingertips, this really shouldn't be a blocker. As we mentioned in the previous point, the goal here is to showcase your engineering insights, not write something that will rival Shakespeare. In fact, simple sentences tend to be best for communicating technical information. And the more you write, the more you'll incrementally improve your command of the language.

If you're accustomed to following each of your written sentences with a "(sorry for my bad English)" disclaimer—stop. There are at least three reasons why it's not a problem, especially when writing a technical blog post:

- Many of your future readers are not native English speakers either. They care about the engineering aspect of your post being interesting, not its grammar and grace.
- Chances are that your company already employs a few native English speakers who'd be happy to review and fix any linguistic inconsistencies.
- If the only negative feedback you receive from your technical blog post is about grammar nitpicks—great job! It's clear proof that the engineering part is flawless.

1.3.3 *No time*

Even if your manager prioritizes writing, your other responsibilities don't magically disappear when you're ready to write. Maybe you get up early to spend some time on it while you're focused and refreshed—but then pesky bug reports and customer problems end up taking precedence. And by the time it all settles down, you're likely not in the mindset to tackle something outside your comfort zone, like writing. But maybe you can carve out some decent blocks of time here and there. For example,

- Waiting for code to compile or tests to run
- That canceled meeting
- When you're blocked on your current task but not ready to take on a new one
- When your vacation starts in two days, so there's no point in starting a major new project now

How much time do you really need? Writing can be a never-ending task if you let it. There's no clear point of completion like the moment when your code compiles and passes some rudimentary test. You could spend days, months, or even years continuously tweaking something far past the point of diminishing returns. Or you could just get it done.

If you're spending months on a blog post, you're either suffering from a crazy corporate communications review process or you're sitting on some prime opportunities to streamline your writing process. Let's hope it's the latter—that means we can help!

1.3.4 *The project isn't 100% completed*

You probably don't need to postpone writing about your project until it's released into production, maybe even a few versions along to make sure it's stable. Of course, reaching a major project milestone is a great time to write about it. You're probably remiss if you pass up the opportunity to share at least a short blog post at every pivotal point.

But releases aren't the only opportunity to write. What about all the discoveries leading up to that point? The architectural decisions behind the design and a discussion of the tradeoffs? The reason why you're working on this in the first place? Some hard-fought lessons learned that your users won't care about but could save your engineering peers some major headaches?

We could go on and on (and we will, as we run through blog post ideas in the next chapter). But the bottom line here is that if it's a nontrivial project, there are probably quite a few interesting angles if you venture beyond the standard "we released it" blog post.

1.3.5   *We don't even have a product out yet*

You certainly *can* write blog posts before you have an MVP or even a clear idea how to build one. But *should* you? The critical factor here is whether your company is in stealth mode or eager to build buzz. If it's the former, you're excused from publishing blog posts related to your product. That doesn't mean you can't start planning and even drafting what you'll publish when the time is right, though.

Once you're ready to start getting some attention, there's a range of blog post angles you could take:

- Announce your existence and vision (likely reserved for founders).
- Tease your vision with a bold what-if article that marks your territory and signals something groundbreaking is in the works.
- Declare your manifesto, the core principles guiding your path forward.
- Start challenging the status quo—with or without explaining what a better approach should involve or your specific vision for a better way.
- Delineate your technical goals.
- Tease some initial breakthroughs.
- Describe what you've selected as your tech stack and why.

You could also get into the various topics mentioned in the previous section. Again, we'll cover more ideas—with examples—in the next chapter.

1.3.6   *It's not new*

There's no fixed expiration date on sharing impressive engineering accomplishments or industry insights. Like cheese or wine, some ideas can improve with age. while others might have already peaked. As a "sniff test," consider whether the topic is still interesting to a reasonable subset of target readers. For example, take an article discussing the engineering decisions behind a longstanding product capability that's a critical differentiator. Although the capability itself is not new, this perspective on it is new—and it's likely to be interesting to your existing and prospective users as well as your global engineering peers. Don't dismiss this as an idea, even if your teammates roll their eyes because they're sick of the topic.

A look back at an older implementation could be particularly interesting as you're working on a new one. For example, say you're in the early phases of reimplementing a Python-based ingestion service in Rust. It could be interesting to write about the rationale behind your original design, what worked well and didn't, and what you're hoping to fix with the new implementation. Later, once the new Rust implementation is completed and you're ready to write about it, you can reference that article on the Python implementation and hyperlink it for readers who want more detailed background.

New perspectives on not-so-new concepts are also totally valid. Different people explain things in different ways. As Phil Eaton put it, "Even if you're writing about a popular topic, there's still a chance your post gets through to someone in a way other posts do not" (https://notes.eatonphil.com/is-it-worth-writing-about.html). For example, two wildly popular Hacker News posts in 2023 were interesting takes on memory allocation and load balancing (https://samwho.dev/memory-allocation/ and https://samwho.dev/load-balancing/, respectively). Those two topics have been discussed for ages. But the author, Sam Rose, invested tremendous thought and time in explaining these concepts in a unique way: with visualizations and even interactive playgrounds. And the effort paid off. The notoriously snarky comment section was actually teeming with compliments.

All that being said, there are some topics you just don't want to touch (like that soft cheese that's been nestled in the corner of your fridge for way too long). Don't waste your time writing about technologies and concepts that are clearly past their prime unless you truly have something groundbreaking to say.

1.3.7 *It's already available as a recorded talk*

Fantastic. Writing a blog post will be simple then!

We can guarantee that everyone in your target audience has not already found and watched your video. Moreover, those who did watch it won't remember every word. Why not consider extending its reach by also making it available as a blog post?

Different people prefer to consume information in different ways. Many people would rather watch a video, where you get a better sense of the speaker's personality and know exactly how much time you need to commit from start to finish.

But others prefer to read. A written article enables considerably more control over how the information is consumed. You can easily reread critical parts and just skim over details that don't seem relevant. There's no need to grab headphones or rely on notoriously poor AI captioning. And you can always copy/paste the actual article text (not poor AI transcriptions) into a tool that translates it into your native language or summarizes it.

> **NOTE** Another advantage of reading versus watching: AI-driven transcription/captioning for technical topics is often comically bad. Here's just one of many gems we've come across in conference video captioning: "It is possible to go to sleep by blocking in io_uring" became "It is possible to go to sleep by blocking and I owe urine." Enough said.

Both written and video formats are valuable, and they can even link to one another to improve the reader's/viewer's comprehension of the topic. We'll cover the "blog post to talk" path in detail later in this book.

1.3.8 *Don't want to leak confidential details*

You definitely should tread carefully here. No blogging benefits are worth the risk of violating a non-disclosure agreement (NDA) or compromising your company's competitive advantage. If you're working in a sensitive environment, you might still be able to write about topics such as:

- Your personal take on a concept, challenge, or trend that affects the broader industry
- Interesting tips and tricks that your team learned about working with popular tools
- How users are applying publicly announced product capabilities and what value they're gaining from them

We're not attorneys, though. Before you invest any substantial time thinking about what to write, talk to your boss and get clarity on what's appropriate.

1.3.9 *Nothing interesting to say*

There are two variations of this: 1) you don't believe that a particular blog post idea or draft is interesting, and 2) you don't feel that you can write something interesting enough to publish. Let's tackle them in turn.

Sometimes you'll hit a wall on a specific idea, and that's fine. Publishing a specific blog post that doesn't add value could tarnish your "brand" as well as that of the blog hosting it. If a particular article just isn't clicking, feel free to set it aside. You can always revisit it later if you have an epiphany. And even if you never publish it, chalk it up as a learning experience.

However, chances are that every engineer has the experiences and/or opinions to fuel at least a handful of interesting blog posts. Please don't give up until you're done reading the extensive "what to write about" discussion in chapter 2.

1.4   *The path forward*

By now, we hope you recognize the value in writing blog posts and admit defeat after our brutal takedown of all your excuses. What next?

First, you need an idea to write about—preferably a healthy pipeline with a variety of different topics you can consider and prioritize over time. We can't tell you what to write. But we can share some triggers that should spark ideas, and we can also help you build a system for discovering and prioritizing topics that align with your focus. If you're already set in this respect, feel free to skip chapter 2 and proceed to chapter 3.

Next, the real work begins: moving from an interesting idea to a compelling blog post. First, what does "a compelling blog post" even mean? We'll share some traits prevalent across a variety of popular engineering blog posts, with lots of examples and explanations. Then, we'll take a systematic look at how to craft your own compelling blog post. We'll share strategies for getting your ideas drafted, tightened, and publishable with as little pain as possible. The focus is on what's most important for a clear, compelling technical article (spoiler: it's certainly not grammar nitpicks).

We hope to provide enough background so that the editorial voice in your head learns to act as a proxy for your reader. We'll cover some simple rules for improving precision by cutting the lard factor and tapping generative AI tools as part of the reviewing and revision process. Knowing that not every blog post warrants extensive revision time, we suggest what to prioritize when you just need to get it done fast as well as ways to give an exceptionally high profile post a little extra polish.

Those core strategies should serve you well across all types of blog posts—across all types of technical writing, really. But sometimes, the devil is in the details. Just like different programming languages have different principles, paradigms, and priorities, so do different types of blog posts. A good "Look at this amazing engineering feat we pulled off" blog post requires a somewhat different approach than a good "Why what everyone thinks about blah is wrong" blog post, for example. That's why we'll go deeper into seven common blog post patterns—sharing targeted best practices for each based on what seems to be resonating in the field.

Once you have a blog post—in any pattern—in progress, it's time to think about things such as promotion, adaptation, and extension. No matter what amazing feats or groundbreaking ideas lie buried within your blog, it will have limited effect if your target readers can't find it. You spent some fraction of your life writing a blog post; why not invest a little more time to maximize its payoff? We'll share a range of options, from easy boosts that take just a few minutes to more extensive refactoring and extension opportunities you can apply to work that you're particularly proud of.

Beyond that, the path leads beyond blogs. An effective blog post makes for a smooth transition into speaking opportunities at industry conferences. And once you've hit your stride with blogging, you might even consider writing a technical book. We'll cover both of those options in detail, sharing commonly overlooked considerations, opportunities, and lessons learned.

No matter which options you pursue, the strategies you learn for planning, creating, and revising technical content with your target audience in mind will help you communicate more clearly and convincingly across

- Async communications with teammates and curious/contentious users
- Doc tasks that inevitably land on your lap
- Proposals and code review comments where you're trying to persuade someone to do something new or differently
- Progress reports (especially as you try to explain that it really *is* much more complicated than everyone anticipated)
- Performance reviews where you're forced to capture a year's worth of work in n words to (hopefully) justify a salary increase or promotion
- The various job application materials and screeners you'll be obsessing over if the performance review did not yield the desired result

Summary

- Writing blog posts offers a broad array of benefits ranging from building connections across the tech community to honing your skills and advancing your career.

- Most of the reasons cited to avoid writing blog posts (not a writer, not a native English speaker, it's not completed, it's not new, and so forth) don't hold up under closer scrutiny.
- This book helps engineers draft compelling blog posts fast by sharing lessons learned from popular blog posts alongside pragmatic writing strategies targeting engineers.

What to write

Selecting a promising topic is the single most important task for creating an engineering blog post that gets read. A catchy title, eloquent sentences, solid code examples, even cool interactive elements—none of that matters if you're not covering a topic that's a good fit for both you and your readers. The flip side of that: if you provide an impressive level of technical insight on a topic your readers truly care about, slight imperfections (like a few rough sentences) will likely be forgiven.

How do you find these perfect topics? They're probably lurking all around your daily work; you just need to start identifying them as such.

This chapter focuses on how to build a healthy list of ideas that you—*you* in particular, not some generic engineer—should be able to develop into compelling blog posts. We start by providing a memorable litmus test for deciding what types of topic ideas have the most potential. The bulk of the chapter focuses on getting the ideas flowing, sharing all sorts of ways you might find inspiration in your daily work and across broader industry discussions. We close by discussing ways to keep a steady flow of fresh ideas on your radar.

2.1   *Prioritizing ideas: The 3 Ps*

There's certainly no shortage of engineering blog posts out there. And with generative artificial intelligence (AI) ready to spin off a virtually endless supply of mindlessly regurgitated ideas, it's getting even harder to rise above all the noise.

You'll get a detailed look at a handful of characteristics that make a blog post stand out, get read, and ultimately get remembered in the next chapter. But as we mentioned at the beginning of this chapter, your topic choice is paramount. If you want to earn a spot in the world of respected engineering blog posts, it's absolutely nonnegotiable that you choose a topic that's rooted in your own experiences—something that you can provide a uniquely interesting perspective on.

To set yourself up for success, remember this handy little test when you're evaluating potential blog post topics. Does your topic meet at least one of the "3 Ps"? Is it about something that you're particularly proud of, pained by, or passionate about?

Let's unpack those a little:

- *Proud of*—What accomplishments are you eager to show off to your engineering peers? What's really going to impress your users or fellow contributors?
- *Pained by*—What challenges have been causing constant headaches and blocking you from forward progress?
- *Passionate about*—What else gets your blood racing?

These are the forces that drive compelling engineering blog posts—giving rise to the unique technical insights that your peers are hoping to gain and the convincing perspective that should keep them hooked.

We can't guarantee that your blog post will bring instant fame if your topic passes this 3 Ps test. But if you try to force a blog post about something that you're not personally proud of, pained by, or passionate about, we can pretty much guarantee that it *won't* yield great results.

A virtually effortless way to test a topic idea

Want a virtually effortless way to test the response to a topic idea? Float it out as a social post. If it takes off, that's a good indicator that a related blog post could gain some nice traction. If it doesn't strike a chord initially, don't despair (yet). Try a few more times and variations before you give up. Social media is fickle.

Here's an example of a playful post that garnered a surprising level of attention (yes, we turned it into a blog post):

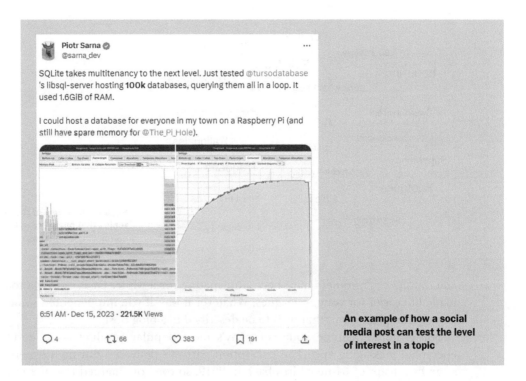

Piotr Sarna @
@sarna_dev

SQLite takes multitenancy to the next level. Just tested @tursodatabase 's libsql-server hosting **100k** databases, querying them all in a loop. It used 1.6GiB of RAM.

I could host a database for everyone in my town on a Raspberry Pi (and still have spare memory for @The_Pi_Hole).

6:51 AM · Dec 15, 2023 · **221.5K** Views

4   66   383   191

An example of how a social media post can test the level of interest in a topic

2.2 Topics, topics, everywhere

If you're working as an engineer, you probably already have a ton of blog post content in your head (even if you don't recognize it as such yet). We hope that as you read this section, you'll jot down some initial thoughts and start seeing blog post topics everywhere.

We focus mainly on topic triggers from the work you're doing every day: not just the cool things you built, but also colossal failures, bug hunts, difficult design decisions, high-stakes architectural shifts, and other fun stuff. We also look at triggers from broader industry controversies and challenges. These will most likely be read by your engineering peers. We close with a few ideas for blog posts specifically targeting your users (far beyond the standard "we released a thing—it's great" blog post). See figure 2.1 for a preview of topic ideas.

This is an extensive, but certainly not exhaustive, list of topic triggers. Consider it a starting point, and let your imagination go wild (as long as you hit at least one of those 3 *P*s!).

2.2.1 That cool thing you implemented

A fairly obvious inspiration, and yet it's often ignored. If you recently implemented something cool, write about it! The definition of *cool* is quite broad, on purpose. It might mean a technological breakthrough so impressive that you'll immediately get a call from the Millennium Prize committee. It can also be a useful feature that your

Figure 2.1   Some of the many topics that might make for compelling blog posts

community or customers have been anticipating for a while. Or it can be a tool that made life easier for your colleagues. Whatever it was, if you implemented something, there's a tangible result that begs to be described in a blog post.

For example, assume your company's most popular product is an end-to-end encrypted messaging app. The encryption part was delivered during a hypergrowth stage by a team of 64 new hires back in 2019, so everyone agreed that the only supported algorithm was going to be ROT13. After all, there's a fair chance nobody would ever notice its questionable security. The implementation is simple, which also makes it rock solid, right? When you joined the team a few years later, you reimplemented the core encryption module with an algorithm that isn't crackable by an average preschooler. Definitely worth a blog post! Also, please be either very diplomatic in the "previous implementation" section or strategically forget to mention the details.

This topic idea feeds the "How We Built It" pattern, which is the subject of chapter 10. It might also lead to the "Non-markety Product Perspectives" pattern (see chapter 13).

2.2.2   A security incident post-mortem

People absolutely love reading about other people's problems. Did you discover a bug that led to a security incident—a personal data leak or data loss? A blog post dissecting such a situation immediately triggers a primitive reflex in your reader's brainstem to grab some popcorn and bask in somebody else's serious trouble, while reveling in the fact that their life isn't so hard after all. And ruthless human nature aside, security incidents are often really interesting from a technical point of view. They are naturally engaging and offer educational value as well. Other developers are encouraged to revisit their own code and see whether their projects could have suffered the same fate if they were less lucky.

For example, imagine that a user logged in as normal and happened to see another user's data. Also assume this was discovered by a decent human being—someone who didn't use the data for malicious reasons and just reported the incident straight to security@your-fancy-company-name.ai. This incident *will* damage your company's reputation, but the penalty will be even more severe if you fail to disclose any details. Your users will find out sooner or later. If your leaders decide to embrace it, they might be desperately seeking someone to write a high-profile article divulging more details. This could very well be you, assuming that you have access to all the interesting technical bits:

- Why did the incident happen?
- How did you discover it?
- How did you fix it?
- How did you ensure it would never happen again?
- Can it affect other projects?

Regardless of the specifics, this is going to be an interesting read. This topic idea feeds the "Lessons Learned" pattern, which is the subject of chapter 11.

2.2.3 *How your infrastructure survived a traffic spike (or didn't)*

Depending on the situation, this could easily go one of two ways. If the stuff hits the fan, you can probably draft a rather compelling "we learned our lesson" type of blog post and hopefully save someone else from the pain that you suffered. A good example of such a blog post is a description of why your system suffered from downtime, for how long, what you learned, how you're preventing it from happening again (you hope!), and how deeply sorry you are for all the affected users. Or, if all went well, it could be a shameless boast of how perfectly you predicted the future, ensuring that the Black Friday spike was drama free and didn't even register as an anomaly in your metrics.

Both are good writing material in their own way. Traffic spikes are common, and their infrastructure-related side effects are common as well. It might sound like bad news, but it's good from the writer's perspective—it just means more inspiration for technical blog posts.

This topic idea feeds the "Lessons Learned" pattern, which is the subject of chapter 11.

2.2.4 *Bug hunting*

Looking for an elusive bug for five straight days is the most infuriating part of computer programming. On the other hand, it's a requirement for achieving the unforgettable peace of mind and blissful state you reach right after zeroing in on the root cause. What's more, a bug hunting adventure is also a perfect plot for a blog post, or even a whole series of them.

Such articles are the computer science world's equivalent of detective stories. Some read them for the thrill; others read them for the educational aspect. In any case, one thing is certain: those kinds of stories often land on the front page of news aggregators.

Note that this trigger is related to the security post-mortem one, but it's much broader. The bug in question can also be a sudden performance regression that happens only on a certain CPU architecture, a mysterious bug that disappears as soon as you try to pinpoint its root cause (a.k.a. a *heisenbug*), or even a really convincing false negative in tests. This topic idea feeds the "Bug Hunt" pattern, which is the subject of chapter 8.

2.2.5   *An open source contribution*

Programmers are often particularly proud of their open source contributions—and rightly so! It shows the world that you're capable of implementing things that aren't covered by five layers of nondisclosure agreements. It's also a public contribution to software that other developers use and appreciate.

The beauty of open source is that since the code is, well, open, it's fine to describe it in detail in a blog post, provide snippets, and even explain how to use it in a pet project. And writing such a blog post not only gives you an avid audience across the project's community, but it also attracts more eyeballs to the project. Talk about win-win!

You could even write about something as simple as a bug fix. Next time you hit an unexpected bug in an open source project and decide to roll up your sleeves and post a fix (instead of just complaining about it online), please share how you fixed it and why. You're a decent human being, and every single maintainer of every single open source project is grateful that you decided to take the "I fixed it!" path rather than the entitled "I need it so you guys need to fix it—so what if you don't get paid for the work" path. (Believe it or not, the latter one gets maintainers frustrated occasionally.)

This topic idea feeds the "How We Built It" pattern, which is the subject of chapter 10.

2.2.6   *A fun weekend project*

A nice tool or gadget that you built in your spare time is perfect blog post material. A weekend project is something that developers do for fun, so just hearing about one evokes positive reactions in your readers. Quite likely, it will also remind many of your readers that it's been quite a while since they worked on an interesting side project. They will probably treat your piece as inspiration and be grateful for it.

Describing how you achieved your goal can be just as much fun as implementing the project. And let's be honest: we've all taken on certain side projects mainly so we could brag about them later. Well, a blog post is a perfect outlet for that bragging.

There's also a pragmatic/professional twist here. Maybe you're worried that you've suffered permanent brain damage from too many days spent shifting around outdated enterprise Java code of questionable quality just to bump up the "passed tests" ratio? And to check whether the synapses are still firing, you spend weekends transforming a Raspberry Pi into a full-fledged DIY home security system? Maybe somebody from the microcontroller industry will read your blog post and reach out with a nice job offer that's much better aligned with your true passion.

This topic idea feeds the "How We Built It" pattern, which is the subject of chapter 10.

2.2.7   *An interesting design decision and tradeoff you made*

Some design decisions are straightforward. If updating your dependencies makes your project both safer and faster, it's a no-brainer. Those kinds of moves can sometimes justify a blog post, but more often, they are only briefly mentioned as part of a larger restructuring. Building your whole article around the idea that "we updated the Java version from one that reached end-of-life five years ago to a slightly fresher one that's still supported" is more likely to trigger a duh reaction in your readers—but you're looking for a wow, or at least a huh reaction. Fortunately, many design decisions require genuine tradeoffs, and those are way more interesting for both the writer and the reader.

For example, latency-minded engineers want to see every last bit of performance squeezed out of a project, even at the expense of developer experience. But many others aren't willing to make that sacrifice; they'd be fully willing to take a hit on performance if it means the product will be super easy for them to use. Sometimes, the tradeoff might seem formidable but be perfectly justified in specific cases. That's great—nonobvious decisions lead to more interesting articles.

More specifically, put yourself in the shoes of someone designing a database. On the one hand, you could let users store unstructured data (looking at you, document stores). That decision would make for a great developer experience, enabling developers to get up to speed fast and change the shape of their data often. Or, you could take a totally different approach and implement strict rules governing how the data is structured. With efficient indexes created in all the right places, the database can perform tenfold faster than the unstructured one previously described. But the tradeoff is the pain inflicted on users: now they're stuck worrying about whether their database schemas are in the right shape.

Each approach has its merits. Why did you choose one option over the other? What do users gain and lose, and how might they compensate for what's lost? That's all great fodder for an interesting blog post, or maybe even two: a technical one for your fellow engineers and a more practical one for users.

This topic idea could feed into a few different patterns: the "How We Built It" pattern (chapter 10), "We Rewrote It in X" (chapter 9), and/or the "Non-markety Product Perspectives" pattern (chapter 13).

2.2.8 *An architectural shift you're making*

Moving off a giant cloud provider to on-premises? Or maybe it's just migrating to a new serverless database in hopes of keeping up with the influx of new users? Describe your experience; your peers around the world have likely also thought about it a lot.

The main blocker against large architectural decisions is that they're large and architectural. That means *everything* can go wrong. And we all know who's going to be blamed for it. Hint: It's not any of the five managers who enthusiastically approved your decision, already imagining how the CEO will be praising them for slashing infrastructure costs.

Engineers facing these decisions rightfully search the internet for similar use cases, trying to estimate the risk-versus-gain ratio. This trigger is also a natural follow-up of "How your infrastructure survived a traffic spike (or didn't)." If it didn't, a shift is in order—and everyone who enjoyed reading about your first adventure will surely be eager to hear how it influenced your architecture and infrastructure.

This topic idea feeds into a variation of the "We Rewrote It in X" blog pattern, which is the subject of chapter 9. It could also feed the "Lessons Learned" pattern (chapter 11) or the "Non-markety Product Perspectives" pattern (chapter 13).

2.2.9 *Frustration and fatigue*

A new programming language appears. Its community grows, it is ergonomic, and it introduces some fresh ideas on how to make programmers' lives better. A few start-ups decide to bet on it as an emerging standard, and you join one of those startups. Quite soon, the honeymoon phase ends, and you realize that you just want to travel back in time and stay with C forever. You really just want to use raw pointers and pass everything by value. You genuinely miss the days spent hunting segmentation faults—it wasn't *that* bad, was it?

This is a common storyline, and it applies to every language that ever became popular, from R and Python to Rust and Zig. But that doesn't make it a bad read, though! In fact, it makes your take on this story even more appealing. If you feel the frustration, chances are that your readers empathize. From there, two things could happen:

- Your readers will feel better—a problem shared is a problem halved.
- Somebody will point out that your problems are already solved in a way you didn't know. Bonus: This presents a great opportunity to write a follow-up blog post where you admit that you were wrong, and the shiny new language is indeed amazing.

Blog posts written by disappointed developers who relentlessly roast some technology often stimulate discussion and occasionally incite flame wars between that technology's zealots and its livid opponents.

Not convinced that the world needs yet another commentary on the same old topic? Then go search for "async Rust sucks." You'll find all sorts of articles such as:

- "It's just me or rust async is still really hard?" (sic!)
- "Async Rust is a bad language"
- "Why asynchronous Rust doesn't work"
- "Think twice before using async Rust"

None of these articles looks particularly distinctive. Yet each time one is published, it attracts a new round of attention on various aggregators and forums. If you can channel your frustration and fatigue into an interesting new angle on a controversial topic, go for it. If you can crank out a draft in the heat of the moment, even better!

This topic idea could feed the "Lessons Learned" pattern, which is the subject of chapter 11, or the "Thoughts on Trends" pattern, which is the subject of chapter 12. It might also follow a blog post on the "We Rewrote It in X" pattern, covered in chapter 9.

2.2.10 *Take a stand on some contentious topic*

This trigger works especially well when your stand doesn't fit the mainstream narrative. If the last 15 most popular articles meticulously described all kinds of problems with asynchronous Rust programming, fat chance yet another one that repeats the same old talk track will stand out. However, a title saying "Async Rust does not, in fact, suck" draws attention and is also very polite to the community.

Technical matters are rarely black and white, and everyone uses and experiences technologies differently. If you disagree with the popular opinion and feel you have good reasons to do so, go ahead and describe it in a blog post! What do we mean by "a good reason"? For instance, if everyone on the internet seems to hate a particular framework, but you have actual hands-on experience with it (and it was a pleasure to work with). For politeness points, be sure to focus on detailing your own experiences, not dismissing others' views or pains. Writing articles on contentious topics is also a nice opportunity to get to know other proponents of your line of thought—they might reach out after reading your article.

This topic idea feeds the "Thoughts on Trends" pattern, which is the subject of chapter 12. It could also feed the "Lessons Learned" pattern, which is covered in chapter 11.

2.2.11 *Sweet numbers*

If your recent contribution sped up user requests tenfold, and you have repeatable benchmarks to verify your claims, by all means share this! Virtually any quantifiable improvement could make for an eye-catching blog post. Beyond speed metrics, you might write about

- Squeezing thousands more virtualized environments into a single computer by optimizing the image size
- Slashing your company's cloud spend
- Reducing the amount of data loaded upon each web page refresh from megabytes to bytes

The technical audience loves numbers. However, these readers also love nitpicking benchmarks and trying to prove they were preconceived, fake, subjective, and "ran on your laptop, so it doesn't count." Wherever the numbers come from, they may be worth a blog post if they are impressive (and look even more impressive in colorful graphs).

This topic idea feeds the "Benchmarks and Test Results" pattern, which is the subject of chapter 14.

2.2.12 *Propose using something in an unexpected way*

Already intriguing, huh? And this is just a vague blog post inspiration, not even a real headline. The key part is "unexpected," which immediately draws attention to your blog post. Many readers will assume your content is educational and valuable, ergo worth reading. Some will visit your blog post only to prove to themselves (and you) that it was not, in fact, unexpected. They thought of it 15 years ago and classified it as a bad idea even back then. Your blog post now offers them the opportunity that they've been waiting for: the perfect comment section for sharing their insight with the world!

What might constitute unexpected usage?

- Encoding data in images to transfer hidden messages. It's called *steganography*, which makes this blog post idea an irresistible combination of a smart word *and* an unexpected usage of something. Use it with caution!

- Compiling a 1990s-era video game to WebAssembly, so it can be played in a browser. Extra points for nostalgia.

- Transforming your Raspberry Pi into a homemade curtain opener to enjoy being woken up by sunlight and the soothing buzz of a $1 DC motor. (If you don't find the sound a cheap DC motor makes soothing, consider a career outside of the tech industry.)

This topic idea feeds the "How We Built It" pattern, which is the subject of chapter 10.

2.2.13   *Revisit past predictions*

Although the annual tradition of publishing tech predictions might seem trite, revisiting *past* predictions about the future sparks retrospection and lively discussion. It's fine if your predictions were ridiculously wrong. In fact, a good rule of thumb is that the further off you were, the better the blog post is going to be!

Articles focused on the fact that the author was right 10 years ago tend to be boastful and boring. People can't help but point out that it might have been pure coincidence (and meanwhile you were probably wrong about hundreds of other things). However, if your predictions were embarrassingly wrong, there's a good chance the article will be funny, with an air of "look how young and naïve I was."

This trigger works best if you can refer back to past predictions published in articles or even social media posts. And if you made a series of past predictions, you now have fodder for a whole series of analysis posts. Continue publishing your annual predictions, and you can keep the cycle going in perpetuity, including high-profile posts that feature milestone anniversaries (e.g., 5, 10, or 20 years).

Maybe you didn't make any past predictions yourself? Feel free to comment on some particularly prescient—or preposterous—predictions that you've stumbled on and feel passionately about. If you're commenting on past predictions by the tech equivalent of an "influencer," be prepared for an attentive (and potentially antagonistic) audience.

This topic idea likely feeds the "Thoughts on Trends" pattern, which is the subject of chapter 12.

2.2.14   *Capability clarification*

You took days or years off your life painstakingly implementing some groundbreaking product capability (such as the one that landed you the Millenium Prize referenced earlier). Then you read or overheard some misguided explanation of it—maybe from a user, maybe from someone on your company's own support or sales team. Maybe it was even something you personally (yet hastily) documented to deem it done-done.

First, take a deep breath. Next, take this as a sign that you should probably dedicate a little more time to ensure that it's properly explained. Remember that you're biased by spending all this time working on that particular feature in that particular field. It might sound obvious to you what cross-entropy or ReLU means and why it's a crucial part of your cool new artificial intelligence model, but the average reader would first need to look up every second word you say. No wonder they misunderstand (and misuse) it later!

Beware that your users probably won't care about all the same things that your engineering peers do. It's totally valid to write about the same capability in two different blog posts for two different audiences: one highlighting your engineering acumen to your peers and the other helping the user understand what's in it for them. Also, don't think that it's ever too late to introduce something or describe it differently. Most readers won't care if you implemented the capability a while ago; they're mainly curious about whether it will make their lives easier, given their specific technical requirements and challenges. And if you still think newness is essential, take a look at the decades-old articles that still trend on Hacker News at least weekly.

Many engineers shy away from writing user-targeted blog posts, particularly if their organization has a dedicated product team for introducing releases and promoting new capabilities. But you, the engineer who knows this thing inside and out, hold the keys to the deeper no-spin information that users *really* want, especially if you're building products for the dev community. Engineers are known to be notoriously bad at marketing (cue the saying that if it were up to engineers, sushi would be described as "cold dead fish.") And that's precisely why skeptical users would just love to read your technical take on product capabilities!

This topic idea feeds the "Non-markety Product Perspectives" pattern, which is the subject of chapter 13.

2.2.15 *Capability comparison*

You probably won't just wake up one day wanting to write "How the XYZ I worked on compares to some other product's ZYX." But you'll likely be forced into it sooner or later. Why? Users like to compare features as they comparison shop. To better understand the differences, they might seek information from the following:

- Online forums, where anyone seeking attention might share their infinite wisdom on how what you implemented compares to what someone else implemented.
- Your sales team, who then taps your product marketing team for their best guess at why yours is the best ever, for anyone and everyone.
- The other company's sales team, which leads to the same thing with a different bias.
- Generative AI, which will spew a few banal paragraphs about each, then politely state, "It's important to note that the choice between XYZ and ZYX depends on your specific use cases and requirements."

As you can imagine, none of these end well. Once this causes your organization enough pain, it will become your own personal pain. You'll get some urgent request for a blog post or presentation, likely as you're struggling to complete your latest project, take time off, or at some other inconvenient time. Why not get ahead of it? Just crank out one of these blog posts each time you implement a capability that might be perceived as similar to something else.

Even if you're not the expert on how every product addresses this somewhat similar thing, you are the world's top expert on how *you* did it. That puts you far ahead of all the previously referenced people who have no clue what *any* of the developers did (but are confidently explaining it anyway). A blog post based on this trigger could start with a quick overview of what you and your teammates already know about the other implementations (or learn after some swift research). Then, it might go deep into why you took your chosen path, why it matters, and what types of technical requirements your approach is best suited for.

This topic idea feeds the "Non-markety Product Perspectives" pattern, which is the subject of chapter 13. It could also feed the "Benchmarks and Test Results" pattern, which is covered in chapter 14.

2.2.16 *Footgun prevention*

You don't love getting interrupted to field yet another incident of users shooting themselves in the foot with some capability you worked on? Perhaps they keep asking for the whole database contents in one piece, even though it's clearly documented as an antipattern. Or maybe users sometimes experience mysterious database concurrency spikes even though the client side has nicely fixed concurrency. After yet another late-night diagnosis, you discover that, yet again, it's because someone "optimized" the default driver configuration that you carefully crafted when you designed the driver—to the point where it ends up resending requests before the original ones were confirmed to have failed.

Next time, jot it down as a blog post idea. Then write it up, once and for all, so you never have to deal with it again. Maybe you can start off with a brief overview of why you implemented that capability in the first place and some of the key assumptions and decisions made as you built it. Then, you can take a detailed look at some of the misuses, abuses, and mistakes that are making your life miserable. Finally, tell them what you'll be doing with all the time you've now saved yourself (or maybe just gloat silently).

This topic idea feeds the "Non-markety Product Perspectives" pattern, which is the subject of chapter 13.

2.2.17 *Why you're building something*

The nature and scope of this trigger varies as wildly as the things you might be building. If you're a junior engineer working on a stable product, it might involve something as granular as detailing why you're extending the query language with a new filtering option. If you've been voluntold to lead a next-generation-of-some-core-component project, write to share the rationale with the users who will ultimately be affected. Bonus: you might also catch the interest of some enthusiastic community contributors who offer their feedback and assistance. Or, if you're a founder or founding engineer, you could line up a series of blog posts that explain the very reason for your company's existence, placing it on the radar of potential users, employees, investors, media, and influencers well before you have a product to show.

In any case, the same core questions should get the blog post ideas flowing:

- What's wrong with the status quo?
- What elements are working well and should be preserved?
- What other attempts have been made to address this problem?
- Did something change recently to make the previous approach less viable?
- What would the ideal approach look like, and what would it enable people to do?
- What are your technical goals and guiding principles?
- How will you implement it?
- Who should be most interested in it?
- How might users apply it?
- How will you measure its improvement over the alternative thing?

Answers to just one of these questions might be fodder for multiple blog posts!

This topic idea feeds the "Non-markety Product Perspectives" pattern, which is the subject of chapter 13.

2.3 Increasing your trigger exposure

People go to great lengths to avoid asthma and allergy triggers. But *blog post* triggers are things to be embraced, not evaded.

It's important to keep tabs on what's new and what people are already talking about in your specific area of interest. This is how you can spot emerging trends and be among the first to start thinking and writing about them. And by keeping your finger on the pulse of a discussion, you can make sure that your take on it actually advances the conversation in some interesting way. Addressing the existing dialogue head-on will win you more friends and upvotes than unintentionally repeating it out of ignorance.

This section provides tips for exposing your brain to a steady stream of blog post topic triggers. Before we get into specific ways to unearth diamonds in the rough across social media, RSS feeds, and the like, here are two overarching recommendations:

- Make sure you have a centralized place to save your ideas! This can be a simple text file or an app designed to save articles and/or social posts across platforms. Scribble them in a physical notepad if you wish! It doesn't matter how you do it; just find some system that works for you.
- Set up reminders to browse these areas at some interval that makes sense for you. Also, timebox this browsing so you avoid getting sucked too deep down the rabbit hole.

2.3.1 Social media

We know, this realm is riddled with problems. But you need to hold your nose and find some tolerable path forward if you want to stay on top of what people are talking about and connect with potential readers. We discuss the connecting angle in chapter 15. Here, let's look specifically at monitoring social media discussions.

The following sections offer a few ideas for making social media more productive (from a blog post topic trigger perspective, at least).

TAKE CONTROL

Figure out how to get ahead of the recommendation algorithms. Does your platform of choice allow you to build and monitor lists of accounts you trust? Can you craft some nice searches (maybe using quotation marks to target precise terms) and bookmark the resulting URLs? Can you use or create tools that yield better results by going through the platform's API? Whatever it takes! You're an engineer; you can certainly figure out clever ways to gain more control over what you see.

CURATE A CIRCLE OF TRUST

Start following a carefully selected group of accounts (perhaps as a list; see the previous section), then expand cautiously from there. It's better to create a list of two people who post a few interesting things per month than get a constant barrage of posts you don't care about. If someone in that initial "circle of trust" reposts something interesting, peruse that other account and add it if it looks promising. Don't hesitate to cut your ties if an account you're following does not understand the concept of TMI (oversharing too much personal information). Carefully monitor what you're fed, especially at first, then prune and shape as needed. Aim for a bonsai tree, not a wilderness.

VENTURE OUT INTO THE WILD (OCCASIONALLY)

If you're ever feeling particularly brave or just have a little time to kill before (during?) a meeting, take a look at what the algorithms recommend for you. Maybe you'll discover something unexpectedly interesting. If nothing else, you can validate your decision to generally avoid algorithm-driven "for you" feeds.

2.3.2 *Virtual communities*

Your best bet here is to find specialized, well-moderated communities that are valuable (or the closest approximation you can find, at least). For help hunting them down, ask around (maybe in that circle of trust you've set up on some social media platform). Or use the broader platform search to see what groups are talking about your topics of interest, and look at the discussion quality, frequency, and civility before you consider tracking it.

Again, it's best to start small and expand cautiously. If you stumble upon a particularly insightful user in one group, do a little detective work and track down other communities they're active in. Maybe some of those are worth your (timeboxed) time as well.

What about the orange elephant in the room (Hacker News)? For better or for worse, this is a highly unfocused discussion where anything could rise to the front page, and a top-notch engineering blog post might be sandwiched between an obituary and a rant about some weird element of popular culture (see figure 2.2). But there's one saving grace here: robust search functionality. Be sure to learn the advanced search syntax and do a little searching across the internet for undocumented Hacker News features.

10. ▲ Scheduling Internals (tontinton.com)
    99 points by signa11 10 hours ago | hide | 9 comments
11. ▲ Scientists find genetic signature of Down syndrome in ancient bones (nytimes.com)
    111 points by bookofjoe 14 hours ago | hide | 59 comments
12. ▲ Talc – A fast and flexible allocator for no_std and WebAssembly (github.com/sfbdragon)
    83 points by excsn 10 hours ago | hide | 20 comments
13. ▲ Children need risk, fear, and excitement in play (afterbabel.com)
    206 points by paulpauper 14 hours ago | hide | 158 comments
14. ▲ I keep making things out of checkboxes (2021) (bryanbraun.com)
    88 points by surprisetalk 7 hours ago | hide | 17 comments
15. ▲ Ask HN: Why is HN so often down?
    107 points by neverrroot 1 hour ago | hide | 72 comments
16. ▲ A Social History of Jell-O Salad (2023) (seriouseats.com)
    8 points by EndXA 5 hours ago | hide | 4 comments
17. ▲ The floppy disk music scene (theverge.com)
    67 points by marban 11 hours ago | hide | 25 comments
18. ▲ The Claro Programming Language (clarolang.com)
    90 points by signa11 11 hours ago | hide | 32 comments
19. ▲ Common Mistakes in Modularisation (two-wrongs.com)
    13 points by thunderbong 5 hours ago | hide | discuss
20. ▲ CT scans show how Heinz's new ketchup cap depends on shear-thinning principles (lumafield.com)
    105 points by viasfo 5 hours ago | hide | 127 comments

Figure 2.2   An example of the range of topics that might be covered on the front page of Hacker News

2.3.3   Feeds and subscriptions

Once you identify reliably solid idea sources through the previously mentioned means, go ahead and follow them directly. Using your aggregation tool of choice, slurp in the source's updates (by means of RSS feeds, ActivityPub, or the AT protocol) and voilà— you get some centralized page or inbox chock full of articles to scan, and maybe even read. Depending on the tool, you might also gain ways to fine-tune your feed, track read versus unread items, take notes, and so on.

And then there's newsletter subscriptions. The very thought of an engineer willfully opting into an email newsletter would have seemed outrageous a few years ago. However, you can now find quite a few high-quality newsletters on dev and tech topics. Some of them are even so valuable that people are willing to pay for them (e.g., *The Pragmatic Engineer* and *Software Design: Tidy First?*). How do you find these newsletters? Ask your peers and keep your eyes and ears open in the previously mentioned areas.

2.3.4   Team chat apps

If you don't already have one, create a channel in your team messaging app for sharing interesting (not necessarily "good") articles and social posts. The internal comment threads will likely be much spicier than whatever was originally shared. Beyond being a good source of blog post ideas, these discussions are also helpful for reading the room. If you decide to write a heated retort to some "future of whatever" blog post that everyone else on your team thinks is the smartest thing ever, it's probably wise to know what you're getting into before you decide to click Publish.

To put this into action, just create a #blog channel and invite everyone to join. That creates mild social pressure on your colleagues to participate. Some people will start slow and only engage in discussions of whether a suggested blog post is a good idea. Others will take the bait and suggest their own ideas right away.

Messages with the potential to become full-blown articles might look like

- "Hey, somebody posted that he's frustrated because there's no decent open source tool for stress-testing GraphQL databases, and we developed one last week."
- "I reverse-engineered my infrared sauna last week—I can post some tech details if anyone's interested."
- "I described our distributed architecture at a local meetup last week, and like 200 people asked me for a write-up."

An increasing number of companies are (still) hiring remote engineers, and chat apps have become the natural successor to coffee breaks in the kitchen. They are also the perfect refuge for programmers who have an otherwise unproductive day (happens to all of us, don't worry). A quick round of email + chat app + GitHub issue tracker checks makes you feel as if you did something important for the company. While lurking for new dad jokes in the #random channel isn't very productive, brainstorming ideas in #blog is!

Additionally, chat apps often allow addressing everyone with an equivalent of Slack's @here, which helps get more attention for the most recent blog post ideas. A chatbot that pings a random user every other week and gently urges them to share a blog post idea is also a good stimulus for keeping the channel alive (and lively).

Summary

- Selecting a promising topic is the single most important task for creating an engineering blog post that gets read.
- The best topic ideas are those that 1) are rooted in your own experiences and 2) you are proud of, pained by, or passionate about.
- You probably already have a ton of blog post content in your head, even if you don't recognize it as such yet.
- Beyond that cool thing you implemented, blog post idea inspiration can come from epic failures, bug hunts, fun weekend projects, difficult design decisions, footgun prevention, and much more.
- A carefully controlled approach to tracking social media, virtual communities, and feeds can yield a steady stream of blog post idea triggers.

Captivating readers
3

This chapter covers

- The difficulties of—and opportunities in—reaching interested readers
- The critical characteristics of blog posts that readers open, read, share, and remember
- How popular blog posts from the past year exemplify these critical characteristics

The previous chapter presented ideas on what to write. Now let's shift focus to what engineers and other technical readers want to read. A compelling topic is essential for getting that initial click. But what will compel people to actually read the complete article, consider it valuable, and hopefully even share it with their colleagues and peers across social media and virtual communities?

A captivating bug hunt article will vary dramatically from an article where a well-known industry expert roasts a highly hyped technology, or one that shares how a team implemented an industry-changing algorithm. That's why this book provides in-depth analysis of these and other blog post patterns, sharing examples, characteristics, as well as specific dos and don'ts for writing your own blog posts in those patterns. We'll launch into those pattern-specific deep dives in part 3 of this book.

But across patterns, several core characteristics are shared by the blog posts that stand out: the articles that engineers talk about and that ultimately become part of the industry's knowledge base. That's what we explore in this chapter.

We don't pretend to know some secret n-step formula for guaranteed success, and this certainly is *not* an attempt at (yet another) spammy "Definitive Guide to Trending on Hacker News." But we did spend quite a lot of time looking at what tends to trend, monitoring industry discussions, and debating this with our engineering peers. Based on that, we're sharing the three core things we believe are essential. We hope our humble proposal gets more people thinking about this topic and ultimately sparks a productive discussion.

NOTE   This chapter focuses on what makes an article stand out. The remainder of this book (particularly parts 2 and 3) looks at pragmatic ways to ensure your own blog posts embody these characteristics.

3.1   Standing out

Consider the following:

- Around 1300 articles are submitted to Hacker News every day (https://news .ycombinator.com/item?id=33454140; "dang" is a Hacker News moderator).
- Anyone can now automatically generate an article on any topic and in any writing style using free generative AI chatbots.
- Any company or individual willing to pay for AI writing platforms can automatically spew thousands of uninspired formulaic articles in an attempt to capture search traffic.

But despite all the noise, engineers with insatiable curiosity still take the time to discover, read, share, and discuss deeply technical articles. And now that everyone has seen the alternative (articles created with generative AI), truly insightful articles are appreciated even more. Reading such blog posts is a primary means of tracking what's new, solving problems, and deepening domain expertise. According to recent estimates, around 10M people visit Hacker News each day, curious to see what's trending (and especially what's controversial, with popcorn in hand). Beyond that, people are also seeking and discovering articles across

- The evolving landscape of social media platforms and other virtual communities
- Various newsletters that share recommended articles
- #techchat-like channels on internal messaging apps
- RSS and Atom feeds they have set up

The opportunity to reach interested readers is definitely there for the taking. So, how do you tap it?

3.2 Critical characteristics

We propose that standout articles share the following characteristics:

- Intriguing topic
- Distinctive educational core
- Smooth delivery

Let's examine each characteristic in turn. Then we'll explore how they're carried out in five real-world examples.

3.2.1 Intriguing topic

An interesting topic is imperative for readers to notice your article. When browsing for their next thing to read, readers look at the title and estimate whether the topic is intriguing enough to engage. In those few precious seconds before switching to another title, they judge whether the topic is valuable, that is, educational, controversial, and/or in line with their field expertise.

DISRUPTIVE

One way to make your engineering blog post stand out is to challenge the status quo. Taking a controversial stand on a widely assumed truth is likely to spark interesting discussions and lure readers in. Even people not generally interested in the topic will be tempted to read it for fear of missing out on the latest global flame war. For example, claiming that async Rust sucks secured a Hacker News front page spot for many blog posts.

EYE-OPENING

While disruptive articles often burn bright and then die out, articles that broaden a reader's perspective tend to snowball in effect. Eye-opening articles might

- Add novel insight into a well-known subject (e.g., a new approach to testing distributed systems)
- Introduce a whole new intriguing topic that the reader never even considered before but now desperately wants to learn about (thanks to your irresistible blog post title)

Both of those approaches invite the readers to explore new territories, a treat no engineer can resist.

RELEVANT

Readers of engineering blogs like to deep dive into their niche. If the topic touches challenges similar to the ones they work with day to day, they're likely to at least skim through it. An article that deepens readers' understanding of a technology they're interested in, or shows an interesting alternative to what they are currently working with, has a good chance of getting read and discussed.

Describing a general problem makes the article relevant to a broader audience, but it's also less relevant to any single reader than a more specific piece. There's a tradeoff. If you want to hedge your bets, consider writing both kinds of blog posts: some touching general subjects (e.g., a programming language) and some very specific to a technical niche (e.g., firmware for smart fridges). Also, try writing some posts geared to experts as well as others that help beginners get started with your area of expertise (especially if it's a growing domain).

3.2.2   *Distinctive educational core*

A good engineering blog post leaves readers with the satisfaction of having learned something new. Readers tend to remember this feeling and will often become loyal readers once you've proven that you have valuable insights to share.

The learned information should be useful, genuine, and transparent. The most grievous mistake is to try and slip in a pure marketing ploy disguised as an informative post. Readers will sense it, publicly shame you for it, and be justified in doing so. Good posts come from authors' genuine motivation to share knowledge. It's fine if that shared knowledge relates to your new product, but there's no place for ulterior motives to mislead.

EXCLUSIVE

Imagine one of those generic articles that's so obviously AI generated you can feel it from the first paragraph. A good engineering blog post should be the exact opposite. Bring some unique value that readers can't easily find, or ask perplexity.ai about: your experience, a controversial opinion, an unorthodox way of accomplishing something technical. A quality engineering blog post should be (much) more than glorified documentation sprinkled with one or two references to Wikipedia articles.

DEEP

Not every reader is interested in complicated technical details (not all the time, at least). And yet, they always appreciate it when authors clearly possess deep knowledge in the area they're writing about. The best articles include insights that stem from a deep understanding of the subject, fun facts, explaining common misunderstandings, and so on. It's fine for an author to be extremely opinionated in a field as long as it's also clear that they're highly experienced in it.

At the same time, great blog posts give readers enough information to form their own views and draw their own conclusions rather than blindly accept the author's. That's why it's so important to provide counterweight—for example, in the form of detailing drawbacks, pitfalls, and antipatterns alongside advantages and recommendations.

PRAGMATIC

Engineers are pragmatic beings. While they love reading purely theoretical academic papers, they love hands-on knowledge even more. This could come in the form of

- A useful script making everyday hacking easier
- A nice open source library
- A list of good practices before releasing software
- A book recommendation
- A list of steps on how to reproduce interesting results at home

If something can be applied immediately after reading the blog post, it's likely to be appreciated by the audience.

3.2.3 Smooth delivery

Reading articles is supposed to be educational, but it's also a form of entertainment. An article shouldn't be boring, painful, excruciatingly long, or otherwise cringeworthy. The audience tends to expect an up-to-date, engaging, and light read.

ENGAGING WRITING

Assuming that your intriguing topic and title lured a reader in, the job is only half done. Before they can learn something, readers need to read the article, and an engaging writing style is key here. A peer-to-peer conversational tone generally works better than being overly formal. Be authentic, and add side notes and personal comments wherever applicable. Last but not least, do not force the jokes; the forced ones are not funny by definition.

If you can find a way to connect with the reader, go for it! Readers appreciate a personal perspective they can relate to (and maybe commiserate with). Clear language, organized structure, and a logical flow also help keep the reader's attention. If the reader gets lost in a chaotic narrative, they might just give up on the article.

APPEALING DESIGN

Aesthetics are important in engineering blog posts. Some might claim that engineers only care about good content and only read blog posts straight from RSS feeds delivered straight to their terminals anyway. In practice, a nicely stylized blog post is more likely to be read to completion and remembered. How do you make it nice?

- Use white space to logically split the paragraphs and sections.
- Ensure that section headers stand out so that readers can quickly scan through the article or navigate to a section they want to read (or reread).
- Make sure the graphics are high resolution, readable, not blurred.
- Use a consistent theme for charts whenever possible.

Some articles are purposely stylized as a single block of text. While cool in theory, that usually just annoys readers, particularly those searching for a specific section. On the other side of the spectrum, an overload of brightly colored charts will make the blog post resemble one of those scammy websites that try to convince you to enter a lottery to win a "guaranteed" iPhone. And if the article, including code samples, isn't readable both in light and dark mode (looking at you, Medium), technical readers will not be pleased.

UP-TO-DATE

Reading blog posts from 2010 is tricky. On the one hand, they are often full of interesting discoveries, still surprisingly applicable to current technologies. On the other hand, half of the hyperlinks are likely to be long dead, and there's no comparison with newer technology. It doesn't have to be like that though! Blog posts can, and should, be updated.

The update could occur as a new section labeled "June 2057 Update," a link to a follow-up article, or just a revival of dead links (e.g., by replacing the bygone ones with their eternal web.archive.org mirrors.) It's also customary for blog posts to retroactively include links to online discussions about them, allowing new readers to join (or at least skim through) the Q and A.

Keeping old articles alive and up-to-date is definitely valuable if they still receive any real traffic. As a bonus, those updates can conveniently lead readers to your newer blog posts related to that same topic.

HANDS-ON ELEMENTS

Judging from online comments, interactivity is highly valued. Clickable charts with customizable parameters, 3D visualizations, step-by-step guides, and games all contribute to your article being truly consumed, shared, and remembered. Readers appreciate when they can engage with the content, zoom into interesting bits, and observe how the results change when they tinker with the parameters. It makes reading the article feel like playing a video game, and it's fair to assume engineers can't resist clicking through it to see what happens.

Bartosz Ciechanowski's blog (https://ciechanow.ski/) is an absolute masterpiece in that respect, with interesting physical phenomena visualized in an interactive way. And Sam Rose (https://samwho.dev/) takes this same spirit of interactive visualization and applies it to foundational programming concepts (e.g., load balancing, memory allocation, hashing).

3.3 *Examples*

To explore how these characteristics converge, let's look at how popular blog posts check all three boxes in one compelling article. We've selected the following five examples from the top 25 engineering blog posts on Hacker News (according to points) in the past year. The wild variation across these examples highlights that there are many possible ways to achieve these critical characteristics. Your own approach will differ based on your purpose for writing, topic, experiences, and personality.

3.3.1 *A Search Engine in 80 Lines of Python*

Author: Alex Molas
Source: Alex Molas' Blog (https://mng.bz/5O0q)

This article is a walkthrough of implementing microsearch, a minimal text search engine written in Python. It describes the theory behind search engines, as well as concrete code implementing all the required features. It's a tutorial on how to write a simple search engine from scratch.

INTRIGUING TOPIC?

The title is already intriguing because it mentions writing something reasonable in 80 lines of code. Combined with "a search engine," which is a rather complicated system, that title becomes *irresistibly* intriguing, regardless of whether the audience has any previous experience with this niche. The content is especially eye-opening for people who are intrigued by search engines, but never dove into specifics. Terms such as "rank" and "inverted index" are patiently explained with examples.

DISTINCTIVE EDUCATIONAL CORE?

This article oozes educational value—it's basically a step-by-step guide on how to implement a search engine, intertwined with theory. The theoretical part is explained in an approachable manner, even for search engine newbies. Code samples are priceless, especially because they aren't just samples; combined, they form a complete implementation of a usable search engine.

SMOOTH DELIVERY?

Clean, clear, and straight to the point. This blog post's appearance and writing style are exactly what you would expect from someone who implemented a functional search engine in 80 lines of code. Within less than 10 centimeters from the top of the page, you can read or access the following:

- What drove the author to start this project and write this post
- The related Hacker News discussion
- The author's background, services, and other writing
- The blog's word count and estimated reading time

The minimalist feel continues throughout the article, which is no small feat given that it's 4,000+ words long. Lengthier code samples are tucked away into expandable elements, making it simple for the reader to quickly parse the article. A quick scan suggests that the article was carefully crafted with the reader experience in mind: crisp headings, short paragraphs, syntax-highlighted code, and even MathJax-embedded formulas that are accessible to screen readers. The author also spares the readers from all the details that *didn't* make it into the final implementation: all the mistakes, dead ends, and the usual trial-and-error casualties. There's no superfluous information here.

From the first sentence, it's clear that this is not ChatGPT. A real person who seems like a rather pleasant human being wrote this. There's no ulterior motive: he was curious, wanted to learn, and decided to share. Even better, he decided to learn by initiating a project that helps the underdog: smaller websites. Throughout, the language is concise yet conversational. It's direct, honest, and confident—walking the reader through the impressive implementation without sounding the slightest bit boastful.

Moreover, the post was apparently updated at least twice in the past few months. It was updated once with a Hacker News discussion link, then updated again to reference a similar implementation that the author discovered after the initial publication.

3.3.2   *Async Rust is a Bad Language*

Author: Matt Kline
Source: Matt Kline's Bit Bashing Blog (https://bitbashing.io/async-rust.html)
This article is a rant (in a purely positive sense) on asynchronous programming in Rust being notoriously unergonomic. It includes a detailed introduction to why asynchronous

programming is useful and how it's designed in Rust as well as other languages. It follows with a list of well-known problems faced by developers who use async Rust.

INTRIGUING TOPIC?

Rant is by definition a disruptive artistic form. The title immediately draws attention as a simple, but heavily opinionated accusation. Rust itself is a polarizing factor in the software engineering community; some people passionately love it, and others passionately dismiss it as too fancy and complex. Thus, a blog post sharing a negative opinion on a whole aspect of the language is automatically intriguing for lots of readers.

DISTINCTIVE EDUCATIONAL CORE?

The first part of the post is an excellent primer on parallelism and concurrency. The post is also full of links to relevant documentation, recommended blog posts (and a book!) about async Rust, and code examples. The author shares his unique perspective as a Rust fan, but not so much an *async* Rust fan.

SMOOTH DELIVERY?

In stark contrast to the previous example, this article takes a bold and dramatic approach. But it's as perfectly suited for a Rust rant as the previous minimalist article was for a minimalist search engine implementation.

   This article is irreverent, through and through. That's clear from the unconventional choice to make the title serve double duty as the first sentence of the article. The headings are consistently (and sneakily) clever—for example, "pain.await." Offbeat images abound, ranging from the always impudent Monty Python, to Mel Brooks' satirical Spaceballs, to CubeDrone comics, and even a child's crayon drawing. The language is colloquial, even saucy at times.

   With so much going on, there's a huge risk of it all becoming an annoying distraction. But that never happens. Every element helps the author to make his point—and to do so in a memorable way. The author's personality is front and center, as it should be in an article in the "Thoughts on Trends" blog post pattern that's covered in chapter 12. Still, he uses "we" throughout to emphasize that we're all in the same (sinking) boat with async Rust.

   Even if you don't care one bit about async Rust, you might be compelled to read this article. It's hard to imagine any reader who would not be curious to see where the bold assertion leads and discover how all these crazy images play out in a deeply technical article.

3.3.3   *Python 3.13 Gets a JIT*

Author: Anthony Shaw
Source: Anthony Shaw's blog (https://mng.bz/6YK5)

   The article is both an announcement that the next version of Python comes with a JIT and an introduction to what it means (just-in-time compilation) and how it can be implemented.

INTRIGUING TOPIC?

The title is intriguing enough just by mentioning a major feature in a new Python release. Python is one of the most popular languages in the world, and JIT is universally recognized as "a thingy that makes programs faster," even by people who aren't deeply interested in compiler internals. The author also argues with "what people tend to think" JIT is, which may be an eye-opening moment for readers.

DISTINCTIVE EDUCATIONAL CORE?

This article is a comprehensible introduction to JIT as a general technique, as well as a specific variant of it: a copy-and-patch JIT. Code samples are clear even though they explain compiling Python programs to bytecode, which is a fairly low-level concept. There are lots of useful links pointing to open source projects (including a Python disassembler implemented by the author), documentation, and academic papers.

SMOOTH DELIVERY?

This one's for you, the reader. The author is serving as the humble interpreter here, working hard to help readers across the massive Python community understand the significance of something they might have never heard of until now.

The headings anticipate the readers' likely questions, and the sections provide clear answers. Acronyms are explained and historical background is recapped. Carefully selected hyperlinks allow readers to go as deep down the rabbit hole as they wish. Readers who pay attention will note a link to a live compiler UI where they can go hands-on and "run all sorts of fun optimizations on the code, like constant propagation and loop hoisting."

The author's deep involvement in the project shines through in his language, as does his optimism about what this means for the Python community. He seems genuinely passionate about this project and eager to help others get the most out of this new development.

A bonus here: the author notes that the pull request for this change was committed on Christmas. If you follow that hyperlink, you'll find what is likely the world's first "'Twas the Night Before Christmas"-themed pull request comment.

3.3.4 I Have Written a JVM in Rust

Author: Andrea Bergia
Source: Andrea Bergia's Blog (https://mng.bz/o0yj)

This article describes the process of implementing a Java Virtual Machine (JVM) in Rust. It explains the general architecture of the project, as well as specific implementation details.

INTRIGUING TOPIC?

Back in the day, publishing an "I wrote <anything> in Rust" post was already intriguing enough to hit the front page of all the engineering news aggregators. In this case, it's doubly intriguing because implementing a JVM from scratch is quite a complex task. It promises a deep dive into Java language internals, but does it deliver on its promise?

DISTINCTIVE EDUCATIONAL CORE?

Yep. This article is actually just a prologue to a series of eight posts. But even on its own, it explains the basics of how Java works, and how one can implement a fully functional virtual machine for it. Code samples are all over the place, and there's a nice visualization of how a simple garbage collection algorithm works. The project is open source, and the post takes advantage of that fact by linking to specific implementations in relevant places. And it's all based on the author's personal project, drawing on his rather unique experience writing a JVM in Rust as a way to learn the language.

SMOOTH DELIVERY?

The playful opening immediately reveals two things:

- The author has pulled off something rather ambitious.
- He's going to be describing it in a fun, somewhat self-deprecating tone.

Who could resist?

The author shares what ran through his mind as he tackled various parts of this task. He provides full transparency into what he did and why, including what didn't work out as expected. The article is nicely organized, with a clean look, clear writing that's informal and conversational, effective visualizations of the GC algorithm, and really sharp-looking code examples.

Even though the article introduces an eight-part blog series, it's not just a tease. Readers leave with a fundamental understanding of all the key elements and also have the chance to zoom in more closely on whatever elements intrigue them most. All articles in the series clearly link back to the series' Table of Contents page. Another nice touch: prominent tags at the top of each article provide easy access to more content on related topics.

3.3.5   *The Return of the Frame Pointers*

Author: Brendan Gregg
Source: Brendan Gregg's blog (https://mng.bz/n0X8)

This article is an odyssey of frame pointers being compiled out of and subsequently restored in Linux libraries and tools.

INTRIGUING TOPIC?

The title is stylized as an operating-system-themed fantasy novel. Like anything that Brendan Gregg publishes, it's full of interesting details. This time, it's even more intriguing than usual because it exposes a timeline of events that not everyone is aware of. (I wasn't aware of these events, even though the details are very much relevant to my experience.)

DISTINCTIVE EDUCATIONAL CORE?

The educational value of this post is (at least) twofold. First of all, it's a lesson on what frame pointers are and why they are useful. Second, it's a history class on design decisions taken in large open source projects. Technical details are, as usual for Gregg, an order of magnitude deeper than an average deeply technical blog post. It's infused with perspective and insight from the author's rather distinctive personal experience. You definitely can't access this elsewhere.

SMOOTH DELIVERY?

This is story time at its finest. The depth of stories behind and within this post truly set it apart from any blog post that any other human could write on this topic. The first sentence, "Sometimes debuggers and profilers are obviously broken, sometimes it's subtle and hard to spot," hints that some interesting story awaits. It does. But first, a Gregg specialty: a flame graph. Two flame graphs, actually. The first one is nicely annotated, calling the reader's attention to the problem that stems from libc compilation without frame pointers. Click that annotated image, and you get an interactive flame graph. Expand the "longer explanation" link for even more details. And this is all just halfway through the article's introduction!

By the time you complete the introduction, you know the crux of the story: frame pointers are back, (re)solving flame graph problems and helping continuous profilers, too. Readers don't have to continue, but they *want to*. Eyes are instantly pulled down the page by two side-by-side stack-trace-walking images from Gregg's famous BPF book. Then the stories continue; for example,

- Quotes and commits that explain why gcc was changed to stop generating frame pointers back in 2004
- His (at the time) colleague's 2004 perspective on why applying this change to x86-64 (64-bit) was a bad idea
- How Java's lack of frame pointer support affected Netflix's performance analysis in the 2010s, as well as workarounds that Gregg created to compensate
- How a seemingly straightforward proposal to bring back frame pointers in 2022 unexpectedly led to a heated debate with 116 discussion threads

Gregg shares each story succinctly yet personably. It feels like a TED-talk-length fireside chat (get comfortable but not too cozy). You can sense the frustration in his narrative, as well as his deep involvement in over 20 years of frame pointer discussions and repercussions.

At the end, Gregg offers an appendix: his detailed writeup trying to persuade Fedora to restore frame pointers. There's also an integrated comments section with uncommonly civil and productive discussion, including some comments that led to post updates. And if you poke around the navigation, you can binge-read his blog posts dating back to 2005. All the posts, old and new, share this same classic layout that perfectly complements Gregg's reputation as a long-standing industry expert.

Summary

- With the onslaught of AI-generated slop, it's harder than ever to get your article noticed, but truly thoughtful posts are even more valued and appreciated.
- Engineering blog posts that get noticed, read, shared, and remembered feature the following critical characteristics:
  - Intriguing topic
  - Distinctive educational core
  - Smooth delivery

- An intriguing topic can be disruptive, eye-opening, or highly relevant to the reader's interests.
- A distinctive educational core provides exclusive, deep, and pragmatic knowledge that readers can't easily access elsewhere.
- Smooth delivery involves engaging writing, appealing design, up-to-date information, and interactive elements when possible.
- Five popular engineering blog posts demonstrate the many possible ways that authors might achieve these critical characteristics.

Part 2

Nailing the writing process

Ready to start writing your own captivating blog post? Part 2 covers pragmatic strategies for optimizing all phases of the blogging process: planning, drafting, revising, reviewing, and publishing. We suggest what to prioritize when you really need to get it done fast, as well as ways to polish the article a bit more when you have the luxury of time:

- Chapter 4 walks you through capturing your ideas and getting to a working draft.
- Chapter 5 helps you optimize the draft, so it resonates with your target readers.
- Chapter 6 is all about getting the feedback you want/need before publication.
- Chapter 7 delineates what to check as you send the post off into the world.

Creating your working draft

This chapter covers

- Starting with your goal top of mind
- Preparing to write
- Cranking out a draft, fast
- Getting past blockers
- Tapping AI for fast feedback on what's missing
- Determining whether your draft is ready to move forward

Once you have a compelling topic idea and understand what's required for a blog post to stand out, it's time to start writing! In this chapter, you will learn how to crank out a working draft, step-by-step. Consider this working draft your MVP (minimum viable product). As with any MVP, you want to focus on getting the core components in place so your work can be reviewed and improved. In this case, that means you need to capture your thoughts in writing as rapidly as reasonable, given your experience and goals. From there, you can step back, take a look, and address any major omissions or oversights. Once all the basics are in place, you can shift focus to criticizing and optimizing what you've captured. That's covered in chapter 5.

Throughout this part of the book, we'll provide concrete examples by planning, writing, and optimizing a fake blog post. The topic is using the Zig language to implement a shiny new database migration tool.

4.1 Focus and challenges

Whether you're writing or programming, you can only make so much headway with what's in your head. Conceptually, it's all crystal clear and flawless. But then, the reality often falls short of your lofty vision. You need to get your ideas on screen, into an editor, before you can start properly checking and troubleshooting them. And translating ideas into words/code tends to surface unforeseen challenges as well as spark new (often better) ideas.

With writing, the most common problem is being unable to start even a single sentence because nothing sounds right. Conversely, it's just as easy to go down the rabbit hole and write three pages of interesting but absolutely unrelated notes. Translating ideas into code has equivalent problems. Sometimes you get stuck at the design stage. Other times, you spend a few hours making the code way more generic and universal than it ever needs to be or wasting way too much time on trivial details such as variable names (i.e., "bikeshedding").

In any case, the initial attempt is rarely a flash of genius immediately manifesting itself as a masterpiece. But once you have something concrete, even if it's messy, you can take the steps required to transform mess into masterpiece (well, the tech blog or code equivalent, at least).

That's why it's so important to quickly complete a working draft—with rough attempts at all the critical elements, particularly the intriguing technical tidbits. There is absolutely zero pressure to make it great at this point. Just make it exist by extracting the ideas from your head. Create a document with the raw materials you can shape into a compelling technical blog post, and complete it fast so you can shift gears to making it good enough for publication. Then, get it done.

> **NOTE** The programming equivalent of this approach is Kent Beck's famous "Make it work, make it right, make it fast." Different stages require different mindsets and different strategies. You can't do it all, all at once (not well, at least).

You might need to unlearn some things to achieve this. For example, you shouldn't delay your progress by obsessing over things such as

- A clever title and catchy introduction
- Eloquent sentences
- Grammar nitpicks
- Pretty diagrams

If those things come to you naturally, great. If not, just move along anyway. Why? Well, that's because

- There are more important things to focus on at this point. If your draft isn't yet providing a distinctive perspective and drawing on your specialized expertise, who cares how nicely your sentences flow? You have other problems to address first.

- Hyperfocusing on superficial details now will delay the completion of a draft, and you need that draft done before you can start identifying and addressing major problems (such as insufficient technical depth).

- It's just too early, and you might be overengineering things that you don't ultimately need. It would be like spending days on performance optimization before you even ran a unit test, or months on perfecting some capability that users don't actually want.

This phase of the writing process is all about creation and addition. The only time criticism is allowed here is to expose major problems and determine what else you should add to resolve them. Once you think your draft contains everything it needs, we'll get it fit for publication. At that point, you will have full permission to unleash your inner critic.

NOTE We're deliberately using the term "working draft" versus "first draft." There's only going to be one draft, which you incrementally evolve based on the time and effort you wish to spend.

4.2 Essential prep

Hopefully, you're so eager to start writing that the thought of preparation annoys you. But we promise: if you spend a little upfront time on this prep (plan for 30 minutes or less), it will pay off in a ton of time saved later, as well as a better draft and, ultimately, a better blog post.

For example, if you define your goal upfront,

- Your initial draft will be better.
- It helps you determine what to cut to improve focus.
- It helps you get more valuable review feedback.
- You'll have some clear criteria for determining when it's good enough to ship.

Before you start, ensure that it's safe to proceed

Before you even begin to develop that great blog post idea, take a few moments to consider if there are any good reasons to hold back. If you're contemplating writing about a topic that might not be well-received by your team, your boss, or anyone else in your organization (or partner ecosystem), feel out the situation. Even if you plan to publish the article on your personal site instead of on the company's engineering blog, be sure to explore any potential resistance before proceeding. This could save you from the pain of spending time on something that's just not feasible, at least not right now.

(continued)

What are some examples of potentially delicate situations?

- You're working in a stealth startup or on an unannounced project and you plan to reference it, maybe even vaguely, in some shape or form.
- You're thinking about sharing even a hint of closed source code in a highly competitive industry.
- You're disclosing an idea that might be submitted for a patent, but your company isn't ready for the "one-year-after-disclosure" clock to start ticking yet.
- You're considering writing about how you discovered a security vulnerability that's not yet safely patched.

Ask questions first, write later. There are many points in your life when it's fine to ask for forgiveness, not permission. This probably isn't one of them.

If you're certain that you're allowed to discuss a topic but still don't want the post associated with your real name and bio, feel free to write under a pseudonym. This shroud of anonymity provides a safe mode for inexperienced writers who are particularly shy about sharing their thoughts in published posts. It allows people to have their content evaluated solely on its own merit—without any bias based on the author's personal identity. And it can provide the freedom required to write the scathing roasts that could be career limiting in certain circles. Regardless of the motivation, be sure to enable Whois domain privacy protection to ensure that details such as the email and address associated with your domain aren't readily accessible. And thanks to Scott Hanselman for this tip!

4.2.1 *Getting a feel for how others approach the topic*

First, set aside a few minutes to search for similar articles on your topic. Don't be alarmed if you see other people writing about the same general topic. That's good—it's a sign that you're going to be adding to a conversation that already has an audience. You don't have to read every word ever written on the topic; you're already an expert on *your* experiences with the topic, and that's what you'll be focusing on, right? If not, go back and reread chapters 2 and 3!

Quickly scan the articles that strike you as similar or interesting companions, then jot down some notes for each:

1. How does the article approach the topic?
2. How does your approach differ?
3. Do you want to read it in full (later!) and potentially reference it in your own blog post?

If there's a lot to cover, generative AI can help you summarize articles for speedy triage. For example, you could use a prompt such as "Summarize this article in 100 words or less. Please state what you believe to be its target audience and its goal." Then, you can use the results of that first-level review to prioritize which ones you want to scan with your human eyeballs and brain.

Example 4.1

We want this book to provide concrete examples. That's why the real Piotr (Sarna) is taking on an alter ego, PretendPiotr, to author a fake blog post about a fake Zig-based data migration tool. Here's an idea of how PretendPiotr might respond to the above questions for one of the (also fake) articles he might have stumbled upon in his research: "Our C++ project is now supported for your architecture—with Zig."

Question 1: How does the article approach the topic?

PretendPiotr: The article starts with a short introduction to the C++ project that was previously supported only for the most popular environment: x86-64 CPU running Linux. Then, it shows how Zig's novel approach to cross-compilation allows the project to be successfully compiled for more processor architectures and operating systems—without changing anything in the source code.

Question 2: How does your approach differ?

PretendPiotr: Both blog posts are going to praise Zig, but with a couple of notable differences:

- My blog post will describe implementing a project in Zig from scratch. The other one uses Zig's compiler to give an existing project cross-compilation superpowers.
- My blog post is also going to have a healthy dose of skepticism—not pure praise.

Question 3: Do you want to read it in full (later!) and potentially reference it in your own blog post?

PretendPiotr: I already read it, twice. Most modern blog posts hardly take more than five minutes to read and less than a minute to skim through the keywords. I'll reference this in my article—in the section that glorifies Zig's design decision to make cross-compilation one of the core features of the language.

4.2.2 Getting a feel for what the site publishes

If you plan to publish this article somewhere other than your personal web site (for example, on your company's engineering blog, or on a community-hosted blog), try to find at least a handful of other engineering blog posts published there. Are they generally the same length and approach that you were envisioning for your own?

NOTE See appendix A for a rundown of some popular sites for publishing engineering blog posts.

If there's a specific human editor you can contact, ask that person if there are any hard and fast guidelines you need to follow with respect to word count, graphics, style, and similar. Also, see if they're at liberty to share what other engineering blog posts were highly successful.

If you do ask about previous successes, be sure to define what you mean by successful. We'll cover metrics much more in chapter 15. For now, just be aware that there are many different ways to measure blog post success, so be clear what you're asking about. You might want to know which engineering blog posts had the most views, best social engagement, or kept people reading the longest. At the same time, the blog editor might be measuring success by a metric such as "conversions": how many people who read your blog post signed up for the free trial. Make sure you're on the same page before you get a list of "top performers."

Also, now's the perfect time to learn about any strict editorial guidelines preventing you from doing what you want to do. For example, if your company is a core supporter of the SomeLanguge Foundation, don't expect to publish your "SomeLanguge is Dead" opinion piece on their corporate engineering blog.

> **NOTE**   If you're planning to write on a delicate topic, please (re)read our "Before you start" note at the beginning of this chapter.

If you stumble upon some condition or restriction that doesn't sit well with you, see if exceptions can be made. If not, consider whether it's worth adapting your approach— or perhaps time to seek out other publication options.

4.2.3   Defining your goal

Writing involves you, your topic, and your reader. That means there are three relationships to consider:

- You + your topic
- Your reader + your topic
- You + your reader

You've definitely got the *you + your topic* relationship covered. But there are two other relationships to think about here: *your reader + your topic* and *you + your reader* (see figure 4.1)

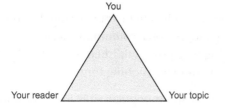

Figure 4.1   It's not all about you + your topic: writing also involves you + your reader and your reader + your topic.

THINK THROUGH THESE QUESTIONS

Before you start writing, spend a few minutes thinking about

1 Who do you want to read this?
2 What do they know about what you're planning to write?
3 Why do they care about what you're planning to write?

4 Why should they care about your perspective on it?

5 What do you want them to do differently or think about differently after reading your blog post?

Example 4.2

Here's how PretendPiotr thought about these questions for the fake Zig blog post.

Question 1: Who do you want to read this?

The audience includes a few social groups:

- *Users of the two databases in question (the one migrated from and the one migrated to)*—They might be interested in using my new tool for migration.
- *Developers interested in learning and promoting Zig*—It's emerging as a possible alternative to C, and lots of people are interested in getting to know it.
- *The "Hacker News crowd"*—Readers who hungrily throw themselves at anything that uses the latest buzzwords. At the time of writing this book, Zig was one of those magic words.

Question 2: What do they know about what you're planning to write?

Let's split it up for each social group described above.

Users looking to move data to the new database should know the fundamentals of working with both databases by this point, and likely know about some existing ways to migrate data from one database to another.

The people who are here for Zig presumably know that Zig is a cool language for new projects. What they don't know is

- Which Zig features were particularly useful for implementing a database migration tool
- If any Zig-specific quirks were annoying to work with
- Whether the project can be considered production ready, even though Zig is a relatively young language with a dynamically evolving standard

The Hacker News crowd likely knows absolutely nothing about the topic, but they are eager to post their vitriol-filled insights in the comment section the second this article lands on the front page.

Question 3: Why do they care about what you're planning to write?

The database users might be looking for a tool that solves some pain points in the existing state-of-the-art solutions, making data migration easier. Even if they don't use this tool, they might be inspired to look for similar ones, or try and create one themselves. The Zig folks are interested in new use cases for Zig and genuinely want to help its adoption to new domains. They probably want to learn more about why I selected it for this use case and how it turned out, from both a performance perspective and a developer experience perspective. And the last (and certainly least [valuable]) category just wants to post passive-aggressive comments.

(continued)

Question 4: Why should they care about your perspective on it?

Well, as the tool author and a database developer (as in, a developer who is skilled in using databases), I'm an expert in the matter. I can write about how it solves a real problem that database users have (data migration) and open problems make for interesting reading.

Zig evangelists are interested in every single user's opinion on the language—and having a pulse, I qualify as such. Zig is still evolving, and its standard is very young, so any user perspective can help shape the language specification. A newcomer's opinion is important for people who are shaping a new industry standard. And since I'm experienced in C, C++, and Rust but new to Zig, I think my perspective on some of the interesting design decisions made by the Zig designers is worth diving into.

Finally, I think we've already established that the comment section raiders just want a new comment section to infest.

Question 5: What do you want them to do differently or think about differently after reading your blog post?

I want database users to use my migration tool. I don't really want to change anything in the Zig folks. But if my struggles make them realize that more users might have problems with some language quirk, maybe they're open to making changes in the specification, and that could make my next Zig project easier to write. Since the last few subsections were all about making fun of the orange site's comment section veterans, let's give them a break here. And jokes aside, the comment section is also quite a great place to discuss the matter online with the post author or get constructive criticism once in a (very long) while!

WRITE TWO CRITICAL SENTENCES

Now that you're done thinking through all that, write down the two most important sentences that will never make it into your blog post:

1 What's the goal of this blog post?
2 Why is your perspective on this topic interesting?

Don't skip this! Seriously, write down your responses before you move on.

The first sentence is something you'll return to quite a few times—for instance, when deciding what more you need to add, what you should cut, and when requesting a review. It should draw heavily from your responses to questions one and five from the previous list (*Who do you want to read this?* and *What do you want them to do differently or think about differently after reading your blog post?*)

The second sentence will help you highlight the angle that sets your blog post apart from all the others that fellow humans (and possibly machines) write about that same topic. This one should be inspired by your responses to questions three and four from the previous list (*Why do they care about what you're planning to write?* and *Why should they care about your perspective on it?*). In addition, it should hint at the "distinctive educational core" attribute referenced in chapter 3. What deep technical details will you be sharing that aren't easily found elsewhere?

Example 4.3

Here are PretendPiotr's responses for the fake blog post.

Question 1: What's the goal of this blog post?

There are actually two goals: 1) convince database users to try out the migration tool, and 2) show that it's possible to create something useful with Zig.

Question 2: Why is your perspective on this topic interesting?

I'm the migration tool author and I've used it for real database migrations—plus I'm an experienced C, C++, and Rust programmer working on my first Zig project.

NOTE Does your blog topic align with any of the blog post patterns discussed in this book? If so, now's a great time to review the related dos and don'ts.

4.3 Optional warmup

If you don't yet feel ready to begin capturing sentences, there are a few ways to start making progress anyway: outlining, mindmapping, working from the model of another article, and copy/pasting your notes. We'll start with outlining, since many people find it helpful to jot down a very rough and informal skeleton to structure their thoughts before writing. But we'll present a few other options, too.

Some people find that mindmapping (visually mapping out how your thoughts are connected) helps them generate and organize ideas. Others find inspiration in trying to imitate the general structure of a model article—something with a similar "story framework" that might be on a totally different topic. And then there's always the ultimate low-effort solution to conquering the curse of the blinking cursor: copy/paste fragments from your emails, issue reports, code commits, and other random notes.

There's no "right approach" here. You might find zero value in the approach that your teammate swears by. And you might find that different approaches are more or less valuable in different scenarios, depending on where your head is at. Sometimes, you might have a burning idea that you know exactly how to approach—so just start writing. But there will be other times when you're simply overwhelmed by all the ideas tangled up in your head. When that happens, remember that a rudimentary outline or mindmap could be a useful tool to unblock yourself.

4.3.1 Outlining

Outlining doesn't have to involve formal-looking Roman numeral hierarchies with multiple levels of indents—though if that helps you, you're welcome to do it that way. An outline is really just a list of the points you want to write about, organized in the order you plan to cover them. The goal is to help you structure your ideas, and you can use any format you wish to accomplish that.

Outline creation is simply a matter of

- Creating a skeleton
- Hanging ideas on the skeleton

You can block out the high-level framework first and then fill in all the details later. Or you can do a detailed mind dump on one section before moving onto the next. And each section of your outline can be as brief or as detailed as you like. Nobody is judging you here. It's totally fine to end up with a multi-layer hierarchy of points for some sections and minimal details in others.

Add your outline to the file that will become your working draft. Then you can later flesh out the various sections without hopping back and forth among tabs. Plus, you instantly become the proud owner of a nonempty "My Great Blog Post" file, so you can honestly say that you've started on it. Consider your outline complete whenever it captures and organizes the main ideas floating around your head. If you think of some other detail later (before you start writing), add it to the appropriate part of the outline so you don't forget about it.

Example 4.4

Here's an example outline for the Zig data migrator blog post:

Zig helped us migrate our data efficiently

- The problem statement
  - Migration costs
  - Developer experience with migrations
  - Proposed solution
- We built it with Zig
  - The good parts:
    C interoperability—priceless for Postgres extensions
    Smooth debugging—all C tools work
    Cross-compilation is s-m-o-o-t-h
  - The not-so-good parts:
    Complicated C macros make the Zig translator choke
    No destructors
    The ecosystem is extremely young
  - The verdict
- Summary

4.3.2   Mindmapping

As shown in figure 4.2, mindmapping visually represents how your thoughts are connected. It's especially helpful for taming chaos. Like outlining, it's partly brainstorming and partly organizing. Unlike outlining, there's no sense of logical flow from a beginning to an end. Despite all the lines in the diagram, it's a nonlinear approach. You start with your main topic and then let it all flow from there.

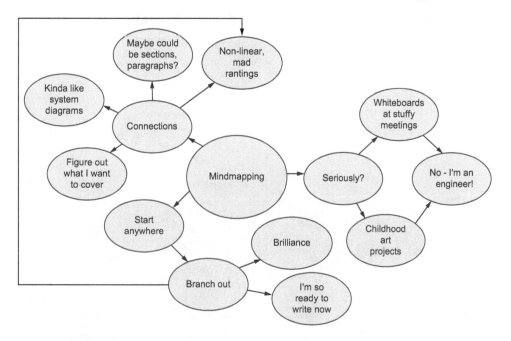

Figure 4.2   Mindmaps might seem awkward, but some people find them helpful.

Top to bottom, right to left, or every which way—it doesn't matter. Just place the main topic somewhere on a screen or actual page, keep branching out from there, and see what you end up with. There's no right or wrong way to do it.

After you complete a mindmap, you might decide to create an outline to give it a more formal structure and linear flow. Or go straight to writing. This is all about whatever feels right—for you, at the given moment, for this particular blog post.

If you've never done it before, mindmapping will likely feel awkward and unnatural at first. Almost everyone has written some type of outline in their life. Mindmapping is a lot less common. You might have been exposed to it via whiteboard exercises in painful group brainstorming sessions, but don't let that scare you away from trying it in this context. Also, mindmaps might feel a bit artsy compared to the clear logic of outlines. If so, think about it this way: you're mapping out the equivalent of a rough system architecture diagram for your blog post.

You can choose from a number of mindmapping tools that offer templates, magic alignment, and other nifty features. If you expect you'll be doing a lot of mindmapping, consider whether such a tool would help you. But don't feel compelled to use a special tool. Good old pen and paper can work just as well for mapping out your ideas for a blog post. And you might very likely find that the ideas flow faster when you're not wrestling with an unfamiliar UI.

Example 4.5

Here's an example mindmap for the Zig data migrator blog post:

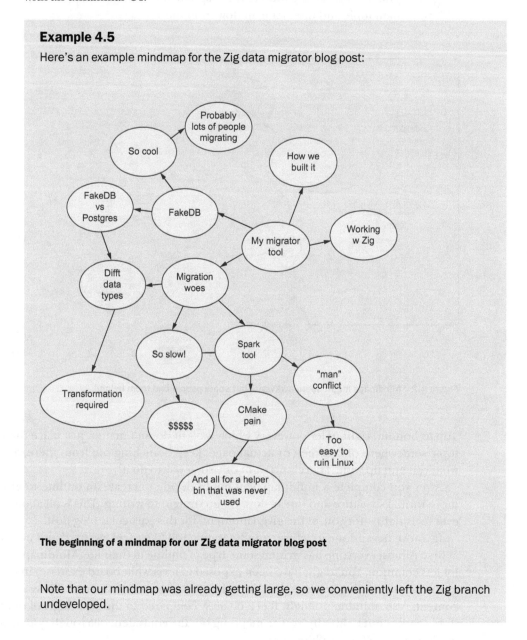

The beginning of a mindmap for our Zig data migrator blog post

Note that our mindmap was already getting large, so we conveniently left the Zig branch undeveloped.

4.3.3   *Working from a model article*

"Working from a model article" is a nicer way to say "stealing someone else's good ideas." But you're not stealing their technical insights, just the way they've opted to organize their blog post. The topic of the model article doesn't have to be at all related to what you plan to write about. In fact, it's probably best if it's *not* related. That makes it even easier to avoid blurring the line between inspiration and imitation.

The key ingredient for getting started here is finding that model article. If you're inspired by multiple articles, even better—you can take the best ideas from each and blend them all into something superior to any individual instance. Take a look at how the model articles are structuring their ideas, abstract it a bit, and reverse engineer an outline.

Example 4.6

Here's how PretendPiotr took a "We wrote it in Rust" blog post and reverse-engineered it into something he could use for his Zig data migrator blog post:

"The Title"

- The problem statement
  - Problem 1
  - Problem 2
  - Proposed solution
- We built it with $LANGUAGE
  - The good parts:
    Good part A
    Good part B
    Good part C
  - The not-so-good parts:
    Bad part A
    Bad part B
    Bad part C
  - The verdict
- Summary

4.3.4 *Copying/pasting your notes*

From a logistical standpoint, it's helpful to have your various notes all in one place. And if that place happens to be in some fenced-off sandbox area of your draft, you've also broken through the blank page barrier. Congrats!

Feel free to copy anything that sparks ideas or includes details you want to cover. For example,

- The Slack thread that triggered this topic idea
- GitHub issues or pull request comments related to your topic
- Your notes on your teammates' comments and questions about the topic
- A summary of test results and links to the files with more details
- A social media discussion about the controversy you're about to comment on

Example 4.7

Here are some tidbits that PretendPiotr might copy in for the fake Zig data migrator blog post:

- A link to Loris Cro's blog post, "Cross-compile a C/C++ Project with Zig" (https://mng.bz/vJYq)
- This screenshot from the Reddit post, "How does zig magically cross compile without target shared libraries" (https://mng.bz/4pzg)

Posted by u/Able_Armadillo491 2 years ago

36

How does zig magically cross compile without target shared libraries

I was rather amazed that I could cross-compile the zig-sokol examples https://github.com/floooh/sokol-zig for a Windows target on a Linux host (WSL Ubuntu). I simply set -target x86_64-windows and copied the executable into Windows and got a nice spinning cube displayed.

The examples need to call down to the target OS's windowing and graphics libraries, as you can see here https://github.com/floooh/sokol-zig/blob/e872e6d26fa57480268715989fd9706076c1ac00/build.zig#L43

How can the compiler even produce an executable, without these libraries (eg d3d11, user32) being present on the host system? What is even happening here https://github.com/floooh/sokol-zig/blob/e872e6d26fa57480268715989fd9706076c1ac00/src/sokol/c/sokol_app.h#L1700 when <windows.h> is not even present at compile time?

- This screenshot from an internal Slack conversation

sarna 1:21 PM
zig cross-compilation is i-n-s-a-n-e, you just build with `-target aarch64-linux` and it works

4.4   *Writing time*

At this point, you're as ready as you'll ever be. Dive in and just do it!

Your mission here is simply to get sentences into an editor: to translate what's in your head into words that you (and others) can review and optimize. As we mentioned earlier in this chapter, you don't need to make it great; you just need to make it exist.

4.4.1   *Getting words on the page*

In fact, you don't even need to write it in the traditional sense of opening a doc and typing out sentences. Yes, some people draft blog posts by grabbing a beverage of choice, sitting down at their desk, and writing an article from start to finish. But that's not always how it happens in reality. Let's look at a few circuitous ways to get words on a page, some of which are better than others:

- Rubber duck dictation
- Chatting with a human
- Writing in your native language

RUBBER DUCK DICTATION

The same rubber duck that led you to that aha moment when debugging is also an amazing writing assistant. Dust off the duck, turn on a voice transcription program, and narrate your blog post idea to your captivated (and captive) audience.

If you're a good verbal explainer, this is a great way to capture ideas in a way that sounds friendly and conversational. But if you're the stereotypical engineer who hates to talk, this option (and the next one) might not be ideal. In that case, stick with the traditional "sit down and type" path.

CHATTING WITH A HUMAN

This is the same idea as rubber ducking, except that you narrate your blog post idea to a real live human instead of a bathtub toy. The advantage: actual feedback. You can tell when your audience seems intrigued, surprised, amused, or just bored to death. And if your human happens to be a trusted colleague, they might question some of your assertions, request clarifications, point out omissions, and offer other feedback that's beyond your rubber duck's innate abilities.

Having this early feedback is great for learning how your readers might react and discovering what questions and objections you should probably address. However, the downside of getting this valuable feedback is that your transcription will likely be choppy and require a bit of reorganization. Not a problem, just prepare yourself. If you're not sure how to get it back into a logical flow, try creating a new high-level outline, then copy/paste the bits into the appropriate order.

WRITING IN YOUR NATIVE LANGUAGE

We're listing this as an option only because we want to address it. It's a *bad* option. Even if your inner monologue runs in your native language, try to capture your ideas in English.

Why? First, the translation will be tedious. Translations for text with technical terms are invariably awkward, and good engineering blog posts should include a healthy amount of technical terms. Moreover, once an awkward translation is imprinted in your brain, it's usually much harder to come up with the natural-sounding equivalent than if you just started with English in the first place. And a final reason: the more you practice writing in English, the more (and the faster) you'll improve. Just write. Remember, there's no need for perfect sentences at this early phase, not even from native English speakers.

By all means, keep your favorite translation app nearby and use it for specific words and sentences when you're stuck. And when it comes time for review, look for a friendly native English speaker who can help you spot and improve the sentences that just don't sound right. Also, rest assured that the grammar checkers and AI tools of the world are actually quite good at spotting and even explaining many common grammatical mistakes and awkward phrasings. Consider them a rudimentary (yet totally free and nonjudgmental) first line of defense.

The bottom line: try to write it in English, but don't spend too much time worrying about grammar or phrasing at this point. We'll get to that later in the process (and in later chapters).

TACKLING GREAT WALLS OF TEXT

Once you have words on a page, spend less than five minutes applying these quick fixes that will help you (and your reviewers) parse what you wrote:

- Scan the doc for paragraphs that are longer than about 2 inches or 5 centimeters. If you can quickly spot some logical breaking point, go ahead and hit the Return/Enter key.
- Zoom out to the page view. If any page has one or zero headings, determine where it might make sense to squeeze in more, then add them.

Don't force it and don't overthink it, especially at this point. We'll look more carefully at both headings and paragraph length in the next chapter. For now, just break it up into manageable chunks so that you will have an easier time seeing what's on the screen. Note that you might need to perform some minor tune-ups later to ensure there's a natural flow in and out of the added headings.

4.4.2 Eliminating blockers

Writing can be hard. The words will not always (not ever?) just flow perfectly. But don't let that stop you. Your goal here is to keep moving toward completion. If you context switch or take a break every time you get stuck, the writing process will drag out much longer than it needs to. Here are tips for making progress, even when you're blocked or just generally frustrated.

RESIST THE URGE TO EDIT

Now's not the time for editing. Once you get something written, you can always go back and fix it later. And you might end up cutting that part anyway, so don't waste time prematurely overengineering it. That would be the equivalent of painstakingly optimizing code that ultimately gets cut because it was solving the wrong problem.

Here are some practical tips for resisting the urge to edit:

- Set some arbitrary (yet highly specific) goal such as "I want to draft these few paragraphs in the next 20 minutes," then set a timer (pomodoro, phone, etc.) and try to beat the clock.
- Disable spell check and grammar check for now if you can't ignore it.
- Become self-conscious about your tendencies to fiddle with the text and try to stop.

- If you catch yourself spending too much time deliberating over particular words or sentences, mark anything that you want to fix later with a color highlight or a comment and move on.

GO OUT OF ORDER

There's no rule that you have to start writing with the introduction. Introductions are often intimidating, even to experienced writers. And sometimes the draft ends up taking a somewhat different direction than you anticipated. In that case, the introduction you wrote for your original plan would have to be reworked anyway.

We'll talk a bit about introductions in chapter 5. For now, here are two recommendations:

- Don't worry about creating some clever hook. Write what comes to mind.
- If you're not sure how to start, just skip it for now and return to it later.

This same strategy applies beyond introductions. You hereby have permission to start anywhere and skip any section that you're struggling with. Do you feel like you can knock off a certain section quite effortlessly? Start there. Maybe there's a test result, concept, or other idea that you're not sure how to explain yet? Skip it.

DROP PLACEHOLDERS WHEN YOU'RE STUCK

To keep your momentum going, you might want to skip more than problematic sections. You could also skip

- Code examples
- Graphics
- References you want to work in
- Details you're hoping a team member will add
- Specific words or phrases that aren't coming to mind right now
- Whatever else happens to slow you down

When you skip something, be sure to drop some sort of prominent "TODO" placeholder in the doc as a reminder. This way, there's no need to worry about forgetting it later.

GIVE YOURSELF A BREAK

"Give yourself a break" can be interpreted in two ways. We mean both here.

First, we mean "stop being so hard on yourself." Remember that you're currently writing the rough draft of a blog post, something that nobody except you will probably ever see in its current state. Even the final version of that blog post does not need to be perfect. No matter how much you labor over it, it won't be fast-tracked to the Smithsonian for display in a glass case. You need to deliver intriguing technical insights to your intended audience in a way that keeps them interested and engaged. You don't need to provide the definitive answer to everything related to your topic. Share what you know at this point, and don't be afraid to admit what you're still curious about. You might end up sparking a discussion in the comment section and/or giving someone else an idea for their next blog post!

Second, we mean "step away from writing for a bit." If you're truly hopelessly stuck and frustrated, work on something else, take a walk, sit in a sauna—whatever helps clear your mind!

4.5 *PretendPiotr's first attempt at the example blog post*

Here's PretendPiotr's first attempt at the example blog post, written with delivery speed in mind and cranked out in under 30 minutes. It's not perfect, nor does it need to be. It exists, and it can get PretendPiotr to the next phase. Also, it provides some nice fodder for our discussions.

> **NOTE**   This is the first working draft, exactly as it flowed. We wanted to show something authentic, so it wasn't proofread or copy-edited like the rest of the book text. In the blog, "we" = PretendPiotr speaking on behalf of his fictional team.

4.5.1 *Zig helped us migrate our data efficiently*

By PretendPiotr

MIGRATING DATA INTO FakeDB

We've been happily using FakeDB for all of our services way before it was cool – some of our early pipelines even ran pre-release versions in production, because we trusted FakeDB's development team so much. Thankfully, the risk of being early adopters paid off, as FakeDB is now the de-facto standard for highly concurrent workloads. There's just one problem though, and it stems from the fact we sometimes need to move data from our legacy Postgres clusters: migrating all data back to FakeDB is S-L-O-W.

MIGRATION COSTS

We don't store massive amounts of data in our legacy Postgres clusters, far from it. The latest migration needed to move ~100GiB out, and that's an amount you can "migrate" from one machine to another via USB stick. If only things were that simple though… Postgres has a well-defined type system, and so does FakeDB. Most of the Postgres data types are perfectly translatable to FakeDB equivalents, but some are not, and as luck would have it, our legacy workloads mostly use the ones that don't translate cleanly. As a result, instead of just blindly moving data from one machine to another, we need to carefully transform it from one format to another, and the existing tools are far from ideal in that matter. The only tool we found for the job, based on Apache Spark, would take us 21 days to finish, if everything goes smoothly, so probably more like 24-25, with a couple of quite expensive cloud machines running full speed. Sounds like a heavy overkill for an amount of data that fits on a 2018 smartphone!

DEVELOPER EXPERIENCE

Costs aside, the existing tool is a pain to use. It took us two days to force it to run in order to make the estimates. The journey included downgrading to an ancient version of CMake in order to compile some helper binary written in C++, which ended up not being used later anyway. The author also decided to helpfully name the tool man, as in Migration Automation eNgine, which is an obvious clash with Linux's existing man tool, which stands for manual. Apparently, the author either used some arcane Linux distribution that didn't come with man preinstalled, or decided his tool is more important and justifies stealing the name, but the fact is, compiling and installing the tool without care is likely to ruin your operating system. In other words, we did not enjoy it. At all.

PROPOSED SOLUTION

It took us the aforementioned two days to establish that the existing migration machinery is far from ideal. Thus, it took us approximately two seconds to reach the obvious conclusion: let's write a tool that actually works and is fun to work with!

WE BUILT IT WITH ZIG

If you read this post's introduction, you already know we're into bleeding edge tech. Zig is an emerging C language competitor, with broad open source community support, dynamically developed – a perfect candidate to write our migration tool in. A fair part of our tool is a Postgres extension, all written in Zig. The rest exports the data we need via HTTP, which, granted, isn't perfectly optimal, but also makes the process easier to debug, load balance, and so on. Since FakeDB is capable of receiving HTTP traffic, that's all we need to perform our migrations.

THE GOOD PARTS

Zig advertises its C interoperability as a core feature, and it really works. It actually feels magical to "import" a C header straight into a Zig program, and use it as if it were a module written natively in Zig. The compiler transpiles (compiles to another language) the header into Zig and exposes it in a developer-friendly way. We were able to use Postgres' official C headers for implementing our extension in Zig. Amazing!

Debugging Zig is also a treat, if you're already used to debugging C. Everything still works – gdb, perf, you name it. On top of that, Zig has a more elaborate system for asserting preconditions and invariants, which makes the debugging process a little bit smoother than C used to be. Zig is not Rust, and it happily lets you dereference null pointers (although its type system tries to prevent obvious cases of that), and use previously freed memory, so we had a dubious pleasure of long debugging sessions – just us, gdb, and the ninth cup of coffee – but it was comforting to see all the existing tools just work.

One of the mind-blowing things about Zig is that cross compilation (ergo compiling the code to target CPU architecture and operating system different than the setup the compiler runs on) is also a core feature of the language. And it's s-m-o-o-t-h. Most of our cloud fleet runs on Arm processors, and our engineers tend to work on x86-64 machines, so it was extremely ergonomic to be able to "just" compile everything locally for a different architecture, and see it work out of the box. Kudos to the author of "Our C++ project is now supported for your architecture – with Zig," who inspired me to try Zig and its cross-compilation superpowers!

THE NOT-SO-GOOD PARTS

Zig is interoperable with C alright, but it's patience has limits. By patience we mean the type system, which is a little more strict than C. Zig also (thankfully) doesn't have C's preprocessor macros that let you do literally anything with program text. Importing the postgres.h header was actually a little bit more complicated than "just" declaring an import, because Zig initially failed to transpile the code, due to layers of layers of layers of layers of complicated C macros. Fortunately, the way it works in Zig is that the generated code is available to the developer, so we were able to fix a few places ourselves.

Another thing we didn't enjoy that much was the lack of destructors. That's one thing we feel C++ and Rust got right: when something goes out of scope, its destructor is implicitly called. Zig doesn't prefer anything implicit, which is fine, but it just doesn't work well in this particular case. Our code leaked memory in a few places precisely because we forgot to spray a few defer calls in all the right places. Note that Zig also enforces all heap allocations to be explicit, which is a fantastic design decision. And it would work great, except we still needed to interoperate with Postgres' code and use its own allocators, and those are not (yet?) hacked in Zig.

One more hopefully temporary downside is that the ecosystem is really young. Compared to Rust or C++ it simply lacks libraries and tools that would be very helpful for programmers. It does come with HTTP support in its standard library, and that's great, but we also wanted to add a thin custom encryption layer, forced down our throats with all the SOC2 requirements, and that we just needed to implement by linking to a Rust implementation.

THE VERDICT

The choice of Zig was 100% worth it! Our tool, named FancyMigratorName, works, is open sourced, and already has a microscopic community around it. We were able to successfully migrate our legacy cluster in 4h, which is a major win over the previous 24 days estimation. Next week we felt a little too optimistic about the tool and almost lost users' data from another legacy cluster, but that's a story for a separate blog post, stay tuned!

SUMMARY

Out of our frustration with the existing tooling, we developed an open source migration tool to move data from Postgres to a FakeDB cluster. We chose Zig to implement it, and the road, though bumpy, was fun and successful! Try our tool, FancyMigratorName, at https://example.com/fancymigratorname, and share your experience with us!

4.6   *Filling in gaps*

Now make some attempt to fill in any missing pieces (e.g., write some tentative introduction and add in rudimentary graphics) and pat yourself on the back. Your working draft is almost done. Wait, almost?

It's time for some healthy paranoia. As a warm-up for the next chapter, you can put your critiquing hat on for a bit here, but only to determine what else you should add before you fully shift gears into the review/revision mindset. Before you move on, consider these three questions:

- Did you actually cover what you intended to cover?
- What else *should* you cover?
- What's preventing it from being viable?

Let's cover each in turn.

4.6.1 Did you actually cover what you intended to cover?

The reality of what you wrote doesn't always match your intentions. That's often a good thing: you probably had new and better ideas pop into your mind as you were heads down writing and intentionally pivoted accordingly. Nice work! But honestly, sometimes ideas just get lost in the shuffle, so be sure to check for that before moving on.

First, return to your prep work. Review the two sentences you wrote earlier in this chapter (your goal and differentiator), as well as any outlines, mindmaps, or other notes you made. Do you feel like you thoroughly covered what you wanted to cover? Did you inadvertently skip some key points? Get it all in there now.

> **NOTE** For example, when drafting the fake blog post shown in section 4.5, PretendPiotr almost forgot about his plans to mention the article "Our C++ project is now supported for your architecture—with Zig." It happens.

Next, let's have some fun. Do the inverse with AI, your speedy, free, always available reviewer. If you're comfortable doing so, feed your blog post to your favorite generative AI tool and see how the AI take on your article matches what you were hoping to get across. Use prompts such as

- What do you believe is the goal of this article and why?
- Summarize this article in one paragraph
- Who do you believe is the audience for this article?

How well do those assessments match your intentions? If it all seems reasonably close, rest assured that you're getting your ideas across. But if there's a significant mismatch, try to figure out why. Maybe the AI is just hallucinating. Or maybe it's picking up on the fact that a certain idea needs additional detail and elaboration. If you believe it's warranted, extend and clarify your draft to get your point across.

EXAMPLE GENERATIVE AI FEEDBACK AND PIOTR'S RESPONSE

Here's the feedback that ChatGPT provided for the current state of the example blog post, along with Piotr's comments.

 Prompt: What do you believe is the goal of this article and why?

 Response: The goal of this article appears to be multifaceted:

1. Informing the Audience: The article aims to inform the audience about the challenges faced by the author's team in migrating data from legacy Postgres clusters to FakeDB. It discusses the limitations and inefficiencies of existing migration tools and outlines the specific issues encountered during their migration process.

2 Advocacy for Zig: The article serves as a platform to advocate for the use of Zig programming language in solving real-world problems, particularly in the context of data migration. It highlights the benefits and features of Zig, such as its interoperability with C, debugging capabilities, and support for cross-compilation.

3 Promotion of FancyMigratorName: The article promotes the author's newly developed migration tool, FancyMigratorName, which is built using Zig. It presents the tool as a solution to the challenges described earlier, emphasizing its efficiency and success in reducing migration time from 24 days to 4 hours.

4 Community Engagement: By inviting readers to try out the FancyMigratorName tool and share their experiences, the article aims to engage the community and potentially grow the user base for the tool. It also hints at the formation of a "microscopic community" around the tool, indicating potential for further collaboration and development.

Piotr's response

It did correctly grasp that I was advocating for Zig and promoting the migration tool. It looks like the blog post's goal is getting across and no changes are necessary in that area. However, it's also interesting to note that the response is riddled with meaningless "points" and borderline tautologies. For instance, the omniscient AI claims that one of the goals of this blog post is "informing the audience." That's true, but that's the goal of every single blog post, so the statement is trivially true.

 Prompt: Summarize this article in one paragraph.

 Response: The article recounts the challenges faced by a team when migrating data from legacy Postgres clusters to FakeDB, highlighting the inefficiencies and frustrations with existing migration tools. In response, the team develops FancyMigratorName, an open source migration tool built using Zig, a programming language known for its C interoperability and debugging capabilities. While Zig presents some challenges, such as strict type systems and a young ecosystem, the team finds it ultimately worth the effort, as FancyMigratorName significantly reduces migration time from an estimated 24 days to just 4 hours. The article encourages readers to try the tool and share feedback, serving as both a solution to a common problem and an example of the effectiveness of Zig in practical application.

Piotr's response

The AI response here is overeager with assumptions. Zig is indeed "a programming language known for its C interoperability," but not really for "debugging capabilities" (and it wasn't intentional to point out debugging capabilities as an advantage of Zig, rather as a side effect of its compatibility with C). The AI response also qualified a "strict type system" as a challenge, while the reality described in the article was more complex. The strict type system was shown as an advantage over C; it was the macros in legacy C code that clashed with Zig's code translation.

Perhaps the blog post can be rephrased to make sure that I send the right message: that the strict type system of Zig is great, and it's the legacy C complicated macros that are the root cause of the problems. Though, when I reread the blog post, it was clear to me. If this was a real article, I would probably ask a colleague to take a look at it before I considered changing anything.

From the author perspective, it is reassuring that the AI review understood the general idea of the article. However, it got some things obviously wrong, which is a bit disturbing. And at times it felt like a subtly broken echo chamber. Even though these particular AI responses didn't do much to help improve this particular article, I think it's still a worthwhile exercise for quickly confirming whether you're on the right track, without bugging any actual humans (yet).

4.6.2 *What else should you cover?*

At this point, you should be pretty certain that what was in your head is represented on the page. But maybe your readers might expect more. For example, readers might feel suspicious (or at least somewhat unfulfilled) when

- You're discussing performance, but do not include any specific performance metrics— numbers, benchmarks, flame graphs, and so forth.
- You're discussing performance and showed benchmarks but don't mention whether tests were run on a powerful server or your old laptop (or you fail to explain why you used something other than a realistic production environment).
- You're discussing an architectural shift, but do not address the migration challenges or the tradeoffs of the new approach.
- You're discussing an internal tool you built, but don't share details on how it affected your real-world processes.
- You're discussing a new approach to a problem but do not cover the challenges with the original one.
- You're discussing a practice with known security risks, but never once mention security.

These omissions would likely surface if you had multiple peers carefully read your draft and provide feedback. In reality, getting decent feedback from just one person is challenging. Getting great feedback from multiple people on a reasonable timeline—don't count on it.

NOTE We'll talk all about navigating the review process in chapter 6.

Peer review by at least one colleague is undeniably valuable, and we'll talk about how to make it faster and more focused in due time. But for this initial review aimed solely at uncovering major gaps and omissions, there's a quick workaround: generative AI.

Driven by large language models (LLMs), generative AI is an expert at knowing what words are typically associated with the words you are using. Since it has likely read millions of tech blog posts and related technical articles, it should have a fundamental understanding of what your human readers might be anticipating.

Feed your blog post to your favorite AI tool (again, only if you're comfortable doing so) and see what it thinks is missing. Use prompts such as

- Does this engineering blog post have any logical gaps?
- What are some problems with this engineering blog post?
- Are there any paragraphs in this engineering blog post that require additional detail?

Don't expect all the feedback to be spot on. Quite likely, it will recommend a lot of things that are either so trivial that you wouldn't bother or so obvious that you already ruled them out (for example, suggesting that your blog post about a shiny new capability should include details about some still-mythical real-world use case). But if you can expose just one valid concern with a 15-second prompt + copy/paste exercise, it's worth a few moments of your time.

EXAMPLE GENERATIVE AI FEEDBACK AND PIOTR'S RESPONSE

Here's the feedback that ChatGPT provided for the current state of the example blog post, along with Piotr's comments.

 Prompt: Does this engineering blog post have any logical gaps?

 Response: While the engineering blog post provides a comprehensive overview of the challenges faced in migrating data from a legacy Postgres cluster to FakeDB and introduces a new solution developed in Zig, there are a few logical gaps worth noting.

Firstly, the article doesn't delve into specific technical details regarding how Fancy-MigratorName solves the challenges mentioned. It briefly mentions using Zig's C interoperability and HTTP support but lacks in-depth explanations or examples of how these features were utilized in the tool's development.

Secondly, there's a lack of discussion about potential risks or drawbacks associated with using Zig for this task. While the article acknowledges some challenges encountered during development, such as dealing with complex C macros and the lack of certain language features, it doesn't thoroughly explore the implications of these limitations or how they were mitigated.

Lastly, the article could benefit from providing more context or comparison with alternative solutions. While it critiques existing migration tools and praises Zig for its advantages, it doesn't provide a nuanced comparison with other programming languages or frameworks that could potentially be used for similar tasks. This would help readers better understand why Zig was chosen over other options and the trade-offs involved.

Piotr's Response

The "no technical details" gap is spot on! The article mentioned the migration speedup from days to hours, but it gave absolutely no proof or description of the reasons why. The blog post should be extended with a paragraph, or a whole section, of details about why the existing solutions were slow, and what made the new implementation fast.

The "Zig risks" gap is a little vague and questionably untrue. The drawbacks of Zig were explained very clearly and the "risks associated with using Zig" can be derived from that.

The "more context" gap can just be folded into "no technical details," and is not very helpful on its own. The part about no "nuanced comparison" of Zig and other languages is technically true, but it's off-topic. The article compared Zig to Rust and C++ a few times, but a nuanced comparison of any of those languages is enough material for a book, not a paragraph in a blog post.

 Prompt: What are some problems with this engineering blog post?

 Response: While the engineering blog post effectively communicates the team's experience in developing FancyMigratorName using Zig, there are several potential problems or areas for improvement:

1. Lack of Objectivity: The blog post appears overly enthusiastic about Zig and the FancyMigratorName tool, which may come across as biased or promotional rather than offering a balanced perspective on the challenges and limitations of the chosen approach.

2. Insufficient Technical Detail: While the blog post provides a high-level overview of the team's experience, it lacks detailed technical insights into how FancyMigratorName was developed, such as specific code examples, architecture diagrams, or performance benchmarks, which could limit its usefulness to developers seeking practical guidance.

3. Lack of Clarity: The article jumps between discussing the challenges of migrating data from a legacy Postgres cluster to FakeDB, the shortcomings of existing migration tools, the benefits of Zig for this task, and the development process of the new migration tool. This lack of focus can make it difficult for readers to follow the main points and understand the overarching narrative.

4. Lack of External Validation: While the blog post mentions the successful migration achieved with FancyMigratorName, it does not provide external validation or testimonials from other users or organizations who have used the tool, which could enhance its credibility and reliability.

By addressing these issues and providing a more balanced, detailed, and informative account of the team's experience, the engineering blog post could offer greater value to readers and stakeholders interested in data migration and software development using Zig.

Piotr's response:

Let's dissect each accusation separately.

- *Lack of Objectivity*—True, but full objectivity was never a goal. The article was intended to be enthusiastic about both Zig and the developed migrator tool. I realize that the unbridled enthusiasm for FakeDB could get the blog post some attention in the Hacker News comments, particularly among the FakeDB lovers/ haters. However, I don't think that's a bad thing since it aligns with the goal of catching the attention of the Hacker News crowd.

- *Insufficient Technical Detail*—Makes sense. This is the same problem mentioned in the "logical gaps" feedback and discussed in the previous section. If this was a real blog post, I would certainly take this into account and revise the article accordingly.

- *Lack of Clarity*—Personally, I think the various threads fit together just fine. But, I'm the author, and the author is always biased by being the expert on the topic. To be safe, I would probably discuss this accusation with a human reviewer.

- *Lack of External Validation*—Lack of testimonials for a brand-new niche open source project is expected. I feel that adding a "testimonial" would make the article look like yet another marketing piece (which is probably what ChatGPT was trained on and how it came up with this suggestion).

P **Prompt:** Are there any paragraphs in this engineering blog post that require additional detail?

Response: Yes, there are a few paragraphs in the engineering blog post that could benefit from additional detail to provide a more comprehensive understanding of the team's experience and the development process:

1 Proposed Solution: While the paragraph mentions the decision to write a new migration tool using Zig, it could provide more insight into why Zig was chosen over other programming languages or frameworks. Additionally, it would be helpful to include some details on the specific features or capabilities of Zig that made it well-suited for the task, beyond just its C interoperability and cross-compilation features.

2 The Good Parts: While the paragraph highlights the benefits of using Zig, such as its C interoperability and debugging capabilities, it could be enhanced with concrete examples or anecdotes illustrating how these features facilitated the development of FancyMigratorName. Additionally, providing specific instances of how Zig's cross-compilation feature was leveraged to target different architectures would add depth to the discussion.

3 The Not-So-Good Parts: This paragraph briefly touches on some drawbacks of Zig, such as its stricter type system and lack of destructors, but could benefit from further elaboration on how these limitations were addressed or mitigated during the development process. Additionally, providing examples of specific challenges encountered and how they were overcome would offer valuable insights for readers considering using Zig for similar projects.

4 The Verdict: While the paragraph concludes with a positive assessment of the decision to use Zig and the success of FancyMigratorName, it could be strengthened by including metrics or data to quantify the improvements achieved, such as the percentage reduction in migration time or the number of successful migrations performed using the tool. Additionally, discussing any lessons learned or areas for future improvement would add depth to the conclusion.

By providing additional detail in these paragraphs, the engineering blog post could offer readers a more nuanced understanding of the team's experience and the factors that contributed to the development and success of FancyMigratorName.

Piotr's response

- *Proposed Solution*—Not very helpful. The description of Zig's advantages isn't "just" C interoperability and cross-compilation features—these are the two major reasons why Zig was chosen, along with the fact it's bleeding edge technology, which was also mentioned.

- *The Good Parts*—Anecdotes are a nice (though generic) suggestion. Their only disadvantage is that they bloat the blog post. If the post is already long enough, it might be better to omit anecdotes that don't really make the article more educational or entertaining. Also, anecdotes should come naturally. If they're forced or forged, they would look artificial and redundant.

- *The Not-So-Good Parts*—It makes sense to point out the lack of details about how the problems with Zig were overcome. The blog post did mention that I handled the issues with incorrectly translated C macros by editing the code manually. I didn't add more details because they would bore the reader. Plus, they're not very human-readable, which is usually an issue with machine-translated code. A good compromise here would be to add a hyperlink to the fixes in order to please any readers who are (over)eager to learn all the details.

- *The Verdict*—It's true that the verdict did not mention a percentage of migration time reduced, but the article did mention four hours vs. 24 days. I think readers get the gist without requiring the exact math. The suggestion to explicitly include lessons learned and areas of future improvement is a very solid piece of advice. If this was a real blog post, I would extend the article to include both.

4.6.3 *What's preventing it from being viable?*

Last but certainly not least, think hard about these fundamental questions and extend the draft to address them before you proceed:

- *Does it highlight your specialized experiences and expertise?* Remember what you wrote in the second critical sentence in the prep phase (Why your perspective on this topic is interesting?). Now's the time to check that you've captured that in your draft. If generative AI or some other engineer with totally different experiences might have written something strikingly similar, strongly consider adding more differentiating elements and more details that draw from your unique experiences (e.g., more context, examples, commentary, and so on).

- *Does it advance your reader's understanding of the topic and include sufficient technical details?* Think back to your intended audience, what they already know about your topic, why they care about your topic—you did think about all that earlier in section 4.2.3, right? Put yourself in your readers' shoes and be honest: is there enough detail to keep them interested and teach them something new? If not, think about what you can add to change that. For example, in some cases, you could add code snippets from one of those online playgrounds that let your readers execute the code and see what it does and why. Or think about the interesting implications of key points or findings you presented and then add that additional commentary to the draft. If you're truly stuck here, look for a colleague who can add more compelling details and make them a co-author.

Don't expect generative AI to help you at all with this evaluation. Look at it critically and trust your gut instinct. If you really have deep-seated doubts, ask a trusted colleague or peer for a quick look. If you take this path, use an angle like "Hey, I wrote this thing to [your_goal]. Do you think [your_target_audience] would find it interesting?"

> **NOTE** If you determine that the draft needs more depth and differentiators, you might want to skip ahead to the "Facts" discussion in chapter 5, which provides strategies and some specific examples.

Consider this the final gate for shifting from creation and addition into review and publication. The hard part is done. Now you can heckle yourself, revise the blog post accordingly, and get it out.

4.7   *If you do nothing else*

In each of these "nailing the writing process" chapters, we're including an "If you do nothing else" section at the end. It highlights the absolute least that you should do in the given phase and is intended as a quick reference for more experienced blog post authors who are impatient and want to get straight to it. And it's also helpful for blog writing emergencies–like when you've been voluntold to write that super high-visibility "incident postmortem" blog post, and it needs to go from vague idea to published within a matter of minutes. Or for when everyone is talking about that new cryptocurrency, which takes an approach so unique they will surely replace the Bitcoin + Ethereum duopoly next week (they promise!), and you want to strike while the discussion is still raging.

Here's the absolute least that you should do to create a decent working draft:

- Think about why you're writing this, what audience it's for, and how it's distinctive.
- Get a hot mess of a draft down fast, add some headings, and break up massive paragraphs.
- Identify and address logical gaps or underdeveloped points—consider using generative AI to help.
- Extend it as needed to ensure it draws on your experiences, adds to the conversation, and is detailed enough to achieve your goal.

Summary

- Prepare for writing by thinking about your goal, your audience, and what interesting perspective you have to offer.
- Tap outlining, mindmapping, and other preparation practices to get the ideas flowing, or skip them and just dive right in.

- If you happen to be more of a talker than a writer, capture your words by talking to a colleague (or your trusty rubber duckie).
- Focus on getting your ideas in writing rapidly, without delaying to deliberate over low-level details.
- Skip things when you get stuck and leave placeholders so you don't forget.
- It doesn't need to be pretty—you just need to get the raw ingredients down so you can move forward.
- You can use generative AI for fast feedback on whether your point is getting across and if you're guilty of any major oversights
- Before you exert any energy optimizing the draft, make sure that it's sharing unique experiences and expertise that advance readers' understanding.

Optimizing your draft 5

This chapter covers

- Shifting from capturing what's in your brain to communicating with your reader
- Catching your target readers' interest and guiding them to the end
- Prioritizing optimizations that matter the most for technical audiences
- Helping your reader better understand what you're trying to communicate

At this point, you're past the hard part: the creation. Most people breathe a sigh of relief, maybe use a grammar checker to resolve egregious errors, and call it done. But you're currently reading a book on writing blog posts, so you're clearly not most people.

This chapter outlines ways to make your blog post more compelling, whether you have just 5 minutes or more than 5 hours to spend whipping it into shape. We tried to capture the essence of the internal monologue that comes naturally after writing and reviewing a healthy amount of engineering blog posts and other forms of technical writing.

Ultimately, it all comes down to taking the brain dump you created in the previous chapter and making it seem custom crafted for your target reader. You want to present your reader with something that fills in any knowledge gaps between what the two of you know, satisfies their curiosity, and makes it simple (hopefully even enjoyable) for them to grasp what they were hoping to learn when they clicked your article.

This chapter is extensive, but don't worry. We don't expect you to consciously think about all these optimizations for any given blog post. When you read the chapter, aim for a general understanding of what's possible. As you're actively optimizing a blog post, return to this chapter and decide what you want to focus on. Over time, you won't need to refer to this chapter at all. You will have developed an annoying critical voice in your head, pointing out problems with all the enthusiasm and snarkiness of those who frequent comment sections—or at least of that annoying teammate who can be a real pain but is usually right. And what you learn is applicable far beyond blogs. For example, it will help you communicate more clearly and concisely as you're

- Interacting with teammates, users, and others across your community
- Sharing your opinions via proposals, reports, or code review comments
- Promoting yourself in performance reviews and hiring processes

To make the discussion concrete, we'll draw on the fake Zig blog draft introduced in chapter 4 (section 4.5) plus reference additional examples as appropriate. And to help you focus your limited time, we're classifying the optimizations into four groups, starting with those we believe have the greatest effect on the typical engineering blog post reader:

- *Core*—Given your goal and target reader, is your draft appropriately focused, logically organized, and sufficiently supported with technical details?
- *Clarity*—Are your sentences clearly and efficiently communicating your ideas to your target reader? And are your paragraphs focused and digestible (tight paragraphs with one idea per paragraph)?
- *Components*—Do the different structural parts do what they need to do? For example, does the title attract the right reader, does the introduction entice them to read on, and does the end tie it up nicely while providing a clear path forward?
- *Consumability*—Does your article sound like a living, breathing human being in conversation with another human being? How can you help the reader better parse the article as 1) they scan it to assess whether they really want to read it; 2) they're actively reading it amid constant threats to their attention; and 3) they return to it later, searching for some interesting tidbit to apply or share?

5.1 Focus and challenges

In chapter 4, we urged you to hold back your criticism so you could focus on rapid creation. Now you can finally unleash your inner critic, but please promise to put it to good use: creating a better experience for your readers!

It's easy to deconstruct and doubt every thought, sentence phrasing, and detail to the point where you just get frustrated and give up. Don't. If you've got a working draft of a blog post sharing your distinctive thoughts and experiences on an interesting topic, you're quite likely sitting on a resource that someone, somewhere would love to read and learn from. Instead of indiscriminately tearing down your work to the point where you feel it's not good enough, try to put yourself in the shoes of your target reader. What will help them find your blog post, understand it, and hopefully appreciate it enough to share it? Questioning and criticizing your draft from that perspective will make it even better.

That focus leads all too naturally to the first challenge: there's a pretty sizable gap between you and your reader at this point. If you selected a topic carefully, you're the world's top expert on the specific information that you're conveying to the reader. That means you're quite qualified to explain it but also that it's easy to forget what the reader doesn't (yet) know. Keeping this gap in mind is critical when assessing whether an introduction is compelling, a statement is sufficiently explained and supported, a sentence is clear, and so on. You will get the best return on your blog writing investment if you make the blog-reading experience easier for your reader. But making something simple for a reader requires some thought and effort on your part. Cue the famous quote by Blaise Pascal: "If I had more time, I would have written a shorter letter."

And that leads to the second challenge of this phase—time management. Given the myriad possibilities for every sentence, indecision and perfectionism can easily suck you into a revision vortex. Even if you somehow have the luxury of time, don't spend weeks or months revising a blog post. It's just not necessary. You will hit the point of diminishing returns soon enough. It's the same as with code: once you make it correct and clear, obsessive refactoring probably won't pay off well enough to justify the opportunity cost.

If you prioritize the types of optimizations that matter most for an engineering blog (for example, supporting your points with interesting technical tidbits versus worrying about split infinitives such as "to boldly go"), you can get it done and move on to the next thing. There's no value in letting a technical article age in a dark cellar. If it's this close, just get it published before some industry shift makes it less interesting or relevant.

5.2   Core (facts, focus, flow)

Roleplaying game time! Remember that target reader you envisioned when planning the blog post? Put yourself in their shoes. You're now that target reader, reading this blog post for the reasons you anticipated earlier. Imagine all the things that might make you

- Doubt that you'll learn what you were hoping to learn
- Suspect that the author is somehow trying to trick you
- Need to reread parts in confusion and/or frustration
- Decide to take "just a quick break" from reading
- Generally think that the author is a rambling, ranting fool

This section is all about prompting you to spot these core issues so that you can improve the reader experience. We'll cover

- *Facts*—Supporting your points with technical details from your own experience, experiments, and trusted industry knowledge
- *Focus*—Concentrating on the material that truly advances your goal and cutting the rest
- *Flow*—Ensuring there's a logical, easy-to-follow path through the parts

5.2.1 Facts

If your technical blog post lacks the necessary technical details, that's the first thing you should address. We're using the term "facts" as shorthand for pretty much anything that a reasonable person in your target audience would accept as true: your experiences, code examples, test results, respected research, and other trusted industry knowledge.

As you probably already know, readers of technical articles are rather snarky and skeptical. You can safely assume that your reader won't trust you. Don't take it personally; they don't trust anyone. But do be proactive and write with this skepticism in mind. That means including an appropriate amount and variety of facts to combat target readers' cries of "That's not true!" and "How do you really know that?"

ENSURE THAT EACH ARGUABLE STATEMENT IS SUPPORTED BY FACTS

If you try to tell technical readers what to think, they'll roast you. Instead, focus on providing enough facts for them to make their own decisions. How does this play out in a blog post? Table 5.1 lists some examples.

Table 5.1 Supporting arguable statements with facts

Instead of just stating	Do this instead (or in addition)
"This optimization yielded an impressive performance boost."	Share the results of fair benchmark tests (before and after).
"NewLanguage is more intuitive than OldLanguage."	Share NewLanguage vs. OldLanguage code examples.
"ShinyNewThing is worth a try."	State: "Our experiences with ShinyNewThing showed that …"
"It's difficult to do [this thing]."	Explain: "Doing [this thing] requires you to deal with [all these other things]," or "We really struggled with [these hard details]."
"Migration is simple and seamless."	Detail the steps required and also call out any conditions that could introduce complexity.
"The code clearly smells."	Highlight the problematic parts of the code and explain why it can be considered an antipattern.

With that in mind, rescan your working draft and look for any arguable statements that aren't sufficiently supported by facts. Specifically, find and review any statement that expresses an opinion or communicates something that a reasonable person in your target audience might doubt or disagree with. Next, ensure that each of those statements is followed by details that could feasibly convince a reasonable person to reach the same conclusion. Grill yourself with a few rounds of *why* to get the juices flowing.

> **TIP** Want the AI perspective? Prompt it with something like "Are there any statements in this engineering blog post that do not seem adequately supported by facts?"

If you find any points that need additional support, there are several options:

- Think about what additional details you can share from your own experience. What specific things occurred that led you to think and write that? While others might have different experiences, nobody can deny the validity of *your* experiences. Weave them into your article as you see it.
- Consider adding code examples, test results, or whatever else could earn the trust of your skeptical target readers.
- Track down external sources that could help: solid research, good explanations of why something is how it is, blog posts that share similar experiences, and so forth.
- Admit defeat and cut it from the article. With a harsh audience, your article is only as strong as its weakest link. Give them just one small thing to attack, and they will move in for the kill, even if the rest of your article is absolutely bulletproof. If you really can't find facts to defend one of your points, delete that point so that it doesn't undermine the credibility of your entire article.

> **TIP** See chapter 14 for details on communicating results from benchmarks and tests.

What about the fake Zig blog post? Does it need any additional facts? Perhaps it would benefit from

- A screenshot with metrics showing how slow the migration used to be with the old tooling
- Code snippets highlighting where Zig worked well
- Code examples of bad Zig produced by the compiler when translating from C
- Another screenshot with metrics showing the improvement brought by the new tool

INVEST IN SHARING FACTS THAT MAKE YOUR ARTICLE STAND OUT

Infusing an article with supporting technical details that are carefully crafted, instructive, and somewhat amusing (if appropriate) is a great way to make it stand out. If you have extra time to invest in your article, spending it here should yield a nice return. Interesting details and examples not only capture peoples' attention, but they also prompt people to remember and share a blog post. Here are a couple examples:

HOW DISCORD STORES TRILLIONS OF MESSAGES

In the Discord blog post "How Discord Stores Trillions of Messages" (https://mng .bz/QVee), Bo Ingram didn't simply state that their database migration solved their problem of unpredictable latencies. He showed this in the context of the 2022 World Cup finals, where Argentina, with Lionel Messi, took on France. Ingram decided to capture monitoring graphs showing 1) the massive spikes in the number of Discord messages sent during each key moment of the game, and 2) how their database handled it all without breaking a sweat. These graphs and the surrounding story were featured in the clutch moment of Ingram's blog post. Since the article was published, there have been countless third-party videos retelling Discord's database migration experience, and that story about the World Cup latencies is referenced in each and every spinoff!

WE PUT A DISTRIBUTED DATABASE IN THE BROWSER – AND MADE A GAME OF IT!

The TigerBeetle blog post "We Put a Distributed Database in the Browser—And Made a Game of It!" (by Phil Eaton and Joran Dirk Greef; https://mng.bz/XVKM) is 100% focused on an interactive example they built to demonstrate how powerful deterministic simulation is for testing distributed systems. The authors brilliantly figured out that since their system is built to allow simulating time and events for testing, the same rules of simulation can be applied to present the tests as an interactive game. It's obviously engaging for readers (duh, it's a game!), but it also sneakily helps people develop an intuition on how deterministic simulation tests work. It's educational content at its finest because lots of readers prefer to play a game with funny beetles rather than read (and try to actually understand) a few long academic papers on simulation testing.

NOTE We analyze this blog post further in chapter 13.

5.2.2 *Focus*

The next thing to focus on: focus. Bloated code could affect performance, but the computer will trudge on. Humans aren't that patient. They started reading based on what your title and introduction promised. Every time you seem to be taking a scenic side trip—or totally bypassing something they wanted to see—you're giving the reader an excuse to lose faith and give up.

CUT WHAT DOESN'T CLEARLY ADVANCE YOUR GOAL

It's fine if you veered off in unexpected directions while you were writing your draft. That's a common part of the creative process, and it often yields better outcomes. But for your reader's sake, please tie in (or cut out) any meandering side paths before you proceed.

Return to that simple one-sentence goal you stated in chapter 4, and make sure it's in your line of vision. Make it nice and big on one of your monitors or scribble it on a separate piece of paper if you like. Also, in case it's not explicitly expressed in your goal, think about the audience you had in mind when planning this article and why they would want to read it. What's in focus for one audience could be entirely superfluous for another.

Now skim the draft section by section, paragraph by paragraph, and hunt down anything that doesn't clearly and logically relate to that goal. Of course, you can make up some crazy connection for almost anything. But if you were forced to justify that connection in front of a jury of your skeptical peers, would you be able to convince them?

> **TIP**   Want the AI perspective? Prompt it with something like "Can you identify any parts of this article that seem less relevant to its main goal of [your goal]?"

In some cases, adding a few words or a new sentence can tie diversions into the core of the article. But if it's too much of a stretch for the specific audience you're targeting, the diversion needs to go. Sorry.

Maybe you're really proud of something you wrote, but it doesn't fit well in this article? Consider repurposing it then. The paragraph that was a distraction in your blog post could have a nice life of its own as a social media post, as a discussion thread, or even grow into its own follow-up blog post. If you truly can't bear the thought of removing some tangential material from your blog post, at least set it apart from the main text (e.g., in a "note" box).

Here are some examples of side paths that could have made it into the fake blog post and how we might have dealt with each:

- *An anecdote about our debugging session*—If we had a specific fun tidbit that was directly related to Zig versus C debugging, we might share it in a separate boxed-off sidebar.
- *More details on our adoption of FakeDB*—If there was already a dedicated article on this, it would be great to just link to it. Otherwise, we would skip these details.
- *A quick tutorial on how to use the new migrator tool*—This extra detail would throw the article out of balance. However, it would be nice to have the conclusion link to a separate page with an easy-to-follow quickstart guide. We already link to the source code, but this would be a nice addition.

PROVIDE AN APPROPRIATE LEVEL OF CONTEXT

Providing a glimpse into your specific project and challenges is a great way to connect with readers. People flock to engineering blog posts to hear first-hand real-world perspectives. Readers with similar backgrounds can't resist comparing notes, and readers from totally different worlds are likely curious about what's going on outside of their daily tasks. Providing an ample amount of context early on in the blog post helps readers decide if they're interested. It's also key for the scene setting that's sometimes required to understand the full significance of the achievement you're sharing.

Does your draft hit the Goldilocks zone of just enough context but not too much? Figuring that out requires remembering who your intended audience is and what they already know about your topic (we talked about defining this in chapter 4).

As the author of the blog post, you're in an odd spot. You probably know more about this particular topic than anyone else alive. This could hurt you in two totally different ways:

1   It could lead you to omit critical information because you forget how little the target reader really knows.

2   It could lead you to overload the poor reader with too much information because you assume they are as enthusiastic about the topic as you are.

As you scan your draft from your readers' perspective, first see whether you've included any background information that your target reader a) would already know or b) might not care about. In either case, hyperlinks are often a good compromise, allowing those who need or want more details to drill down, while keeping the article succinct and focused.

Returning to the fake Zig blog post, things that would qualify as too much context might include:

- Details on why the team moved from Postgres to FakeDB
- An explanation of FakeDB (assuming it truly is as popular as the article claims) and Postgres
- A comparison of database migration strategies (online or offline)

Next, think hard about what background information you're missing. We performed a broad and very rudimentary "what's missing" exercise like this at the end of chapter 4 with the help of AI. Here, think specifically about what background is really required to help your target audience understand and appreciate your article. For example, would the reader benefit from more background on

- The project you're working on, such as who uses the project and what sets it apart from alternatives?
- Your tech stack, maybe with an architectural diagram or two?
- Some hint of who you are, and why your perspective on this topic is worth reading?
- Somewhat esoteric tools, technologies, and concepts they must understand to get your article's main point?

Again, feel free to tap hyperlinks whenever possible to keep the context-setting concise.

> **TIP**   Want the AI perspective? Prompt it with something like "Are there any parts of this engineering blog post that could benefit from more context or perhaps some hyperlinks for additional information? The target reader is [your target reader]."

Looking back at the fake blog post, one major oversight stands out: the article never defined who "we" are. Who developed this migration tool? Trusted industry veterans or some newbies playing around? Data migrations are stressful business-critical projects. The blog post wants to convince readers to adopt this tool for their own data migrations, but the readers will probably be hungry for some background on who wrote the tool. Assuming that "we" actually refers to a small team of well-known engineers, fresh off some famous exit, this can be resolved pretty easily. We could change the first sentence to something like "The team at AwesomeNewCo, a spin-off from NowRichyRich, has been happily using..." Then, we could hyperlink "team at AwesomeNewCo" to the web page that showcases the team's true awesomeness.

CONSIDER CROPPING TO HIGHLIGHT THE MOST INTERESTING PART

Shift your focus to photography for just a moment. Sometimes, upon reviewing your photos, you notice that one detail is particularly interesting, and you want to feature it more prominently. Other times, some tourist photobombed your once-in-a-lifetime shot, and you need to salvage it somehow. Cropping is your friend.

This applies to writing, too. After a blog post is drafted, the writing equivalent of some quick photo cropping might help make your original take more eye-catching and compelling. Feel free to do a little cropping around the edges to focus your readers' attention on the details that will be most interesting to them.

For example, the fake Zig blog post could be cropped in a few different ways:

- Crop out most of the Zig material and focus solely on the data migration tool.
- Crop out most of the database migration tool material and focus on lessons learned during that first foray into Zig.
- Crop that Zig-focused version even further and make the post all about working with Zig's strict type system (this would require substantial expansion of that topic as well as cropping out the unrelated material).

5.2.3   *Flow*

Finally, consider flow: how the different parts of your article are ordered and appear to relate to one another. Your reader will certainly appreciate your work on improving the focus—that's like reviewing your standard "cool local things to do" recommendation list and customizing it for your weekend guest's interests and abilities. By also optimizing the flow, you ensure that everything is logically organized and ordered. Continuing the analogy, that's like crafting a step-by-step itinerary that covers all of your guest's interests, while making the best use of their limited time. But enough analogies—let's get into it.

MAKE SURE YOU CAN EXPLAIN THE ORDER

Here's the first and most fundamental test of whether your reader will understand the article's flow: Can *you* explain it? If you, the mastermind behind this article, can't clearly articulate how it moves from one part to the next, it's highly unlikely that the reader could possibly figure it out.

Try to walk your anticipated target reader through the flow at a high level. Speak through it or write it down—it doesn't matter. Cover details such as

- Why you're starting where you start
- What you cover first and why
- What you shift to next, and how that relates to the previous thing

And then continue until you reach the end.

For example, "The fake Zig blog post begins by presenting the problem that drove us to this Zig project: we were frustrated with the available options for migrating data, so we decided to build our own tool. We share that we decided to build that tool in Zig, and then we present the good and bad parts of working with Zig. We present a verdict that considers the Zig pros and cons we encountered, and then we wrap up by inviting our readers to try out the tool we built in Zig."

If that was easy for you, fantastic. Now you just need to ensure the reader can understand the underlying flow (as discussed in the next section). If not, you might be able to address the problems by

- Shuffling some parts around
- Thinking more about the connections and adding some sentences (or even paragraphs) to clarify
- Eliminating any sections that don't really connect (as covered in the focus discussion from the previous section)

PROVIDE CLEAR SIGNPOSTS TO THE READER

Once you're at a point where the flow makes sense to you, ensure that the connections in your head are coming across to the reader. The best place to start is the start.

When a reader clicks your article, it's as if they stepped off the subway in a new location. They're not certain this is where they want to be, and they're unsure of the path forward. If you really want them to proceed through your post, orient them a bit in your introductory paragraphs. Help them immediately understand where they've landed, where they're going, and what they're going to experience along the way.

The fake Zig blog post doesn't orient readers at all. It jumps right into a database discussion without any mention of Zig. The readers who clicked the article solely because they saw Zig in the title might initially wonder if they landed in the right place.

In contrast, Gwen Shapira does a superb job of orienting the reader in this introduction-ending paragraph from her blog post, "Transaction Isolation in Postgres, explained" (https://mng.bz/yo0E). She writes, "I'm going to start by explaining what problem transaction isolation is even trying to solve. Then I'll explain the standard isolation levels as they appear in the SQL92 standard and are still mostly used today. Then we'll talk about the problems with SQL92 levels and how Postgres handles isolation and these problems today. Grab some tea and we'll start."

Next, check if your headings give the reader a good sense of the flow you just explained to yourself in the previous section. They should call out the different parts of the article in terms that make sense to the reader. Headings that are heavy on terms the readers don't yet understand won't help your readers orient themselves. When in doubt, try to anticipate what question is running through your reader's head at that point in the article and work that into a heading (see table 5.2 for examples).

Table 5.2 Helpful vs. unhelpful headings

Unhelpful heading	Better option
pg_fakedb	Why we built a FakeDB <> Postgres migration tool in Zig
@cImport and translate-c	How we achieved C interoperability
catch unreachable	Comparing Zig's error handling to Rust's

Here are a few starters you can use for heading inspiration if you're stuck:

- A brief primer on…
- Why we decided to…
- Earlier evolutions of our…
- How we previously…
- The problem(s) with…
- How we're approaching…
- So why…
- What we learned from…
- What's next for…

The fake Zig blog post does a nice job of using helpful headings. Perhaps the heading "The Verdict" could be revised to "The Verdict: 100% Worth It" to provide a lot more information with just a few more words.

Finally, within the paragraphs and sentences of your article, be sure to overcommunicate how each new idea relates to what came before it. Every part and every sentence should be clearly connected if you want the reader to follow along to the end. This can be a lifeline for a reader who gets distracted or lost. Connect the dots for them.

> **TIP** Want the AI perspective? Prompt it with something like "Are there any awkward transitions" or "Do you see any places where the target reader, ([your target reader]), might get lost?"

Here are some examples of ways that you can connect new ideas to what you were talking about before (we'll abbreviate this as $WYWTAB):

- To achieve $WYWTAB, we had to…
- By implementing $WYWTAB, we…
- $WYWTAB allowed us to…
- But there was a problem with $WYWTAB…
- The hardest part of $WYWTAB was…
- After $WYWTAB, we decided it was time for…

It can also be helpful to link individual sentences together using transitional words and phrases. They help the reader quickly assess where you're going next. While phrases such as "moreover" or "as expected" indicate that everything is unfolding without drama, phrases such as "remarkably" or "interestingly" alert the reader that they should pay (even closer) attention to what follows. It's like when you're watching a horror movie, and the ominous music starts to play.

Here are some words you could use to help your perpetually distracted readers prepare for the next idea:

again / as expected / certainly / consequently / essentially / evidently / fortunately / furthermore / interestingly / moreover / naturally / nevertheless / regrettably /

remarkably / significantly / similarly / surprisingly / typically / ultimately / undeniably / understandably

The fake Zig blog post connects sentences together quite smoothly. Each sentence flows naturally from the previous one. This is apparent right from the first paragraph. We've bolded the transitions here for emphasis:

> *We've been happily using FakeDB for all of our services way before it was cool—some of our early pipelines even ran pre-release versions in production, because we trusted FakeDB's development team so much.* **Thankfully,** *the risk of being early adopters paid off, as FakeDB is now the de-facto standard for highly concurrent workloads.* **There's just one problem though,** *and it stems from the fact we sometimes need to move data from our legacy Postgres clusters: migrating all data back to FakeDB is S-L-O-W.*

FRONTLOAD AS MUCH AS REASONABLE

If you're writing the movie script for a summer blockbuster, you can get away with saving the big reveal or plot twist for the very end. Once your audience has paid who-knows-how-much for a ticket and popcorn, they're most likely going to be sitting there until the credits roll.

You shouldn't assume such a captive audience for your blog post though. Even if you set up nice guideposts to lead readers through, some people will inevitably click away or just lose your post in a sea of open tabs. That's why it's so essential to place critical information at the start of your blog post (i.e., to "frontload" it). This is also known as using an "inverted pyramid" structure. For more on the inverted pyramid approach, see Amy Schade's "Inverted Pyramid: Writing for Comprehension" article for the Nielsen Norman Group (https://mng.bz/aVBY).

> **NOTE** Bug-hunting blog posts are an exception to this rule (as discussed in chapter 8). Don't prematurely reveal the culprit; it deprives the reader from experiencing the thrill of the hunt!

At the very least, you want your readers to grasp what your blog post is about and whether it's interesting and useful to them. Ultimately, you want to make sure it registers in their brain as something worth reading now or revisiting later. Don't make them read through 2000 words to realize that you accomplished something truly amazing. Every detail shouldn't be revealed upfront, but do try to offer tidbits that entice the reader to continue.

Somewhere in the introduction, be sure to touch upon the two critical questions you answered in chapter 4:

- *What's the goal of this blog post?* Your introduction should clearly restate your goal in terms of the reader. What's in it for them? What will they get out of reading this?
- *Why is your perspective on this topic interesting?* Again, restate this in terms that the reader cares about. For example, maybe you could work it into an explanation of why you're writing this article.

There are usually ample opportunities to mention details about who you are and what you've been working on in the course of a natural introduction. For example, consider the following excerpt from Liz Fong-Jones's blog post, "Scaling Kafka at Honeycomb" (https://mng.bz/M1ym). Liz is a well-known engineer, currently Field CTO at Honeycomb, so her byline alone already piques the interest of many readers. She also shares some specific technical details on why her perspective on scaling Kafka is so interesting:

> *When you send telemetry into Honeycomb, our infrastructure needs to buffer your data before processing it in our "retriever" columnar storage database. For the entirety of Honeycomb's existence, we have used Apache Kafka to perform this buffering function in our observability pipeline. In this post, we'll review the history of how we got here, why we're so picky about Kafka software and hardware, and how we qualified and adopted the new AWS Graviton2-based storage instances. Lastly, at the end of this post, we'll discuss the decrease in price per megabyte of throughput after the cumulative optimizations we've made in the past two years. Let's dive in.*

Note that her introduction concludes with a nice preview of what's ahead, similar to the one in the Gwen Shapira blog post referenced earlier.

Also, if part of the reason why your perspective is interesting comes from the fact that you're working at ReallyCoolStartup that's known for XYZ, don't assume that everyone who reads your blog post will know about ReallyCoolStartup, even if your blog post is published on the ReallyCoolStartup company blog. If your article happens to take off on social media or Hacker News, it's likely to be read by many people who have no clue what ReallyCoolStartup is or does (and few will take the time to learn before they start commenting). Strongly consider providing a super short overview of what's so cool about ReallyCoolStartup, even if it's just an aside within a broader sentence. For example, you could write something like "At ReallyCoolStartup, which focuses on XYZ, we recently…"

> **TIP**   Want the AI perspective? Prompt it with something like "Do you think the introduction of this article would motivate [your target reader] to read this engineering blog post? Why?"

How did the fake Zig blog post perform with respect to frontloading? Not so well. This article is backloaded more than frontloaded. It doesn't

- Tell the reader what's in it for them
- Mention Zig, which is a primary focus of the article
- Provide any context about who is writing it
- Share any differentiators whatsoever

Based on that introduction, the reader can only glean that this article will cover something about a faster way to migrate data from Postgres to FakeDB.

5.3   *Clarity*

Your sentences are *how* you achieve the goal that you set for this article. You need to express your ideas and experiences in sentences that the reader can understand. Otherwise, the ideas from your brain aren't going to make it all the way over to your reader's brain. Consider the coding equivalent. You can have the most impressive idea, but if you can't implement it in code that the compiler understands, you won't be able to make that idea a reality.

When you wrote your working draft, you captured your thoughts in sentences on the page. Great, that was a critical first step. Now it's time to reread those sentences with your reader in mind and tighten them up as needed to ensure that your meaning isn't muddled.

You don't need to spend tons of time revising every sentence to the point where it's so eloquent you'd want to print and frame it. But your reader will appreciate any time you spend making sure that your ideas are communicated clearly and concisely. It will make their reading experience faster, simpler, and more enjoyable. For example, consider the difference between reading the original and revised examples that follow. (The original is extreme, but it's actually a real excerpt from a draft we came across).

> *Original:* *To overcome the scaling challenges we were facing, such as the lack of a centralized system interface for keeping and managing the growing number of business rules, as well as a previously loosely coupled infrastructure of third-party services whose many failures were impacting our sales process, around two years ago we decided to create a single platform to manage all aspects of our process for selling directly to consumers.*

> *Revised:* *Two years ago, we decided to build a centralized B2C sales platform. As the business scaled, we wanted to centrally manage the growing number of business rules and cut the dependencies on unreliable third-party services.*

The original was difficult to process—but it captured his ideas and led the way to a clearer statement later on. It provided something we could debug.

Think of your dear readers. If you can convert clunky sentences into clear ones, your readers can understand your thoughts better and reach the end of your article faster. And this scales. Assume that with 15 minutes of sentence tuneup, you can save each reader 1 minute of reading time. Now assume a blog post that attracts 1,000 readers (or over 20,000, if it trends on Hacker News). The 1,000 to 20,000+ minutes (over 333 hours!) you've saved your global engineering peers is a nice return on investment from your 15-minute sentence tuneup.

After you read this section, you should be able to quickly improve sentence clarity by

- Reading sentences out loud, with the takeaways from this section in your head
- Applying the method we introduce for improving the clarity of the clunkiest sentences
- Using a tool such as Grammarly to spot any mechanical problems you've overlooked

Before you begin, remember that sentences, like code, can easily be overengineered past the point of diminishing returns. Don't overdo it. You could spend hours or days rewriting every sentence, but you have other things to do, and perfect is the enemy of good. Focus on making fast fixes to the following categories of sentences, and move on:

- Most prominent (e.g., the introduction)

- Most important (e.g., key findings and takeaways)
- Most muddled (e.g., whatever came out embarrassingly awful the first time)

5.3.1 *Targeting unclear bulky sentences*

Let's start by talking about unclear bulky sentences: the written equivalent of code bloat. It's all too easy to write convoluted sentences. When you're writing your draft, the words don't always pop into your brain in the ideal order, and sometimes, they're not even the right words at all. But as long as you end up with *some* words, *any* words to remind you of what you were thinking, you achieved your initial goal of extracting your thoughts from your brain. You still need to clarify your thoughts for your reader, though.

Before you can improve the article's overall clarity, you need a good grasp of what types of sentences are the top candidates for optimization. Here are some high-level traits to look out for:

- Overly long sentences (e.g., any sentence you can't read out loud, start to finish, without wanting to take a second breath)
- Sentences with multiple prepositional phrases (e.g., "We were collaborating *on* integration *across* environments *from* the start *of* our project...")
- Bureaucratic-sounding sentences built around a weak, passive verb (e.g., "The bug was then located." versus "We found the bug!")
- Any other time the action (the verb) and the actor (the subject performing that action) are unclear, too far from one another, or revealed too late in the sentence (e.g., "Ultimately the problem, which we later realized was actually a great opportunity for improving our process, was that coding standards were neither defined nor followed.")

Some sentences might check multiple boxes!

5.3.2 *Optimizing unclear bulky sentences*

Now comes the fun part: optimizing your clunkiest sentences. Think of it as a sentence engineering challenge, and there's even a process you can apply to do this methodically. That process is based on the Paramedic Method introduced by Richard Lanham, a professor at UCLA.

We wanted some nicely convoluted sentences to workshop throughout these steps, so we asked ChatGPT to badly rework a paragraph from the fake Zig blog post. It did not disappoint! Here's the AI-"enhanced" example that we'll use:

> *An additional drawback with Zig is the young state of the ecosystem, though we hope that this is not going to continue over the long term. Juxtaposed with Rust or compared against C++, there is a conspicuous dearth of libraries and tools that would be very helpful to programmers. It is great that it provides HTTP support within its standard library. However, with all the SOC2 requirements, it needed to be secured by means of a thin custom encryption layer. In the end, it was decided that the best solution was implementing it by means of a link to an existing Rust implementation.*

NOTE Don't plan to perform these steps for every sentence in your article! It's most likely overkill. Use this strategy as a tool to tighten your most important sentences (e.g., your introduction, and the paragraph stating your findings).

STEP 1: BOLD THE PREPOSITIONS

Looking at excessive prepositions and "to be" verbs (the focus of step 2) is a great way to identify unclear bulky sentences. It's also your best source of clues on how to improve them.

Prepositions are connector words that tie an object to the rest of the sentence. Each preposition precedes the object that it's talking about. But this isn't a grammar book. Here's what's important: clusters of prepositions and prepositional phrases inevitably make sentences difficult to read. They're often a sign that you're trying to tack too many things onto one poor sentence (aim for one sentence, one idea, period). It gets monotonous, and it adds dead weight that buries the sentence's main point. Sentences with lots of prepositions sound like they were written by committee, with everyone tacking on some part just to show that they contributed.

NOTE If you can say "[the_word] my desk" or "[the_word] the meeting," then [the_word] is probably a preposition!

To complete step 1, find the prepositions in a sentence or paragraph you want to optimize, then bold them. Just guess—you don't have to be 100% accurate.

Here's an example of bolding the prepositions, using the ChatGPT-"enhanced" excerpt:

> *An additional drawback **with** Zig is the young state **of** the ecosystem, though we hope that this is not going to continue **over** the long term. Juxtaposed **with** Rust or compared **against** C++, there is a conspicuous dearth **of** libraries and tools that would be very helpful **to** programmers. It is great that it provides HTTP support **within** its standard library. However, **with** all the SOC2 requirements, it needed to be secured **by** means **of** a thin custom encryption layer. **In** the end, it was decided that the best solution was implementing it **by** means **of** a link **to** an existing Rust implementation.*

Now read that aloud, overemphasizing each of the bolded words. Do this a few times with a few different examples, and you won't be able to unhear it. Then don't be surprised if you instinctively start using fewer prepositions as you write.

Common prepositions

Not sure what's a preposition? Here's a list of common ones for fast reference:

about / above / across / after / against / along / among / around / as / at / before / behind / beneath / beside / between / by / during / for / from / in / into / like / near / of / off / on / out / over / through / to / toward / under / upon / with / within / without

---

Even a single preposition can muddle the meaning. For example, a phrase such as "a careless way of coding" could be stated much more directly as "careless coding." "Is indicative of" could become "indicates." Prepositions are not evil per se. But in excess, they're often a symptom of a larger problem.

STEP 2: HIGHLIGHT THE "TO BE" VERBS

Like excessive prepositions, "to be" verbs commonly figure into unclear bulky sentences. They often perform the inglorious task of burying the sentence's real action and actor (the person or thing performing that action).

"To be" verbs (e.g., is, was, has, had) vaguely highlight a state of existence rather than express a real action. Sentences that revolve around such verbs often use passive instead of active voice, which shifts the focus from the subject *performing* the action to the thing *receiving* the action. It sounds suspiciously like it's trying to hide something or avoid assigning blame (which it often is). Here's the difference:

- *Passive*—"The bug was then located."
- *Active*—"We found the bug!"

> **NOTE** Another fun rule of thumb: if you can add "by zombies" to the end of a sentence and it still makes sense, then your sentence uses passive voice. For example, "The bug was then located *by zombies.*"

There's nothing wrong with using passive "to be" verbs in moderation. In fact, it's the preferred option when you don't know who did something or you don't want to mention who did it (e.g., "The build was broken, so we started to investigate why.") Just don't overuse and abuse them. You can often find a better alternative: a stronger verb that shares more information, more concisely and directly.

To complete step 2, identify and highlight the forms of "to be." Use color highlighting if you're working in an editor that allows it, or just use italics if you prefer.

"To be" verbs

Not sure what a "to be" verb looks like? Here's a quick reference:

am / is / are / was / were / be / being / been

Here's that same ChatGPT-"enhanced" excerpt with "to be" verbs underlined:

> *An additional drawback* **with** *Zig* is *the young state* **of** *the ecosystem, though we hope that this* is *not going to continue* **over** *the long term. Juxtaposed* **with** *Rust or compared* **against** *C++, there* is *a conspicuous dearth* **of** *libraries and tools that would* be *very helpful* **to** *programmers. It* is *great that it provides HTTP support* **within** *its standard library. However,* **with** *all the SOC2 requirements, it needed to* be *secured* **by** *means* **of** *a thin custom encryption layer.* **In** *the end, it* was *decided that the best solution* was *implementing it* **by** *means* **of** *a link* **to** *an existing Rust implementation.*

We could certainly make this paragraph more direct and readable by tackling some of those "to be" verbs. Read the sentence aloud again, lingering and cringing on each of the underlined verbs (as well as the prepositions). Do it a few times, and this will be stuck in your head forever, too. If all goes well, you will naturally catch yourself when you find yourself leaning on a lazy "to be" verb when there are much better alternatives.

> **NOTE** You don't need to change anything in your sentences (yet). This step, and the previous one, are designed to help you target sentences that could benefit from optimization, provide clues on how to fix them, and make you start wincing whenever you read a sentence that abuses prepositions and "to be" verbs.

STEP 3: FIND THE ACTOR AND THE ACTION

Now it's time to rein in those sentences. At its core, a sentence communicates some action: a subject did a thing. If your reader can't immediately tell who/what is performing some action and what action they're performing, then you're burdening them with extra work to unravel what you really meant. This won't be appreciated.

To complete step 3, think about the actor and the action in your flagged (and now marked-up) sentences. Then find a verb that concisely captures the actor's action. Try to look beyond the weak "to be" verbs and find something more precise and powerful.

For example, let's look at the first sentence in the ChatGPT-"enhanced" excerpt: "An additional drawback with Zig is the young state of the ecosystem, though we hope that this is not going to continue over the long term." Who or what is the subject? Some candidates are

- The drawback
- Zig
- The ecosystem
- The author's team (the "we")

After thinking about it, it seems like it's really about "Zig's young ecosystem." So what is that young ecosystem doing? Based on the context, it seems like it might be "complicating adoption." Now let's put it together using an active verb. That yields:

> *"Zig's young ecosystem complicates adoption"*

For another example, consider the final sentence: "In the end, it was decided that the best solution was implementing it by means of a link to an existing Rust implementation." Where's the actor and action here? Hidden. With all the prepositions and "to be" verbs, we have a lot of words but no stated actor and a buried action. It seems the actor is actually "we" (the author's team) and the action is "implementing it by means of a link," which could be expressed simply as "linked." That gives us a new core of

> *"We linked to an existing Rust implementation."*

STEP 4: REBUILD THE SENTENCE AROUND THE ACTOR AND THE ACTION

Now expand on that core and reintroduce any remaining essential elements from the original sentence. Try to avoid adding too many words at the start of the sentence; generally, the faster the reader reaches the subject and verb, the better. And while you're tacking the original bits back on, you might as well try to simplify them, particularly by eliminating excessive prepositions and rethinking "to be" verbs.

In our first example, we might end up with, "Another drawback: Zig's young ecosystem complicates adoption. We hope this improves." In the second one, we might end up with, "Ultimately, we implemented that encryption layer by linking to an existing Rust implementation."

STEP 5: CUT (OR REPLACE) THE REMAINING USELESS WORDS

Finally, think hard about what else you might cut. Are there any words that aren't adding value—either enhancing the readers' understanding of the subject or making the article more pleasant to read? If so, strongly consider cutting them.

> **NOTE** Sometimes, there's a tradeoff between being ultra concise and achieving the desired authentic tone. As we cover in section 5.5.1, a conversational tone makes the article much more consumable than some bland impersonal article would be. If words add value in that respect, they're not "useless," and you shouldn't feel compelled to cut them.

In our first example, we ended up with "Another drawback: Zig's young ecosystem complicates adoption. We hope this improves." Does it add any value to share that the team *hopes* this improves? Not really. It would be more interesting if it were supported with some facts, like the project's GitHub star history showing a nice trend up and to the right (see figure 5.1). For example, we could incorporate that detail as follows: "Another drawback: Zig's young ecosystem complicates adoption. But this could change soon given the surging interest in Zig."

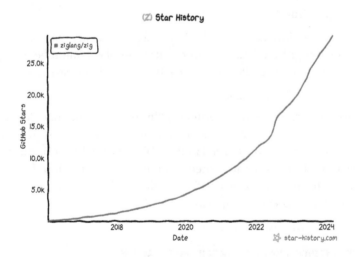

Figure 5.1   **This image could be added to the fake Zig blog post to demonstrate the surging interest in Zig.**

Revisiting the second example, there's not too much to cut in "Ultimately, we implemented that encryption layer by linking to an existing Rust implementation." "Ultimately" is not essential, but it's a nice linking word that indicates the team considered multiple options first and determined this was the best approach. We'll keep it.

But we could safely kill "existing." After all, the team couldn't just link to something that did not exist. However, it might be more interesting to replace "existing" with the name of the specific implementation that was used, plus a link. For example: "Ultimately, we implemented that encryption layer by linking to the RustyEncryption Rust implementation." Now, readers considering similar projects have a starting point for their own encryption library research. But wait: Do we *really* need to say "the RustyEncryption Rust implementation"? "Rust implementation" can be inferred from the context, and if readers want to know more, they can click the hyperlink we're adding. Let's simplify it: "Ultimately, we implemented that encryption layer by linking to RustyEncryption." Table 5.3 recaps how those two sentences have evolved.

Table 5.3 Original vs. revised sentences

Before	After
An additional drawback with Zig is the young state of the ecosystem, though we hope that this is not going to continue over the long term.	Another drawback: Zig's young ecosystem complicates adoption. But this could change soon given the surging interest in Zig. [Star History image]
In the end, it was decided that the best solution was implementing it by means of a link to an existing Rust implementation.	Ultimately, we implemented that encryption layer by linking to RustyEncryption.

And for fun, let's tackle a couple other unwieldy sentences from the fake blog post, too, as shown in table 5.4:

Table 5.4 More original vs. revised sentences

Before	After
Zig is not Rust, and it happily lets you dereference null pointers (although its type system tries to prevent obvious cases of that), and use previously freed memory, so we had a dubious pleasure of long debugging sessions, just us, gdb, and the ninth cup of coffee – but it was comforting to see all the existing tools just work.	Unlike Rust, Zig happily lets you dereference null pointers (but its type system tries to prevent egregious offenses). It also lets you use previously freed memory. We abused these freedoms, which led to the dubious pleasure of long debugging sessions: just us, gdb, and the ninth cup of coffee. At least all the existing tools still just work.
One of the mind-blowing things about Zig is that cross compilation (ergo compiling the code to target CPU architecture and operating system different than the setup the compiler runs on) is also a core feature of the language.	Zig's cross compilation is mind-blowing. You can compile code to a target CPU architecture and operating system different than the setup your compiler runs on.

Note that we didn't remove every "to be" verb or preposition, and you don't need to either. Taking a hard look at them is a means to an end (sentence clarity), not a goal in and of itself. Also note that we left a few nonessential words because we very deliberately wanted to preserve the author's friendly and personable voice rather than make the article seem too detached and dull. The discussion of why and how to make it sound human continues in section 5.5.1.

Calculating the lard factor

Richard Lanham uses the "lard factor" to measure success in revision with the Paramedic Method. To calculate it, take the word reduction you achieved and divide it by the original number of words. In the case of the second example (linking to RustyEncryption), we get a lard factor of 57%:

23 - 10 = 13 / 23 = .5652 or 57%

Plus, we ended up adding a link that readers might find useful!

Don't cut words for the sake of brevity. Just ensure that every word is justified and pulling its own weight.

When you're hunting down words to eliminate or replace, pay special attention to the following:

- *The "blah blah is that" opening*—This is also known as "throat clearing" or "the slow windup." It's just extra words that you're forcing the reader to read before reaching your point. It manifests itself in sentences such as "the fact of the matter is that…" and "what is most notable here is that…"
- *Redundancies*—Don't use two words when one can achieve the same effect (e.g., basic fundamentals, end result, merge together, past history, new innovations).
- *Very + word*—Given the hundreds of thousands of words (at least) in the English language, there is likely one that's a better match to whatever you're trying to express than "very + whatever." This is one place where generative AI excels. Just prompt it with something like "Please suggest 30 words that mean 'very strange'" and select the one you like.
- *The phrase that should have been a word*—Why force your reader to read three or four words when one would do the trick? For example,
  - In light of the fact that > Since
  - Despite the fact that > Although
  - In the event that > If
- *Double negatives*—Double negatives require twice as much brain power to process than the alternative. Moreover, it's generally easier for the brain to process something in the affirmative. For example,
  - It's not impossible for… > It's possible that… (or *Possibly*)
  - No tests without failures… > Only failing tests…
- *Superlatives and extremes*—Never use superlatives or extremes; it's always the worst approach. But seriously, it's usually difficult to prove that you are indeed the only, best, fastest, or easiest whatever or that you always or never do something. And if you can't prove it, you *will* lose your readers' trust. Plus, you're likely to incite the comment section vitriol that we've mentioned many times by now. If you do

choose to use superlatives, know that they will be perceived as "fighting words," so be prepared for the fight that follows.

STEP 6: WATCH OUT FOR OTHER CLARITY KILLERS

Even after all of that, there are still a million more things you *could* fine-tune. But what else should you focus on? If you have the time and desire, we recommend looking for the following clarity killers that are common in engineering blog posts.

- *Muddled modifiers*—Clarify what modifiers are modifying. Otherwise, the reader might misinterpret your meaning. For example,
  - Debugging the code, the error became clear. (The error was debugging the code for you? Great!)
  - Coding quickly makes you a better programmer. (Do you need to code with blazing fast speed to become a better programmer? Or will any pace of coding make you a better programmer before long?)
  - I'll read the proposal and schedule your presentation tomorrow. (What's happening tomorrow? The reading? Or should you be ready to present tomorrow?)

- *Disconnects*—If you start saying something, finish it before you move on to the next idea. Don't leave your reader hanging. Keep your subject close to your verb and your verb close to its object. For example,
  - We weren't entirely shocked that John, after six months of frustration with endless feature creep, changing deadlines, and stakeholder turnover, quit.
  - The new algorithm, which can significantly reduce the computational complexity and memory footprint of deep learning models by surgically removing redundant connections, had a serious bug.

- *Vague/incorrect it/that references*—Unless the context makes it totally clear what each "it" or "that" refers to, you might want to specify. For example,
  - It's somewhere in the repo but it's broken. (What's broken? The thing someone is looking for or the repo itself?)
  - The report mentioned a major issue, but it lacked a resolution (Did the report fail to include a resolution? Or was the major issue unresolved?)

- *Punctuation overload*—A sentence that's technically correct could be made intimidating by the sheer amount and variety of punctuation. For example,
  - Push more logic into the database itself: letting it process as much as possible locally—which is (usually) great for "performance"—and then return the results to the users... or some middleware.
  - Some databases (e.g., PostgreSQL) implement their own binary format on top of the TCP/IP stack; others (e.g., Amazon DynamoDB) build theirs on top of HTTP—that's a bit more verbose, but also more versatile (as well as more compatible with browsers).

- *Startling shifts*—Choose your verb tense and how you're addressing the user, then keep it consistent throughout the article. For example,
  - Starting with "This provides you with" then shifting to "Users gain the ability to"
  - Starting with "We were in the middle of a meeting" then shifting to "And then everything suddenly stops"
- *Inconsistent tech terms*—If something is known by multiple terms, by all means include them all in the article, ideally when you introduce the thing. This helps the readers determine if you're really talking about the same thing if you say "po-tay-to" and they "say po-tah-to." But don't arbitrarily change terms throughout the article. For example,
  - Define it upfront as "The blah (also known as *blahblah* and *blahblahblah*)."
  - Don't randomly switch around by calling it "the blah" in one sentence and "the blahblahblah" in another.
- *Perplexed paragraphs*—One paragraph, one idea. If you can't clearly state the point of a paragraph, you can't expect your reader to grasp it. A paragraph could have one big idea with supporting facts and details. Or it could unite several closely related ideas that build on one another. But if a paragraph randomly wanders off into an orthogonal idea, start a new paragraph so the shift is clear to the reader.

Common errors in English

Every language has its quirks. English certainly has its fair share of similar words with distinctly different meanings. Fortunately, there's a great reference you can tap if you want quick clarification: Paul Brians' *Common Errors in English Usage* (https://brians.wsu .edu/common-errors/). Can't remember the difference between adverse and averse? It's and its? Less and fewer? This site explains all that and much more.

GIVE AI A CHANCE?

Now for fun, let's take a look at how AI would revise the entire convoluted paragraph that we started with. When prompted "Make this more direct and clearer," it did a fairly decent job. It got us from this

> *An additional drawback with Zig is the young state of the ecosystem, though we hope that this is not going to continue over the long term. Juxtaposed with Rust or compared against C++, there is a conspicuous dearth of libraries and tools that would be very helpful to programmers. It is great that it provides HTTP support within its standard library. However, with all the SOC2 requirements, it needed to be secured by means of a thin custom encryption layer. In the end, it was decided that the best solution was implementing it by means of a link to an existing Rust implementation.*

to

> *Zig's ecosystem is still young, lacking compared to Rust or C++. The shortage of libraries and tools is noticeable, though we hope this changes in the long run. While it does*

offer HTTP support in its standard library, we needed to add a custom encryption layer to meet SOC2 requirements. After evaluating options, linking to an existing Rust implementation emerged as the most effective solution.

It didn't introduce the two more substantial improvements that we made (replacing the "we hope" bit with the GitHub star history and providing a link to the specific Rust implementation used). A human brain is required to realize that those additional details might be interesting—and weave them in. Still, the improvement is decent given the low effort required. We certainly don't recommend that you feed your work to AI and then blindly copy in the revision. But if you're stuck, you might want to see what AI suggests. Even if it doesn't suggest something better, seeing some potential revisions might trick your brain into generating more of its own ideas.

In appendix B, we'll have a little more fun with using generative AI for revision.

5.3.3 Grappling with grammar

Your grammar does not need to be perfect, but it certainly helps to have a good reference handy in case you want to check something—especially if you're not a native English speaker. One that we recommend is *A Writer's Reference* by Diana Hacker (no Hacker News pun intended). It's available as a nice spiral-bound book with tabs and indexes to help you quickly answer whatever question you have. It's a classic, and any used edition should work fine for your writing purposes. Once you see how the book is organized, it will be faster to find your answer here than by searching the internet.

What about writing tools like Grammarly and lesser-known alternatives (we provide a rundown in appendix A)? They don't find everything. Sometimes they even suggest the *wrong* thing and then tell you to change it back, sending you in an infinite loop. But you'd be remiss not to use one. They do catch many mistakes (particularly incorrect punctuation, misspelled words, and missing words) faster and more accurately than most humans could.

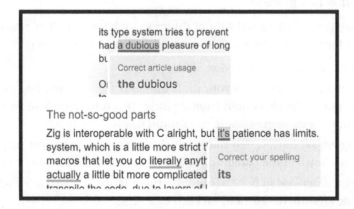

Figure 5.2 In the fake Zig blog post, Grammarly instantly caught two things we would correct: incorrect article usage and a simple mixup between it's and its.

Consider whatever option you select as an essential but fallible tool. Like a static analysis checker that's not yet tuned for your needs and preferences, it will report problems you don't care about, and it's dangerous to assume that the absence of reported problems means everything is just perfect. Always scan the findings to see if it caught something interesting. But certainly question anything that seems fishy, and know that it will inevitably miss things.

Another option is to tap generative AI. You can ask an AI chatbot to clarify specific grammatical points (e.g., "Please explain the rule for when to use an article.") This is usually spot on. Also, you can feed it a sentence or even your entire article and ask it to point out grammatical errors. But beware; based on our experiences

- It likely won't report everything in one try. You might need to go through a few iterations of finding and fixing, or use a very carefully worded prompt, before it reveals everything it noticed.
- The recommendations are sometimes nonsense and implementing them would actually make the sentences worse.

Our take: it's worth seeing what AI reports, just in case it happens to catch something that's clearly valid. As long as you can quickly spot the real problems among the noise, it's a means of free checking that might quickly surface something you missed. But always review the results with suspicion. We'll discuss this more, with examples, in appendix B.

Honestly, the best way to find missing words and other awkwardness is to read your draft out loud. If that's too embarrassing or impractical, at least whisper it audibly to yourself. You might feel silly doing a dramatic reading of your own blog post. But you'd be surprised by how many things you catch when you mouth it and hear it out loud versus when it's just a voice in your head. Keep your trusty grammar guide nearby in case something sounds weird and you want to investigate further.

5.3.4   *Putting it all together in a process*

Throughout this section, we discussed a lot of things to look for, as well as a variety of ways to find and fix them. Here's how we recommend putting it all together:

1 Review the targeting criteria in section 5.3.1.
2 With those criteria in mind, read your draft out loud (really!) and flag any sentences that could obviously benefit from revision. If you have trouble reading a sentence naturally, in a single breath, you should flag it.
3 Of all the flagged sentences, determine which ones are most critical (e.g., sentences from your intro or the paragraph revealing your most impressive findings).
4 Use the process described in 5.3.2 to optimize those target sentences. Timebox it to a reasonable amount of time and stick to it.
5 Look at the problems your grammar-checking tool reports and fix what makes sense. Consider asking generative AI for a grammar check, too.

6 Read the blog post out loud again, as slowly and dramatically as you can bear. If anything else critical jumps out at you, pause to fix it, and then proceed with your soliloquy.

Congratulations, you've done your due diligence! Now onto the next.

5.4 Components

Zooming out a bit, let's look at the various components of the blog post: the higher-level components that either include or enhance the sentences we just looked at are

- Titles
- Introductions
- Endings
- Headings
- Visuals
- Code

As with sentences, you could go down the rabbit hole overengineering these components well past the point of diminishing returns. Instead of trying to make them perfect, aim to make them effective. To get you there, let's focus on what each component should achieve, then look at some tips for accomplishing that goal.

5.4.1 Titles

Titles need to draw in your target readers. If your title doesn't catch the reader's attention, pique their curiosity, and intrigue them enough to click, then your blog post won't get read, no matter how great it is.

There are exceptions, of course. If an industry luminary happens to share your article in a social media post that's something like "This is the most important thing on BLAH that I've ever read—check it out: LINK," then your title matters much less. But it's generally safe to assume that the weight of the world rests on your title.

Let's be realistic. Sometimes you'll feel that your working draft ended up "good enough" based on your intuition, and you'll skip all the review/optimization steps for core and clarity. That's fine. In fact, that's great—with enough practice, that will all come naturally. But don't ever publish without spending at least a few minutes thinking about the title. It's too important, and it's also a very fast and easy way to make a big difference.

Try to force yourself to create a long list of title variations, at least 10 or so. Don't keep overwriting the same title; you risk losing good ideas that you might want to mix and match into a final title. In some separate area in the same doc, a different one, or on a good old piece of paper, just try to crank out title variations that follow these recommendations (which we will explore in turn next):

- Intrigue your target readers without misleading them.
- Would catch your target readers' attention in a random list of blog post titles (think Hacker News).
- Feature at least one term that your target readers might be looking for.

Before we dive into the details, note the focus on target readers. Chapter 4 prompted you to consider and define who you expected to read the article. This should be a primary consideration for your title. If your target audience is truly "anyone on Hacker News," you'd want to go with a broad, maybe somewhat mysterious title. But if you're writing specifically for readers who obsess over the nuances of consensus algorithms in the context of database internals, you're going to need a rather specific terminology-laced title. A title misfire will prevent you from reaching the right readers, and attracting the wrong readers is a surefire way to stir up negative comments.

INTRIGUE YOUR TARGET READERS WITHOUT MISLEADING THEM

When technical readers judge the article by its title, they consider whether they believe the article will help them learn about a topic that interests them. Otherwise, they won't bother spending their time on it.

For your title, aim to highlight a challenge, pain, technology, or engineering feat that lies at the intersection of 1) what your target readers care about and 2) what your article addresses. Remember how the last chapter urged you to define what's so special about your take on your selected topic and why your reader would be interested in your perspective on it? That should be your guide for what to feature in your title.

Don't bury your differentiators. If your article presents something surprising or counterintuitive, a unique perspective, a contrarian opinion, or a new way to approach a longstanding problem, then definitely mention that in the title! There's no shame in enticing people to read by highlighting what's special about your article.

However, never tease something that you don't ultimately deliver on. For instance, if you promise a result like "Read This Post to Learn a Shocking Truth About A/B Testing" and your blog post doesn't actually include any groundbreaking information, people will notice. You'll not only lose readers for this blog post. You'll get snarky comments referencing clickbait. And you'll breed distrust that could very likely deter people from reading your subsequent blog posts.

Consider ad blockers too. You're targeting a technical audience, experienced in creative ways of avoiding ads when they browse the internet. The following qualities can get your title filtered out (for a good reason!):

- Profanity
- WORDS IN ALL CAPS
- Excessive exclamation marks!!!!!!!
- Emojis ☺✈🐶
- Words with erotic or obscene connotations
- Hyperlinks directly in the title (yes, it happens)

The above traits also make the title seem clickbaity to a human. If you use them in your title, ad blockers are actually doing you a favor by preventing you from getting purely negative online feedback. The bottom line: don't do it.

What should you do instead? The most intriguing titles tend to be

- *Short and crisp*—No "fluff" words that don't pull their own weight.
- *Playful, provocative, or mysterious*—If you enjoy wordplay, this is your chance.
- *Technical and targeted*—Something a broader audience would never "get."

Here are a few examples of particularly intriguing titles:

- "Moore's Scofflaws" by Bryan Cantrill (https://oxide.computer/blog/moores-scofflaws)
- "Ship Shape" by Kerry Halupka and Rowan Katekar (https://mng.bz/gA5n)
- "Is Something Bugging You?" by Will Wilson (https://mng.bz/eVxZ)
- "Dumpster Diving the Go Garbage Collector" by Natalie Serrino (https://blog.px.dev/go-garbage-collector/)
- "Lies We Tell Ourselves to Keep Using Golang" by Amos Wenger (https://mng.bz/pxm0)

Another strategy is to use a multipart title—a short catchy phrase and a more descriptive phrase, separated by a colon. For example, "Herding elephants: Lessons learned from sharding Postgres at Notion" (which we'll discuss in chapter 11). The initial part, on its own, would attract people looking to herd large animals—presumably not the target reader. The analogy is a fun introduction to the descriptive title that follows the colon.

ENSURE THE TITLE CAN STAND ALONE

Once your blog post is published, you can't control where it shows up and with what information. The only thing you *can* control is that its title will (most likely) be shown. Read your title with that in mind. If your target reader sees your title, without any context in some random list or feed, would that title alone get them to click?

If your article happens to hit the front page of Hacker News, readers will decide to click—or not—based only on your title and the domain of where it's hosted. No cool image, no description, nothing. And it's the same in many other news aggregators and newsletters, at least the ones that attract the technical audience you're presumably trying to reach. Some popular lists (e.g., This Week in Rust) don't even display a domain.

If you're working for a household-name tech leader, you can probably publish a post titled "How [BigTech] [anything]," and people will be curious enough to click. Not so if you're at a little-known startup. In that case, you probably need to add more descriptive and/or intriguing words.

THINK ABOUT WHAT YOUR TARGET READER MIGHT BE LOOKING FOR

Blog posts have a predictable life cycle. Upon publication, they're shared across aggregator and social sites, where they take off (or not) based on upvotes and endorsements. In this arena, having a catchy, somewhat mysterious title might help you stand out within a sea of options.

Once the newness wears off, your blog post likely won't be featured on lists or feeds. Still, any time someone searches for a matching term, it could have a chance to draw attention.

Highlighting appropriate search terms (a.k.a. keywords) in the title is especially important at this point of the blog post's lifecycle. If you want your blog post to live a long and healthy life, keywords matter. You don't need to resort to the tricky search engine optimization (SEO) strategies that, along with AI-generated content, are responsible for most of the junk you receive in search results. But you really should

- Think about what terms your target readers might be searching when they're exploring a question or problem that your blog post addresses
- Consider featuring at least one of those terms in your title (and the others in your introduction and headings)

TIP   If you feel strongly about using a catchy title without a recognizable keyword, you could try launching with that catchy title, then retitling the article later.

Don't pander to machines. But if your article covers topics that people are searching for or talking about, be sure to highlight that so it can be found by interested humans and the machines they use to surface information. For example, if you're writing about something many developers are following (say, Rust), don't forget to include that technology in your title.

A quick search will yield many SEO-optimized listings for many SEO optimization tools—all promising to guide you to the precise winning combination and placement of keywords you need to win the SEO game. If you have a solid article, you shouldn't need them. Just make sure your title highlights the most critical term(s) and the others are featured prominently (maybe in your headings).

NOTE   We'll cover keywords a bit more in chapter 7. Skip ahead if you're really not sure what to highlight in your title.

Example 5.1

There are many specific title compliments and critiques throughout the example blog posts we'll be discussing for each pattern. Here's a quick preview of a few title-related comments:

- *How a Single Line of Code Made a 24-core Server Slower Than a Laptop*—It seemed a bit clickbatity at first, but the article delivered on its promise.
- *How Prime Video Updates its App for More Than 8,000 Device Types*—It mentions "over 8,000 device types," introducing an impressive level of awe.
- *Rust After the Honeymoon*—Intriguing in its technical ambiguity as well as emotional connotation (honeymoon).
- *How We Built Scalable Spatial Data and Spatial Indexing in CockroachDB*—It wouldn't jump out at the average reader, but it is well-suited for the target audience.

Let's also return to the fake Zig blog post. In the initial draft, the title was "Zig helped us migrate our data efficiently." Zig was a key focus, so it's good to have that featured quite prominently. Making it the first word gives it extra emphasis.

But who is "us"? Do many people care about Zig helping the unknown "us" migrate data? (Well, since it's Zig, maybe.) Fans of this "us" might not notice the article unless they also see and recognize the domain. And didn't the author (PretendPiotr) want users of FakeDB and Postgres to read this blog post? They're unlikely to notice or find this blog post unless FakeDB and Postgres are included somewhere in the headline.

With that in mind, here are some alternate title ideas:

- Zig Helped Us Migrate to FakeDB Efficiently
- Zig Helped Us Finally Migrate Off Postgres
- How to Migrate Data from Postgres to FakeDB...with Zig!

TIP You could ask AI to generate some additional title options for you. It most likely won't spit out the perfect title, but it might get you thinking about different approaches and spark some new ideas in your own human brain.

5.4.2 Introductions

Once readers are lured in by your title, they'll likely scan your introduction to assess whether the article delivers on the title's promise. Is it worth reading now (or at least saving for later)? At this point, they're wondering

- What exactly they'll get from reading this article
- What angle you're taking on this topic
- How it compares to everything else they've read on the topic
- If you seem qualified to address this topic
- If it's really worth their time

Don't be shy—tell them! Provide the information they want and let them decide if they wish to continue. Technical readers never want to feel tricked. If you're upfront and transparent about your angle and intentions, readers who aren't interested can just leave now and move on with their lives. They'll appreciate that you saved them some time, and you'll appreciate that they didn't end up flaming you for wasting their time on something that didn't meet their expectations. Win-win!

NOTE Introductions are also discussed in section 5.2.3, particularly the part about frontloading your article. And section 5.2.2 covered the importance of providing context, which is critical in an introduction.

Also, plan to think hard about every sentence (ideally, every single word) in your introduction. We've said quite a few times that you don't want or need to overengineer every sentence in the article. Ensuring that the introduction is clear and concise, however, should pay off immensely in catching the target readers' attention and motivating them to continue. The introduction is the perfect place to put all the sentence-tightening lessons you learned from section 5.3 into action. Here are our recommendations for a solid introduction, tying together some earlier threads on context and frontloading, and introducing some additional tips.

UNLESS YOU HAVE ANOTHER IDEA, JUST START WITH THE BACKSTORY

Don't fret over coming up with some famous first line. If you have some electrifying hook in mind, use it. If you want to try something intriguing, you could start off with a startling fact or outcome, a provocative statement, or an anecdote. But really, if you're not so inspired (like most of us, most of the time), just start at how it all began.

Something happened to prompt you to do (or think) this thing and write about it. Begin your article by sharing what that was and why it drove you down this path. This immediately starts to close the gap between you and your reader. It offers a great opportunity for you to share a bit about why you're qualified to speak about this topic and what's so unique about your perspective on it. Plus, it saves you from the frustration of trying to write some clever opening under pressure. If you're feeling particularly creative, first channel it toward writing a catchy title. It will have a much larger effect there. Plus, it's a lot fewer words to worry about.

TELL THE READER WHAT TO EXPECT AND WHAT'S IN IT FOR THEM

Remember the goal you stated for your article, the one sentence you defined in chapter 4? The introduction is a great place to let the reader in on what you're trying to accomplish here. That way, they can either click away or set aside time to dive in.

But remember that everything is now about your reader, not about you. Your reader cares mostly about what's in it for them, so restate your goal in terms of them. Will they discover a new technique for alleviating a key pain point? Gain the wisdom of your lessons learned without having to endure the pain you suffered? Vicariously experience the fun of your latest weekend project? Don't force them to guess; just be open and share.

Also, it's a nice gesture to tell them what they'll experience along the way, like a proper tour guide. For example, if you're talking about how you built something cool, will you also be providing source code and explanations so they can later experiment on their own? That might factor heavily into someone's decision to read your article. If you want to build trust and avoid (at least some) nasty comments, transparency is the best policy.

MAKE SURE YOU'VE INDICATED WHY YOUR TAKE ON THIS TOPIC IS INTERESTING

In chapter 4, we also urged you to write down why your perspective on this topic is so interesting to your target audience. That's likely the second thing that your reader wants to know before deciding whether to read your article. Don't force them to scan the whole article and guess. Just reveal it in the introduction.

Is your take interesting because you're writing about something you personally designed and/or implemented? Because you ran an extreme scale scenario that nobody else dared to run? Because you have extensive experience working with something in production and want to share the reality versus the hype? Whatever sets your take on this topic apart, don't let the reader leave the introduction without knowing it.

BE HIGHLY AWARE OF WHAT YOUR TARGET READER DOES AND DOESN'T KNOW

Think about the range of people who might stumble onto your blog post:

- They might not know anything about you, your company, or your project.
- They might not know much about your topic.
- They might already know way more about your topic than you expect, maybe even more than you know.

You can't please everyone. And if you try, you end up pleasing no one. So who do you write for? It 100% depends on who your target audience is. Who did you have in mind when you wrote it? That's the person you should cater to. This is important throughout the article, but it's especially important at the beginning. If the target reader finds that the first few paragraphs are too overwhelming or too basic for them, they're likely to leave before they read the rest.

Provide whatever context is required to give the target reader a soft landing. Even a short (several words) description of your project when you first introduce it could really help orient a reader. And avoid explaining things that your target reader should already know. Hyperlinks are your friend here. They let you abstract away details that would turn off the advanced reader, while still offering learning options for those who would appreciate a little more background. Don't go into hyperlink overload, though. That looks immediately unappealing and gets distracting fast. Use your best judgment on what's most helpful for your target reader.

Example 5.2

How did the fake Zig blog post stack up on the criteria we set forth here? Not well, as shown in the table. As we briefly mentioned in section 5.2.2, PretendPiotr went straight into the meat of the article, without really considering what the reader knows or cares about.

Criteria	Verdict
Provide the context required to help the reader understand where they've landed	No, it jumps right into the middle of the story.
Help the reader understand your goal, stated in terms of what's in it for them	There were two stated goals: 1) convince database users to try out the migration tool, and 2) show that it's possible to create something useful with Zig. Neither is reflected in this introduction. Still, the reader can probably guess that they'll learn a faster way to move data from Postgres to FakeDB.
Give the reader a taste of what they'll experience along the way	Not at all. The title mentions Zig and the bulk of the article is about Zig, but the introduction doesn't mention Zig once.
Share why your perspective on this topic is interesting	Nope. It doesn't even provide any context on who "we" is.

(continued)

If this were a real article, we'd recommend adding a paragraph or two before the current start; that new intro could then cover the key points.

TIP   Section 5.2 shared excerpts from a couple rather effective introductions by Gwen Shapira and Liz Fong-Jones.

5.4.3 Endings

Many readers will drop off before the end—they lose interest, or life happens. But those who stuck it out should be rewarded for their perseverance. Here are some parting gifts you can leave them with.

SUMMARY/TAKEAWAYS

Even if the reader has been following along, it's nice to offer them a concise summary, tying it all together for them. In the ideal world, every reader would read every word carefully, then write down their own summary/takeaways in some notes file. That way, they could force themselves to synthesize everything they learned and restate it in their own words for better absorption and retention.

But in reality, that doesn't always (or ever?) happen. So help out the reader and do it for them. Don't repeat every key point; instead, synthesize the main ideas and touch on why it all matters. Bonus: it makes it very easy for the reader to share your key points with their colleagues or social network, potentially giving you additional readers later on. Also, look back at your introduction and see if it makes sense to revisit any of those threads in the conclusion. It could be a nice way to close the loop for the reader.

IMPLICATIONS/EXTRAPOLATION

Try and place your experiences and findings in the context of the broader industry, beyond your project and company. In other words, directly address the "so what" question. Thinking about how your specific work ties into the broader tech world is always interesting; it could be inspiring, humbling, rewarding, or all that at the same time.

Moreover, it's a conversation starter. It could spark a discussion in the comment section, and maybe some small percentage of those comments lead to a thoughtful discussion. Maybe someone will write a follow-up article focused on one of those threads and link back to your article as their inspiration.

WHAT'S NEXT (FOR YOU)

Many blog post patterns covered in the next part of this book wrap by discussing what's next for the project. This is especially common in posts that follow the "How We Built It" and "We Rewrote It in X" patterns. Projects rarely have a clear-cut ending; there's almost always more work to be done. Giving your reader insight into this is a nice transparency touch. And if something significant is planned, mentioning it here can help build anticipation for the next blog post that you'll write when that aspect of the product is ready to share.

NEXT STEPS (FOR THEM)

Do you have an ask or invitation for the highly interested reader who reached the end of your article? Would you like them to provide you feedback on something, maybe contribute to a project? Or can you give them a way to apply what they learned or learn even more? Ending by giving them something, as well as asking for something, is a mutually beneficial way to wrap it up.

Example 5.3

The example blog posts in our pattern chapters showcase many different approaches to endings. One of the most fun ones is the Discord post "Why Discord Is Switching From Go to Rust," which will be featured in chapter 9. In closing, the author

- Links to another blog post about Discord's use of Rust
- Shares how Discord's dev process has changed as a result of this project
- Invites Rust devotees to consider joining the Discord engineering team
- Reveals that while Discord relies on Rust, the Rust community relies on Discord as their primary communication channel
- Provides a direct link to the Rust Programming Language Discord Server

Although the fake Zig blog post really missed the mark on the introduction, it wrapped with a satisfying conclusion. It tied together all the various threads: the Postgres to FakeDB data migration, the new data migrator, and the adventures in Zig. It also offered easy access to the new tool and invited users to share their feedback.

5.4.4 *Headings*

Your headings are signposts that help the reader scan and navigate your article. They should call out the different parts of the article in terms that make sense to the reader. We covered this, with some examples of hits and misses, in section 5.2.3 (on flow). To summarize the key takeaways from that discussion

- Make sure the headings focus on terms that the reader understands.
- Strongly consider crafting headings that answer the questions that are likely in the reader's head at that point in the article.

Here are a few additional tips for helpful headings.

LESS IS MORE

Aim for the shortest possible set of words that will help orient your reader. Headlines should break up the paragraphs. If you have super long headings, in big bold fonts, it's likely to overwhelm the reader more than help them.

PLACE THE CRITICAL WORDS AT THE START

Readers scan from left to right. Don't force the reader to read through a lot of filler words to reach the important ones. For example, assume you're writing up a benchmark and you have a few sections on how configuration A compares to configuration

B: one covering throughput, the other covering latency. Don't use headings like "Configuration A vs. Configuration B: Throughput," "Configuration A vs. Configuration B: Latency." Instead, go with "Throughput Results," "Latency Results."

AVOID UNNECESSARY COMPLEXITY

Sometimes you really need multiple layers of headings to convey the structure of an article. But often, the complexity ends up disorienting the reader, especially if it's hard to visually distinguish one level of the hierarchy from another. You don't need to avoid it; just be very deliberate about it. And consider numbering sections if it would help readers understand where they are in the hierarchy.

> **TIP** Want the AI perspective? Try prompting a few different chatbots with something like "Can you recommend ways to improve the existing headings in this article?" Note that some provided much more helpful feedback than others at the time of writing. If you really want recommendations and feel like the feedback you're getting is inadequate, it might be worth trying another chatbot.

5.4.5   Visuals

The visuals you add can be just as important as your words, sometimes even more so. Images such as architectural diagrams, graphs quantifying your optimizations, and screenshots of the clues you encountered along your bug hunt can make or break the article for some readers. Done well, they convey complex information with impressive efficiency.

Engineering blog posts commonly use visuals to tell stories about data. Exploring data visualization best practices is well beyond the scope of a section in a chapter of a book. In fact, there are entire books written on data visualization. Two recent examples include *Everyday Data Visualization* by Desireé Abbott and *Fundamentals of Data Visualization* by Claus O. Wilke. Also, the series of books by Edward Tufte are classics in that respect. If you're going to be designing your own images, we strongly recommend that you consider learning from those experts.

Even if you're just grabbing screenshots or integrating basic charts from a spreadsheet, there are a few basic considerations to keep in mind with visuals.

THINK ABOUT HOW THE READER WILL EXPERIENCE IT ON THE PAGE

A screenshot of a full-screen dark mode dashboard isn't going to convey much information to a reader viewing it in a typical web template. You can probably have the image explode into the full size (we'll cover options like this in chapter 7). But it might be better to create an image that shows the exact part of the dashboard you're talking about, at an instantly readable size. You will focus your reader's attention and also save them a couple clicks.

CAPTION CAREFULLY

If you decided to spend time creating and adding an image, just spend another minute writing a caption that tells readers why it's there and what they should be focusing on.

It's an easy way to help readers get the most out of it. It also makes the meaning clear to readers with visual impairments, or whenever the image is not loading.

CONSIDER COLOR-BLIND READERS

If your image conveys meaning through colors, consider if color-blind readers can still grasp the meaning (you can find free color-blind simulators online). Colorblindness is much more common in men than women (8% versus 0.4%). Given the tech field demographics, your article is likely to reach a lot of male readers, and thus a fair amount of color-blind readers.

TAKE COPYRIGHTS SERIOUSLY

This is another case of ask for permission, not forgiveness. It's the right thing to do, and even an innocuous mistake could be tremendously costly. We once had a teammate unknowingly use a copyrighted image in a blog post. The copyright holder discovered that and contacted the company. Our company immediately took it down, but we also had to pay damages in the amount of tens of thousands of dollars. Lesson learned.

> **TIP** Want ideas on what visuals to add? Prompt AI with something like "Can you think of any visuals to add to this article?"

5.4.6 Code

Last and certainly not least, code examples. Code examples should be used strategically to show how something works, why something has improved, why an optimization is necessary, and so on. We'll talk about how code excerpts are displayed in chapter 7. For now, let's focus on the code itself.

If you're including code examples, ensure that they are

- *Shareable*—If your project isn't open source, make sure you have clearance to share any real code examples. We've said this a few times by now, but it's important. If there's any doubt as to whether you can share closed source code, ask for permission, not forgiveness.
- *Well-vetted*—Few things are more embarrassing than sharing a blog post and having the comment section take you to task for a careless coding mistake. Even if the code is already in production, give it a careful look and get another pair of eyes on it as well.
- *Realistic*—If you're making up code for the sake of an example, ensure that the examples are realistic and secure even if they're not real (people will copy/ paste). They should be syntactically correct and compile—you can check that with one of those online language playgrounds, if your language has one. Better yet, share the link to the playground snippet so that readers can easily play with the code.
- *Concise*—If you're showing code that you don't expect anyone to run, consider if you can omit any parts that just aren't relevant to what you're discussing. If you take that path, use ellipses (...) to indicate where code was omitted.

5.5   *Consumability*

Finally, consider the overall experience of what it's like to be a reader sitting down and reading your article. What else can you do to draw them closer into your world? To connect with them at a human-to-human level and evoke emotion? To motivate them to continue even if they're getting tired? And to help them dive back in if they get torn away and really do want to pick up where they left off? That's what we cover in this section, the last of things to consider when optimizing your working draft.

5.5.1   *Keeping it human*

Show your reader that you're human; not by demonstrating that you can select all the traffic lights in an image grid, but by being authentic and relatable in your writing.

Blog posts are not research papers. Shunning that austere formality is not only acceptable in this context—it's expected. As shown in many of the example blog posts we've referenced in this book, some of the most educational blog posts are friendly and also a bit fun. Would you rather learn from friends sharing their personal trials and tribulations over lunch—or from a suit-and-tie professor delivering a scripted lecture to a room of 500 people? Keep that in mind as you write and review your blog post. Here are some tips for keeping it human.

BE OPEN

Emotion equals engagement. If you can connect with a reader in a way that makes them feel curious, inspired, excited, nostalgic, or empathetic, chances are they will be more likely to complete, share, and remember your article.

But how do you do that? Forced attempts to evoke emotion will be detected as such (and likely ridiculed). Instead, just be real. Ensure that you're not eliminating or downplaying authentic elements that could help your reader connect with you. More specifically, don't be afraid to

- Share a little about your background when relevant to the discussion
- Reveal what was going through your head throughout your triumphs and tribulations
- Admit your worries, frustrations, mistakes, and imperfections
- Be open about what you don't (yet) know
- Poke fun at yourself

These are the things that will keep your reader engaged and also clearly distinguish you from a machine.

WRITE IN YOUR AUTHENTIC CONVERSATIONAL VOICE

Your writing should sound like some version of you. How do you sound while chatting with familiar work colleagues over lunch? That's a good tone to aim for. Also, feel free to incorporate elements of your text-chatting persona or even your interior monologue.

Your written words should mimic this voice with respect to things such as

- *Word choice*—Use words that you'd normally use. Don't raid the thesaurus and select words that you've never actually uttered.

- *Sentence length and complexity*—If you're a very direct person who naturally speaks in short sentences, great. Those are typically easy to read. If you tend to speak in longer and more complex sentences, you still want to capture that style—but be extra vigilant to ensure that it's clear and consumable for the reader.

- *Tone*—If you're enthusiastic, sarcastic, snarky, irreverent, serious, reserved, playful, witty, whatever in reality, your writing should reflect this. If one of your close friends were to read your article, would they recognize your personality or think "who *is* this person?"

- *Formality*—Authors of engineering blog posts commonly use contractions and colloquialisms. They take liberty with grammatical rules because that's how they sound in casual situations. However, if that's not how *you* speak, don't force yourself to be informal. Do what's authentic, whatever that means for you.

TIP   Without training, AI can't detect if your article sounds like you. But you could get some feedback on tone by prompting a chatbot with questions like "How would you describe the author's voice in this article?" and "Does it sound like it came from a human?"

If a sentence doesn't sound like you, try explaining what you really meant out loud, imagining your target reader sitting in front of you. And keep a voice recorder running in case you utter the perfect phrasing.

ADDRESS THE READER DIRECTLY

Envision your blog post as a conversation between you (or your team) and the reader. The author is either "I" or "we," and the reader is "you." Referring to them as "people," "users," or some other impersonal entity creates an invisible barrier between you and the reader. And given that you are already trying to communicate deeply technical information to some unknown person somewhere around the world, you don't need any more barriers.

You could even engage with the reader during the article, asking them to analyze a problem or consider what they would have done at a given point. This faux dialog is especially common in the "Bug Hunt" pattern (see chapter 8), where it's used to prompt readers to consider the evidence before them and draw their own conclusions. It can be a fun way to pull the reader into the scene.

SPEAK THE READER'S LANGUAGE

You're naturally going to describe the same thing using different language if you're messaging one of your teammates, presenting to experts in your field, or attempting to explain your work to your family. For example, you vary your

- Formality and tone
- Level of explanation
- Use of technical terms

- Cultural references and inside jokes
- Comparisons and analogies

This adaptability should also carry over to your writing.

In chapter 4, we prompted you to think about your audience: who you are writing for, what they already know, and why they care about what you're writing. Remember all this as you review your language!

For example, when you're writing primarily to users in your community, you're likely to be friendly, fully transparent, and highly technical. But if you're targeting potential investors, you might use language that's more crafted, value oriented, and aspirational.

5.5.2 *Making it scannable by humans*

If your blog post makes the readers' eyes hurt, only the most committed readers are likely to trudge through it. In contrast, if it's a clean balance of text, headings, and white space, with a nice spattering of thoughtful visuals, your reader can immediately recognize that you've thought about their experience. This might earn you a few minutes of their time, a chance to convince them that the article is indeed worth a read.

Think of the difference that unreadable code makes. If the function definition spans six whole screens, it's a red flag. Simple things like inconsistent indentation or very long lines of code never fail to make reviewers frown. Modern graphical IDEs (integrated development environments) often show a preview of the whole file for easy scrolling; this makes it readily apparent whether the code is in nice, human-readable shape, or quite the opposite. When it's the former, the associated code is invariably easier to reason about, spot errors in, and modify.

Scannability is equally important in your reader's interactions with your blog post, but for somewhat different reasons:

- When they first encounter your blog post, they likely scan it to determine if they want to read it.
- As they read it, they scan guideposts like headings to understand where they are and to check if they're understanding it correctly.
- If they get distracted, they use those same guideposts to try to pick up where they left off.
- If they later decide to revisit some fact or finding in your article, they want to rapidly relocate whatever it is they were looking for.

How can you help the reader better parse the article in these situations? Here are a few tips.

REVIEW THE ARTICLE AT THE MACRO LEVEL

Don't worry about the words for a moment. Just think about the balance of headings, visuals, and sentences on the page. Does it look enticing or intimidating? What can you do to change that?

TEAR DOWN WALLS OF TEXT

Making the article easier to parse almost always boils down to some angle on breaking up walls of text. Toward the end of chapter 4, we offered a quick fix: find the longest paragraphs and hit Return/Enter at the most logical point in the middle. That's actually one of the fastest and easiest ways to help your reader better process your article. The rule of thumb here: each paragraph should feature one main idea, no more. In chapter 4, we also suggested that you consider having at least a couple of headings per page.

But don't stop there. Also consider

- *Converting paragraphs to lists*—If you have a paragraph that's essentially gluing together a set of related items, consider making it a list. Use numbered lists if ordering matters (e.g., steps that must be processed sequentially or a prioritized list). Otherwise, use bulleted lists. Apply a parallel structure to the items in your list to facilitate human parsing and processing. That really just means "start them off in the same way." For example, look at the first word in each bullet within this list (e.g., converting, using, adding). Decide how you want your lists to be structured, then stick with it.
- *Converting paragraphs to tables*—This is a great option if you're comparing things (different options, before and after). It's much simpler for the reader's brain to note the similarities and differences when the items being compared are sitting beside one another in a highly structured table.
- *Using boxes for extra information*—In section 5.2, we urged you to eliminate information that detracts from your focus. But maybe a few tidbits didn't quite fit into the article's natural flow, and you couldn't bear the thought of eliminating them? Fine. Set them aside in a box (could be a single-cell table) so that the readers can tell that it's somewhat orthogonal to the core text.
- *Adding decorative images, maybe even memes*—Sometimes the brain can only take so much text. If you still have a lot of text, consider breaking it up with one or two additional images: maybe something you created with generative AI or a relevant meme. Don't go overboard with gratuitous graphics, of course. But a carefully crafted image that evokes a little smile offers a nice brain break in a deeply technical article.

BOLD KEY POINTS

Finally, consider bolding key points within the remaining paragraphs. This is a great tool for focusing the reader's attention, as long as you use it deliberately and judiciously. It's better to have a few key phrases or complete (short) sentences highlighted than to have isolated bolded words scattered throughout. For example, consider the difference in figure 5.3.

5.6   *If you do nothing else*

We've covered quite a lot in this chapter. But our recommendation for the absolute least you should do if you're experienced, or just crazy short on time, is a fairly simple six-step process:

Debugging Zig is also a treat, if you're already used to debugging C. Everything still works – gdb, perf, you name it. On top of that, Zig has a more elaborate system for asserting preconditions and invariants, which makes the debugging process a little bit smoother than C used to be. Zig is not Rust, and it happily lets you dereference null pointers (although its type system tries to prevent obvious cases of that), and use previously freed memory, so we had a dubious pleasure of long debugging sessions, just us, gdb, and the ninth cup of coffee – but it was comforting to see all the existing tools just work.

Debugging Zig is also **a treat**, if you're already **used to debugging C**. Everything still works – **gdb**, **perf**, you name it. On top of that, Zig has a more elaborate system for **asserting preconditions** and **invariants**, which makes the debugging process a little bit **smoother than C** used to be. Zig is not Rust, and it happily lets you **dereference null pointers** (although its type system tries to prevent obvious cases of that), and **use previously freed memory**, so we had a dubious pleasure of long debugging sessions, just us, gdb, and the ninth cup of coffee – but it was comforting to see all the existing tools just work.

Figure 5.3   In the first paragraph, the clean bolding focuses the reader's eyes. In the second paragraph, it's overkill and becomes an annoying distraction.

1 Read the article in your head with a focus on how the reader will perceive the content. Imagine that the most critical person in your target audience is sitting in front of you staring at you:

 – What are they most skeptical about?

 – Where do they want more context, detail, or supporting facts?

 – Where might they get lost, distracted, or disoriented?

2 Spend a few minutes thinking about the title.

3 Spend a few minutes ensuring that your introduction clearly conveys what your target reader will get out of your article and why they would care about your take on this topic.

4 Make sure you have enough headings and not too many long paragraphs.

5 Read it out loud with a focus on how it sounds. Think about sentence clarity:

 – What sentences are so long that you need to take another breath?

 – What sentences stand out as being clunky or unclear?

 – What sentences just don't sound like you?

 – Are any words missing?

6 See if your grammar-checking tool notices anything you immediately recognize as a real problem.

Summary

- Your ultimate goal is to make the target reader feel like the article was written with them in mind.

- Be obsessive about considering what your target reader already knows, doesn't know, and wants to know.

- Your top priority should be providing the target reader the facts required to earn their trust.

- When you rework sentences, think about making it more convenient and pleasant for your reader to understand your thoughts.
- Target the clunkiest sentences in your most prominent paragraphs for revision.
- Highlighting weak "to be" verbs and prepositions can help you find and fix suboptimal sentences.
- Aim for writing that's clear and concise, but still personable and conversational.
- Your writing should sound like how you speak or chat with colleagues.
- Spend a few minutes crafting an intriguing title.
- Ensure that your introduction is upfront about your goal (in terms of what's in it for your reader) and what's so special about your take on the topic.
- Break up big blocks of text to make the article more scannable.
- Reading your draft out loud is a great way to spot problems.

Getting feedback

6

This chapter covers

- Comparing the code review and article review processes
- Determining who should review your work and when to start the process
- Preparing your reviewers
- Responding to comments

Let's be honest: when you ask your peers to review something, your code or your writing, the only response you really want is "Wow, this is absolutely perfect—ship it!" Critical feedback inevitably stings, at least at first. But if you're not sold on its value, think back to just a few of the many times a peer code review comment saved you from a much worse fate than that initial humbling. It's no different with writing. Just do it. Your bruised ego will recover, your blog post will be better, and you'll likely learn a few things in the process.

This chapter provides tips on how to make the article review process more valuable for you, as well as more straightforward for your reviewers. We'll explore how article review compares to code review and then get into the logistics of applying the "four eyes" principle to your blog posts. Who should be reviewing your blog post, when, and how? How can you set the stage for more valuable feedback? And how do you handle tricky situations such as when you disagree with a reviewer's suggestions?

NOTE If you're writing for a company blog and your organization has an established article review process, follow that by all means! Hopefully, this chapter provides some additional tips for making that process faster and more valuable.

6.1 Focus and challenges

A review process can turn into a massive source of frustration if you and your reviewer aren't fully aligned. A simple "Hey can you look at this" might be fine if your reviewer is a close teammate who has been involved from the start of this blog post's lifecycle. But otherwise, you might end up with headaches as the reviewer is

- Trying to remold your entire article to reflect their vision
- Obsessing over details that are no longer up for debate
- Just nitpicking grammar when you really want a technical review
- Procrastinating because they feel overwhelmed by the task

And that leads to the greatest challenge: getting valuable feedback promptly. Put yourself in the reviewer's shoes. They probably weren't planning to review a blog post you wrote. Now that you've asked them to be "the reviewer," they might feel responsible for finding and fixing everything they consider wrong. If the article is a success, you get all (or at least most) of the credit. But if a major problem slipped through to publication, they're likely to feel remiss for not noticing and flagging it. It's not a glorious task.

As we'll explain shortly, overcommunication can address these challenges. By spending maybe 5 extra minutes defining the scope of what you expect, you lighten the load on your reviewer and absolve them of full responsibility for everything wrong with the article. Moreover, by declaring certain things (such as the topic angle itself or the specific tests that were run) "off limits," you further reduce the scope of things the reviewer has to worry about. You also reduce your chances of getting feedback that's not valuable to you at this stage of the writing process.

6.2 Comparing writing review with code review

Having your blog post reviewed is in some ways similar to receiving code review:

- Feedback from another person familiar with the topic is very useful.
- Typos are pointed out mercilessly.
- Lots of the review comments are purely stylistic:
  - "Looks good, but please split this function into three."
  - "Looks good, but please split this paragraph into three."

- Different opinions on how something should be designed lead to long discussions.
- Negative feedback can be taken a little too personally at times.

Blog post reviewing is also distinctly different in a few respects:

- Feedback from someone not even remotely familiar with the topic can be extremely useful for a blog post, but not that often for code.
- When there are long discussions on how something should be written, they often settle on the author's original approach, especially when the author's subjective opinion is a vital part of the blog post. For code, what's often discussed is "the ultimate truth," ideally proven with formulas. That means the discussions tend to be longer and might even involve arbiters when no consensus is in sight.

Many code review practices carry over to article review, so code review best practices are the perfect place to start when thinking about how to introduce the article to your reviewer and how to interact with them. In both cases, clearly describing your intent when you submit a pull request or article review request helps the reviewer get into your head. That, in turn, helps you get more valuable feedback. For example, in both cases, it's helpful to cover

- The underlying rationale
- The alternatives
- Why the alternative you selected is best

When it comes to interacting with the reviewer, the recommended protocol is exactly the same with article and code reviews. You don't need to timidly cave in to every request and suggestion. If you disagree with something a reviewer seems to be insisting on, feel free to start a discussion and share more details about why you took your approach and/or why you disagree with what's suggested. Maybe the reviewer is actually right. Or maybe you are. Either way, someone learns something in the process.

But some code review practices *don't* carry over to articles:

- With code review, you can usually placate a reviewer by promising to implement a nonessential suggestion later. With writing, the article most likely won't be continuously evolving like a code base does, so that's usually not a viable option here.
- With code review, it's nicest to work with small, self-contained changes. That's not feasible with an article, which should generally be reviewed as a whole, from start to finish.
- With code review, it's risky to make even a tiny change after the review is complete—even fixing a typo or moving a block around. But with articles, a small tweak isn't going to break the build. Postreview optimizing here is totally fine.

6.3   *Selecting your reviewer(s)*

The first decision to make is who should be reviewing your article. Ideally, you want two different reviewers:

- *Technical reviewer*—Someone close to the topic, perhaps a teammate or a peer who works on similar projects and technologies. They can point out inadequate detail, factual errors, omissions, irrelevant technical digressions, and similar.

- *Clarity reviewer*—Someone who is not deep in the weeds of your project and can play the role of the curious target reader. They can point out places where additional context is needed, the flow seems to take giant leaps or go in circles, or sentences just don't make sense. Even better, maybe they are willing to perform some editing for you.

> **TIP** If someone is editing the text of the article, make sure the changes are tracked (or you view them via version history). That way, you can review the changes carefully, check that they didn't change your meaning, and just generally ensure that you're comfortable with any proposed changes. Otherwise, it's like trying to review code updates without access to diffs.

As you choose, consider who can give you the most brutal feedback (we promise, you'll appreciate it after the sting wears off). This is likely someone you know fairly well. If you've already endured late-night debugging sessions, team offsites, and all other sorts of actual or forced fun with someone, chances are they won't be afraid to tell you what they really think. But don't limit yourself. There might be others in your company, community, or network who are fully willing to share honest feedback. If you're a senior or staff engineer and really want to torment a junior new hire, you might even consider asking them under the condition that they shouldn't hold anything back.

Once you select a reviewer, let them know immediately. Consider this a "save the date" type of thing: you don't need to give them all the details yet. But letting them know in advance is a nice touch. That way, you don't surprise them with an urgent review request at a time when they might be overwhelmed with other projects.

Not sure what to say? For a teammate, it could be as simple as this:

> *I'm working on a blog post about {topic} and would really appreciate your feedback on it when it's a little further along, maybe in {some general timeframe}. No action required now—I just wanted to get it on your radar.*

Or for someone you're not as familiar with (perhaps someone on a different team), you could say:

> *I'm working on a blog post about {topic}. I heard {namedrop if appropriate} that you've done a lot of work on {blah}, so I would really appreciate your perspective on the article. Do you think you could spare 30 minutes or so to provide feedback when it's a little further along, maybe in {some general timeframe}?*

6.4 Deciding when to start

There's no standard best time for getting a draft in front of a reviewer. Start too early, and reviewers might feel like you're wasting their time. Start too late, and it might not be feasible to fix any fundamental problems raised by reviewers. And what's perfect for one blog post might be disastrous for another.

Here are some things to consider as you determine when to start the review process.

6.4.1   *How important and/or controversial is the topic?*

Are you writing something that's likely to generate a lot of debate, either internally or externally? "How We Built It" articles, benchmarks, and controversial "Thoughts on Trends" articles definitely fall into this category. Others might as well; in some companies, even innocuous-seeming ideas end up being contentious. In these cases, you might want to begin the review process even before the first draft. Make sure you have a decent outline, and share it with key stakeholders as well as your technical reviewer before you start fleshing out the actual article.

The reviewers can't nitpick over low-level details because none exist yet. They're forced to focus on the high-level content and flow, which is great to have early feedback on. As with software defects, the earlier you expose a critical issue in an article, the faster and easier it is to fix. You don't want to get to the point where you've tidied up all your clunkiest sentences and then find out that your boss hates the fundamental idea of the article.

When the actual draft of this blog post is ready, consider sending it off for technical review as soon as you feel the core (focus, flow, facts—see chapter 5) is solid. There's no point in spending too much time worrying about specific sentences when your reviewers might ask you to scrap entire sections and add different ones.

Also, plan extra time for clarity review here. Maybe even have a few different people read it with clarity in mind. Although readers might easily excuse small imperfections in the quick blog you wrote sharing your weekend project, high-profile blog posts will be held to a higher standard. You don't want the blog announcing your company's greatest engineering achievement ever to contain even a single sentence that the target audience can't easily parse.

6.4.2   *Do you have a true "blocker" question?*

Sometimes you can't move forward with the draft until you get the answer to a critical question. For example,

- Are we happy with the results of these tests, or do we need to try something different?
- Do you think I should also include a section on the details of {blah} or continue without it?
- Are the details introduced in the best order for the average reader, or should I restructure the article?
- Are we really going to deliver on what this section promises in the next few months, or should I rethink that whole part to avoid empty promises?
- Do you think the target reader can follow this tutorial without getting stuck somewhere?

In these cases, it's time for at least a preliminary review. When you request a review (described in section 6.5), include some verbiage like this: "I'm not yet done with the article: I still plan to {do X, Y, and Z}. But I'd like you to take a quick look at what I have so far and lmk if {big question}."

6.4.3 *Do you feel like you've done what you intended to do?*

As soon as you feel like you've completed everything you intended to do for this dear draft, send it off on the review process! Don't wait for the point where you feel every sentence is positively poetic. Instead, aim for the point of having done your due diligence:

- You feel everything that was in your head is reflected in the draft.
- You've thought about core concerns (focus, flow, facts).
- You're confident your sentences are reasonably clear.
- You gave your title and introduction some tender loving care.
- You revisited the goal you defined for this blog and feel that you've achieved it.
- You revisited the reason why your take on this topic is compelling, and you feel it's reflected in the article.

If you've checked all those boxes, the draft is definitely ready for more eyeballs.

6.4.4 *Will there be time for another review cycle after your tech reviewer finishes?*

Ideally, you'd send the draft for technical review, revise it accordingly, and then have your clarity reviewer take a look. But that's not always practical. Sometimes you need to speedrun the whole process, or sometimes the technical review takes longer than expected.

If you anticipate publishing quite soon after you receive the tech review feedback, go ahead and see if someone can read it for clarity now (in parallel). Then, if you need to change anything after the tech review, be sure to track your changes. Maybe a final round of clarity review is possible. If not, be sure to give those revised bits some extra scrutiny yourself.

6.5 *Preparing your reviewers*

Once you've identified some reviewers, and you're ready to throw your draft over the wall for review, what do you do? "Email it to them with a note like 'Please review this blog post draft'" is the most common response but also the wrong one.

As we mentioned earlier in this chapter, just about 5 minutes spent on preparation can make the review process significantly less daunting for your reviewer and much more valuable for you. Here are a few tips followed by an example of how you can put them into practice.

6.5.1 *Providing background*

By now, you're probably sick of looking at your blog post draft. But remember that it's quite new to your reviewer. Tell your reviewer the essentials about what you're writing, why, and where you are in the writing process. That includes

- What's the goal and who's the target audience
- Where it is in the process
- What's nonnegotiable

Let's look at each in turn.

WHAT'S THE GOAL AND WHO IS THE TARGET AUDIENCE

Think back to your planning work from chapter 4. Share that one-sentence statement of the article's goal with your reviewer, and if the audience isn't already clearly highlighted in that goal statement, add it here. Telling the reviewer what you're trying to accomplish should guide them to provide feedback accordingly. For example, they might offer totally different comments if they know you're trying to help an end-user understand why your product works the way it does than if the article is intended to share your design decisions with fellow infrastructure engineers.

WHERE IT IS IN THE PROCESS

Are you sending them a rough draft for technical review, which will be followed by revision and then a clarity review and edit? If your technical reviewer knows that, they're less likely to worry about missing words, rephrasing things for you, and so on. Are you sending out a super early draft for feedback on the fundamentals? Or have five people already read it, including your direct boss and the CTO, and said they love the overall direction but want actual engineers to double-check the technical details? Be transparent and let your reviewer know.

WHAT'S NONNEGOTIABLE

Did your boss declare that no more benchmarks should be run? Did a partner sponsoring the project require tests to be run in a certain way? Did you already ask for permission to include code examples, only to be denied? Mention it here and save your reviewer the grief of writing a detailed comment on something that doesn't matter because it's just not up for debate.

6.5.2   *Specifying what you want*

What do you really want to learn from this reviewer for this particular article? You might not always get what you wish for, but you're more likely to get it if you ask than if you don't.

HIGH-LEVEL REQUEST

The message where you send them the doc for review should include a high-level request explaining the scope of what you're looking for. For technical reviewers, the standard request could be something like "Please keep an eye out for technical issues such as inadequate detail, factual errors, omissions, irrelevant technical digressions, etc."

You might also ask specific questions that apply to the whole article. For example: "Is there anything we can't include in the blog post because it's not officially released yet?" For clarity reviewers, you might ask "Please note places where you think the target reader {specify} might want additional context, where the flow seems to take giant leaps or go in circles, where sentences don't make sense, etc."

NOTE When you write your request, avoid asking in a way that stifles feedback. For example, we've seen review requests come in with comments like "How do you like it?" or "I think this is ready to go—let me know what you think." That puts the reviewer in an awkward position and makes them feel bad for giving you constructive criticism. If you write a message as we recommended previously, such comments would likely seem out of place. Still, we wanted to mention it because it's a common way to start the review process off on the wrong foot.

SPECIFIC QUESTIONS AND REQUESTS

Additionally, feel free to feed your reviewers some specific questions that you want answered. If your questions refer to the article in general (e.g., "Do you think I need more technical detail throughout?"), mention that in your review message. Whenever you have questions related to a specific part of the article, add them as comments in the doc. In-doc comments are perfect for questions and comments like`

- I know we're planning a dedicated blog on this. Should I hold off on mentioning it here?
- I debated also mentioning the {blah} here. WDYT?
- I'm worried that this point might be unclear. WDYT?
- Can you double-check that this code sample is free of features we deprecated in the last release?
- I added this "details" section when I thought I wasn't going to have enough to write about, but the article actually landed pretty long. I'm absolutely fine with nuking the whole section. Do you think I should keep it or cut it?
- I feel like having six straight throughput graphs is probably overkill here, but they each show something interesting, so I'm not sure which to cut. Which one or two do you think are most intriguing?
- Do you know of any good resources I can link out to on this?
- You implemented this feature—did I capture its description right?
- Can you rerun this example on your Mac? I want to make sure it runs fine on more operating systems.

TIMING

A task without a deadline is usually the first one to get pushed back (and rightfully so). Even if there's no hard and fast deadline for when you need the feedback, go ahead and specify when you'd like to receive the feedback. For example, "I'm looking to get this published by {some date}—do you think you could get me feedback by {another date}?"

What if you hit the very common scenario where you don't receive a response by that date? Time for the "friendly reminder." For example: "I'd still really appreciate your feedback on the {topic} blog post. Any questions I can answer at this point?"

Example 6.1

Here's a message that PretendPiotr might send to his technical reviewer when he shares the fake Zig blog for review:

> *Hi, can you take a look at my blog draft about writing fancymigratorname in Zig?*
>
> *The goals were 1) convince FakeDB users to try out the Postgres migration tool, and 2) show that it's possible to create something useful with Zig.*
>
> *You're perfect audience material since it's likely the first time you've seen Zig code, and at the same time you're a Postgres pro. Please let me know if anything looks unclear. No rush per se, but Big Boss will obliterate me if it's not shipped by the end of next week (:*

And here are a few comments that the reviewer might make:

- In "The good parts," you mention "Postgres" official C headers," but that's ambiguous. All Postgres codebase is in C. Maybe just add a link to the extension API or mention that you mean the header for writing extensions in C.
- Nitpick: s/it's patience/its patience/ in "The not-so-good parts."
- Since you so gracefully mentioned I never read Zig code, I feel obliged to inform you that I still haven't seen any after looking at the draft. A snippet or two wouldn't hurt.

6.6   *Responding to reviewer comments*

Your reviewers finally responded! It's exciting that the process is moving forward, but how do you deal with their feedback?

Try to resist diving right in, ready to defend your article to the death. Find some time when you can thoughtfully review the comments. If you can stand it, read all the comments before you respond to a single comment. It's not uncommon to fall into despair reading a seemingly endless onslaught of comments, then reach some final comment like "This is great—I really enjoyed it and think it's a valuable resource!" Do everyone a favor and at least skim through all the comments before you respond to any of the comments.

Now take a deep breath and start responding. You don't need to make every change the reviewer suggested, but you should at least consider and acknowledge them all. Review them with curiosity, not combativeness. Perhaps the reviewer is saving you from public embarrassment or at least helping you sharpen your argument in ways that prevent a few snarky comments.

TIP   What if a reviewer's comment overlooks the "constructive" part of the "constructive criticism" term? If you truly want to learn what he was hoping for, try responding with something like a nonconfrontational "Okay, what changes do you think would be helpful here?"

As noted in the discussion of code review best practices (section 6.2), feel free to respectfully disagree with an article reviewer, just as you might with a code reviewer. The same general principles apply:

- For each suggestion, either a) implement a change and note that in the response, b) promise to do it later, c) explain why you don't think a change is required, or d) at least acknowledge it with something like "comment noted."
- Don't just give in if you believe your approach is correct. Initiate a discussion, and at least one of you will learn something.
- Be open to the fact that your approach might not be correct. Someone with fresh eyes and a totally different set of experiences might notice different problems and opportunities. That's the whole point of the review, after all.

Also, if you don't understand something, say so. The reviewer would much rather clarify what they meant than have you ignore the feedback they spent time thinking about and communicating.

What if your reviewer went above and beyond, providing you more feedback than you asked for (e.g., a technical reviewer pointing out ways to improve sentence clarity)? Thank them and be extremely grateful! Take *all* of their feedback seriously; consider every comment an opportunity to improve or harden the article.

6.7 Special steps for special cases

But as with programming, edge cases occur. Finally, let's look at additional steps you might consider in special situations.

6.7.1 Nonnative English speakers

We've stressed that your technical readers will likely forgive some grammatical imperfections. And if someone reviewed your draft for clarity, your article should be in pretty decent shape by now. But if you want to be extra sure that it sounds right, feel free to tap a native English speaker who's willing to perform a light edit for you.

Ideally, you can find someone in your company or social network who has at least some basic understanding of a) the general topic and b) what *you* sound like. Most likely, they'll do this for free as long as you've been moderately nice to them (or at least have earned a reputation as a decent human being). You could also consider hiring an editor on a site like Fiverr, but the quality could vary, especially for technical topics. Another option: ask your colleagues and network for recommendations.

6.7.2 Don't know who to ask

If you're writing about an independent project or just want to keep your blog post writing separate from your work life, finding reviewers might require a little extra creativity. Feel free to throw the request out on social media or pop a note in an appropriately themed discussion forum. For example: "Hey, I'm writing an article on {your specific topic} and would really appreciate feedback from some {the general topic} experts. Any volunteers? :-)"

There's no guarantee, of course. But you might get some independent feedback and make a few connections along the way.

6.7.3   *Other organizations involved*

Does your blog post feature a specific tool or project managed by another organization? If so, consider running it by that other organization before you publish. Even if you're not required to get their approval, they might provide helpful feedback (e.g., something you overlooked with respect to the tool/project that they're the experts on). Plus, this puts your blog post on their radar. If they're interested, they can prepare to share it on their social media handles, perhaps republish it on their blog, include it in their newsletter, and so forth.

6.8   *If you do nothing else*

Here is the absolute least that you should do for the review process:

- Check any applicable company review protocols.
- Prepare a brief message summarizing your goal for the article, where it is in the process, and what you want from the reviewer.
- Flag any specific sections or sentences you have specific questions or doubts about.
- Find at least one trusted person to give it a look.

Summary

- Constructive criticism might sting at first, but it's a valuable tool for optimizing and "hardening" your article.
- You can and should apply some code review best practices to the article review process (e.g., clearly describing your intent and using comments you disagree with as a springboard for discussion and learning).
- In the ideal world, you'll have one reviewer (close to your subject) who can point out technical flaws and another (further from your subject) who can be the reader advocate and point out what requires additional context or clarification.
- The best time to start the review varies; sometimes you even want to have the outline reviewed; other times you can wait until you feel "it's ready."
- A few minutes spent upfront providing reviewers with background and specifying what you want will pay off in better feedback and less frustration all around.
- Be open-minded and curious when responding to reviewer comments, and never shy away from initiating a discussion.

Ship it

7

The finish line is in sight! You're so close to shipping it. But even if you're tired of thinking about this article, there are a few additional details to consider as your work is transformed into an actual blog post on the internet.

The little things do matter. For example, you don't want to end up with your carefully crafted code examples being rendered in colors that make a reader's brain hurt—or skipping the few minutes it would take to add a thumbnail image that helps your article stand out on social media feeds.

This chapter walks through the final details to consider as the blog post is staged and published. If you're writing for a company blog, a lot of this might be handled by someone else. Even so, it's good to know what to look for. It's hard to imagine a blog editor who would not appreciate additional interest and input from a contributor.

And if you want to consider publishing on your own someday (why not), you might as well start thinking about these low-level details sooner rather than later.

7.1   *Focus and challenges*

At this point, you can shift focus from the article itself, which should be nicely vetted by now, to the various logistical details surrounding its publication. This is often a nice mental break, different from most of the writing process, as well as your daily work. But there can be a lot of unknowns, especially when it comes to things such as optimizing for findability.

The best practice for rising to the top of search engine results is continuously evolving, to the point that there's a whole industry of search engine optimization (SEO) that revolves around trying to game the system. Don't focus on that. A little fun with Google Trends plus a few minutes of reflecting on how humans really think should do the trick. We'll share some high-level considerations that will help across search engine platforms and algorithm updates, even as the precise nuances of Google's rankings continuously shift inside their black box.

The main challenge at this phase is making fast decisions and just getting things done. You could easily waste hours having too much fun with AI-generated thumbnail images or browsing articles in the various tags you're considering for your article. As we've mentioned quite a few times by now, there's limited value in overengineering such things. Find the fastest path to a solution that meets the need, then move on. More blogging opportunities await!

Does publishing here limit your options?

Do you have dreams of seeing your article featured in a tech publication (e.g., *The New Stack*, *InfoQ*, or *ACM Queue*)? Taking this path has a number of advantages (such as extended reach and promotion, which could be especially important to lesser-known authors). It also has a few drawbacks, particularly some lack of control. We'll explore the pros and cons, plus tips for getting your articles into the editorial review process, in chapter 15.

However, it's important to consider this now because many such publications only publish original content. If you publish the article elsewhere now, you will need to revise it substantially before a tech publication will consider it. If you really want to see this specific version of this article published somewhere where original content is required, strongly consider delaying your own publication so you don't limit your options.

Note that this consideration applies specifically to tech publications that rely on editors and strict editorial review processes to curate original content for their target audience. It does not matter for aggregators (such as dev.to) that let you publish existing content without passing through a traditional editorial process.

7.2   *Read through the core content one final time*

If you've been following along, your blog post should be well planned, written to withstand technical readers' healthy skepticism, and vetted by humans as well as pointed AI prompting and spelling/grammar checkers. If you still have doubts, look back to your original goal for the blog with the clear mind that comes after a little time has passed. After all the review and revision, is there any rational reason to feel that you didn't achieve this goal? Any reason why your target reader would not get the main learning you want them to walk away with? If you believe there's a problem, first get another opinion and then determine whether it's a fatal flaw (unlikely at this point). Really, after all this, your blog post is probably quite ready to go out and meet the world.

Want a final sanity check that you've caught mistakes like typos, missing words, grammatical errors, and so on?

- Review the findings from a spelling/grammar checking tool again, or maybe even use a different one (e.g., the native Google Docs spell checking with Grammarly disabled).
- Try a few different AI chatbots with a few different prompts. For example,
  - Point out all grammar errors, spelling errors, and punctuation errors in this article.
  - Point out any verb tense errors or inconsistencies in the article.
  - Point out any inconsistent terminology usage in this article.
- Read it out loud one more time, slowly and dramatically.

Finally, do a quick internet search for the topic of your article and the key related terms. You might want to tweak your article if you learn that

- One of the technologies or companies you referenced just changed its name
- A major security vulnerability was discovered in a library you're promoting
- The exact thing you ranted about for 3000 words is now happily resolved

For example, if you discovered that Zimbabwe just released a new gold-backed currency named Zig (it did!), you might want to rethink a headline such as "Zig: A New Gold Standard for Low Latency Programming."

Now rest assured that you've done way more than your due diligence!

7.3 *Preview in place*

Sometimes the item that looked perfect in the home improvement store needs a little adjustment once it's actually in your home. The same can happen with blog posts. Once you get the content into the template, you might find that a heading needs a trim, an image is displayed at a size that makes its labels illegible, and so on.

This section covers the surface-level things to consider and review once your blog post is in place. We'll get into metadata concerns in the following section.

> **NOTE** If feasible, try to check how everything looks on mobile devices and the top few browsers you anticipate your readers might use. If that's not feasible, be sure to check it there as soon as it's published.

7.3.1   Title and headings

Does the title that seemed perfect in your doc look awkward in whatever template you're using? Is it sprawling across two lines of massive text, maybe even three? Is one word dangling, all on its own (as in figure 7.1)? If so, think about trimming it.

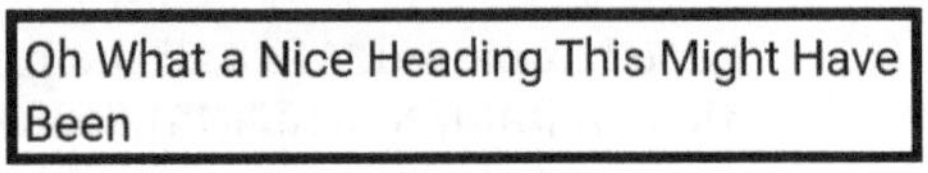

> Oh What a Nice Heading This Might Have Been

Figure 7.1   The dangling word on the second line just isn't a good look.

To be fair, your title's most important job is to catch the eye of your target reader out in the wild, on feeds, lists, and so on. Once people click in, they have probably already read the title. But, first impressions do matter. The first thing readers see on the page shouldn't look careless or downright ugly.

Also, skim your headings. Headings that extend over multiple lines won't be as scannable as shorter ones. If all words are absolutely essential, so be it. But if you can find a way to make headings crisper without changing their meaning, then trim away.

> **TIP** Don't change heading levels to make heading text appear smaller. Stick to the recommended hierarchy (one H1 per document>>H2s>>H3s>>H4s) to avoid problems with accessibility (e.g., via screen readers) as well as search engines.

7.3.2   Code

Is your code legible and copy/pasteable (or even better, immediately executable)? You can find a number of visualization tools that create pretty images based on a code snippet, but don't use them for adding code to the body of your blog post. Let readers touch and grab your code, and let machines read it too. Save the code visualization tools for decorative images (for example, thumbnails for social sharing), and link to the GitHub repo whenever feasible so that readers can see the code in context.

Sometimes, even code that's in standard blog code embeds looks atrocious. For example, consider the Rust function code in figure 7.2 (using Medium's dark mode).

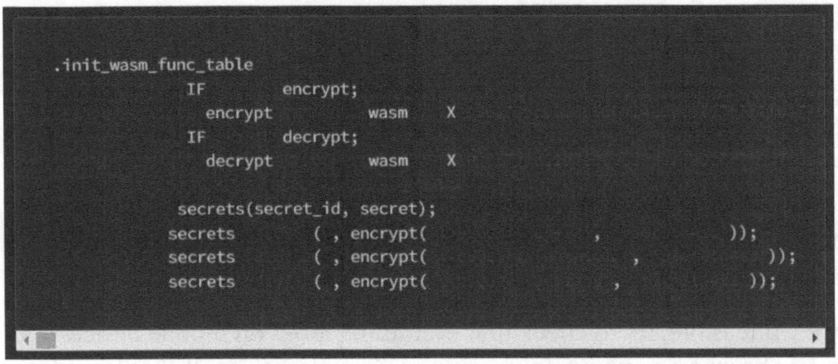

```
.init_wasm_func_table
        IF          encrypt;
          encrypt           wasm     X
        IF          decrypt;
          decrypt           wasm     X

        secrets(secret_id, secret);
        secrets        ( , encrypt(                ,            ));
        secrets        ( , encrypt(                ,          ));
        secrets        ( , encrypt(                ,          ));
```

Figure 7.2   A highly illegible code excerpt in Medium's standard "dark mode" code embed

Even in full color, it's virtually unreadable. Figure 7.3 (best viewed in color) shows how using a different framework makes a huge difference for code legibility.

```
.init_wasm_func_table
DROP FUNCTION IF EXISTS encrypt;
CREATE FUNCTION encrypt LANGUAGE wasm AS X'0061736d0100000001410b60037f7f017f60
DROP FUNCTION IF EXISTS decrypt;
CREATE FUNCTION decrypt LANGUAGE wasm AS X'0061736d01000000013a0a60027f7f017f6003

CREATE TABLE secrets(secret_id, secret);
INSERT INTO secrets VALUES (1, encrypt('libSQL is great', 's3cr3tp4ss'));
INSERT INTO secrets VALUES (2, encrypt('libSQL is fantastic', 's3cr3tp4ss'));
INSERT INTO secrets VALUES (3, encrypt('libSQL is amazing', 's3cr3tp4ss'));
```

Figure 7.3 The same code displayed in a different blog framework

Here are some specific tips:

- Prefer options that provide syntax highlighting, and be sure to specify the language. GitHub gists do the job and can easily be embedded into third-party sites (e.g., Medium). Code syntax highlighting libraries (Shiki, Prism, highlight.js, etc.) are another option if you're publishing on your own blog site.
- Even better, embed an interactive playground (e.g., Stackblitz or Sandpack) where users can play around with the code within the blog page.
- Inspect how the code is rendering in the new environment, especially indentation problems and any characters that might have been skipped at the start or end of the copy/paste.
- Aim for short lines—wrapping at 80–120 characters or so. Maybe that requires configuration, or maybe it requires another code display option altogether (refer back to the first bullet point).

7.3.3 Core images

Are the screenshots, diagrams, graphs, and other images in the body of the post shown at an appropriate size in the template? Large images will likely be automatically resized to accommodate the template's width (figure 7.4). But is that really the ideal size for the reader?

You could let users click to open a full-sized version of any image that's smaller than it really should be. But it's even better to crop or redesign the image so that the initial view shows all the appropriate details.

If the blog is heavy on images, consider resizing images to the precise width needed, as well as compressing images. The sweet spot to aim for is the smallest file size that provides the highest image quality. Keeping images under 100KB is a good target.

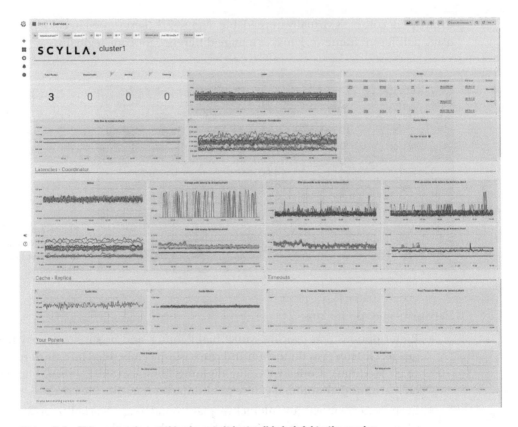

Figure 7.4 This screenshot at this size won't be terribly helpful to the reader.

> **TIP** You can find free image compressors (e.g., tinyPNG) quite readily across the internet. Command-line tools such as ImageMagick's "convert" also offer size-reduction features.

7.3.4 *Header image*

Does the template require an image at the top of your blog post? Many personal engineering blog sites opt to skip this and go with a minimalist design. However, many company blogs and blogging platforms require an image, and some individual blog site maintainers prefer to use such images, too.

If you want or need to use a header image, try to preview (or at least approximate) how it's going to be displayed:

- At the top of the blog post itself
- In other positions (e.g., as a thumbnail image in lists or grids of posts)

An image that looks great at 1200 pixel width might not be ideal for a more condensed tile in a grid of available blog posts. Pay extra close attention to this if your image includes text or other elements that shouldn't be arbitrarily cut off. In some cases, you might be able to specify a different image for the header and the grid tile. Other times, you might be forced to have the same image serve dual purposes, so use one that works in both contexts.

7.3.5 Videos

We haven't talked specifically about videos until now, but many blog authors use videos to add quick demos, visually explain concepts, or share a conference talk that's relevant to the topic at hand. If you're embedding any videos into your article, check the following when you preview the post:

- *Is the sizing appropriate?* As long as you can adjust the source code of your blog, you don't need to accept the default size. Fiddle with it until you're satisfied.

- *Does the video display even if you're not logged into the video platform?* Check this in incognito mode or equivalent. If you find and fix the settings problem now, your readers won't ever see the ugly "Video unavailable" message shown in figure 7.5.

- *Is the video available in the major regions where you expect your blog post to be shared and read?* You can find various tools online to check this, or you could recruit some human beta testers across your network.

Figure 7.5 Check if the video plays for people who are not logged into your video platform account.

7.3.6 Tables and lists

As mentioned previously, tables and lists are great tools for breaking up great walls of text. But they don't always turn out as planned in HTML—not at first, at least. If you have complex tables or multilevel lists, check how they're rendering. And don't be surprised if some adjustment is required to achieve the effect you originally envisioned.

Elective elements to consider if you're running your own blog

How to set up your own blog site is beyond the scope of this book (though we do have a few quick notes in appendix A). If you are running your own blog site, consider whether you want to add the following elements to each blog post page:

- "Table of contents" links that jump directly to each heading and subheading
- Links to share/discuss the article on relevant forums, aggregators, and social media sites
- The latest related articles that share the same tags

(continued)
- Links to other popular articles on the site
- An RSS, Atom feed, or other ways for people to track what you're publishing
- A link to your bio, GitHub repo, and social handles

7.4   *Manage metadata*

Next, go below the surface and focus on the metadata. It's easy to forget what's not readily apparent ("out of sight, out of mind"). But metadata can make a big difference in terms of findability, accessibility, and shareability. Let's touch on each of those before we move into the recommendations.

- *Findability*—Humans rely on machines to find information, and machines rely on metadata (as well as your article's text) to understand and classify your article. Highlighting key terms in your metadata helps machines connect interested readers with your article.
- *Accessibility*—Not everyone experiences your article in the same way. Some of your target readers might be relying on assistive technologies such as screen readers or Braille displays to understand your article. Little things such as ensuring that hyperlinked text is meaningful and images are carefully described can make a huge difference. Those same things also help search engines.
- *Shareability*—If someone decides to share your article on their social media platform of choice, how will it appear in their followers' feeds? You might take the time to manually upload an image when you're sharing your own article. But will your readers? Help them out by specifying a default.

Throughout this section, we're focusing on high-level, broadly applicable principles because

- Not everyone uses the same search engines, social media platforms, and so forth.
- The array of available options is shifting.
- Many low-level implementation details (e.g., thumbnail image expectations or what to click to do anything anywhere) are also constantly evolving.

TIP A great place for details on how all this metadata affects Google's search rankings is the Google Search Documentation, available at https://developers .google.com/search/docs. And for details on how they affect accessibility, see *All WCAG 2.2 Understanding Docs*, available at https://www.w3.org/WAI/ WCAG22/Understanding/.

7.4.1   *Your keywords*

First off, determine the handful of keywords you want to prioritize while populating your metadata. Put yourself in your readers' shoes. What might motivate them to seek an article on the topic you wrote about? And what terms might they search for as they attempt to learn more about it? Likely, there will be at least one big broad search term (e.g., "Java" or "Rust") and one to three qualifying terms (e.g., "performance," "concurrency," "pitfalls"). That mixture should help you balance reach and relevance.

Consider the top three to five terms "your keywords." You want your article to appear when people search on these terms, so be sure to highlight these terms in the metadata when it's logical and natural. Include them in your meta description and URL unless you have a good reason not to. Also, consider these keywords top candidates for your tags or topics. (All these terms are explained more in the following sections.) Beyond metadata, consider mentioning these keywords in your headers and subheaders, too.

> **TIP** Want the AI perspective? Prompt it with something like "What are some good SEO keywords for this blog post?" It might suggest a few decent options as well as spark more ideas in your brain.

USING GOOGLE TRENDS TO HELP DECIDE

Not sure what terms people are actually searching for? Google Trends (https://trends .google.com/) is your friend. Use it to determine

- If one term is searched more often than a similar term
- If interest in one term is rising, while interest in another is flat or dying out
- What related terms people are searching for (These might be points to address in a follow up blog or hints as to what questions could surface in the comments section.)

Let's look at a quick example. Assume we're writing about a Kafka-like tool, and the team is torn between featuring "streaming data" or "event streaming." We plug both into Google Trends, expand the region to Worldwide, expand the range to Past 5 years, restrict the category to Computers & Electronics, and voilà. There seems to be significantly higher interest in "streaming data" (see figure 7.6).

Further down the page, the list of related queries for "event streaming" shows things like "apple event california streaming" and "apple event live streaming." This indicates that the "event streaming" results include queries about livestreaming events such as Apple conferences and announcements. And even with that inflation/dilution, there's still less interest in "event streaming" than in "streaming data."

All that being said, if the blog post focused on sharing experiences with different event processing patterns (publish–subscribe, event sourcing, Command Query Responsibility Segregation [CQRS]), it might be better to focus on "event streaming" despite the relatively lower search interest.

Here are some tips for using Google Trends:

- Know that you're looking at the popularity of search terms over time. The data is normalized and scaled on a range from 0 to 100, with 100 representing the peak popularity of a term within the specified period and location.

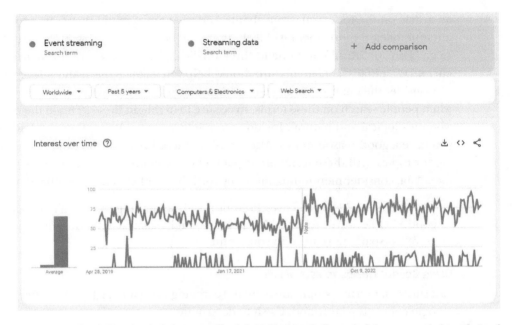

Figure 7.6   Google Trends result for comparing interest in two similar search terms: event streaming and streaming data. There seems to be significantly higher interest in streaming data.

- When selecting terms, avoid the one labeled "search term" unless there are no other options available. Anything that's not a search term is a "topic." Topics are language agnostic and account for misspellings. You will likely get more accurate results with topics than with search terms. For example, choose "Rust: Programming Language" over "Rust: Search Term" (which could include results for the movie, the metal, the game, etc.).

- Compare topics to topics and search terms to search terms.

- Expand the timeframe to at least a couple of years to get a better understanding of how interest is trending and to discover seasonal spikes (e.g., around conferences).

- Look in the "Related Topics" and "Related Queries" area. If it mentions relevant terms, consider if those are better options. If it mentions crazily irrelevant terms (e.g., "reebok zig") consider excluding them with a negative search term like "zig –reebok."

You can use the following search operators:

- *Quotation marks*—Gets data for the precise term within the quotation marks:
  - *"streaming data platform"* will include data for "open source streaming data platform" but not for "streaming platform."
- *Plus sign*—Gets data for search phrases with one or the other keyword:
  - *Postgres + PostgreSQL* will include data for Postgres as well as for PostgreSQL.

- *Minus sign*—Excludes data containing the keyword indicated after the minus sign:
  - *Rust –movie* will exclude results related to the Rust movie starring Alec Baldwin.

You can learn more about Google Trends in the following resources by Google:

- FAQ about Google Trends data: https://mng.bz/OmaO
- Basics of Google Trends: https://mng.bz/YV9Q
- 15 tips for Getting the Most out of Google Trends: https://mng.bz/GNP8

> **Example 7.1**
> One top keyword for the fake Zig blog would be "Zig," of course, and maybe "examples" as well. But it should also target "FakeDB" and "Postgres," and maybe "migrator," too. After all, if anyone in the world is searching for a Postgres to FakeDB migrator, this is the blog for them!

7.4.2 Title tag

The title tag (`<title>`) sets the title that browsers display as the tab title and bookmark text. For people navigating the web via screen readers, the title tag is what's read aloud as the person navigates among tabs.

This tag also determines the title shown in social media link previews (unless it's overridden by platform-specific metadata, which we discuss more later). And it's usually—though not always—used as the hyperlinked text in search results. Google admits that it sometimes opts to use different text in its results, but what you specify in this tag is your best shot at influencing what's shown there.

Additionally, the title tag is one of the factors determining how search engines understand and rank your blog post. If your "target keywords" appear across your title tag, URL, or meta description, as well as in your article, your post is more likely to show up when people search for those terms.

Usually, the title is just automatically copied over from your H1 (the title shown at the top of the blog post). Assuming you already put a lot of thought into your article title, that's probably fine. However, you might want to adjust it if

- *It's long.* Browsers truncate the title at around 50–60 characters. This shouldn't be a problem if your H1 is fairly short and features the most eye-catching terms at the start rather than at the end. But if that shortened version isn't ideal, tighten the title a bit. You might be able to get a few more characters to display by replacing "and" with "&" and replacing long em dashes (—) with pipes (|) or colons (:).
- *You want to highlight an additional detail.* If you have a short title and some breathing room before the 50–60 character cutoff, you could add your own name, site name, or company name at the end. For example, the "How We Built It" pattern blog titled "Ship Shape" (chapter 10) uses "Ship Shape—Canva Engineering

Blog" as the title tag. If you're a known brand, or want to become one, why not use the extra real estate to highlight that brand? Note that Google is currently showing the site's brand name at the top of each search result (above the URL), so the extra branding might not be so critical.

Although the title doesn't need to match the H1, it must be similar. If not, the search engine might suspect that you're trying to trick it and end up penalizing you by burying your blog post deep down where your target audience will never find it. (Cue the joke that the best place to hide a dead body is page 2 of Google search results.)

> **Example 7.2**
>
> Assume that the fake Zig blog ended up being titled "We Built a Postgres to FakeDB Migrator with Zig." That's only 47 characters, so we could extend it in the title tag as follows: "We Built a Postgres to FakeDB Migrator with Zig | ACME blog." Now it's 59 characters. The word "blog" might get cut off, but that's not critical.
>
> The following title would be risky: "Why and How the ACME Engineering Team Decided to Build a New Data Migrator (Postgres to FakeDB) with Zig." It could quite likely get cut off at or before the word "Build." That means all the important terms (Postgres, FakeDB, Zig, migrator) would be skipped.

7.4.3   Meta description

The meta description (`<meta name="description"`...) specifies the blurb used in link previews and influences the blurb shown in search results. Google might select different text (as it sometimes does with the title), so there's no guarantee that what you add is what readers will get.

The effect on search engine rankings is allegedly minimal. But the effect on users deciding what to read is significant. Along with your title, this is your best chance to hook the target reader—your opportunity to tell them what your article is about and why it's so interesting. Focus on writing a clear and compelling description, including your keywords if appropriate. You have around 150 characters to work with here.

Note that Google typically bolds any user search terms that appear in its description blurb (figure 7.7). If the reader is scrolling through results and notices that your blog post clearly addresses their search terms, they might trust it enough to click through.

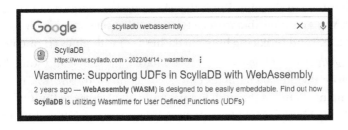

Figure 7.7   A screenshot of an article's meta description as displayed in Google search results. Note how the user's search terms are bolded in the description.

Some platforms (like Medium) will automatically create a meta description using the first 140–150 characters from your article. Don't just accept the default! Craft something carefully, ideally highlighting the technologies you discuss and what interesting angle you take.

Once you have a tight statement to attract the target reader, strongly consider adding it at the very start of the blog post, maybe prominently in bold. That gives the reader a super fast way to see if your blog post is a good match for their interests and to move on immediately if it's not.

Example 7.3

Here's a sample meta description for the fake Zig blog: "ACME built a Postgres to FakeDB data migration tool in Zig. Learn how Zig compared to C, C++ & Rust and access the open source tool."

Here's what you *don't* want to do: "In this article, ACME staff engineer PretendPiotr shares his experiences creating a new data migration tool that enables faster migrations from Postgres to FakeDB. And he built it in Zig." What's wrong with it?

- Postgres will likely get cut off, and FakeDB and Zig will definitely get cut off.
- It's loaded with a lot of words the reader won't care about.
- It's all about PretendPiotr and the article, not about what's in it for the reader.

7.4.4 *URL*

Most platforms automatically generate a URL (often labeled "permalink" in the UI) based on the title you specify. If you want to modify it, change it right away. If you change it after you publish, you'll need redirects, and your analytics will become more difficult to track—just think about it upfront and save yourself grief later.

Per Google's John Mueller (Google Search Advocate), having keywords in a URL is a "very, very lightweight ranking factor" (Mueller mentioned this in Google SEO office-hours: https://mng.bz/0MPW). Even if there's not much benefit, adding your keywords there doesn't require much effort, so just do it.

Use lowercase throughout and separate words with hyphens, not underscores. To keep things tight, you might want to use a URL that's shorter than the title. The URL length won't affect your search engine ranking at all (Mueller mentioned this in an episode of AskGooglebot: https://www.youtube.com/watch?v=WmEpP9aPq8o), so don't shorten it in hopes it will help you in that respect.

NOTE Some platforms (looking at you, Medium) add an autogenerated hash to the URL for tracking purposes. Some people have created and shared scripts for removing it, but it's probably safest to just let it be.

What about dates? Should your URL include the publish date? It's a personal preference, but the general consensus is that dates don't add value and they clutter the URL. Many readers want to know when the article was published, so definitely include a publish date within the article itself. An extra benefit of a dateless URL is that if you update the post, you can just update the body of the blog with an "Updated: whenever" blurb. You won't have to deal with a clearly outdated dated URL.

> **Example 7.4**
>
> Assume the fake Zig blog is titled "We Built a Postgres to FakeDB Migrator with Zig." A clean URL that includes our most important keywords would be "/postgres -fakedb-migrator-zig."
>
> A bad option would be "/we_built_a_postgres_to_fakedb_migrator_with_zig"—particularly due to the underscores instead of hyphens. Another bad option would be "/database -zigzagging" since our "Zig" keyword might not be recognized as a separate word in that context.

7.4.5   *Hyperlinks*

In chapter 5, we touted how hyperlinks help you provide details to extra curious or less experienced readers without diluting the focus of your article. Now's the time to nail the execution.

First, think about what text to hyperlink. The answer is never "here" (as in "learn more *here*") or the URL itself. Instead, ensure that the hyperlinked text describes the linked item and tells your reader what to expect. Why?

- It helps your readers determine if they want to click through.
- It provides search engines clues about how your content relates to other sites. Note that linking to other sites likely won't help your own ranking, but it could pass on some good "search engine karma" to those you're linking to.
- It's absolutely critical for those experiencing your site through assistive technology such as screen readers. People using these devices commonly access the links out of context, tabbing to jump from link to link or pulling up a list of links when they're done with the article. Imagine how frustrating it would be to request a list of links and hear something like "here, click here, here, read more, here," capped off by a few GitHub URLs tortuously spelled out one character at a time (H-T-T-P-colon...).

Finally, take the time to manually confirm that all links actually lead to the expected pages. It's a pain. But sending readers off into dead ends won't foster goodwill and motivate them to share your blog post. Even if you checked the links last week in your doc, check them again in the HTML page:

- You might have copied something over incorrectly. If you're just one character off, your readers get to experience the site's clever 404 page.
- The links might have changed, particularly if you're linking to documentation pages (which seem to move around way more often than any other type of web page in existence).

Example 7.5

In chapter 5, we proposed revising the fake Zig blog to include a link to the RustEncryption library. The best way to handle that would be to make the bolded text the hyperlink:

*"Ultimately, we implemented that encryption layer by linking to **RustyEncryption**."*

Something like "Ultimately, we implemented that encryption layer by linking to Rusty-Encryption, which you can **access here**" would probably still make sense to people reading the link in context. But the out-of-context "access here" wouldn't be meaningful if an assistive technology was reading out all the page's links to a visually impaired reader.

7.4.6 Images

Earlier in this chapter, we discussed how images look to human eyes. Now let's shift focus to how their metadata is used by machines—search engines trying to understand your page as well as screen readers and other assistive devices trying to describe them to humans.

Image metadata is important for

- Helping people with visual impairments understand the meaning and purpose of your images
- Helping search engines better understand the page's overall content
- Helping search engines determine if the image should be displayed for relevant image searches
- Telling readers what they're missing in case the image fails to load (e.g., due to low bandwidth)

Focus on two elements here: the file name and the ALT text description (a short text blurb that describes the image). For the file name, the recommendation is quite simple. Just use something more descriptive than IMG123.png—for example, original-acme-architecture.png. For the ALT text descriptions, use text that

- Describes this specific image (what's important about it and how does it relate to your blog post?)
- Avoids filler words (e.g., "This screenshot is an image that shows...")
- Doesn't exceed 125 characters (the cutoff for many screen reading tools)
- Mentions any relevant keywords (e.g., key technologies in a system diagram)

Note that you don't need to add an ALT description for purely decorative images.

Example 7.6

The fake Zig blog ended up with one image, the following Zig GitHub star history:

(continued)

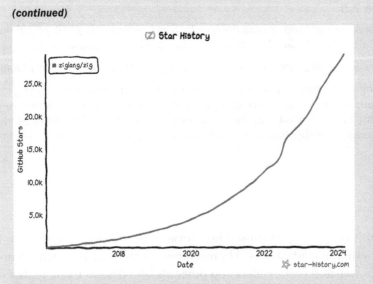

An image for the fake Zig blog. It needs an ALT text description so readers who can't see it will understand what it's communicating.

A good file name might be "zig-star-history.png." And a good ALT text description might be "The ziglang/zig GitHub star history from 2016 to 2024. Between 2022 & 2024, the stars surged from 10K to 30K."

7.4.7   Taxonomies: Categories, tags, and topics

Many blogs use categories and/or tags to organize information. If the site you're publishing on uses them, don't forget to apply them to the article. When a reader completes an article and is hungry for more, they might skim through categories or tags that catch their interest. If articles aren't properly categorized and tagged, the curious reader won't have easy access to those related articles.

Note that there are two distinctly different schools of thought when it comes to tagging. One is to tag every key term that's mentioned. The other is to apply a tag only if someone hoping to learn more about that term would find value in this article's discussion of it. A fleeting mention of a term would not pass that test, but a respectable reference that's at least a paragraph might. Follow whatever approach is used throughout the blog site.

In Medium and other platforms, there's also the concept of a "topic." Topics have two purposes:

- Influence what content is recommended to a reader (readers can declare their topics of interest and algorithms will suggest content within those topics)
- Allow readers of a given article to drill down into additional articles on that same topic

When you publish an article on Medium, you can specify up to five topics. At the time of writing, you can specify the topics in two different places (Change Topics, More Settings). The Change Topics area displays a number next to each topic but the More Settings area does not. Regardless, that number (seen in figure 7.8) is not terribly valuable.

You might assume that the number Medium shows next to a topic would be the number of followers for that topic. No. It's actually the number of articles currently tagged with that topic. So what if a topic has 46K articles? There's a big difference between

Figure 7.8 **What's this number (46K) telling you about the Database topic? You might assume it means 46K people follow this topic. Wrong. It's the number of articles tagged with this topic.**

a topic with 5K followers and 46K articles and another with 3M followers and 46K articles. To see how many people are following a particular topic, use the Medium "search by topic" functionality. For each topic, you'll see the number of followers as well as the number of articles. Ahh, much better.

With that knowledge, weigh your options, considering both relevance and reach. Do you want to be a small fish in a big pond (appear in a broader topic with many followers but also many articles) or the big fish in a small pond (appear in a more specialized topic with a smaller, more focused set of followers and also fewer articles to compete with)? With up to five options, you can likely target the most relevant specialized topics as well as a broader topic or two.

Example 7.7

If the fake Zig post was being published on the company blog, it could fall under the "Engineering" category and might be tagged with Zig, tools, data migration, Postgres, and FakeDB.

If we were publishing it on Medium, here are some related topics.

Potential Medium topics for the fake Zig blog

Topic	Followers	Articles
Zig	107	122
Ziglang	50	29
Postgres	1.4K	7.3K
Postgresql	1.7K	7.3K

(continued)

Potential Medium topics for the fake Zig blog *(continued)*

Topic	Followers	Articles
FakeDB	Too fake for followers	Too fake for articles
Programming	6.9M	404K
Software Development	2.6M	287K
Software Engineering	2.2M	98K
C	977	6.1K
Cplusplus	609	2.7K
Rust	7.2K	9.3K
Rust Programming Language	2.3K	1.6K
Database	5K	46K

We would definitely want to select "Zig"; it's a major focus, even though few people are currently following it. The people following "Ziglang" are probably also following "Zig," so we could skip that.

We'd also select "Postgresql" and "FakeDB" since they're important keywords (we're targeting Postgres users migrating to FakeDB). It seems "Postgresql" has slightly more followers than "Postgres," even though they're two different words for the exact same thing. We might as well select the one with more followers.

What else? Let's try "Programming," which could provide exposure to a broad audience who might be curious about Zig even though they don't follow it yet. 6.9M followers is quite attractive.

That leaves us with one more. "Database" has a lot of stories, but very few followers. It's also likely quite broad. There's a low chance that someone who declared themselves interested in "Database" would care about this highly specialized migration tool—or in the lessons learned working with Zig. Maybe "C," since the blog post talks at length about Zig's C interoperability? Or "Rust," since we mention it briefly and it has a healthy amount of followers? Or do we target another big broad one like "Software Engineering?" Decisions, decisions.

There is no right answer. Weigh the options, make an educated guess, and adjust it later if needed.

7.4.8   *Featured (thumbnail) images*

Some articles stand out in a bad way on social media feeds. Instead of an image that's either compelling, nondescript, or repulsive, they just have a sad gray box, as shown in figure 7.9. Don't be that article.

Figure 7.9 Don't want this drab image representing your dazzling blog? Then specify an og:image thumbnail in the metadata.

When you share your own article on your social media platform of choice, you will likely take the time to manually upload an appropriate thumbnail image. But will the people who happen to share it take that extra step? You can just set it in the metadata, and rest assured that your preferred image will display whenever someone shares the article.

To set a default image and avoid the fate of the sad gray box, ensure that your post has og:image metadata set to the desired image. In many cases, if you specify something called the "Featured Image" in WordPress or Medium, it will automatically set the appropriate og:image tag for you. If your blogging platform doesn't automatically add the og:image tag for you, please do it yourself. In fact, add the complete set of Open Graph metadata while you're at it.

But what's Open Graph? It's a protocol, created by Facebook, that controls what's shown when your article is shared on social media. Most platforms respect Open Graph. And some platforms have their own paradigms that can override Open Graph settings on their domain (e.g., so you can set an image that uses the dimensions they prefer). For example, "X" still provides documentation on using "Twitter cards" as of this writing. You can learn more about the Open Graph protocol at https://ogp.me/. For Twitter cards and any other platform-specific metadata, search on the appropriate sites.

If you wanted to add a mix of Open Graph and Twitter card data, you might add something like the following `<meta>` tags in the `<head>` of your page.

Listing 7.1 Adding meta tags for social media

```
<meta property="og:site_name" content="http://www.mysite.com">
<meta property="og:locale" content="en-us">
<meta property="og:type" content="article">
<meta property="og:url" content="https://www.mysite.com/my/great-article">
<meta property="og:title" content="My great title">
<meta property="og:image"
content="http://www.mysite.com/img/great-article-thumbnail.png">
<meta property="twitter:site" content="@my_handle">
<meta property="twitter:title" content="My great title">
<meta property="twitter:card" content="This is the best article ever.">
<meta property="twitter:image"
content="http://www.mysite.com/img/great-article-x-thumbnail.png">
```

Finally, note that the LinkedIn Post Inspector (https://www.linkedin.com/post-inspector) is a great tool for checking how posts will display on LinkedIn (and likely other platforms). Beyond the display preview, it explains how it selected the values for each element and describes how to change the displayed elements by modifying the associated metadata (figure 7.10).

Metadata that we gathered about this page:

Property	Value		Image
			Note: We used the value from the provided Open Graph tag on the page.
Title	Enhancements to ScyllaDB's Filtering Implementation		How to change the image
			Provide a metadata tag for the og:image in the page's head section. For example:
Type	Article Lorem Ipsum		`<meta name="image" property="og:image" content="[Image URL here]">`
Image	https://www.scylladb.com/wp-content/uploads/800x400-blog-allow-filtering.png		Alternate values we considered
			Other values from the page that our scraper could have used for the content's image:
Description	In this post we discuss the enhanced filtering support coming in ScyllaDB 2.4 and compare it to the recommended alternatives and their performance.		https://www.scylladb.com/wp-content/uploads/mc-lp-piotr-sarna-150x150.png
			http://i4.ytimg.com/vi/dyWZRjtPI2s/0.jpg
Author	Piotr Sarna		https://www.scylladb.com/wp-content/uploads/blog-ad-data-performance-book.png
Publish date	No publication date found		https://www.scylladb.com/wp-content/uploads/logo-scylla-horizontal-RGB.svg
			https://www.scylladb.com/wp-content/uploads/1200x628-fb-lkdn-scylla-3-0.jpg

Figure 7.10   The LinkedIn Post Inspector shows what your post will look like, why, and how to change key elements.

Another option: once your blog post is published or you have a publicly shareable preview, just do a quick test post on your platform of choice.

Not sure what to use for a thumbnail image? Think about what would catch the eye of someone in your target audience. Flame graphs, other cool data visualizations, and images of code are always nice. They don't have to be fully readable in tiny thumbnail size, just readable enough to make them intriguing. You could use some custom article-themed artwork created by a human, or attempt to generate an image with an AI tool (we'll talk more about this in appendix B). If you have a recognizable personal brand, consider featuring your brand logo here.

Or, if you're just not into graphics and want to immediately draw attention to your words, take a screenshot of the article itself (figure 7.11). If you do this, plan to play around with screenshot sizes to find a nice balance between compactness and readability.

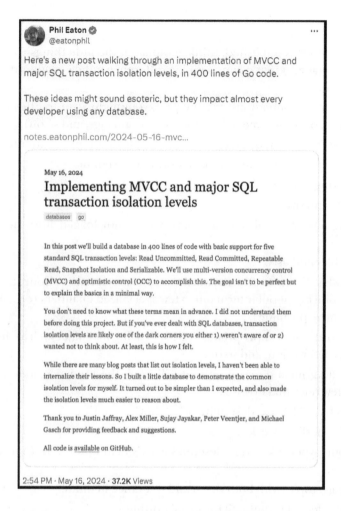

Figure 7.11   An example of using a screenshot of the article as the featured image for social media sharing.

Example 7.8

For the fake Zig blog, a fun featured image might be the Zig lizard with one hand on a Postgres elephant and the other hand on the FakeDB mascot (whatever that might be— a Chupacabra perhaps). A more serious approach would show a screenshot of the article itself.

7.5   *If you do nothing else*

Honestly, all these little things make a big difference, and there's not much you can reasonably skip. Before you ship it, run through the checklist in the Summary section to ensure you're not overlooking some tiny detail that could have an outsized effect on your post's overall readability, findability, accessibility, and shareability.

Summary

- Before your blog post is published, think about all of the little things (both surface level and metadata) that can make a big difference in how readers discover and experience it.
- Even if you're not the one publishing the post, you might want to offer recommendations (e.g., propose a meta description, relevant tags, and so on).
- Preview the post (ideally on both mobile and desktop) with special attention to
  - Whether the title and headings look awkward in the template
  - Code rendering and copy/paste errors
  - Image clarity and size
  - Video sizing and availability (make sure you're not logged into the video platform)
  - Complex tables and lists
- Think about what three to five keywords are most relevant to your article—usually at least one big popular term plus a few specialized qualifiers (e.g., Async, Rust, performance, profiling).
- Use those keywords when appropriate, while specifying metadata such as the title tag, URL, meta description, and so on.
- Craft a compelling meta description that will hook the human reader, ideally with at least a few relevant keywords.
- Ensure images have ALT text describing what they're showing.
- Check that all hyperlinks work.
- Check that your hyperlinked text describes what's behind the link (not "here" and not a URL).
- Think about tags/topics with both reach and relevance in mind.
- Give your blog a decent thumbnail for social posting.

Part 3

Applying blog post patterns

Part 2 took a broad, systematic look at how to write a captivating blog post. But just like different programming languages have different conventions, so do different types of blog posts. A captivating bug hunt article will vary dramatically from an opinion piece roasting a highly hyped technology, or an article that shares how a team implemented an industry-changing algorithm. Part 3 involves in-depth analysis of these and other blog post "patterns" exploring real-world examples, characteristics, and dos and don'ts for each:

- Chapter 8 analyzes "Bug Hunt" blog posts that share the thrill of finding and fixing some elusive bug.
- Chapter 9 analyzes "Rewrote It in X" blog posts that are all about rewriting an app in a new programming language, library, or framework.
- Chapter 10 analyzes "How We Built It" blog posts that share your most impressive engineering achievements.
- Chapter 11 analyzes "Lessons Learned" blog posts that share lessons learned from technical challenges.
- Chapter 12 analyzes "Thoughts on Trends" blog posts that are highly opinionated takes on industry trends.
- Chapter 13 analyzes "Non-markety Product Perspectives" blog posts where the product is embedded into a genuinely intriguing and educational article.
- Chapter 14 analyzes "Benchmarks and Test Results" blog posts that share various flavors of benchmarks and tests.

The "Bug Hunt" pattern

8

This chapter covers

- Blog posts that share the thrill of finding and fixing some elusive bug
- Their purpose and audience
- How various authors approached this type of post
- Key elements of successful "Bug Hunt" posts
- Dos and don'ts for your own "Bug Hunt" post

The "Bug Hunt" blog post pattern is the programming world's equivalent of a detective story. It has a theme, a main plot, side plots, a protagonist (you), and an antagonist (usually also you, having introduced the bug two weeks ago in the first place). It's captivating, keeps readers in suspense, and ends with a satisfying plot twist or a tactical cliffhanger. And the best part is that it's even more fun to write than to read!

8.1 Purpose

Writing a bug-hunting article serves a few purposes, depending on the success of the hunt, where the fault ultimately fell, and a few other factors. Let's tackle the potential purposes one by one.

8.1.1   *Knowledge dump*

The fact that a bug appeared and was fixed is undeniably important. But what's way more important is reducing the chance that it happens again and knowing what to do if it does. While hunting for a bug, it's likely you encountered

- A few dead ends
- A very convincing red herring
- A tool that looked helpful at first, but ended up being unrelated
- Another tool that proved immensely useful
- Some blog post from 2014 that led you to discover the root cause

All those steps are incredibly useful for the future debugger of another similar problem (likely you again, two weeks older). Awareness of the past dead ends and distractions is especially helpful here. Quick identification of a known red herring can save the future debugger (you) a few hours of unproductive research. You can treat bug-hunting blog posts as scrolls of ancient knowledge (two weeks or older), created by your predecessors (you) to pass it on to future generations (also you).

8.1.2 Global bug awareness

It's give-back-to-the-community time! Chances are, the bug that you fixed doesn't uniquely apply to your project. Instead, it was caused by a sneaky pitfall in your language of choice, one of the libraries, or specific hardware. Your article can genuinely inspire others to think "Huh, we do have exactly the same setup—makes me wonder…" It might also motivate the team behind that technology to consider ways to stop others from making the same mistake.

As a result, writing a story about how you fixed an interesting bug may cause a few other bugs of the same category to be fixed worldwide. It's a superpower! This purpose is especially important if the bug is related to

- Bleeding edge software
- Novel hardware
- A young open source community

Those tend to develop dynamically and have very little test coverage compared to industry standards simply because they are too young to be implemented in a critical mass of projects. You can think of this purpose as an external version of the previously described "knowledge dump"—it's a knowledge dump that you write for everyone, not just for yourself or your team.

8.1.3 Bragging

Set aside the negative connotation of the "bragging" word. Tech world bragging at the right dosage is good for you and your peers. Bragging about doing something interesting, like hunting and resolving a bug, helps you as well as your readers:

- *It's educational.* Your audience can presumably learn something by reading how you achieved your goal.
- *It broadens your professional network.* People intrigued by similar technologies and challenges will likely reach out to you, as outlined in chapter 1.
- *It feels good.* There's no shame in acknowledging that attention is one of the benefits of telling the world that you did something.
- *It yields free criticism—hopefully constructive criticism, but valuable either way.* The (often illusory) sense of anonymity on the internet makes it easy to criticize others, so you can count on lots of comments and nitpicks after your article goes public. But after filtering out the vitriol, you can often learn something new, or even revisit your whole approach to the problem.

8.2 Audience

Bug-hunting is a technical topic, and the audience for bug-hunting blog posts is inherently just as technical. Categories of interested readers include

- People with a similar background (which means they are potentially susceptible to introducing or suffering from similar bugs in their systems)

- People whose job is finding and fixing production bugs
- People in the middle of a similar bug hunt
- People who might be able to prevent this class of bug from recurring (those behind the technology where the bug occurred or working on defect prevention tools)
- Detective fiction aficionados
- Your colleagues
- Professional internet critics specialized in unsolicited advice

It's safe to assume that the audience is someone who

- Already has sufficient professional background to understand the technical terms and idioms you use in the article
- If not, is willing to look them up and learn
- If not, is absolutely fine with just pretending that they understand it

Therefore, it's fine to treat a bug-hunting blog post as one addressed to intermediate level (or above) readers and not newcomers. Advanced technical terms are fine because you're not trying to make the article accessible to the wider public. Just expand any arcane acronyms as you see fit and provide hyperlinks as needed.

8.3   *Examples of "Bug Hunt" blog posts*

Because bugs can occur anywhere, so can bug-hunting blog posts. In the wild, you can find bug-hunting posts published across a variety of blogs: Big Tech, unicorn, startup, and personal blogs. In general, bug-hunting posts published by large high-profile companies are unsurprisingly less common (and more guarded) than those by startups as well as individual contributors writing about open source contributions and weekend projects.

Here are some prime examples of blog posts that apply the "Bug Hunt" pattern, along with Piotr's commentary on each.

8.3.1   *Hunting a NUMA Performance Bug*

Author: Michał Chojnowski
Source: ScyllaDB Blog (https://mng.bz/KDPE)

SUMMARY

The article describes a performance regression happening on modern hardware with NUMA (Non-Uniform Memory Access) design. The regression seemed to occur randomly on half of the runs, which made it much harder to pinpoint. The article shares a few failed (but nonetheless skillful and impressive) attempts to diagnose the problem. Then, one of the observations leads straight to a breakthrough and a surprisingly small fix – measured with lines of code.

COMMENTARY

This is the pinnacle of bug-hunting blog posts. It's deeply technical, but at the same time simple to follow. The less experienced readers can skip some of the nitty-gritty details and still learn a lot. All of the failed attempts to diagnose the issue are educational, and surely usable in future debugging.

The casual expertise that the author shows while editing executable binaries directly as if they were text files makes the blog post an extremely enjoyable read. The solution to the problem is also very satisfactory, especially to a programmer's mind: just one seemingly innocent line of code changed, and all the performance regressions are eliminated.

8.3.2 Why Is My Rust Build So Slow?

Author: Amos Wenger
Source: fasterthanlime Blog (https://mng.bz/9oP0)

SUMMARY

This extensive blog post investigates compilation time problems for a Rust project. It shows multiple techniques for how to profile the compiler itself, decompose the compilation process into manageable pieces, and measure how long each piece takes and why. It's full of images, code snippets, and descriptions of concrete tools you can use. The article's conclusion is not really any single breakthrough, but rather honest advice to apply all the described extensive techniques if you're unsatisfied with your Rust build times.

COMMENTARY

Compared to an average technical blog post, this one is a hog in a purely positive sense! It can easily take a skilled reader half an hour to read through it, and it's probably a good idea to digest it in three or four parts, taking breaks from the screen to avoid dizziness and diplopia.

This is a positive trait because it makes the article stand out. Many tech articles try to squeeze as much information as possible into 4–6 minutes of reading. And that's fair, considering the average attention span of a human being raised on smartphones rather than playing outside all day with occasional cartoon breaks. Yet, a long article will appeal to the old school folks who were once capable of reading a book in a single sitting.

The article has a unique style featuring the author's alter ego, Cool Bear (figure 8.1), who regularly adds short humorous comments, keeping the reader engaged throughout the (lengthy) reading process.

This type of a bug-hunting blog post also serves as an encyclopedia of techniques for debugging the Rust compiler. I have it bookmarked, just in case I ever need to refresh my knowledge of how to measure linking times in my projects. The conclusion is also quite unconventional: instead of building tension and finally presenting readers with a surprise solution, it's simply an honest summary with encouragement to reach out.

8.3.3 How a Single Line of Code Made a 24-core Server Slower Than a Laptop

Author: Piotr Kołaczkowski
Source: Piotr Kołaczkowski's Blog (https://mng.bz/j0lV)

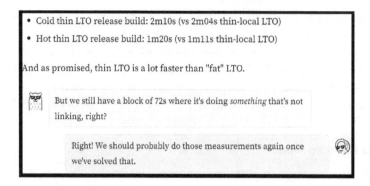

- Cold thin LTO release build: 2m10s (vs 2m04s thin-local LTO)
- Hot thin LTO release build: 1m20s (vs 1m11s thin-local LTO)

And as promised, thin LTO is a lot faster than "fat" LTO.

But we still have a block of 72s where it's doing *something* that's not linking, right?

Right! We should probably do those measurements again once we've solved that.

Figure 8.1   This article highlights insights from the author's alter ego, Cool Bear, sometimes in dialog with the author's own interior monologue.

SUMMARY

The blog post describes how local benchmarks detected a bottleneck on machines with lots of CPU cores. The author shares a performance analysis, performs some profiling, then offers a few explanations of how modern CPUs work under the hood and how the processor caches manage memory. The suggested fix is a natural consequence of the conclusions reached earlier in the article: minimizing the amount of state shared between processor units eliminates the bottleneck.

COMMENTARY

This is another stellar example of a bug-hunting blog post. Its title is a little clickbaity, but still elegant enough to avoid being rejected by the average ad-blocking software. The technical details are much more universally understood than the ones in Chojnowski's NUMA blog post (described earlier in this section).

The article is sneakily educational, digressing on things like "How many nanoseconds does L3 cache access take on average on Intel Xeon." That's great practice; it leaves those details imprinted in readers' minds without them realizing it. Who knows, maybe one day that tucked-away tip might help fix a performance bug in another project. Overall, the article leaves readers satisfied with the result and also a tiny bit smarter in the field of CPU architecture and performance.

8.3.4   *Lessons from Debugging a Tricky Direct Memory Leak*

Author: Sanchay Javeria
Source: Pinterest Engineering Blog (https://mng.bz/WVyd)

SUMMARY

Pinterest's development team shares their experience hunting a stream processing code memory leak that led to cascading failures in their distributed system. It goes over debugging techniques for the Java environment and then finally pinpoints a bug in application code that caused the memory leak.

COMMENTARY

This is a classic bug-hunting article, so much so that it could be used as a blog post template for hunting down almost any problem in Java code. It contains the customary investigation steps, along with screenshots from observability tools. Also following custom, the culmination paragraph is called "The Fix." It explains that the culprit was yet another memory leak problem caused indirectly by garbage collection mechanisms in Java. Hint: it always is!

In this context, the conclusion isn't really an earth-shattering breakthrough, but it definitely meets the readers' expectations. I bet the majority of the readers think "ah, I knew it from the start" right after learning the root cause.

8.3.5 *ZFS Is Mysteriously Eating My CPU*

Author: Brendan Gregg
Source: Brendan Gregg's Blog (https://mng.bz/86PW)

SUMMARY

The blog post describes a hunt for the cause of mysterious higher-than-expected CPU usage. It shows how to narrow the candidates down to a single function call with analysis tools and concludes with a surprising performance bug in ZFS—a file system implementation.

COMMENTARY

The title itself is captivating, but then something in the URL jumps out at you: it's by Brendan Gregg, the flame graph inventor! This is a prime example of why personal brand matters so much. When I see "Brendan Gregg," I immediately assume that the article is interesting—and I wasn't mistaken in the slightest.

Given Gregg's expertise, the problem analysis naturally involved flame graphs. The root cause is quite a surprise, and Gregg described it in a very informal and funny manner. The blog post is also very concise (a 3-minute read, even if you reserve some time upfront to look at the flame graph screenshots). It clearly shows that you don't need to write thousands of words to squeeze in lots of knowledge, tips, and interesting technical details.

8.4 Characteristics

Bug-hunting blog posts can vary as wildly as the actual bug hunts, but they tend to share the following characteristics:

- They recount the story chronologically, from the moment the evil bug manifested itself, to when it was pronounced dead.
- They focus primarily on the thrill (and pain) of the hunt.
- They freely share the evidence collected along the hunt so readers can put on their detective hats and play along.
- They're largely geared to experienced developers who know the technologies being discussed (or are ready to learn as they go).
- They offer technical nuggets that could be interesting now, lifesaving later.

Let's examine each in turn.

8.4.1   Crafted chronologically

Bug-hunting blog posts often follow a specific structure since they are the technological equivalent of detective stories. (If you want an intro or refresher on the structure of a detective story, generative AI does a decent job here). The introduction paragraph does not reveal too many details and certainly does not provide a spoiler on the solution. Often, the authors just elaborate on the (properly mysterious) title with a few more words.

Once the problem is defined, the hunt begins, usually with a few failed (but educational) attempts. The tension builds until the author reaches their aha moment, which is followed by the fix description (and that section is customarily titled "The Fix"). After the solution is revealed, the blog post concludes by describing preventive measures to stop this bug from recurring, and often a concise apology to any affected users.

8.4.2   Heavy on the hunt

The meatiest part of the article is the path toward identifying the problem. Spending around 80% of the post explaining the investigation process is a good rule of thumb. For example, here's how much time each of the example blog posts spent on the investigation (based on word count):

- *Chojnowski*—85% hunt
- *Wenger*—83% hunt
- *Kołaczkowski*—83% hunt
- *Javeria*—82% hunt
- *Gregg*—93% hunt

8.4.3   Evidence everywhere

Bug hunt blog posts are usually full of forensic evidence. Readers want to see flame graphs, numbers, charts, scripts, and code samples. This lets them step into your detective shoes and try to figure out the riddle before the big reveal.

For example, here's some of the evidence shown in the example blog posts:

- *Chojnowski*—Database monitoring graphs (writes per shard), network and disk performance graphs, CPU stats, flame graphs and instruction-level breakdowns, the CPU's performance measuring monitoring unit (PMU) events, and a variety of attempted code fixes
- *Wenger*—Cargo build timings, a timeline of compilation units, CPU usage and concurrency graphs, debug information, flame graphs, tracing through Chromium and Perfetto, attempted code fixes, dependency graphs
- *Kołaczkowski*—A look at the benchmarking tool's design, throughput results (on his 4-core laptop vs. a 24-core server), flame graphs
- *Javeria*—Out-of-memory error details, backpressure tests, and multiple forays into memory monitoring
- *Gregg*—Flame graphs (of course!), ZFS mount details, arcstats, and all the source code, via a GitHub link

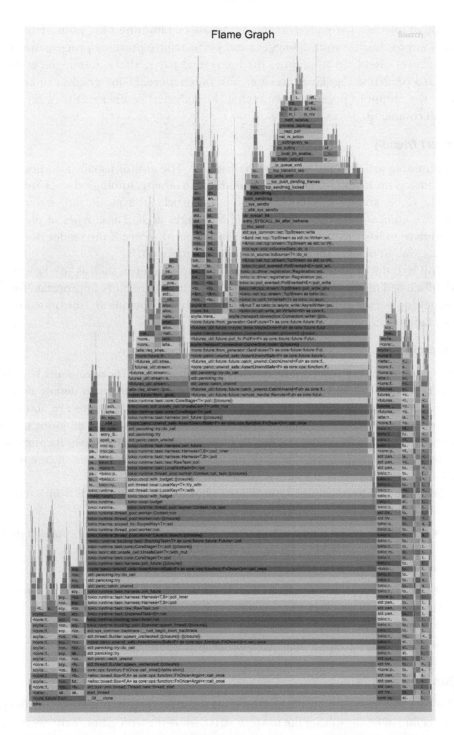

Figure 8.2   Example of an eye-catching flame graph. You can interact with this flame graph at https://scyllabook.sarna.dev/perf/fg-before.svg.

Flame graphs are particularly common across bug-hunting blog posts. They offer a great way to visualize your debugging and performance profiling process. And they're interactive—users can zoom in to the interesting parts, filter out only the events that match a particular regular expression, and much more. Flame graphs can be created from the output of popular tools, such as Linux's perf profiler or Rust's cargo flame graph command.

8.4.4   *Expert friendly*

Bug-hunting articles tend to be expert friendly. The author usually assumes that the audience is proficient in (or at least familiar with) the technological stack used in the article. Code samples and scripts shared in the article are typically targeted to readers who are familiar with the programming languages used. These types of posts aren't conducive to basic explanations of core language concepts; if the reader doesn't "get it," they might need to soldier through it or just move on.

This is distinctly different than in other blog post patterns, such as "We Rewrote It in X" (discussed in chapter 9). Blog posts in that pattern are more appropriate for those just getting started with the given technology and often include an "Introduction to the New Language" section.

8.4.5   *Educational*

Blog posts following this pattern can be quite educational for developers beyond the affected team. The meaty part, bug identification, is abundant in details about how to inspect similar problems. Even more importantly, these sections are abundant in reproducible details: ones that are likely to be useful for solving all kinds of similar problems that readers might face in the future. The blog post serves its purpose if it leaves the reader equipped with a few more tricks they can apply, just in case they ever encounter a similar bug at some point in their life.

For example, here's a high-level view of what readers could learn from each of our example blog posts:

- *Chojnowski*—The kinds of problems you might encounter with complex memory architecture (NUMA), especially with ARM processors.
- *Wenger*—Ways to improve your Rust build times.
- *Kołaczkowski*—How modern CPUs work under the hood and how the processor caches manage memory.
- *Javeria*—Java is evil.
- *Gregg*—How to apply analysis tools like an absolute expert.

8.5   *Dos and don'ts*

The best blog posts are born from the most torturous bug hunts. Driven by the glorious feeling of finally solving the mystery, strike while the iron is hot. Write your impressions before the high of the hunt wears off and help your peers solve their next case faster. Here are some tips for writing your own bug hunt blog post.

8.5.1 Check if anyone (your boss, your boss' lawyers) will be upset by your transparency

This is especially important if you hunted a bug that had a notable effect on users or if the disclosure of this bug could negatively affect your company's reputation and/or the all-important stock price. Open source or source-available projects usually don't impose any legal considerations (except maybe trying to avoid getting your code infected with one of the GPL licenses and its copyleft terms). Not all code is open source, though.

Before you publish code snippets of your heavily guarded corporate secrets, make sure that your boss and any interested parties are fine with it. Even if you skip the code, your superiors still may be averse to making certain information public, especially if the bug was related to security, or ended with an unfortunate data leak. Use this rule of thumb: ask first, write and publish later.

8.5.2 Do a technical deep dive

Technical details are a must in any, well, technical blog post. If your article lacks details such as code samples, specs on the exact technology used, step-by-step instructions, and so forth, many readers will leave unsatisfied. Even worse, they might doubt your integrity. Perhaps the inconvenient bits were deliberately omitted to make the product look better? If you worry that you might be adding too many technical details, err on the side of more. Readers can always skip over them if they don't find them interesting.

Bug-hunting blog posts are especially expected to be loaded with tips, tricks, code, benchmark results, as well as links to open source repositories and documentation. Otherwise, you rob readers of the fun opportunity to draw their own conclusions from the copious evidence. As noted earlier, it's fine to be expert-friendly here. You can assume that the audience is either already familiar with the technology described or willing to catch up (with the help of your blog post).

8.5.3 Be brutally honest about all your failures

Your failures and misery provide readers with the cathartic effect that brought them to your blog post in the first place! They also give rise to the most educational aspect of bug-hunting articles. After all, it's great to learn from mistakes, but it's even better to learn from somebody else's mistakes first.

Bug-hunting blog posts are usually written after the root cause has been identified and the bug fixed. The more pain and suffering are described in the first paragraphs, the better the final breakthrough looks. Readers who struggle with similar problems are going to actively search the internet for descriptions of similar problems, so all the sorrowful keywords such as "broken," "fault," or "FUBAR" serve dual purposes—they're an emotional outlet for the author's frustration, plus they make the blog post easier to find online.

Don't try to convey a perfect, pristine bug hunt. Dead ends and failed attempts bring in tons of educational value. Programmers (which is of course a synonym for "great minds") think alike. That means some readers could get stuck in the same dead ends, unless they read your cautionary tale first.

8.5.4   *Include numbers, benchmarks, metrics, and flame graphs*

Benchmark results, metrics, and all kinds of numbers are the equivalent of clues and proofs from the detective fiction world. Bug-hunting blog posts look less legit if they use vague phrasing such as "our system is now much faster." Readers will immediately think "Yeah, but how much faster?" followed by "Dear author, if you were *really* proud of the results, then you would have posted them." Screenshots from your metrics (or even better, interactive figures like flame graphs) catch readers' eyes, making the article both more credible and more enjoyable to read.

8.5.5   *Don't give away too much, too soon—keep the tension building*

For most blog posts, we recommend sharing the TL;DR early on so readers can quickly decide if they want to continue. Not here! With bug hunt blog posts, avoid spoilers at all costs! The tension should be patiently built until the aha moment occurs and the fix is revealed. This is key for allowing readers (those not in a hurry, at least) to vicariously experience the thrill of the hunt, with all its twists and turns. They probably already suspect that the article concludes with a happy ending, because otherwise it wouldn't be published. But aren't most detective stories like that anyway?

8.5.6   *Don't make overeager readers hunt too hard for the fix*

That being said, some readers will get impatient. Maybe they drew their own conclusion after just a few paragraphs and want the immediate gratification of confirming that they got it right, right away, unlike silly old you. Maybe this is the twelfth Java bug-hunting blog post they've come across this month and they want to see if this is yet another one where the garbage collector is ultimately to blame. Be kind and mark "the fix" with a nice prominent heading so they can skip ahead to the smoking gun.

As a bonus, having a clearly labeled fix is also helpful to those who are returning to your blog post because they're now suffering a similar problem. Back when they were reading this for fun, they enjoyed following along with the thrill of your hunt. But now that the tables have turned, they want to go straight to your fix and see if it will save them in their own moment of despair.

8.5.7   *Add breaking points wherever necessary*

Bug hunt articles can get long, especially if you're covering every little twist and turn (as you absolutely should!). If you end up writing a blog post that will take over 20 minutes or so to read, consider adding a few clear breaking points for readers, in case they opt to consume your article in more than one sitting.

For example, you could provide a short recap of the progress of the investigation so far. You might add an explicit note that the steps previously described led to a dead end, leading to a new thesis. Or you could simply use subheadings such as "Phase 3," subliminally suggesting to the reader that it's fine to take a short coffee break here without losing context.

8.5.8 Don't suck the life out of it

Readers aren't here to read an official failure report. The captivating bits are the personal story, the struggle, and the final joy of figuring out what was wrong. The best bug-hunting blog posts use an informal conversational tone, and anecdotes are very much welcome.

Narrate it from your personal point of view. Don't hesitate to share what was going through your mind as the mystery unfolded. Also, rants are borderline mandatory and expected—in reasonable doses, of course. Deep down, most humans enjoy reading about other people's frustrations and feeling the indirect relief that it didn't happen to them (yet).

The "building tension" and "providing full access to clues" approaches described earlier are two fundamental ways to keep readers engaged (yes, they *are* shamelessly stolen from real detective stories). In addition, you might want to

- Write in an extremely casual tone, sacrificing "proper" grammar as needed to keep it conversational.
- Create a faux dialog with the reader: ask them questions so they're encouraged to step back and form their own hypotheses (which you will proceed to confirm or disprove).
- Write as if you're in the thick of the hunt (e.g., "Let's see if …" versus "Then we checked if…").
- Share exactly what popped into your head (no matter how silly it seems in retrospect) as you encountered each new piece of information.
- Explicitly call out critical moments such as "plot twist," "dead end," and "the aha moment" to ensure readers are in the right mindset at every point.

8.5.9 Don't forget to thank those who helped along the hunt

The most important reason for publicly acknowledging your collaborators is pure kindness. Bug hunts are among the most infuriating parts of computer programming, and misery loves company. Your collaborators probably made the pain a bit less excruciating; if you appreciate that at all, do thank them here. For the not-so-empathetic folks, there are also pragmatic (read: selfish) reasons for thanking your collaborators. Your acknowledgment could make them more likely to assist in the next bug hunt. Also, if you name someone in a blog post, you can pretty much guarantee that they will read it, and maybe they will even share it. Perhaps someone they know will be the person to start it trending on Hacker News.

8.5.10 Extrapolate

Feel free to extrapolate from specific errors (e.g., "Our Rust code had a bug.") into more general problems (e.g., "Rust standard library makes it easy to deadlock in this particular use case.") Bug-hunting blog posts are also opportunities to shine some light on pain points you have with a particular technology. You've managed to attract a captive audience, interested in what you have to say. Why not take advantage of that? If you noted something particularly problematic with the language or library you used, bite the bullet and suggest that something should be fixed upstream. Programming language and library maintainers appreciate constructive criticism that helps improve their projects.

Summary

- Writing a bug-hunting article serves to share knowledge, raise awareness about bugs you encountered, and showcase your achievements.
- A bug-hunting blog post targets a technical audience, from experts to enthusiasts, usually assuming (at least) intermediate knowledge of the terminology.
- Bug-hunting blog posts are typically heavy on investigative details, showcasing technical evidence in the form of numbers, benchmarks, results, and graphs.
- Top tips:
  - Check for transparency problems.
  - Do a technical deep dive.
  - Be brutally honest.
  - Include numbers and benchmarks.
  - Avoid spoilers.
  - Clearly mark the fix.
  - Make it personal.
  - Thank your collaborators.

The "Rewrote It in X" pattern

This chapter covers

- Blog posts that are all about rewriting an app in a new (and trendy!) programming language, library, or framework
- Their purpose and audience
- How various authors approached this type of post
- Key elements of successful "We Rewrote It in X" posts
- Dos and don'ts for your own "We Rewrote It in X" post

To clarify, X stands for a wildcard to be replaced with a programming language or framework of your choice, not rebranded Twitter. With that important legal disambiguation out of the way, let's proceed with the pattern description.

"We Rewrote It in X" has long been prevalent in the technical blog space. Lately, it became exceedingly trendy during a wave of Rust rewrites (to the point that a new acronym, RIIR [rewrite it in Rust], was coined). By the time this book is published, we might be in the middle of or long past a rush of "We Rewrote It in Zig" blog posts, or even a language that wasn't designed at the time of writing.

Aside from language evangelism, articles about porting a project to another language, library, or framework are often juicy with problem statements (why the rewrite was needed in the first place), technical details, and new unexpected problems that arose only after the rewrite was already past the point of no return.

9.1   Purpose

There are a few reasons to write a blog post in this pattern (beyond simply having some "Rewrote It in X" masterpiece associated with your name):

- Encourage your peers to consider adopting the new language or framework
- Discuss the improvements you were able to make to your own projects
- Strengthen the community supporting the selected open source language
- Vent your own rewrite frustrations in a way that helps others avoid them

9.1.1   Evangelism

One key purpose of this pattern is to advocate for the selected language or framework. New programming languages are spawned daily (or so it seems), but only a select few ever achieve the level of sustained interest and adoption that makes them a valid choice for real-world projects. Thus, it's in the best interest of language inventors, maintainers, and excited early adopters to promote real-world use cases and show that the language actually improves the existing developer experience.

The language might be focusing on a particular niche that benefits from a specialized approach. For example,

- Internet of Things (IoT)
- Artificial intelligence (e.g., see the Mojo language)
- Querying a graph database

It also might be a brave attempt to overtake a general-purpose language such as C++ or Python (good luck).

Whatever the target use case, a programming language is only considered alive if real-world projects actually use it—preferably open source ones, so that a broader community can see and verify the code. And what better way to kickstart more projects in language X than to publish an article that describes a cool use case and shares how this new approach resolved the technical problems plaguing previous implementations. This is honest authentic evangelism, not marketing propaganda.

9.1.2 Project promotion

The previous section focused on the "X" part of the pattern name; this one focuses on the "it" component. Obviously, something got rewritten to another language, and a substantial part of the article will cover how "it" is now better. Common improvements cited when discussing a rewrite include

- Performance boost
- Availability on more platforms (e.g., operating systems, CPU architectures)
- Easier maintenance, with the optimistic anticipation of fewer bugs in the future
- Better test coverage
- Better user experience (e.g., it's now much easier to install and start using the project)
- Better developer experience (e.g., it's now much easier to contribute to the project; tooling is improved)

The improvements are usually attributed to the new programming language's characteristics. It might be faster by nature because it compiles to native assembly instead of running on a virtual machine. For example, think of migrating from Java to C++. Other times, it might have facilitated a more efficient implementation. For example, think of migrating to Rust and its safe concurrency primitives (as opposed to the previous tricky C implementation, unchanged from 1989 for fear of breaking some intricate, long-forgotten assumptions).

At first glance, it looks like the article is just praising the language. However, in reality, it's the speed *of the product* that improved, and it's *the product* that's now less prone to bugs. That's an indirect invitation to start using the product in question because it just became better.

9.1.3   Community development

Language implementations are often open source. And when the language is open source, writing a blog post on how it made your life easier is a nice "thank you" note to the community behind it. Based on your freely given testimonials, you also encourage other people involved in language evangelism (described in section 9.1.1) to write their own blog posts on the subject. Perhaps they will even refer to your blog post as one of their sources.

This is especially important and visible with rising technology, and the everlasting example of Zig applies here as well. Its community is still relatively small at the time of writing this book and revolves around a few large projects that adopted it early, such as Bun (the JavaScript runtime) and TigerBeetle (the database). At this early stage of community development, it's clearly beneficial to write interesting articles about writing or rewriting applications in the new language. Bun and TigerBeetle did it, and now they are considered the default examples of large, production-ready Zig projects. Win-win!

> **TIP**   See if the team or foundation behind the project you support is open to guest blogging opportunities. This helps you reach interested readers and helps the other team/foundation get attention.

9.1.4   Ranting

Rewriting a project to another language is hardly ever a smooth process. Moreover, there's no guarantee that the story has a happy ending! Some blog posts following this pattern are actually quite grudgy and end up being a "lessons learned" type of story.

One therapeutic effect of writing a rant about a failed (or bumpy) rewrite is venting the accumulated anger. But that alone should not justify publishing your experiences. As with virtually every technical article, you should offer some educational value. In the case of a rant, that could be a warning to others (and your future self): "Be careful next time you rush to rewrite something instead of trying to improve the status quo first." The article might also add value by sharing how to avoid the mistakes and pitfalls you stumbled into, ideally making someone else's rewrite process considerably smoother.

9.2   Audience

This pattern usually includes the programming language's name in the title, and that naturally attracts this language's enthusiasts. The following groups are likely interested:

- Evangelists of programming language X, including authors, maintainers, and other enthusiasts
- Evangelists of the programming language you rewrote it *from*; they likely consider these posts a form of an exit interview (sharing candid feedback, areas to improve, etc.).

- People interested in learning about the latest and greatest programming languages.
- People interested in writing their own programming language.
- Users of the now-rewritten software who want to learn about what improved.
- Competitors of the now-rewritten software who are here to check if they should consider a rewrite as well.
- Professional internet critics specialized in unsolicited advice.

Given this varied audience, articles describing a rewrite process should consider dedicating an entire section, or at least a paragraph, to introducing the new language. We cover this more in section 9.4.1.

9.3 Examples of "We Rewrote It in X" blog posts

In the wild, you can find "We Rewrote It in X" blog posts (or slight variations thereof) pretty much anywhere. The most common place to spot one of these posts is on the corporate engineering blog for a Big Tech company or unicorn who has outgrown their original tech stack on a particular project. The burden of evolving a legacy tech stack for an application that the world depends on makes for a great story (and also shows potential engineering recruits that they remain on the forefront of innovation, right?). But you can also find similar posts written by startups, as well as individual contributors working on weekend projects. Many of these take the angle of "We Wrote It in X" since the authors had the luxury of reading so many of their peers' recent "We Rewrote It in X" blog posts before selecting the initial technology for a new project.

Here are some example blog posts that will give you a good feel for this pattern, along with Piotr's commentary on each.

9.3.1 Why I Rewrote My Rust Keyboard Firmware in Zig: Consistency, Mastery, and Fun

Author: Kevin Lynagh
Source: Kevin Lynagh's Blog (https://kevinlynagh.com/rust-zig/)

SUMMARY

The author describes his experience rewriting his own keyboard firmware from Rust to Zig. The introduction briefly mentions that Rust was originally selected as the language for the keyboard firmware and then shifts to how the author was eventually convinced to try Zig. The main part of the blog post shows concrete code snippets that are problematic and/or ugly in Rust. The bad examples are later followed by their Zig counterparts, which are clearly cleaner and more readable. At the end, the author expresses excitement about the future of Zig. However, he also notes that Zig's ecosystem is not yet as mature as Rust's, so early adopters should brace themselves for a few compiler bugs and sparse documentation.

COMMENTARY

This article is a pleasure to read for so many reasons. The author needed to rewrite firmware for keyboards he produces himself, which is a fascinating technical topic on its own. The article contains backlinks to his other writings on creating his own hardware, which makes the whole blog a rabbit hole (in a purely positive sense).

The code snippets are informational and easy to read, even if you're not fluent in Zig. The Rust code snippets are substantially harder to parse, but that's deliberate and done masterfully. After all, the whole point of the article was to show that the rewrite resulted in much clearer code.

The author concludes that in his case, there's simply no upside to choosing Rust over Zig, which makes the rewrite a complete success. The author's satisfaction and optimism come across throughout the post, making it an enjoyable read. And the fact that he wraps up by crediting a few people who are well-known in the Rust and Zig worlds adds credibility to the whole article—and is simply a nice gesture. This is a great example to follow!

9.3.2 *How Turborepo is Porting from Go to Rust*

Authors: Nicholas Yang, Anthony Shew
Source: Vercel Blog (https://mng.bz/znNg)

SUMMARY

This blog post describes how the Turborepo project was ported from Go to Rust. It starts by disambiguating porting versus a full rewrite, briefly discussing the advantages and disadvantages of both approaches. It follows with a few examples of problems caused by the porting process and how the team decided to overcome them. The authors conclude that porting was the right decision, one that benefited the team. Finally, the blog post ends with a short promotion of the Turborepo product.

COMMENTARY

Reading this blog post was quite an ambivalent experience for me. The first few paragraphs were sparse on technical details, which is something I generally look for. Instead, I began to suspect I was reading a marketing whitepaper, sneakily presented as a technical post.

Thankfully, more technical details appeared over time, and the described road bumps were quite educational. I didn't find that any of the solutions were particularly creative or surprising though. From a purely technical point of view, the solutions looked more like workarounds. That's perfectly fine, of course. Practical solutions should be applied during an incremental port to another language. They are just not particularly captivating for readers like me (i.e., those who delude themselves into thinking they're so smart that only the hardest programming problems could possibly be of interest).

On the bright side, I did appreciate the educational value of the post—for example, learning that compiling a program written in Go and statically linked with the *musl* C library can cause nonobvious runtime issues.

9.3.3 *Why Discord Is Switching From Go to Rust*

Author: Jesse Howarth
Source: Discord Blog (https://mng.bz/0M8W)

SUMMARY

The article starts off by describing Discord's latency problems with one of their services implemented in Go. Next, it explains how rewriting the whole service to Rust helped alleviate all spikes, as well as improve the general performance. The rewrite was done iteratively, with the first version already fixing the latency spike problem, and the next iterations further improving the service's performance. The article concludes with a fun fact about the symbiosis between Discord and Rust: the language powers lots of Discord's services, and the Discord platform is also the Rust maintainers' main means of communication.

COMMENTARY

This blog post is a solid example of the "We Rewrote It in X" pattern. It starts with a clear problem statement, showing why the previously chosen language no longer met the requirements of the scale Discord was then operating at. The technical bits are interesting, and in some cases intriguing. For example, it was interesting that they decided to replace a HashMap with a BTreeMap, while customarily it's done the other way around. In my humble opinion, one missing bit is code snippets showing some of the details. But they might have had their hands tied due to legal issues associated with sharing closed source code. It was a nice touch to share the metrics from before and after the rewrite, showing a clear improvement.

9.3.4 *From Zero to 10 Million Lines of Kotlin*

Author: Omer Strulovich
Source: Engineering at Meta Blog (https://mng.bz/KDJE)

SUMMARY

This article is a detailed report on how Meta coordinated a huge rewrite of their application code from Java to Kotlin. It starts with an extensive rationale of why the rewrite was needed in the first place and then presents the two approaches they considered: iterative migration or full rewrite. After justifying the full rewrite option, the author explains multiple intricacies with the existing tools dedicated specifically to migrating from Java to Kotlin. The blog post also discusses the approach of using the official migration tools combined with a few custom practical scripts and a testing phase. That combo allowed Meta engineers to translate millions of lines of production code from Java to Kotlin. The article concludes with an optimistic vision of the future of Kotlin at Meta.

COMMENTARY

Even though this report is relatively long, it's dense with technical details, practical advice, and measurable results. All of those traits are welcome in an engineering blog post. The code samples are short and helpful. This article is also full of links to open source projects, documentation of external tools, and related blog posts. That's a good sign. However, in this particular case, the sheer number of hyperlinks could be a bit overwhelming if you opt to act on them. You will end up with an overload of open tabs if you start drilling down to line up articles for later reading.

This blog takes an interesting angle: it states from the start that although rewriting Java to Kotlin is largely automatic, their massive migration incurred enough caveats and subtle problems to justify developing a custom pipeline of scripts and tests. The numbers are also impressive and optimistic—if Meta managed to rewrite millions of lines of production Java code to Kotlin, your pet project is safe to port as well.

9.3.5   *Why We at $FAMOUS_COMPANY Switched to $HYPED_TECHNOLOGY*

Author: Saagar Jha
Source: Saagar Jha's Blog (https://mng.bz/9ox0)

SUMMARY & COMMENTARY

This particular blog post is satirical, and hilarious at that, but also fits the pattern extremely well. It actually fits the pattern too well, because its sole purpose is to mock all the overly promotional blog posts boasting about switching to the newest hyped technology. Anyone attempting to write about their rewrite process should read this one before they start writing:

- It's structured well, moving from the rationale, through the rewrite details, to the final conclusion.
- It contains a balanced amount of graphs and fun facts.
- It turns you into a self-conscious writer. If you reread your blog post and it looks deceptively similar to this one, consider rewording (unless you don't mind seeing the link to this parody post endlessly spammed in your post's comment section).

Don't feel discouraged by this article though. What allowed it to be funny in the first place was the surge of "We Rewrote It" blog posts trending on the front page of Hacker News for months. That's a clear indication that readers still enjoy them!

9.4   *Characteristics*

The main class of "We Rewrote It in X" blog posts tend to follow a pretty standard template—so much so that it inspired Saagar Jha to author the parody blog referenced in the previous section (and us to add a chapter section [9.4.3] calling out the common pieces and flow). But there are a few corner cases to note:

- Some teams choose to zoom in on the decision to abandon the original language, with titles like "Why We Sunsetted/Retired X."
- There's a growing trend of posts sharing the inside scoop on why they decided to take the contrarian path and *not* rewrite their app in the trendiest new language.
- One subtle variation is "We Wrote It in X," where teams who made their language selection quite recently share which of the current trendy languages they selected, why, and how it worked out (basically, the same pattern minus the migration part).

Blog posts in the standard "We Rewrote It in X" pattern tend to have the following characteristics.

9.4.1   *Suitable for language newbies*

Articles about rewrites are often motivated by specific features or guiding principles of the new language. It's common practice (and a good idea) to dedicate a section, or at least a single paragraph, to introducing the language in case any readers are not yet familiar with it.

This section might include details such as

- A short overview of the language's mission, core concepts, and intended use cases
- The advantages over the previously used language
- The most interesting (or important) known disadvantages
- Examples in the form of code snippets (interactive ones that users can run and edit are particularly engaging and educational)

For the segment of readers who are new to the language, this dedicated intro section will help them onboard themselves. It also benefits the language experts in your audience. By clearly marking this introductory material as such, you're alerting these readers that it's safe to just skim over this part.

9.4.2   *Practical*

There's a whole category of readers who are desperately looking for context before they start their own major rewrite. For their sake, posts in this pattern tend to include a reasonable helping of helpful details, such as

- Tools used for automating the rewrite
- Tools used for verifying the rewrite was correct
- Custom scripts for fixing incorrectly rewritten code (e.g., with these tools)
- Code samples in the old language, idiomatically rewritten to the new one

For example, here are some of the practical elements featured in our example "We Rewrote It in X" blogs:

- *Lynagh*—Code examples in both old and new languages, links to related posts, (e.g., https://mng.bz/j0MV), and direct links to Zig (new language) documentation
- *Yang and Shew*—A link to a known issue related to migration (https://github .com/golang/go/issues/13492) and graphs visualizing the migration procedure
- *Howarth*—A link to Go (old language) documentation explaining a failed attempt to fix the issues prior to the rewrite (https://pkg.go.dev/runtime/ debug#SetGCPercent)
- *Strulovich*—A reference to a presentation about issues with Kotlin (new language) (https://mng.bz/aV0Y), a reference to their own fix of a related open source tool (https://github.com/pygments/pygments/pull/1699), and a reference to their own open source helper tools (https://github.com/facebook/ ktfmt; https://github.com/fbsamples/kotlin_ast_tools)

> **NOTE**   This one is the single most practical "We Rewrote It" blog post I've ever seen. Congrats!

Assuming that the rewrite is considered a success and the authors want to encourage their peers to follow suit, it makes sense that they provide readers a useful toolkit to start with.

9.4.3   *Tremendously templated structure*

Although there's unfortunately no easy-to-follow recipe for pulling off a successful rewrite, there *is* one for writing a blog post about it. Given the continued popularity of these posts on sites like Hacker News, the standard formula works, so why reinvent the wheel?

The standard "We Rewrote It in X" blog post contains the following elements, usually in the precise order listed:

- *Templated title*—The title always includes the new language name and usually uses some form of "rewrote," "moved," "switched," or "migrated." The minimalist "We Rewrote It in X" is used quite a bit. Some opt to define the "we" and call out the original language (especially if it is remarkably old and/or impressively complex). This gives you something like "Why ACME moved from COBOL to Zig."
- *What are we doing here*—A little background on the project. For example, how long it's been around, how it's evolved, who it serves, what's most important (e.g., ability to iterate fast, achieving crazy low latencies, or something else entirely).
- *Why it's time to move on*—This is often a proactive response to positive problems such as catastrophic success (e.g., "Our original Typescript server served us well for a few years, but now our service is so popular that we needed to rewrite it in Rust"). Sometimes it's because the original language turned out to be a poor fit for the project and the team couldn't bear it any longer. And it's occasionally because someone on the team wanted an excuse to play with a shiny new language, but that's not usually written.
- *Also ran*—Covers what other options were considered and why they didn't make the cut. It's usually fairly brief, keeping the article's focus on the dearly departed old language and the fascinating new one.
- *Meet the new language*—This is the section where we learn why they chose the new language and all the greatness that it has to offer. As noted above, this is often targeted to people new to that particular language and can be conveniently skipped by those who are already sold on it.
- *Migration nuts and bolts*—Here's where you get most of the practical elements referenced in the previous section: all the challenges faced and the tools and strategies used to move past them.
- *The verdict*—Did the gain outweigh the pain? This is the place where authors reflect on the overall process and maybe showcase some specific effects, quantitative (benchmarks) or qualitative (happier and more agile teams).

- *Join us*—A not-so-subtle reminder that the team is on the forefront of innovation and that they would love for interested readers to join them (insert link to careers page).

The "We Rewrote It in X" pattern is by far the most predictable of all the patterns covered in this book. And it's also why Saagar Jha's parody is such a brilliant and hilarious read.

9.5 *Dos and don'ts*

Writing your own "We Rewrote It in X" blog post is a great opportunity to validate whether the rewrite is justified, show a few tricks you're particularly proud of, and add a tribute or two to the new language's authors and maintainers.

These blog posts are typically written and published after the rewrite is deemed done, ideally with some reportable results demonstrating that it was indeed worth it. You could feasibly start writing at any point during or after the rewrite process. If you start writing about it early, you could even turn it into a whole series of blog posts. For example, you could write "Why We're Rewriting It in X" once you've made the decision, "How We're Rewriting It in X" as you're in the middle of the rewrite, and "Our X Rewrite: Results and the Verdict" after it's completed. Of course, if your team's rewrite turns out to be an utter disaster, you might regret having told the world about it. On the bright side, the resulting "Our Failed X Rewrite: Lessons Learned" blog post could make for a gripping read!

Here are some tips to keep in mind while writing your own "We Rewrote It in X" blog post.

9.5.1 *Start by explaining your rewrite motivation*

Pointless rewrites from one language to another are a plague. The internet is already full of half-baked rewrites of popular open source projects, long abandoned and forgotten. Rewriting a project "just because" usually doesn't warrant a blog post about the experience—unless the rewrite yielded some surprising and absolutely stunning benefits that the author never anticipated.

Be aware that there's a good chance your average reader is a programmer who's sick of telling junior colleagues that even though the new language is really shiny and groundbreaking, they shouldn't just go ahead and rewrite everything in it. By explaining your motivation thoroughly, including specific technical reasons, you calm that average reader down and perhaps earn his readership for a few minutes. You might win him over on the value of migration, or you might provide him additional ammunition for his anti-rewrite campaign.

If you're considering writing a "We Rewrote It in X" blog post, try to write (at least) one convincing paragraph justifying the rewrite. If you have trouble with this task, you might want to reconsider writing on this topic. If you're able to write something interesting, fantastic! That's an indication that the rewrite has merit, and should make for an interesting read. Bonus: now you've already got your blog post started.

A few sample questions to ask yourself:

- Why did you (or someone else) select the original language?
- Why did you decide to ditch it?
- What alternatives did you consider?

Your answers to the above questions can help you populate the explanation paragraph (or an even lengthier justification section).

9.5.2   Provide background on your project

Sounds obvious, right? But it's often overlooked in practice. Authors of "We Rewrote It in X" blog posts sometimes get so caught up in the marvels of the new language that they end up delivering a paean of the language's features instead of a down-to-earth analysis of how it helped their project. Remember that if someone clicks your "We Rewrote It in X" post, it's because they want to learn why and how your specific team (the "we" part of the title) made this shift. If they wanted to read a generic profusion of praise for a language, they could simply get that through AI (e.g., "Tell me why X is so great.").

> **NOTE**   If you really want to focus on sharing your praise for a language, that's fine. Just don't mislead readers who expect a "We Rewrote It in X" post. Write it up as a "Thoughts on Trends" pattern type of post instead (covered in chapter 12). And make sure it's not as generic as something from generative AI.

Across patterns, sharing project context is a key element for making blog posts appealing and distinctive. Readers with similar experiences to yours are naturally curious about how you approached common challenges—and, of course, evaluating who did it better. At the same time, readers working in different worlds want to keep tabs on what's happening across the wide wide world of engineering, beyond their day-to-day duties. Providing context about what you're working on and why helps stir up emotion—be it empathy, envy, arrogance, or something else—and that will help get your blog post read.

Project context is particularly important for the "We Rewrote It in X" pattern because the decision of what language to select depends so heavily upon the project's technical requirements. For example, while Rust is a reasonable choice for implementing a highly efficient database, it's likely to be counterproductive for frontend development. A very good way of introducing that project perspective is to dedicate the first section of the blog to describing *your* case and explaining what motivated your specific rewrite.

9.5.3   Don't gloss over the rough parts

Technical blog post readers are generally not a trusting lot. If all they see is advantages and excitement, they are likely to immediately dismiss your blog post as a marketing piece (or a thinly veiled engineering recruitment attempt, at best). Interesting technical details might help, but that assumes that your readers actually reach those details. More likely, they will have already left the blog post and switched to another browser tab.

Statistically, it's highly unlikely that every aspect of a real-world production rewrite was completely smooth. Really, you encountered *zero* challenges—with the language itself, or its tooling, dependency management, state of its documentation, and similar? Balancing pros and cons is important to make the blog look credible (as well as to help your readers learn, of course).

Be fully transparent about the things that went wrong (unless your dear superiors object, of course—again, it's better to ask permission than forgiveness in these matters). In particular, list all the caveats and footguns you experienced when rewriting software from language A to B, as well as how you dealt with them. Some of your readers, even those who have already weathered other types of rewrites, might not be aware that a naive rewrite from A to B can cause subtle problems such as inefficient memory management or undefined behavior in their applications. If your blog post makes them realize that they need to step back and check all the millions of lines of code they've already rewritten to look for a new class of errors, you helped reduce the total number of software bugs in this world. Thanks!

Moreover, constructive criticism of a new and/or rising language is generally welcome in technical blog posts. If you draw attention to practical problems with the language, you get them on the community radar, increasing the chance that the language's maintainers might recognize and fix them.

9.5.4 *Share the resources you used*

A rundown of any and all resources you found helpful during the rewrite (or conversely, the ones you found embarrassingly unhelpful) could be priceless to others who are considering a similar rewrite. "We Rewrote It in X" articles are expected to be both entertaining (reading about somebody else's failures) and educational (learning from somebody else's mistakes). A list of the resources that you tried to tap, annotated with your candid commentary on each, could help you accomplish both. Or take the high road and just focus on highlighting the resources that were most valuable—whatever you're comfortable with.

A simple bulleted list with a sentence or two commentary on why you found each item helpful (or not) would help readers navigate the vast sea of resources. It could also save them hours of scanning through search-engine-optimized results to unearth the handful of hidden gems that truly add value.

In addition to helping your readers, a positive endorsement here is a nice way to share your appreciation for the people behind the resources you relied on. Whether they developed a really cool tool or wrote a detailed article that saved you from some nasty mistake, they deserve a bit of public praise and positive feedback.

Summary

- The "We Rewrote It in X" pattern became (in)famous lately during a surge of Rust rewrites.
- Blog posts in this pattern promote both the rewritten project and its new language, library, or framework.

- Readers interested in adopting the new language are a primary audience, and the new language's authors and maintainers are likely to read for constructive criticism.
- "We Rewrote It in X" blog posts are typically suitable for those new to the new language and full of practical tips, code snippets, and tools; they're also rather formulaic in structure.
- Top tips:
  - Provide a good rationale for the rewrite: what's wrong with the old language, why the new language solves the problems, and which alternatives were considered and discarded.
  - Explain your project's goals and technical requirements upfront.
  - Don't gloss over the road bumps or headaches, or else the post will be dismissed as too promotional.
  - Pay it forward by sharing what resources helped you and why.

The "How We Built It" pattern

This chapter covers

- Blog posts that share your most impressive engineering achievements
- Their purpose and audience
- How various authors approached this type of post
- Key elements of successful "How We Built It" posts
- Dos and don'ts for your own "How We Built It" post

Engineers are natural builders, a curious and constantly tinkering bunch. When we're not scratching that itch by building something ourselves, it's always fun to see what others are building—for pragmatic learning, inspiration, and really just pure discovery.

First and foremost, engineers writing about how they built things creates a valuable knowledge base for the community, brick by brick (pun intended). Such blog posts might be triggered by a range of experiments and achievements:

- Using a rising technology as one of the early adopters. For example,

- A new database specialized for a niche (e.g., adopting the TigerBeetle database for your brand-new banking system)
- A new framework for creating web pages (e.g., Rust's Leptos)
- A new programming language (e.g., writing your software in Zig)
- Successfully using the same technology (e.g., Postgres) for decades
- Using a novel system architecture (e.g., one trying to serve billions of users)
- Improving an existing architecture to cut cloud costs by millions of dollars per year
- Implementing an algorithm previously known only from academic papers
- Inventing a new algorithm (or improving an existing one) and implementing it

These blog posts are sometimes published in a multipart series because the building process, just like the situation on actual construction sites, can take years. They are sometimes cryptic on details (to avoid helping the competition too much) but at the same time informative enough to give readers a general idea of how a successful system can be built.

10.1   Purpose

The "How We Built It" pattern is often (at its essence) an abbreviation for "How We Built It Better Than Anybody Ever Imagined Possible." That brings us to the first purpose on the list.

10.1.1 Pioneering

Writing a detailed article on a technical innovation is a great tool for establishing leadership. If you describe a particular idea first, you earn a long-lasting legacy as the pioneer. That gives your project (or the whole company) extra visibility. Now, whenever somebody mentions that new algorithm, they're going to associate it with you.

Note that the innovation doesn't have to be a mathematical breakthrough worthy of the Millennium Prize. On the contrary, it can be a small improvement to a decades-old algorithm that works great for your particular use case. It can also be an unusual setup for an existing technology (e.g., running your entire storage infrastructure on a fleet of used corporate laptops with discounted USB sticks). Any unusual decision, be it architectural or algorithmic, can be the one that earns you recognition as an inventor or early adopter.

10.1.2 Flexing muscles

Publicly sharing how a product was built is a not-so-subtle way of highlighting how much better it is than any of its alternatives. That usually sends the following messages:

- Proof that the authors believe their solution is incomparably better than any existing solutions. It can be a literal mathematical proof or just an architectural design backed by tests, model checkers, and benchmarks.
- A healthy amount of confidence that even though the authors are hereby sharing the recipe for success, they're still pioneers and experts in the matter (which makes their product a default choice).

Describing a novel way of solving a problem is also simply a nice gesture. Readers tend to appreciate the authors' transparency, as opposed to keeping interesting ideas as corporate secrets. To sum up, writing an article on an interesting way of building something makes you look smart and confident—what's not to like?

10.1.3 Free peer review

One thing is certain after publishing a "How We Built It" blog post: it will ignite a spirited comment section discussion on why another approach is actually much better. After filtering out the snarky comments (and ones that just blindly recommend using Postgres without even reading the article first), what's left is hopefully a fair dose of constructive criticism.

A few examples of valuable comments are

- Pointing out a known security problem with one of the libraries used for the project, as well as which dependencies should be upgraded to avoid problems
- Suggesting that the team switch from one of the services they're relying on to a compatible one that's more modern and cost-efficient
- Recommending a tool for improving the project's test coverage
- Pointing out a bug in the academic paper that the implementation was based on (yes, it really happens; see Avinash's case: https://mng.bz/gAEn

- Suggesting how to improve the project's performance just by tweaking the database configuration

Not many people are fans of unsolicited advice, but publishing a "How We Built It" article is often seen as a broadcasted review request.

10.2   Audience

"How We Built It" blog posts may appeal to a mixed lot:

- Developers of similar projects, who might be interested in implementation details, design decisions, and architecture. They may come looking for inspiration to creatively "borrow" the intriguing bits back into their projects.
- General tech enthusiasts, who enjoy learning about the latest tools, frameworks, and techniques used in real-world projects. They may not be professionals in this particular field, but they're eager to expand their knowledge far and wide.
- Startup founders and investors, who are interested in learning from other teams' approaches as they feel out potential new opportunities. They can use these blog posts to assess whether there's room for yet another approach (theirs!) in this niche and to inform their own teams about what the competition is up to (refer back to the first bullet point).
- STEM students, Ph.D. candidates, and post-docs, who are all still in the habit of reading scientific papers and exploring new algorithms.
- Users of the product, driven by curiosity to deeply understand why the thing they use works the way it does.

10.3   Examples of "How We Built It" blog posts

Most popular blog posts about building new things come from large companies. Yes, the mere mention of a recognizable logo does help reach a broader audience. But it's more than that. Projects from large companies naturally involve an impressive scale that piques the curiosity of every engineer. It's inherently more interesting to learn how Amazon coordinates updates for over 8,000 device types than to read a post about somebody successfully coordinating updates for his two Raspberry Pis.

Of course, that's not a hard rule. There are lots of intriguing "How I Built It at Home" blog posts out there, as well as impressive "How We Built It Even Though We're Just a Humble Bootstrapped Startup" posts, so don't let that discourage you. We just wanted to explain in advance why this examples section is dominated by stories showcasing impressive scale!

Here are some prime examples of blog posts that apply the "How We Built It" pattern, along with Piotr's commentary on each.

10.3.1   *How Prime Video Updates its App for More Than 8,000 Device Types*

Author: Alexandru Ene
Source: Amazon Science Blog (https://mng.bz/eVWZ)

SUMMARY

The article explains how Amazon updates its entertainment system for all the devices it supports. There are over 8,000 distinct types of devices, ranging from gaming consoles to USB streaming sticks. Each device has its own hardware and architecture, which creates quite a technical challenge.

The introduction praises WebAssembly and mentions that this technology enabled a substantial performance boost. The body of the article kicks off by explaining the system's specific architecture, split into a performance-oriented part and a lightweight easy-to-update-often part. Then there's an explanation of the new architecture, which is partially based on WebAssembly. The author sheds light on how the switch to the new code was performed without breaking backward compatibility. Finally, the article wraps by detailing the impressive performance and space utilization improvement—and also adding a short "thank you" note to the Rust and WebAssembly communities.

COMMENTARY

The first brilliant move by the author is already in the title—mentioning "over 8,000 device types" introduces an impressive level of awe. The article is full of interesting insights, including architecture graphs and references to used tools (e.g., egui and a Rust GUI library). I also really appreciate the anecdote explaining how they needed to implement some of the bugs from their previous architecture because existing users relied on those edge cases—reminds me of https://xkcd.com/1172/. It's written in a conversational tone, and yet it's full of technical and educational details. Overall, a very enjoyable read.

10.3.2 Twitter's Recommendation Algorithm

Author: The Twitter Team
Source: X Engineering Blog (https://mng.bz/pxA0)

SUMMARY

This blog post explains the technical and architectural details of Twitter's algorithm for selecting which Tweets to show users. The recommendation algorithm is split into stages:

1. Candidate sourcing
2. Ranking
3. Heuristics and filters

Each stage is explained with a dedicated section including links to Twitter's own academic papers presenting research on recommendation algorithms. Also, for full transparency, Twitter open sourced its algorithm's implementation; the article mentions this and shares the link to the open source code repository. And the customary "We're hiring—apply for a job" invitation is tacked on after the conclusion.

COMMENTARY

Casually mentioning that you're a tech giant in charge of one of the largest social networks worldwide is a great hook for a catchy title. This particular title is also short and intriguing, which sets a high bar for the contents.

The contents don't disappoint. On the contrary, they exceed expectations for a few reasons:

- The hyperlinks lead either to academic papers or open source repositories. I was sufficiently impressed after seeing that the first hyperlink was a scientific paper (Real Graph), and then the second one led to a paper as well (GraphJet), then the third (SimClusters)…

- The article is heavy on technical details, but those are often hidden under the aforementioned links to academic papers. The main flow is quite simple to understand, even for people not experienced in social networks, graphs, or machine learning.

- Images and text are perfectly balanced to give readers' eyes a well-deserved break after every few paragraphs.

- The article contains lots of meaningful numbers, which also emphasizes the scale at which Twitter operates. For example, "The pipeline above runs approximately 5 billion times per day and completes in under 1.5 seconds on average."

The cherry on top is open-sourcing the entire algorithm, which breaks a pattern that tech giants often follow when "publishing" their ideas. The pattern is to do *only* one of the following:

- Release a huge amount of open source code
- Thoroughly explain the architecture and design decisions

As a result, the "great idea" is unusable because

- Nobody can really understand the code without enough context and documentation, or
- (When the code isn't released) People are left trying to implement it based on a bunch of scientific papers, which often conveniently leave the hardest implementation details as an "exercise for the reader."

In this article, Twitter both explained and released the code. That's admirable.

10.3.3 How We Built Notification Rate Limiter for Eight Billion Notifications Per Day for 400 Million Monthly Active Users

Authors: Akshit Verma and Ayush Gupta
Source: ShareChat Blog (https://mng.bz/Om5O)

SUMMARY

The article describes how to implement a system for handling user notifications in a mobile app at a large scale (for hundreds of millions of users). After describing why a rate limiter is required, the authors delineate the challenges to overcome when building such a system. Two choices for overcoming these challenges are presented: one for the rate limiter algorithm and one for the underlying database. Then, they explain the reasoning behind why they selected their approach (a combination of both fixed window rate limiting and event-based paradigms). The next section, "Design & Implementation," covers the chosen database schema and implementation details. The article concludes with a rationale for why the solution is considered fast and scalable. There's also a glossary at the end, explaining a few niche terms.

COMMENTARY

The title of this one is four lines long, so it's quite a hog compared to the succinct title in the Twitter example. On the other hand, it shows interesting numbers (two of them), which is a nice touch.

The article itself features lots of specific technical details such as concrete database schemas. That encourages users to try and implement similar systems themselves. It's nice to see in a blog post.

Initially, I was also grateful that the authors provided a glossary at the end. But ultimately, the unexplained acronyms and niche words are my number one problem with the article. The first few terms I needed to look up were DAU (presumably Daily Active Users), OKR (presumably Objectives and Key Results), and FCM (presumably Firebase Cloud Messaging). I was especially amused by the fact that I found FCM in the glossary, but it was mentioned only to explain yet another niche term. Another minor problem is the images; they're a bit too detailed for the template's display size, which makes them difficult to read. Fortunately, you can just click them to open a full-sized image, which is a viable workaround. Overall, it's still a solid example of a "How We Built It" blog post, especially because users can immediately try out the database schemas in their own setups.

10.3.4 *How We Built Scalable Spatial Data and Spatial Indexing in CockroachDB*

Author: Sumeer Bhola
Source: CockroachLabs Blog (https://www.cockroachlabs.com/blog/how-we-built-spatial-indexing/)

SUMMARY

The blog post describes CockroachDB's implementation of spatial indexing, a feature customarily used for geographical searches (e.g., "Am I in Pruszków right now?", or "Is this restaurant nearby?"). It explains two of the most popular techniques for spatial indexing, namely dividing the objects (e.g., geographical locations) into smaller areas, or dividing the space itself. The article further explains that the latter approach (dividing the space) better fits CockroachDB's architecture, and that's why it was chosen. The article dives into the index's implementation details and how the database had to change to accommodate it (for example, a new distributed query processor was developed). The article concludes with a detailed list of roadmap items related to the feature.

COMMENTARY

First things first: the title. It's not very exciting, but it is self-explanatory. It wouldn't jump out at the average reader, but it is well-suited for the target audience:

- Anyone looking for a database with spatial indexing support

- Anyone interested in implementing their own spatial indexing
- CockroachDB users who are eager to learn about new database features

The article is a helpful spatial indexing primer. It introduces the idea, explains the most popular approaches, and shares implementation details with respect to CockroachDB. It educates readers without gratuitous promotion of CockroachDB. You can walk away with a good grasp of spatial indexing implementation, even if you don't really care about using CockroachDB.

The visualizations are key for explaining the algorithms. Spatial indexing algorithms work with two-dimensional data, and that's much harder to imagine and visualize in your brain than the one-dimensional arrays that programmers' brains are accustomed to (my brain, at least). The visualization based on a real-life map of Paris and its suburbs is an especially nice touch, showing how this technology can be put into practice.

The roadmap items are a little confusing for a spatial indexing newbie (again, me), but I felt fully excused to ignore them and take pride in the fact I'm now loosely aware of what practical geographical algorithms look like.

10.3.5 *Ship Shape*

Authors: Kerry Halupka, Rowan Katekar
Source: Canva Engineering Blog (https://mng.bz/GNJ8)

SUMMARY

The article describes how Canva implemented a real-time shape recognition feature that works entirely in the browser. The authors explain the previous implementation (computer vision heuristics), followed by its limitations and rationale for a new approach: applying a machine learning model. The idea is explained in detail, including the algorithms they used and their parameters. The article concludes by stating that the feature is a great success, followed by acknowledgments.

COMMENTARY

Brilliant. I'm tempted to stop the commentary right there, but let me dive into more detailed praise. The title is brilliant because it's two syllables long and very intriguing. I'd say it was specifically optimized for landing on the front page of Hacker News, knowing full well that only a very composed individual could resist the urge to click the title and figure out what it means.

The next brilliant thing is the images, which isn't a surprise given that Canva's flagship product is an online graphic design tool. The images are engaging and really help readers grasp the presented ideas, even without reading the paragraphs explaining them.

The technical details go very deep for somebody not experienced with machine learning (e.g., me) and the article includes hyperlinks to algorithm descriptions for those who want to go even deeper. I don't think those details are required to understand the main flow, though. I felt that I understood the model based on the images and text in the main article (but maybe that was just a comfy illusion and I was deluding myself).

Either way, reading the article left me feeling a little smarter regarding machine learning. The numbers are quite impressive, too: the model fits into 250 kilobytes, with the accompanying implementation of 300 lines of code and running under 10 milliseconds on a laptop.

10.4 Characteristics

"How We Built It" articles featuring the most impressive feats (e.g., unique industry-shaping approaches, novel approaches to commonly experienced challenges, or solutions accommodating extreme needs and scale) tend to feature the following characteristics:

- They offer practical tidbits although the achievement is likely still not easily reproducible.
- Nevertheless, they create an interesting and valuable industry knowledge base.
- They're more formal than the average blog post, adopting the majestic plural (also known as "royal we").
- Expecting (at least) their fifteen minutes of fame, they anticipate and answer the most likely questions and objections.

Let's cover each in turn.

10.4.1 Not always reproducible

"How We Built It" articles are often full of practical tidbits like code snippets, the tools used, and diagrams. However, that doesn't mean the reader will be able to achieve the same result even after a thorough study of the article. In fact, those most willing to share are often those most confident it won't help the competition in any substantial way.

The extended subcategories of this pattern include:

- How We Built It Because We Are a Huge Company with Lots of Resources
- How We Built It Because We Needed to Scale for Millions of Users
- How We Built It on Top of Our Closed Source Tech Stack
- How We Built It After Years of Confidential Research

The contents of all those articles can still be immensely educational though, which leads to the next section.

10.4.2 Serve as a knowledge base

A long journey precedes the point where it's feasible to publish a "How We Built It" blog post. Along the way, the author(s) discovered useful resources, tried different approaches, and evaluated related projects and tools. That's all deeply practical knowledge, often applicable to projects that are barely, if at all, related to the titular "built" project. A nonexhaustive list of interesting things one can find in a "How We Built It" blog post includes

- References to academic papers
- Practical tips about a programming language (e.g., "how to efficiently manage short-lived memory in Zig")
- Practical tips about a specific tool (e.g., "how not to lose your mind trying to manage Kubernetes via its command-line interface")
- Approaches to planning and executing a long-term project

The important bit is that the knowledge is often general, in the "good to know" category. That makes the "How We Built It" articles worth reading even for people not directly involved with the described technology.

10.4.3 *Pluralis maiestatis*

"How We Built It" blog posts tend to have a slightly more formal tone than other patterns like the Bug Hunt. As the name of the pattern suggests, the use of majestic plural is prevalent. Instead of informal jokes and digressions, these posts are commonly characterized by a pristine storyline and an extensive list of acknowledgments at the end.

Of course, those rules are not set in stone, but they come naturally because the author (or, more often, authors) usually represent the whole company, or at least a team of relentless programmers and researchers who made the venture possible. The blog post examples discussed in this chapter are actually the following:

- How we, the Amazon Web Services team, built…
- How we, the Twitter folks, built…
- How we, at ShareChat, built…
- How we, the CockroachDB team, built…
- How we, Canva engineers, built…

Since speaking on behalf of a whole company is a weighty responsibility, it makes sense that the authors adopt a somewhat formal tone to rise to the occasion.

10.4.4 *inb4*

"How We Built It" articles often include baked-in responses to the questions that the curious and critical masses are likely to ask, suggesting that the authors anticipate their blog post will be popular enough to spark heated online discussions. They are usually correct. Even if they're not, the preemptive responses create a FAQ section that makes the article more interactive.

When the authors assume that their articles will be relentlessly reviewed by lots of professional and unprofessional online critics, they provide the following upfront:

- Extensive explanations of why a decision was made, especially if it wasn't an obvious (e.g., "industry standard") choice.
- A list of previous attempts, along with short notes on why they failed.
- Bold challenges to things once considered "common knowledge" or "good practice." Noting that times and technology have changed, the author shares reasons

and options for moving beyond the accepted ways (which are now diplomatically deemed "legacy.")

- A short note backlinking to the online discussion as it unfolds. This isn't published right away, but it's often popped into the article the second it gains traction and ends up on a front page somewhere.

All of these make the articles look fresh and more personal. Lots of readers question the nonobvious choices made by blog post authors. When the nonobvious choice is followed by a rationale starting with "You might wonder why we decided...," the readers are likely to appreciate it and give the authors extra credit for their clairvoyance.

10.5 Dos and don'ts

If you're the one designated to drive the "How We Built It" post for your team's latest achievements, congratulations! Consider it an honor. But be sure to set your expectations appropriately. This isn't something you can (or should) knock off in a day, given the planning, graphics, approvals, and whatnot that will be required. By all means, get started right away. But also be patient. This is likely to be a work you feature on your CV/resume. Take the time needed to fully think through everything from the initial scope to the comment section response.

10.5.1 Agree on the scope early

Blog posts describing how things were built are often written on behalf of the company, assuming that whatever's written in the article is also officially endorsed. To avoid misunderstandings, it's good practice to discuss the scope of the article first:

- What's alright to reveal
- What's legally not alright to reveal
- What's tactically not alright to reveal

Educating others is truly a worthwhile goal. But in reality, you can't risk publishing blog post content that's not acceptable to whoever the titular "we" actually refers to.

10.5.2 Make graphics a first-class citizen

When writing an article on how things were built, it's important to avoid the author's skew: decisions, design, and all kinds of details are much less obvious for people who didn't write the code. In that case, it's a good idea to outsource part of the explanation process to the readers' occipital lobes. In other words, make sure your blog post abounds in colorful images and graphs.

Diagrams make it easy to visualize the architecture of a complex system or a nonintuitive algorithm, which the article is most likely about. (If it isn't, it doesn't bode well; it seems the most popular "How We Built It" blog posts are about something grand, groundbreaking, unintuitive, or otherwise impressive). At the same time, those same readers would prefer to have the details laid out as simply as possible. Images, graphs, diagrams, and even screenshots are a good compromise for being educational versus too complicated to understand.

10.5.3 *Don't rush it*

"How We Built It" articles tend to describe a long-term project that took an uncanny amount of effort to complete. Unless there's pressure to publish as soon as possible, don't. Blog posts of this kind deserve at least a fraction of the meticulousness the project received. With the hardest part (coding, deploying, designing, formally proving correctness, you name it) completed, it might be tempting to brag about the results immediately. However, a sloppy blog post including mistakes such as

- Incorrect links to references
- Logical fallacies
- Code samples with old bugs, even if already fixed in the linked repository
- Typos (yes, really!)

may diminish the grand moment of showing the world the achievement. People will notice, and they will also bring it up online, which brings us to the next subsection.

10.5.4 *Prepare for (un)constructive criticism*

As mentioned in section 10.4, anticipating future questions and undermining attempts is especially important in this pattern. On top of that, it's advised to brace for a heated online flamewar. The following things can help:

- Show the blog post's beta version to a limited trusted audience (e.g., all colleagues) and ask for a brutal and nitpicky review.
- Prepare a list of questions that might come up but are at the same time petty enough to omit from the article. Then, prepare answers to those questions upfront.
- Carefully plan the blog publication time and ensure that everyone is ready for a discussion the minute it lands on a front page.
- Periodically monitor the likely front pages (Hacker News, lobste.rs, subreddits, etc.) so you don't miss the opportunity to officially insult other people online as the blog post's author. And jokes aside, the discussion is likely to last only for a couple of minutes and then move on to the next hot thing. It's a shame to miss it; sometimes, it's actually informative!

Summary

- Writing a "How We Built It" blog post is a great opportunity to share your greatest engineering feats with the world.
- Readers always love insight into how some well-known company achieved something impressive at scale, but a blog post about a smaller startup victory or weekend project can also trend as long as it's intriguing.
- Such blog posts tend to have a more formal air than most (especially if written on behalf of a team), anticipate lively online discussions, and share with extreme

care (avoiding anything that might compromise a precarious competitive advantage).

- Top tips:
  - Get early consensus on what (if anything) is acceptable to share.
  - Use visuals to help the reader efficiently grasp the algorithms, system architecture, or other achievements—at a high level, at least.
  - Know that the planning, review, and approval process might take longer than for other types of blog posts due to the importance of the topic and the number of stakeholders involved.
  - Prepare for a heated online flamewar: preemptively answer questions in the blog if applicable and/or rally the troops to respond after it's published.

The "Lessons Learned" pattern

This chapter covers

- Blog posts that share lessons learned from technical challenges
- Their purpose and audience
- How various authors approached this type of post
- Key elements of successful "Lessons Learned" posts
- Dos and don'ts for your own "Lessons Learned" post

Attention, aspiring technical influencers: this is the chapter for you! The "Lessons Learned" pattern is all about sharing your personal experiences and process of drawing conclusions from your trials and errors. It is the perfect starter engineering blog post because the only real requirement is having encountered a technical problem of any sort.

Technical audiences love to learn. And one of the few things they love even more than learning itself is learning from other people's mistakes instead of their own. "Lessons Learned" posts often contain condensed knowledge about how somebody else dealt with a problem. This is something many readers hold dear because it's a lightweight version of having a mentor who can walk you through a problem.

Start with a humble "Lessons Learned" post, and you'll be serially applying the "Thoughts on Trends" pattern (chapter 12) like a professional industry luminary in no time! (Conditions apply: "no time" is a euphemism for "sometimes a considerable amount of time, if ever.")

11.1 Purpose

People have been recording their personal experiences for ages. "Lessons Learned" blog posts serve a similar purpose as the good old diary, letter, or folktale. For the author, the process of recording, pondering, and structuring past experiences can be enlightening and cathartic. And their audience can simply sit back, grab some popcorn, and learn from others' struggles.

11.1.1 Self-reflection

One of the best ways to learn from your actions (especially mistakes) is to write down your experiences early, while all the details are still fresh in your memory. There are several benefits to doing that:

- Because your actions are recorded, you can review them in retrospect a bit more objectively after some time has passed. At that point, you're likely to notice patterns and details you initially overlooked—so you can continue learning from that initial mistake.

- Memory gets skewed over time, so writing down all details and reflections early tends to make them more realistic than how they're remembered after a few days or weeks. It's even better to cross-check both the on-paper version and the in-brain one!

- Writing down your experiences includes more than producing a stream of text; it also might involve creating diagrams, side notes, arrows pointing from one paragraph to another and forming a complex graph of thought patterns, underlining important bits, and so on. All of this helps organize the experience and prepare it for scrutiny.

Once you complete those notes, it's probably easy to convert them into a nice educational blog post, images included! Some of the best articles on lessons learned include hand-drawn diagrams; that's not a coincidence but rather a natural consequence of how they came into existence.

11.1.2 Storytelling

Writing about the lessons life has taught you is a unique grandfatherly experience. Sharing your experiences in a way that helps others avoid your mistakes simply feels good—and for a good reason. As with articles in the "Bug Hunt" pattern, you're helping your readers save time and maintain their mental well-being if they ever find themselves in similar distress. Also, the fact that you're now sharing this story gives you a great excuse to subtly color it—leaving all the technical details intact of course, but perhaps sharing perspectives, commentary, and anecdotes that make it more enjoyable and engaging.

11.1.3 Kickstart

As noted in the introduction, "Lessons Learned" is the perfect pattern to follow as you begin your journey as a writer. Virtually anyone with some interesting lessons in their portfolio (so any programmer) meets the prerequisites for a "Lessons Learned" blog post. This pattern has a much lower barrier to entry than "How We Built It," which requires something to be built first, and "Thoughts on Trends," which requires a certain level of recognized expertise. In most cases, there's simply no excuse *not* to write at least one article following the "Lessons Learned" pattern in your lifetime, so you may just as well check that box early!

11.2 Audience

There are two main classes of audience for "Lessons Learned" posts:

- The technical equivalent of a circle of children sitting around you and listening to your wise, personal story from the old times, full of wonder and delight—that is, anybody interested in knowing your experience on the subject.

- Professionals from related fields (e.g., programmers working on similar projects and DevOps folks using the same database) who likely need exactly this kind of lesson—so they can file it away for some time in the future or to cross-check against their own experience with a similar problem.

This pattern is quite general and likely to be read by a whole spectrum of readers. It's usually light, engaging, and occasionally humorous, which makes it a perfect read between compilations.

11.3 Examples of "Lessons Learned" blog posts

Databases play an important role in the programming world, being a scapegoat for all too many production failures worldwide. Catastrophic events are commonly related to databases in one way or another: being unable to connect to one, overloading the database, getting malformed data from it, and so forth. Thus, it shouldn't be a surprise that so many compelling "Lessons Learned" pattern examples are database-centric!

Here are some prime examples of blog posts that apply the "Lessons Learned" pattern, along with Piotr's commentary on each.

11.3.1 25% or 6 to 4: The 11/6/23 Authentication Outage

Author: Mark Smith

Source: Discord Blog (https://discord.com/blog/authentication-outage)

SUMMARY

This blog post is a post-mortem analysis of an authentication system outage at Discord. It begins with a disclaimer that it was an outage, not a bug. While service availability was affected, no security breach occurred. Next, the article presents an overview of Discord's authentication layer architecture.

The main part of the article is a detailed log of how the degradation was

1 Discovered
2 Investigated
3 Diagnosed
4 Fixed

The log entries are annotated with the exact minute they occurred. They are also intertwined with screenshots from observability tools to visualize the investigation progress. The post concludes with lessons learned and potential plans for implementing prevention mechanisms to ensure similar situations are properly handled next time they happen.

COMMENTARY

On the title front, it's interesting to note that this blog post's canonical link is shorter than its actual title, without using any link shorteners. To be extra picky, "Authentication Outage" is a nice title with a simple, yet powerful message. Once most people see those words associated with the discord.com URL, they're in. Also, I didn't originally get all the out-of-context digits in the title. I later learned that it's actually a reference to a song by the rock band Chicago.

Nitpicks aside, this is a rock-solid technical article. The introduction lets readers peek into the architectural decisions of a massive production-grade messaging system, providing educational value from the start. The absolute best part is the detailed log with timestamps. It really keeps the tension building, like watching one of those thriller movies where every few minutes you see that "HOUR 5. STILL NO SIGN OF THE ABDUCTEE" interlude. It's enjoyable to track the team's progress in real time, experiencing how fast decisions need to be made to restore the service's availability. The stakes are quite high, with Discord and its ever-growing user base. The lessons learned and future plans look well-thought-out and structured.

This article is in many ways similar to the "Bug Hunt" pattern. There's an introduction, a mystery, an investigation, and (in a way) a fix. It's not a complete fit, though. The outage wasn't caused by a software bug. Rather, it stemmed from a series of infrastructure decisions that in hindsight might be called "negligence" but in practice were borderline impossible to predict. Also, the fix was not a single breakthrough, but rather a series of actions taken to alleviate the problem—and partially just waiting for the system to recover. And while every second counted with a Discord availability problem, bugs in "Bug Hunt" blog posts are usually not investigated under such intense time pressure. Thus, this article fits better into the slightly broader "Lessons Learned" category.

11.3.2 *Herding Elephants: Lessons Learned from Sharding Postgres at Notion*

Author: Garrett Fidalgo

Source: Notion Blog (https://www.notion.so/blog/sharding-postgres-at-notion)

SUMMARY

This article describes Notion's process of migrating from a single monolith database to a sharded setup. It starts by announcing the success early, establishing that the whole process went smoothly and that Notion's users are happy with the result. Stepping back a bit, the article then explains what sharding is and how Notion decided to apply it. The author covers

- Which data to split into smaller sets
- How to categorize the data (in database nomenclature, "what's the partition key")
- How many logical shards and physical databases should be created

He also describes their strategy to avoid prolonged downtime by using techniques such as double writes, backfilling, and integrity checks. The article wraps up with a paragraph that lists lessons learned during the process.

COMMENTARY

Another title longer than the blog post's URL! This title is rather compelling though. It's a nice example of balancing catchiness and details by using two elements:

- A main title that's short and intriguing
- A subtitle that explains what the article is actually about

The body of the article covers many of the things technical readers enjoy in a blog post: lots of technical details, easy-to-grasp pictures, and interludes explaining the decisions in more detail.

Another interesting point to note: despite its "Lessons Learned" title, it's actually a solid example of the "How We Built It" pattern. Still, we wanted to put its summary and commentary here for two reasons. First, it's futile to try and classify every single blog post into one of the handful of patterns we chose to cover in this book. Many fantastic blog posts do not fit into any of them, and some share elements of multiple patterns. Second, the concluding paragraph is actually a nice, compressed example of a mini "Lessons Learned" blog post. In fact, it could also serve as a very good first working draft for a full-fledged "Lessons Learned" article.

11.3.3 *Something You Probably Want to Know About if You're Using SQLite in Golang*

Author: Piotr Jastrzębski
Source: Turso Blog (https://mng.bz/XVMM)

SUMMARY

The article describes a pitfall related to using the SQLite database in a program written in Go. The introduction explains why this problem is often hard to recognize—because it doesn't manifest itself by any error, but rather in excessive storage overhead. The next section introduces SQLite's storage layer details, including the write-ahead logging mode. Then the problem is teased out through code samples, intertwined with checking how much storage the database occupies while running the code. The problem: when the database runs in write-ahead logging (WAL) mode, something prevents a checkpoint operation from clearing excessive disk space. The article concludes with a clear explanation of the problem (ultimately, failure to close rows in WAL mode), a rule of thumb to remember when working with SQLite and Go, and a bonus side note mentioning that this problem also affects another SQLite operation: vacuum.

COMMENTARY

The title is a bit lengthy, but it's also a perfect teaser. It's hard to resist the temptation of seeing what the problem is here, even if you don't use SQLite or Go at all. The code samples followed by checking how much storage is used while the code executes is a nice touch—it makes the blog post feel interactive and easy for readers to reproduce on their own. This article is actually part of a larger anthology on pitfalls related to Go and SQLite, and it's preceded by another post explaining how to avoid deadlocking your code when using both.

What I especially appreciate here is the recursive nature of why this blog post fits well into the "Lessons Learned" pattern. As the author explains in the very first sentence, this particular lesson was learned because of a discussion sparked by another blog post that also happened to fit into the same pattern. It makes the first blog post twice as educational!

11.3.4 *Lessons Learned Scaling PostgreSQL Database to 1.2bn Records/Month*

Author: Gajus Kuizinas
Source: Gajus Kuizinas' Blog (https://mng.bz/yoXE)

SUMMARY

This article describes the author's experience using the Postgres database for multiple purposes at large scale. The introduction explains the rationale behind using Postgres instead of a more complicated technology stack, as well as the expected use cases for the database. The next section goes over the multiple cloud providers used to host the database, sharing the experience with each and reaching the conclusion that a self-hosted database cluster is the way to go. That's followed by a section devoted to materialized views and the author's multiple attempts to apply them. Next comes a section on using the database as a message queue, then an aggregation of useful tips and tweaks to make working with Postgres easier. Finally, the author advertises a new open source Postgres client (Slonik) that's also designed to improve the experience with Postgres. The article concludes with extensive acknowledgments.

COMMENTARY

This article is very, very, very, very long. Fortunately, it's also nicely split into small, distinguishable paragraphs. Moreover, it follows a structure of introducing the problem, presenting a few solutions to it, and concluding the section with takeaways. That makes it easy for readers to consume the blog post in multiple reading sessions. The takeaways are educational and practical. Most users are likely to learn at least one more thing about Postgres' internals and good practices. Overall, it's a great compendium of condensed practical Postgres knowledge, and the list of good practices at the end looks especially useful.

There's one nitpick though. Code samples are always appreciated, but these SQL queries require at least two full-finger scrolls, which is a little traumatizing. The fact that the samples lack syntax coloring aggravates the feeling (that's usually the blog platform's fault though), but my main concern is the complexity of the queries. On the one hand, it's great to be transparent and share real-life queries. However, in this particular case, the details are likely too overwhelming for an average reader.

11.3.5 *Lessons from Stripe*

Author: Mark McGranaghan
Source: Mark McGranaghan's Blog (https://markmcgranaghan.com/lessons-from -stripe)

SUMMARY

This article is a short overview of the author's experience while working at Stripe. It covers three main areas: optimism, ambition, and recruiting. Learnings from each of the areas above are covered in dedicated paragraphs. The article concludes with a short recommendation of Stripe as a workplace.

COMMENTARY

This is a perfect example of how a nontechnical blog post can cover lessons learned for a purely technical audience. By now you're probably dead tired from an endless stream of database-related blog post reviews, so here's the long-awaited break. This article is really short but also densely packed with practical information. Who can benefit from reading this article? People who

- Might apply to Stripe
- Have a job offer from Stripe in hand
- Wonder if their own toxic work environment is actually that bad
- Want to improve their employees' lives

The article covers lots of nontechnical areas important for people working technical jobs. The lessons learned are well-structured (three simple paragraphs with intriguing headlines: Optimism, Ambition, Recruiting) and full of interesting details. Great post!

11.4 Characteristics

"Lessons Learned" blog posts are highly focused on turning the authors' personal experiences into educational lessons for readers. Given that, it's not surprising that introspection, reflection, and storytelling are common characteristics.

11.4.1 Diary-like

Some articles in the "Lessons Learned" pattern almost feel like they should be prefaced by "Dear Diary." The author is freely sharing inner frustrations, and the reader is looking over their shoulder, ready to learn vicariously through the author's experiences. Accordingly, these articles don't tend to adopt the pluralis maiestatis airs used in "How We Built It" pattern articles. They're a bit more informal, raw, and introspective. For example:

- Kuizinas' article begins with "This isn't my first rodeo with large datasets" and shortly thereafter links out to a comedy video.
- From start to finish, the McGranaghan article is quite open about what working at Stripe was really like and how the company's priorities affected him personally.
- Jastrzebski starts off with a casual account of how his publication of a separate article sparked conversations that led to the discovery of a nasty bug that's "close to [his] heart."
- Fidalgo begins by hinting that there's much more to one of Notion's officially announced "five minutes of scheduled maintenance" than meets the eye, then launches into "Let me tell you the story of how we sharded and what we learned along the way."
- Smith's is probably the most guarded of the bunch; the first few paragraphs seem highly reviewed by legal/corporate communications departments. But as soon as the article shifts to the technical details, the language loosens up and the real story begins.

Much like diary entries and "Bug Hunt" articles, "Lessons Learned" articles are commonly organized chronologically. Many feature real-life timestamps (see the Discord piece) or key milestones (the Notion blog's callouts of "Decision 1," "Decision 2," and so on) that allow readers to step into the author's shoes and follow the drama as it unfolds.

11.4.2 Imprintable

Lessons become memorable through their story. Readers are more likely to remember a particular pitfall or interesting technical detail if it's nicely wrapped in

- A playful anecdote
- A mysterious detective story
- A suspenseful debug session on a live system

Having such stories imprinted in your mind can actually avert problems. It's quite possible that someone, in a data center somewhere, has already uttered the words "No, we're not continuing the upgrade—remember that blog post about what happened to Discord." Even if the blog post does not prevent a problem, it can still help solve one. Once it dawns on you or a teammate that the problem you're currently suffering through was discussed in a post they once read, that post gets shared, you apply the relevant tidbits, and you're hopefully much closer to alleviating your own headache. The lesson becomes more memorable through the story, but the story also becomes more memorable through the lesson.

11.4.3 Reflections and ruminations

Generally, "Lessons Learned" posts are not written in the heat of the moment but rather after a fair amount of time has elapsed, allowing for analysis and reflection. For example,

- The Notion article seems to have been written a full six months after the downtime (which was itself months after the project, and lessons learned, actually began).
- The Discord blog was published a week after the incident. That might not seem long compared to the Notion example, but remember that Notion was ruminating over a months-long project ,while Discord was digesting a 50-minute outage.
- Both the Kuizinas and McGranaghan articles seem to be drawing lessons learned based on multiple years of experience.

In many cases, this extra time for reflection provides the objectivity and clarity needed to deduce more, and broader, lessons learned than you might find in a "Bug Hunt" article. For example, the database lessons learned by Discord and Notion can be broadly applied across many different database technologies and deployment scenarios. That's a stark contrast to most bug hunt lessons learned, which tend to be discrete solutions bound to a specific technology and setup.

However, this is a trend, not a rule. For example, Jastrzębski's lesson learned didn't require lengthy reflection. It seems like a "Eureka moment," and it's quite specific, related to unexpected behavior that's endemic to Go plus SQLite. Like life lessons, some tech lessons hit you fast, while others require more distance and deliberation.

11.5 Dos & don'ts

Articles on lessons learned come in many styles, from a short note about a single lesson to a compendium of lessons learned by the author throughout the years. The broad range of what's possible here might make it easier or harder for you, depending on whether you love or hate structure. Virtually anything with a bit of personal perspective and another bit of educational value is likely to work.

11.5.1 Be humble

"Lessons Learned" is not a good pattern for boasting. For that, go with "How We Built It" or maybe a heroic "Bug Hunt." "Lessons Learned" posts are more about an honest examination of conscience, rethinking one's actions in retrospect, and analyzing what went right and what went terribly wrong. Of course, be sure to highlight all the good decisions. However, remember that most of the educational benefit comes from dissecting the bad ones, especially bad decisions that seemed right at the time.

Exposing all your failures and wrong turns is expected here. Readers are here to learn, not to judge (except those notorious ones, lurking across the internet for new articles to disparage in the comment sections).

11.5.2 Don't forget

Timing is a delicate dance when writing posts in this pattern. On the one hand, you want to start recording the details while everything is still fresh in your mind. But on the other hand, sometimes you need a little time and distance before you can recognize the full implications of what you just experienced.

If you just survived a learning experience, start recording copious notes immediately, even if you're still not sure what it all means yet. Then, let it simmer until ready, which is not the same as indefinitely. Don't expect that an epiphany will strike you when you least expect it. Set a reasonable deadline and force yourself to distill some meaning from your past tribulations before you're too deep into new ones.

11.5.3 Don't turn on full diary mode

Even though these posts share personal experiences, it's important to maintain the balance and avoid going "full personal diary mode." Ultimately blog posts are written for the readers. Although sharing your personal experience is welcome, the following are less so:

- Using acronyms without unrolling them at least once—your readers might not be used to them, and if they open another browser tab to check yet another cryptic acronym, they might never return to your post.
- Mental shortcuts, omitting details that you already know, but your readers most likely don't!
- Mentioning that you learned something, but without actually explaining how the readers can apply the lessons learned. Ultimately, the readers want to know your personal perspective, but also learn something themselves.

11.5.4 Encourage interaction

There's a good chance that some readers of your "Lessons Learned" article have already experienced a similar problem before they click through to read how you approached it. Now that they're here reading your article, why not take advantage of the opportunity to engage with like-minded individuals? Leaving your contact information (or just the usual litany of social media links) as part of the conclusion, along with a note like "Don't hesitate to reach out if you found this blog post useful" can build connections across the community.

NOTE   For tips on initiating and engaging in a community discussion, see chapter 15.

Summary

- The "Lessons Learned" pattern is a timeless classic for capturing and sharing what you learned from frustration, fumbling, and failure.
- Although the primary goal is educating the reader, writing such posts can also be edifying and cathartic for the writer.
- Anyone who has ever faced a technical problem is qualified to write a blog post in this pattern, and the different shapes and forms it could take vary as widely as the technical problems programmers learn from.
- Top tips:
  - Be open about all your failures and missteps; this is not the place to brag.
  - Start recording details right away, and start writing the blog post once you've had time to reflect on your experience and distill it into clear lessons learned.
  - Although these posts have a "Dear Diary" feel, remember that they are indeed going to be read by someone, which means that an appropriate level of explanation and context is required.
  - Encouraging your readers to contact you is a nice way to connect with peers who have similar interests and experiences.

The "Thoughts on Trends" pattern

12

This chapter covers

- Blog posts that are highly opinionated takes on industry trends
- Their purpose and audience
- How various authors approached this type of post
- Key elements of successful "Thoughts on Trends" posts
- Dos and don'ts for your own "Thoughts on Trends" post

"Thoughts on Trends" articles are highly opinionated, far more than any other pattern, because the author's opinion is the core feature of the article. This pattern works best if you've already established a position as an expert, either in a niche or technology in general.

Note that the term "an expert" is not limited to industry luminaries and popular social media figures. For example, given an article about new trends in web development, an expert author could be

- A web developer with a few years of experience
- A contributor to a popular web development framework
- The author of a few blog posts about web development
- The host of a podcast about web development
- A conference speaker who has delivered a few talks about web development

Across patterns, articles that go viral are likely to be authored by a known technologist, although exceptions certainly do occur. But in the "Thoughts on Trends" pattern, that bias is particularly pronounced.

Don't let that discourage you, though! In this chapter, we look closely at how established experts approach this challenge so you can pull off this pattern like a master whenever you're ready.

12.1 Purpose

Blog posts in this pattern can serve a variety of purposes, from reflecting on the past, to shaping the future and sharing thoughts on whatever everyone is obsessing about today. This pattern is commonly (but not exclusively) applied by experienced writers who maintain a personal engineering blog.

12.1.1 *Continuous delivery*

Something is always trending. Here are some examples:

- A new language
- A new programming paradigm
- A new type of hardware (e.g., the AWS Inferentia chip dedicated to AI workloads)
- A new leather jacket in the NVIDIA CEO's wardrobe
- A series of layoffs
- A new zero-day vulnerability in a library that everybody relies on

That's great news for engineering blog writers—a never-ending supply of trends continuously gives authors the opportunity to publish an opinion on something new and shiny. It's also great news for blog maintainers. Posts on trending topics tend to attract many new readers to a blog, and at least some percentage of these new readers are likely to explore previously published posts, as well as the one currently in the spotlight.

12.1.2 *Retrospection*

Publishing opinions on current trends also creates an opportunity for the author to revisit the article in 2, 3, or maybe even 10 years to comment on the accuracy of that original take. This is especially intriguing if the author also played clairvoyant and expressed their opinions on how the future would unfold. If the prediction actually turned out to be correct, a follow-up article is downright crucial! But even if it wasn't, a healthy dose of self-criticism gives the article an authentic vibe. Publishing blog posts on trends is a clear twofer—write one, get the second one (almost) for free after an appropriate amount of time has elapsed.

12.1.3 *Shaping the future*

Some "Thoughts on Trends" blog posts are powerful enough to influence the future they are commenting on. For instance, an honest, non-markety endorsement of a new language published on a popular engineering newsletter can be the driving factor in that language's adoption. Conversely, if a new language gets mercilessly roasted, it might encourage the maintainers to work twice as hard to fix the obvious mistakes and deliver something of better quality. Or, it could discourage the authors and push them toward orphaning the project. Either way, the article makes a difference.

12.2 *Audience*

"Thoughts on Trends" articles are often posted by experienced authors running popular engineering blogs and/or newsletters. The first obvious group of interested readers are subscribers to the aforementioned. The most succinct description of this pattern's target audience is just everyone, though. Trends are by definition popular, and those posts are addressed to anyone interested in them.

12.3 *Examples of "Thoughts on Trends" blog posts*

The examples selected here are a natural consequence of the fact that opinionated takes tend to come from well-known industry experts. Every featured author is a serial writer, with multiple successful blog posts in their portfolio. The chances of your "Thoughts on Trends" article becoming popular rise exponentially based on how well-recognized you are.

Here are some prime examples of blog posts that apply the "Thoughts on Trends" pattern, along with Piotr's commentary on each.

> **NOTE** If you haven't been following and reading all the mentioned authors, it's time to catch up! All of them have a track record of fantastic technical blog posts.

12.3.1 *I Want Off Mr. Golang's Wild Ride*

Author: Amos Wenger
Source: fasterthanlime Blog (https://mng.bz/QVoe)

SUMMARY

This article is a self-proclaimed rant on a variety of problems with the Go language. The introduction candidly admits that this article will be a rant and announces the upcoming list of problems. The main sections cover

- Why Go language constructs are not simple, even though that alleged simplicity is explicitly mentioned in the language design and core concepts
- How the dependency-solving system tends to pull lots of redundant data, bloating even tiny projects beyond proportion
- How Go failed to solve a seemingly simple issue with its standard library functions for time management

Wenger often contrasts the Go code with Rust to show how "the Go way" is worse than its alternatives. The final section concludes that even a single issue has multiple severe root causes in the Go ecosystem, which doesn't bode well for Go's future. It also refers to another web page describing Go idiosyncrasies and calls out that a tricky "footgun" in the API is casually mentioned as a footnote in the documentation instead of being properly checked at compile time.

After that conclusion, there's a bonus update from April 2022 (two years after the original publication). Here, the author emphasizes that they still haven't changed their mind and also raises a few more interesting points.

COMMENTARY

Rants done right, like this one, are extremely enjoyable to read. It's written in a light tone, even though you can practically feel the years of frustration that the author expertly enchanted into the words. I hereby classify this article as a roast. I really appreciate the clickable table of contents, especially since this article is quite long.

The length is expected though, judging by the author's other popular articles. One microscopic nitpick is that the table of contents is rather coarse grained, with two giga-sections (Simple is a lie; Lots of little things) covering most of the article.

The blog post features an abundance of interesting code examples and graphics, as well as lots of pseudo-interactive conversations with the cool bear, the author's alter ego. As usual, it makes the article way more engaging and easy to read even though it doesn't fit into the average attention span of 5–10 minutes reading time.

The April 2022 update is a splendid cherry on top:

- It makes the whole article more current.
- It emphasizes the verdict reached in the original contents.
- It adds a few links to related articles and docs.

I had high expectations since the bar was set quite high by the author's previous articles, and I wasn't disappointed one bit. Yet another great read from this author.

12.3.2 *How to Think About WebAssembly (Amid the Hype)*

Author: Matt Butcher
Source: Fermyon Blog (https://www.fermyon.com/blog/how-to-think-about-wasm)

SUMMARY

This blog post is an essay on what WebAssembly (a.k.a. Wasm) is, used to be, and was originally designed to be, plus how it's evolving. The introduction lists a few perspectives on what WebAssembly actually is, followed by its technical definition (a standardized bytecode format). The next section describes WebAssembly's origins as a more efficient alternative to JavaScript. It's followed by the proposition that WebAssembly can be useful beyond web browsers due to the following features:

- Security
- Robustness
- Compactness
- Interoperability
- Fast loading times

The main new application of WebAssembly is revealed to be virtualization and standardized plugins. Next, the author places WebAssembly on a timeline of programming languages and explains what's needed to make WebAssembly truly universal: a new specification of a system interface, WASI (WebAssembly System Interface).

COMMENTARY

Anyone even remotely familiar with the author's other posts (highly recommended!) would expect this blog post to be a truly philosophical essay. It is! At the same time, its casual style makes it really pleasant to read (unlike most philosophical posts). As a huge fan of succinct titles, I would have preferred the one from the article's URL ("How to think about Wasm"), but that's the only nitpick that comes to mind.

The introduction is overloaded with contrasting definitions of WebAssembly (including hyperlinks to each). But that's not a flaw—it's a brilliant trick to emphasize that lots of people are confused about what WebAssembly actually is. After the intentionally induced confusion, Butcher presents a purely technical and concise definition: "WebAssembly is a bytecode format that any WebAssembly-capable runtime can execute."

The initial confusion contrasted with later disambiguation makes the reading process dynamic and enjoyable. The author has a quite unique style; I wholeheartedly recommend reading his other pieces to compare and learn.

12.3.3   *Rust After the Honeymoon*

Author: Bryan Cantrill
Source: Bryan Cantrill's Blog (https://mng.bz/vJvq)

SUMMARY

The blog post revisits the themes from the author's previous post on Rust, published two years earlier. The introduction refers to the original article and explains that the author's feelings toward Rust remain positive. Cantrill highlights Rust language features such as

- Good support for embedded systems programming, allowing easily opting out from the standard library
- Built-in developer-friendly formatting options
- Support for debugging formats (available in the ecosystem as independent libraries)
- Data-bearing enums, a compact way of expressing data types
- Unsafe Rust, which offers a way to bypass strict compiler checks for specific use cases
- Error handling

The conclusion admits that Rust isn't perfect, but emphasizes that Rust is an amazing language despite its minor imperfections.

COMMENTARY

This article is packed with interesting technical insights. It's also very well structured, with paragraph headings forming a list of features the author likes in Rust for easy scannability. The title is perfectly balanced between clickbaity and technical:

- *It's intentionally ambiguous.* It's teasingly unclear whether the author still likes Rust. The "after the honeymoon" term is a great way to catch the eyes of curious readers.
- *Rust!* It's Bryan Cantrill's thoughts on Rust. Anyone even the slightest bit interested in Rust won't pass up Bryan Cantrill's perspective on it.

Cantrill includes an ample amount of code examples to demonstrate what he loves about Rust, and encourages readers to catch up with its predecessor post, "Falling in love with Rust" (another compelling title). The author, his achievements, and the blog post's domain are all recognizable in the niche of performance-oriented programming, which gives this article even more authority and traction.

Another distinctive element is that the article was a rather early perspective on Rust, and from an intriguing angle on top of that. Specifically, it explores Rust through the lens of embedded systems, where efficiency matters more than usual due to limited available resources. Overall, a great example of a "Thoughts on Trends" article!

12.3.4 *Software Architecture is Overrated, Clear and Simple Design is Underrated*

Author: Gergely Orosz
Source: The Pragmatic Engineer Blog (https://mng.bz/n0V8)

SUMMARY

The article reflects on standard software architectural patterns and compares them with an opposite approach: simple design. The introduction covers the author's experience building large distributed systems, along with an observation that none of those successful projects were based on any kind of standard pattern. There were also no people titled "architects" on the teams who delivered the projects.

The next section explains the alternative approach, applied by large companies as well as startups. That approach is based on defining a business problem, brainstorming a solution, and iterating through feedback loops. The author then notes that this system does not specifically match any of the patterns popular in the technical literature; yet, it's extremely efficient. Next, the author emphasizes the importance of simple design and simple code. Architectural patterns are considered "good to know," but not an ultimate goal of any developer. The final section is a collection of advice for designing systems; it covers approaches such as

- Discussing it with colleagues over a whiteboard
- Using a shared online document for brainstorming
- Creating multiple designs and contrasting them
- Reviewing other people's ideas

COMMENTARY

This is a 2019 article by Gergely Orosz, the engineer and engineering manager who went on to launch *The Pragmatic Engineer* newsletter (a long-term #1 newsletter on Substack) and write the bestselling book, *The Software Engineer's Guidebook*. Given that, his name and brand attract attention regardless of topic, but this is one topic that particularly resonates with me as a startup engineer. I also like that this blog post is a gentle, professional roast, but a roast nonetheless.

Overusing architectural patterns is a true concern. Lots of readers (me included!) sympathize with anyone who dares say they aren't actually essential for a good commercial project. A considerable percentage of programmers have had the dubious pleasure of working on an overmanaged project, sticking to an architectural design that doesn't make much sense but was already approved by someone more senior in the corporation. On the other hand, some programmers have only worked at startups and are intimately familiar with the simple design culture. This blog appeals to their egos as well, validating their experiences and beliefs. Readers are likely to be both happier and smarter after reading this.

12.3.5 *How io_uring and eBPF Will Revolutionize Programming in Linux*

Author: Glauber Costa
Source: The New Stack (https://mng.bz/o0xj)
This article was originally published on The New Stack, then later reposted (with their permission) on the ScyllaDB blog.

SUMMARY

The article dissects two relatively new technologies related to the Linux kernel: io_uring and eBPF. It begins with a detailed history of input/output system call API design in Linux—from blocking system calls to first attempts at an asynchronous API. It's followed by an equally detailed technical description of a new interface: io_uring. The new interface is explained both from a design perspective and by concrete code samples.

Next comes a series of benchmarks, showing io_uring's superiority compared to the legacy APIs. The first series of benchmarks is performed with a specialized tool. After that, the author shares real-life examples of improvements measured by running a ScyllaDB database.

The following section is devoted to eBPF, a mechanism originating from a network packet filtering system, but now getting more universal. The conclusion reassures the audience that both technologies are likely to revolutionize the paradigms of programming in Linux.

COMMENTARY

I have a soft spot for blog posts related to io_uring, for a few reasons:

- It's brilliant technology, which sounds like an obvious good idea once you compare it with its predecessors, but it wasn't obvious at all before Jens Axboe figured it out.
- It has the right level of low-level programming, which my brain can still follow, but is also sufficiently expert-friendly to make me feel proud that I can understand what happens under the hood.
- It truly is revolutionary, allowing more programmers to write efficient systems easily.
- Its name is a homophone of "I owe urine," which never stops being hilarious.

Personal preferences aside, this article is a goldmine of technical details and can be used as a primer for io_uring out-of-the-box. The eBPF section is substantially lighter but still very informative.

The article was released when io_uring was still a relatively young project and rapidly gaining traction. Perfect timing for a "Thoughts on Trends" blog post, especially by one of the luminaries in the field of Linux kernel and I/O, and especially with such abundant technical details about "the new thing." People were already talking about io_uring before this article was written, but only in very general terms. This article was one of the first that actually provided practical information on how to use it, as well as first-hand experience from applying it to a project heavily reliant on I/O performance (ScyllaDB).

12.4 *Characteristics*

Like the opinion columns you might find in a newspaper, "Thoughts on Trends" articles are written to announce and justify some bold assertion that a fair proportion of readers are likely to disagree with. Sparking a discussion is a primary goal. However, like other compelling engineering blog posts, these posts are highly technical. Even if each argument is not directly supported with a code sample, they are nevertheless rooted in deep experience with the technology that's the target of the author's advocacy, roasting, or spicy speculation.

> **NOTE** For tips on initiating and engaging in a community discussion, see Chapter 15.

12.4.1 *Opinionated and persuasive*

Articles following this pattern are generally either an opinion or an assorted collection of opinions. The authors might not have any vested interest in you adopting their views, but they are doggedly committed to making a solid case that could sway many minds. Table 12.1 shows our best guess at the core opinion the authors are trying to communicate in the example blog posts.

Table 12.1   The opinion in each example blog post

Title	Opinion (our best guess)
I Want Off Mr. Golang's Wild Ride	Go's alleged simplicity is actually its curse.
Rust After the Honeymoon	The more I worked with Rust in production, the deeper my appreciation grew.
How to Think About WebAssembly (Amid the Hype)	WebAssembly's most interesting opportunities are beyond the web, but we need WASI to tap its potential.
Software Architecture is Overrated, Clear and Simple Design is Underrated	We should move past the industry's unreasonable obsession with architectural patterns.
How io_uring and eBPF Will Revolutionize Programming in Linux	If you work with Linux, you better learn about these oddly named technologies.

In this pattern, opinions aren't simply stated. They're elaborated, supported, even defended against imaginary counterarguments to create a bulletproof argument. For example,

- Matt Butcher applies his broad and deep industry perspective to become the respected voice of reason on the "what is Wasm" debate. But despite the profound knowledge density infused into each highly readable sentence, it's never about sharing how much he knows. It's all spun toward anticipating and answering what's running through the readers' minds as the carefully constructed argument unfolds.

- Amos Wenger pulls you inside their mind for a condensed version of all the trials and tribulations that led them to regret using Go. And Wenger brings the receipts! Beyond extensive Rust vs. Go code comparisons and some painful package dependency details, they also highlight specific issues filed and share screenshots of debates with the Go core team. It's hard to imagine how anyone might come up with a "Yeah, but" response after digesting all of this.

12.4.2 *Provocative*

Opinions stated in "Thoughts on Trends" articles often touch on controversial subjects (e.g., Async Rust Sucks) or take controversial stances on topics that might not ordinarily raise any eyebrows (e.g., Database Isolation Is Broken and You Should Care). Writing a strong opinion about the former means inheriting an already-polarized audience. And writing a pointed takedown of something that many hold dear might create a newly polarized audience. Even if the vast majority of readers might not care that much, there's likely a loud minority at both extremes ready for a fight, either against you or against those who declare war versus your position.

Roasts are provocative by definition, but paeans (expressions of high praise) set people off, too. Nothing triggers heated online discussions more than posting a positive comment about something that another person passionately hates!

Note that provocative elements of paeans might surface as jabs at what they're replacing. For example, in Bryan Cantrill's article about why he personally loves working with Rust, there is no shortage of zingers targeted at replaced (and adjacent) technologies. For example,

- "But the nothing that C provides reflects history more than minimalism; it is not an elegant nothing, but rather an ill-considered nothing that leaves those who build embedded systems building effectively everything themselves—and in a language that does little to help them write correct software."
- "Lest I sound like I am heaping too much praise on DWARF, let me be clear that DWARF is historically acutely painful to deal with. The specification (to the degree that one can call it that) is an elaborate mess, and the format itself seems to go out of its way to inflict pain on those who would consume it."
- "After nearly three decades working in C, I thought I appreciated its level of unsafety, but the truth is I had just become numb to it; to implement in Rust is to eat the fruit from the tree of knowledge of unsafe programs—and to go back to unsafe code is to realize that you were naked all along!"

12.4.3 *Idiosyncratic*

Opinions aside, one feature that makes "Thoughts on Trends" articles stand out is the unique style of the author leaking through the lines. For instance, I'm relatively sure I can recognize Matt Butcher's philosophical hand in written text without looking at the byline. Same for Bryan Cantrill's racing mind.

This is a natural consequence of this pattern being a popular tool for experienced writers. By now, they've already developed a distinctive writing voice. And since stating opinions is also quite personal, the style is especially visible in this pattern. In some cases recognizing the style is as obvious as seeing a "Cool bear's hot tip" interlude and connecting the dots. In the others, it's the specific sense of humor, or lack thereof.

12.5 Dos & don'ts

By the time you're writing your own "Thoughts on Trends" blog, you've probably mastered the blog-writing basics. But a "Thoughts on Trends" post is a different beast than, say, a "Lessons Learned" article—and not everyone is comfortable sharing their opinions so overtly. Before you step onto your soapbox, read a variety of opinionated takes and think about what approach suits your personality as well as your angle on the topic. As long as you see an authentic path forward, start thinking about the following tips for pulling it off.

12.5.1 Be famous

Being recognized as an expert on a topic is by far the strongest first step to creating a "Thoughts on Trends" article that gets attention. Although that recommendation might sound ridiculous at first, each engineering blog post you write brings you closer to recognizability. With a track record of a few blog posts related to your niche, you're already in a decent position to try and post your ruminations on current trends.

Keep in mind, though: "Thoughts on Trends" articles require a distinctly different approach than the other patterns you might have become accustomed to writing. They're the only ones that bring persuasion into play. And that leads to the next tip.

12.5.2 Consider the elements of persuasion

Ready to persuade an audience? Consider the following three core means of persuasion (rooted in Aristotle): ethos, pathos, and logos.

ETHOS

Ethos emphasizes your credibility: why people should care what you have to say about this topic. Of course, the more famous you are, the easier this is. If you're not (yet) known by everyone in your target audience, think about how you can convey your authority. You clearly don't want to come off as pompous or narcissistic. But look for subtle ways to sneak in details that prove you have solid experience related to the topic at hand. For example, if you wanted to highlight your vast expertise with C, you might drop in a phrase like "Back when I was wrestling with C," and hyperlink it to a related blog or project.

PATHOS

Pathos appeals to people's emotions, such as their frustrations, fears, excitement, or curiosity. For this one, try to put yourself in your reader's shoes. Why are they reading this article? Maybe they're worried that the proposed rewrite in X will be a massive distraction with no clear benefit. Maybe they've heard the hype about ShinyNewThing and are eager to build a case for adopting it. Or perhaps they're insanely frustrated with something and are looking for solace in their peers' misery. Then, think about what you can share to resonate with those emotions. Storytelling, sharing what was running through your own head at critical junctures, a little humor and self-deprecation as appropriate—all this can help you connect with the reader at an emotional level.

Logos

Logos involves making logical and rational arguments, and it's likely the element that comes most naturally to the stereotypical engineer. Persuading readers in this way involves ensuring that your arguments make logical sense and are supported by an appropriate level of "facts," which might include your first-hand experiences, code examples, test results, details on industry trends and shifts, and so forth. To cover this angle, think about all the statements a snarky reader might argue with, and ensure that each and every one is supported by irrefutable facts. Also, try to explain the high-level flow of your argument to yourself, your teammate, or your trusted rubber duckie and see if it makes sense at that level.

> **NOTE** Chapter 5 went into much more detail on ways to achieve all these strategies.

12.5.3 *Be bold*

"Thoughts on Trends" blog posts are the perfect outlet for strong, controversial opinions. In fact, if you can't imagine reasonable people arguing with your main point, you might want to rethink it. Readers especially appreciate comments coming from far ends of the judgment spectrum, be it overly positive or overly negative. The example blog posts could be classified as shown in table 12.2.

Table 12.2   Classifying the example blog posts

Title	Type
I Want Off Mr. Golang's Wild Ride	Roast
Rust After the Honeymoon	Paean
How to Think About WebAssembly (Amid the Hype)	Paean with a grain of roast
Software Architecture is Overrated, Clear and Simple Design is Underrated	Gentlemen's roast
How io_uring and eBPF Will Revolutionize Programming in Linux	Paean

Determine what approach you want to take, and run with it—from a provocative start to a tight, powerful finish. Both the introduction and the conclusion should express arguable opinions using concise, powerful sentences (covered in detail in chapter 5).

12.5.4 Roast

If you decide to share a negative opinion on a topic, make it a show. Roasting is an especially entertaining form of criticism. Pulling it off requires the right amount of mocking and exaggeration, while still keeping it humorous rather than aggressive.

12.5.5 Don't just roast

Pointing out the downsides is easy, but a good "Roast on Trends" article needs to be extra careful to back up all the accusations with hard evidence. Mockery is acceptable but it can't be based on baseless claims. Ultimately, treat the roast format as a convenient container for packaging up your technical insights—a means to an end, not a goal in and of itself. The core of the article still needs to contain all the relevant technical details, as any respectable engineering blog post should. Without solid arguments, the roast will itself end up roasted in the comment section.

12.5.6 Don't just praise

For completeness, the same rule applies to the positive opinions of paeans. Praise should be backed by credible results. Otherwise, your article could be dismissed as a paid promotion or just an attempt to get on the hype train.

Summary

- "Thoughts on Trends" posts provide established experts an outlet for sharing predictions, praise, or problems related to a topic they're highly familiar with.
- These posts might reflect on the past, shape the future, or comment on whatever is catching everyone's attention today.
- Readers include both fans of the author and those passionate about the topic being discussed.
- These posts are bold, provocative, and individualistic, while still rooted in deep technical experience.
- Top tips:
  - Establish expertise on this topic first.
  - Consider what elements of persuasion you want to use, and how.
  - Announce a strong, potentially provocative, stance and stick to it.
  - Roasts are especially fun to write and read, but praise and prognostication are also valid approaches.
  - Keep it balanced, especially if you roast or praise, or else you will be roasted for bias, unfounded attacks, and/or overly enthusiastic promotion.

13
The "Non-market Product Perspectives" pattern

This chapter covers

- Blog posts where the product is embedded into a genuinely intriguing and educational article
- Their purpose and audience
- How various authors approached this type of post
- Key elements of successful "Non-market Product Perspectives" posts
- Dos and don'ts for your own "Non-Market Product Perspectives" post

The pattern's name, "Non-market Product Perspectives," is itself a marketing trick to deceive you into thinking this pattern is not about marketing. It actually *is* about marketing, at least in a way. The "non-markety" part is there to distract you from the "product" keyword, which is a clear indicator that somebody is ultimately trying to sell something.

Fortunately, this kind of marketing works by educating readers about fascinating technical tidbits, groundbreaking designs, and other impressive achievements that just so happen to be available in the product that's casually mentioned a few dozen times in the post. The selling part tends to be noninvasive, sometimes even borderline subliminal. In the best of the bunch, no purchase is necessary for readers to walk away with useful learnings—but now they're so intrigued that they want to try the product anyway. That's what makes this pattern so valuable for companies and readers alike.

"Non-markety Product Perspectives" engineering blog posts are especially valuable for companies marketing products to developers. An engineer-authored piece that provides an inside look at a product might be the only way to bypass developers' primitive gag reflex to all things marketing. But these posts can be especially tricky to pull off. As an author, how do you share something valuable related to your product without facing the wrath of your fellow snarky developers, all too eager to accuse you of "marketing fluff"? That's what we'll explore in this chapter.

13.1 Purpose

In the introduction, we mentioned that the "Non-markety Product Perspectives" pattern is mostly driven by marketing. That includes marketing the company as an employer and technology leader, as well as marketing actual usable products.

13.1.1 *Product placement*

The ultimate goal of this pattern is to encourage readers to try out the product (or at least recognize that your product exists in case they're ever in the market). It's achieved not by flashy advertisements, but rather by focusing on a remarkable engineering achievement related to the product. For example,

- Something used to be annoying for developers, but we know how to fix it (with our product)
- Here's how a specific protocol works in detail (with example usage in our product)
- There's an important thing to remember when implementing a distributed system (and we did remember it when working on our product)

Embedding the product into a genuinely intriguing and educational post is a highly effective way of getting the attention of programmers.

13.1.2 *Teaser*

Quite a few articles following this pattern describe a product feature that isn't yet delivered. Sometimes the product isn't generally available at all, being hidden under a "private beta" label or only observed in an obscure heavily edited demo video from a few months ago. Promising things that aren't even close to being implemented is a cornerstone of technical marketing, so it's absolutely acceptable! Releasing a "Non-markety Product Perspectives" blog post is a good way of announcing an innovative idea that will (eventually) get productized and become part of the company's offering.

13.1.3 *Hiring*

Engineering blogs are generally honeypots for talent. The readers already demonstrated initiative by reading a blog post about the company's products, processes, or culture. Placing a modest note about open positions at the end rewards those with the curiosity and initiative to reach the final paragraph.

"Non-markety Product Perspectives" articles are especially great for hiring purposes. Looking for candidates who stay up-to-date with technology? The fact that they discovered and devoured your entire blog is a good test. It's fair to assume that anyone who applies after reading one of these blog posts is already aware of what the company does and has (presumably) bought into the vision. That's a promising start.

13.2 *Audience*

People who already follow a specific company, or an entire industry branch (e.g., embedded systems, AI, cloud infrastructure) constitute one social group particularly interested in product perspectives. This group can be further divided into

- Aficionados of a specific product (e.g., their favorite web development framework)
- Aficionados of an entire concept (e.g., web development frameworks in general)

- People considering job opportunities with the company that posted the article

Another curious category is the competition: developers working for companies in a similar niche, as well as startup founders, developer advocates, and their marketing folks. They're likely wondering about

- What their competition is up to these days
- If the competitor's good ideas can be creatively reused

"Non-markety Product Perspectives" usually offer a peek into the described product's technical details, but that doesn't mean they cater only to existing or prospective users. Done well, they're solid engineering blog posts in and of themselves, leaving readers with learnings and technical tidbits that are valuable beyond the user community. Done really well, they might convert an aficionado of the topic into a potential product aficionado or job applicant.

13.3 Examples of "Non-markety Product Perspectives" blog posts

In the wild, "Non-markety Product Perspectives" blog posts live primarily on company blogs, likely just a click away from the product being mentioned. Existing users who might be poking around the site for docs, a new product version, and similar are likely to stumble upon these posts. They're also commonly the fodder for social media feeds and newsletters—a way for the company to remind the world that they exist without seeming egregiously salesy.

Here are some prime examples of blog posts that apply the "Non-markety Product Perspectives" pattern, along with Piotr's commentary on each.

13.3.1 We Put a Distributed Database in a Browser—And Made a Game of It!

Authors: Phil Eaton, Joran Dirk Greef
Source: TigerBeetle Blog (https://mng.bz/mRr0)

SUMMARY

The article shows how TigerBeetle's specific distributed system architecture can be compiled to WebAssembly, running in a browser as a game anyone can play. It begins by introducing TigerBeetle's deterministic simulator. This design allows the database to be tested in a simulated environment, abstracting away input/output, networking, and also clocks. The web browser game is built on top of the very same code that the distributed database system uses, compiled to WebAssembly with the Zig language toolchain.

The next paragraphs describe three difficulty levels in the game, which also correspond to real-life problems that can impact distributed systems:

- *Level 1*—Uninterrupted replication
- *Level 2*—Network and storage failures (but no corruption)
- *Level 3*—Network and storage failures including on-disk corruption

Then, the authors share a short history of how the game idea came to life, along with tributes to the contributors. The final paragraph, pointedly named "Law of Demos," redirects readers to a video just in case the game doesn't work in their environment.

COMMENTARY

TigerBeetle squeezed an entire distributed system in a browser as a game, forever raising the bar for what an impressive technical blog post looks like. Just take a look at it, and you'll see why further commentary is really unnecessary.

But if you happen to be reading this book in some lovely off-the-grid location, or just don't want to visit the internet right now, here are a few reasons why this is so captivating:

1 The web browser game runs the same code as the distributed system. It's mind-blowing to realize that although it's intended for large fast servers, it can also run inside a web browser after being compiled to WebAssembly.

2 It shows a complicated distributed replication algorithm in a visual way, making it way more comprehensible than an academic paper on that exact algorithm.

3 It's interactive, allowing readers to try and prove the algorithm wrong by injecting faults into the distributed system: isolating nodes from the network, forcing them to restart, and so on.

4 It does the above by letting you

   a Smash animated anthropomorphic beetles with a hammer (node failure)

   b Electrocute them (disk corruption)

   c Freeze them (network partition)

Do I really need to continue, or can we just roll back to "just take a look at it, and you'll see why further commentary is really unnecessary" and call it a day?

13.3.2 *32 Bit Real Estate*

Author: Kurt Mackey
Source: Fly.io Blog (https://fly.io/blog/32-bit-real-estate/)

SUMMARY

This article is a primer on how the market of IPv4 addresses works. The introduction presents a problem that's often ignored: IP addresses can be quite costly for infrastructure companies like Fly.io. Early on, the article explains that the global pool of IP addresses is owned and managed by five public benefit entities: ARIN, RIPE, APNIC, AFRINIC, and LACNIC. They can be leased by individuals and companies, but not bought.

After acknowledging IPv6 as a standard that solves many of the IPv4 shortcomings, the author explains that IPv6's still stunted adoption means it's not yet a viable alternative. He continues to provide a peek into the IPv4 address exchange market, which is deceptively similar in principle to how cryptocurrency exchanges work. Then, the article explains that you can take out the equivalent of a mortgage on a block of IPv4 addresses, as well as lease them for fixed terms. IPv4 addresses can also be considered an investment, with appreciating value, at least as long as IPv6 is not widely adopted.

The conclusion sums up that IP addresses are surprisingly expensive and still very important for an infrastructure company. The final sentence wraps it all up with a playful comparison between the decades-old IPv4 market and scammy cryptocurrency-related markets.

COMMENTARY

Great title: short, technical, intriguing. The contents are insightful as well. The number of IPv4 users is huge compared to the number of people who understand how it works underneath (a handful of public entities administering the whole address space and a rather ancient BGP [Border Gateway Protocol]).

Although the topic isn't all that complex from a technical perspective, it's a really engaging and nice read. For many readers, it will induce the "ah, so that's how it works" revelation, which makes the blog post memorable. The company's product is mentioned quite a lot, but in a rather noninvasive way, related to the technical content. Still, you walk away with a general idea of what fly.io is all about and will have that filed in the back of your mind in case you ever need such a product.

13.3.3 *System Dependencies Are Hard (So We Made Them Easier)*

Author: Misty De Méo
Source: Axo Blog (https://blog.axo.dev/2023/10/dependencies)

SUMMARY

The article is an overview of cargo-dist—a tool developed by Axo, the company behind this engineering blog. It starts with the problem statement that managing dependencies in the Rust ecosystem is harder than expected. The next section explains that cargo-dist can automatically install dependencies for multiple programming environments. The article then shifts to cargo-dist's ability to figure out link-time dependencies of a package (so that they can be installed automatically along with the rest of the project).

The intricacies of actually installing a package on Apple hardware are covered next—along with a look at how cargo-dist makes the process easier. Next, the author explores the complexities of linking on different platforms, complete with more technical details. The article wraps by simply encouraging readers to try cargo-dist and letting them know about a new release.

COMMENTARY

The title is intriguing, and the problem stated in the introduction makes total sense. It's nice to see code snippets and concrete technical examples of how cargo-dist solves a particular problem (here, detecting which packages must be installed along with the original project).

My only complaint is that while the title and introduction appear to be describing a universal tool (which cargo-dist actually is and strives to be), the blog post is very Apple-centric. For a person who doesn't own any hardware produced by the aforementioned company (we exist), it quickly gets less captivating, and whole paragraphs can be skipped. There's of course nothing wrong with focusing on a specific environment, but I'd appreciate realizing that earlier than halfway through the article.

Nonetheless, I appreciate that the Apple-specific parts are very detailed, and it's nice to be able to follow the author's thought process of overcoming the build-stage problems step by step. The conclusion paragraph is amazing, straight to the point: here's our product, give it a try.

13.3.4 Why fsync(): Losing Unsynced Data on a Single Node Leads to Global Data Loss

Authors: Denis Rystsov, Alexander Gallego
Source: Redpanda Blog (https://mng.bz/5OPq)

SUMMARY

This article warns readers that unsynchronized data is a serious problem in distributed systems. The introduction briefly presents a list of measures that Redpanda (a faster Apache Kafka) takes to make the product more robust with respect to consistency. Next, it explains the titular `fsync` and how it contributes to data consistency on disk. That's followed by a brief look at replication's purpose in distributed systems.

Once all that's covered, it's time for the problem statement: replication does not guarantee data safety if data isn't synchronized with `fsync`. The problem description spans beyond a single paragraph. There's a proof of impossibility as well as a concrete counter-example to support the thesis. The article concludes that the thesis is considered proven, and encourages users to try Redpanda and join its community.

COMMENTARY

The title is both eye-catching and very explicit, which is a great maneuver. The "Why `'fsync()'`" part is intriguing enough for any reader even remotely concerned with data consistency, and the rest is a succinct summary of the whole article.

The level of detail is quite satisfactory for a deeply technical audience. Often, articles about data consistency are either purely theoretical academic papers or hands-on examples. This particular article has both. It provides

- A theoretical proof of why replication is not sufficient to guarantee consistency
- A reproducible example of data loss

It's especially nice to see a step-by-step guide on how to reach the same results, in case a reader doesn't take the authors' word for it. This article uses detailed technical insights to implicitly advertise the product (Redpanda): it shows the steps that were taken to provide better consistency guarantees for its users. This is precisely what the "Non-markety Product Perspectives" pattern can be used for.

13.3.5 So You Think You Want to Write a Deterministic Hypervisor?

Author: Alex Pshenichkin
Source: Antithesis Blog (https://mng.bz/6YP5)

SUMMARY

The article is a follow-up to the Antithesis launch post, which announced their main product: a deterministic hypervisor for testing and debugging complex systems. The first part of the article explains what determinism is and why it's not trivial to emulate it on modern hardware due to complexities such as

- Speculative execution with branch predictions
- Instruction pipelines
- Interrupts
- Processor parallelism

Next comes a sneak peek of the design, revealing that the hypervisor is based on existing software—bhyve, FreeBSD's stock hypervisor. That's followed by a deep dive into a few things that had to be adjusted, including time management and deterministic I/O (including disk and network access). Finally, the author announces that more details are coming and encourages readers to apply for a job there if they enjoy solving similar problems.

COMMENTARY

This article is especially noteworthy when you connect the dots and realize it comes from the founding team of FoundationDB, a database with a very specific and holistic approach to testing distributed systems. At first glance, this blog post is a decent candidate for the "How We Built It" pattern, due to its level of technical details and (partial) product design description. But ultimately, the technical details are used to pique interest in an impressive product that brings distributed system testing to a new level.

Just like its predecessor post (the launch post titled "Is Something Bugging You?"), this post is masterfully written in a way that

- Shows that the authors are experts in their field
- Conceals enough technical details to make readers
  - Crave more posts
  - Want to get in touch and use Antithesis against their software
  - Want to apply for a job so they can join the aforementioned team of experts

There's a very delicate balance between showcasing solid engineering and making a post look markety. I think the Antithesis team nails it just right. I also like how they make a pattern out of using a provocative question as a blog post title. That makes it feel immediately interactive.

13.4 *Characteristics*

"Non-markety Product Perspectives" share some characteristics with their more magisterial cousins, "How We Built It" blog posts:

- The product plays a leading or support role.
- They're providing a peek into implementation details, as well as their processes.
- The engineering tidbits shared expand the overall industry knowledge base.

However, "Non-markety Product Perspectives" tend to focus on a much narrower niche, usually either how they tackled a highly specialized challenge related to building the product or a deep dive into a particular use case for the product. A company will typically publish "Non-markety Product Perspectives" posts quite regularly but reserve "How We Built It" posts for special occasions.

13.4.1 *Technical*

This is the most markety pattern of all the ones covered in this book, but it's nonetheless still an engineering blog pattern. The best litmus test of an effective "Non-markety Product Perspectives" article is whether someone with zero interest in your product learns something they might jot down in a TIL (Today I Learned) file or share with their colleagues. Otherwise, it's likely just a marketing piece in disguise, something that the online mobs are particularly great at detecting and publicly shaming.

It's impossible not to bring up TigerBeetle as a good example, again. Readers have an opportunity to learn and understand a distributed system replication technique by playing an online game. Good luck getting more technical and educational than that!

13.4.2 *Behind the scenes*

One nice part of bringing the author's own product into a blog post is that the author can offer unique behind-the-scenes perspectives that make the post more engaging and distinctive. For example, authors might include unique tidbits such as

- An amusing anecdote explaining why the blog post's main topic is related to the product in the first place
- A few product implementation details that may not be obvious to the audience— Easter eggs, specialized tricks specific to a programming language, hacky scripts, and so forth
- A short rant on why something didn't work when trying to integrate it with the product

Readers leave privy to information that was never before published. And they likely feel a stronger connection to the product after being granted this behind-the-scenes access.

A perfect example of such a technical sneak peek is in Antithesis' article on their deterministic hypervisor. It provides exclusive details such as a screenshot showing parts of a comment block from their otherwise closed source code.

13.4.3 *Subliminal*

This characteristic is closely related to the product placement purpose referenced at the beginning of this chapter. Ideally, the urge to try out the product is induced on a subliminal level, without explicitly advertising the product in each paragraph. The audience should be subtly nudged toward trying out the product simply because it's related to an intriguing engineering subject in one way or another.

For example, consider Fly.io and their article on the IPv4 address space. Their introduction has this subliminal effect where you skim through it and don't really remember the contents after reading the rest of the article. And yet, it sticks in your mind: Fly.io manages IP addresses at an impressive scale, and they have a product you can try.

13.5   Dos & don'ts

Beware: Almost any engineer is at risk of being "voluntold" to write one of these posts at almost any time. When that request arrives, don't panic. If you focus on full transparency, the deep technical details that stem from your unique engineering point of view, and providing a balanced perspective, you'll be fine. Here are some specifics.

13.5.1 Introduce yourself

You don't really need to introduce yourself as an author, but it *is* good practice to clearly tell the readers a little bit about the company behind the article: what overall category you're in and what's distinctive about your product. That way, you're upfront about the fact that the article was written by someone with a vested interest (maybe literally) in this product's success. Nobody should feel tricked. Readers who wanted a purely technical piece with no product affiliation can turn around now. It also gives readers additional context upfront. Now that they have an inkling of what the company does, technical bits from the article are easier to imagine in a real-world scenario.

For an example of how this might be done, look at a few different fly.io blog posts. They seem to have a rule to put a short description of what the company does on top of each engineering blog post. The exact wording varies, but it's always a short summary of what the company is up to at the time of writing.

13.5.2 Don't sell

Avoid making the product the central point of the article. Otherwise, the article will likely be immediately qualified as marketing fluff and ignored by everyone except people who are already excited about the product.

Instead, the product should just be part of the theme. For example,

- The product relies on the technology described in the post
- The product is a proposed solution to a known technical problem
- The product suffered from a notable technical pitfall

It's absolutely fine to directly encourage readers to use/register/download/try the product somewhere in the intro or outro. However, the article still needs to be first and foremost an engineering blog post, not product propaganda.

You might wonder if the TigerBeetle post mentioned earlier makes the product the central point of the article. Well, yes and no. While it's clear that everything in the article is very specific to TigerBeetle and its implementation, the central point is explaining a complicated distributed consistency algorithm via gamification. It's fair to assume most readers aren't in desperate need of a fast and correct financial transaction database. Still, they can certainly grasp a new concept from the distributed systems category while venting frustration on animated beetles with hammers and thunderbolts.

If you want to be crazy cautious that you won't be perceived as "selling," run through this checklist:

- *Targeted topic*—Does this really require an engineering perspective, *your personal* engineering perspective, in fact? If not, rethink the focus, or try to pawn it off on someone else.

- *Total transparency*—In addition to the "what our company does" disclaimer noted in "Introduce yourself," make sure the reader can immediately determine what they'll get out of your post and what role your product plays in that. Don't make them hunt for it and certainly don't spring the product on them without warning mid-post or even later.

- *No gratuitous material*—After you reveal what the reader will get from this post, stick to it. Ruthlessly cut anything that's not essential for accomplishing that. Are you tempted (or being pressured) to add details about some other cool capability, pop in some impressive but unrelated test results, etc.? Don't. Save it as an idea for another time (and maybe another author).

- *Distinctive details*—A good 80% or so of your article should focus on details that could only come from your unique engineering perspective. Provide quick background if absolutely necessary, but keep the focus on "behind-the-scenes" access to details that aren't available elsewhere.

- *No arguable statement left unsupported*—Hunt down any statements that a reasonable person in your target audience might question or argue with. Ensure that they are all supported by facts: technical details from your own experience, experiments, or trusted industry knowledge. This is covered extensively in section 5.2.1.

- *Watch your language*—Excessive adjectives or adverbs, buzzwords, superlatives, and extremes will raise red flags. An extreme example (credit to ChatGPT): "Our revolutionary software offers state-of-the-art features that leverage dynamic algorithms for a seamless, world-class user experience. This represents a paradigm shift in the industry with its transformative capabilities and next-gen technology, ensuring optimal performance and scalability for all users." If in doubt, look back to the image at the start of this chapter. If the words might come out of that gentleman's mouth, cut or rethink them!

13.5.3 *Be balanced but don't bash*

While a "Non-market Product Perspectives" blog post is not an overt marketing technique, it's still expected to showcase something in an impressive and intriguing way. It's important to provide a realistic and honest look at the product. If appropriate, do share what it's *not* built for, when it *shouldn't* be used, and similar. But avoid placing too much emphasis on the product's shortcomings, sharing users' negative experiences with it, and so on.

Negative feedback will look out of place, making the readers wonder why on Earth the company agreed to release a lampoon against their own creation. More importantly, the article will most certainly get a red light at its review stage. There are other forms of articles in which honest criticism of the product's weak points is appreciated (see, for example, the "Bug Hunt" pattern). But "Non-markety Product Perspectives" post isn't the place for it.

Summary

- Embedding the product into a genuinely intriguing and educational post is one of the best ways to introduce a product to programmers.
- Blog posts in this pattern not only draw attention to working products but also sell the company as a technology leader and attractive employer.
- Readers include your most dedicated users, potential users, people with no intention of ever using the product, and competitors who want people to use their product instead.
- These posts should be just as technical as other engineering articles, provide exclusive behind-the-scenes details related to the product, and subliminally educate the reader that the product exists and is backed by a cool engineering team.
- Top tips:
  - Disclose your company's purpose upfront for transparency and to help the reader better understand the article.
  - Ensure the product is part of a larger theme that's intriguing even if a reader has zero interest in that specific product.
  - Actively avoid and root out "marketing fluff"—use the "Don't sell" checklist in the chapter for specifics.
  - Be honest and realistic about the product, but don't go overboard and leave the reader with a negative impression.

The "Benchmarks and Test Results" pattern

Skepticism about benchmarks is so trendy right now that "All benchmarks are wrong" could become an entire pattern chapter in this book. This herd skepticism against benchmarks is actually a positive trend. Why not pay closer attention to whether benchmarks and test results shared in engineering blogs truly make sense? On the flip side, writers beware. If you're writing one of these blog posts, it's more important than ever to do your homework and ensure that the published benchmarks are truthful, reproducible, and not too synthetic.

"Benchmarks and Test Results" articles tend to fall into at least three distinct categories:

- Tests that compare the company's product against its competition
- Tests that compare something (such as cloud infrastructure or hardware) using the company's product
- Measuring something independent of the company's products (e.g., an open source project or a new graphics processing unit)

The tests comparing the author's company's product versus its competition are most likely to face a low level of trust and stir up online debate. They are still ubiquitous, though; showing measured numbers is one of the few effective ways to promote a project to engineers.

The second variety (using the author's company's product to test/compare something else) brings valuable third-party conclusions about something shiny, like a new generation of processors or new energy-efficient cloud machines. At the same time, it's a noble way of featuring the company's product—showing it as a real-life "user" of the tested technology.

Tests that don't involve the author's company's product at all are often admired and sought after since they are less likely to be biased (assuming that the author is not affiliated with *any* of the compared technologies). They're also significantly rarer. Tests consume considerable time and resources, which makes them a quite demanding independent weekend project. And the author's company is unlikely to sponsor the project if it doesn't benefit that company in some way.

14.1   Purpose

Each flavor of the "Benchmarks and Test Results" pattern serves a slightly different purpose:

- *Benchmarketing*—Tests that compare the company's product against its competition
- *Subtle benchmarketing*—Using the author's company's product to test/compare something else
- *Community service*—Measuring something independent of the company's products (e.g., an open source project or a new graphics processing unit)

14.1.1   Benchmarketing

When companies compare their own products with alternatives and share the results publicly, it's typically to highlight where their product performs better. Of course, most technical readers bring a healthy dose of skepticism to such reports. They immediately assume that the benchmarks and test results are highly biased in the vendor's favor. Still, developers gravitate to numbers, so they'll likely read the article anyway.

14.1.2   Subtle benchmarketing

Interweaving the product into a benchmark focused on something else is a subtler form of marketing that targets developers. Using the company's product to test and compare different things has two main benefits:

- Tests are typically more practical and realistic. It's more interesting to see how a real product behaves when using technology X versus technology Y than to see how it performs using synthetic programs written only for testing purposes.
- It's a more socially acceptable way of marketing through numbers. Between the lines, the message can still be "Our product is fast regardless, but it's way faster when it runs on technology Z."

Benchmarks and test results are sometimes a side effect of genuine curiosity and experimentation. The company already decided to evaluate new hardware or a new software library—then they decided to share the results with the community. The benchmarks born from this process generally make for more authentic benchmarking blog posts, compared with "us versus them" posts.

14.1.3   Community service

Benchmarks and tests powered by the pure will to share are highly appreciated. Independent benchmarks might be created as weekend projects because the author is curious about which technology is more efficient. They can also be incidental, with the author noticing a strange result while implementing something and then subsequently deciding to measure it and write a blog post about it. Either way, those articles are perceived as the most objective and trustworthy because the author is not invested in any side of the comparison.

14.2 Audience

Let's dissect the target audience by the pattern flavor. Benchmarks and tests performed *by* the company *for* the company are likely read only by 1) people who are generally interested in the company's technology, or 2) those evaluating it for a future use case. Beyond those groups, these posts are unlikely to sneak past the ad-blocking software automatically burned into most readers' brains.

When the company uses its own products to test and benchmark *another* technology, the audience expands. Of course, it still lures in people interested in the company one way or the other. But it also appeals to readers who care about the tested technology. When a software company evaluates a brand-new chip dedicated to AI inference, for example, the target audience spans well beyond just people intrigued by what software the company produces. Anyone intrigued by the numbers for the tested technology might also be curious enough to read.

The last flavor, independent tests, brings in "everyone." A technical audience appreciates transparent research and gladly reads an independent benchmarking blog post, even if it isn't directly in their field of interest. Independent tests are often driven by dedication and curiosity, which automatically makes them more engaging than all the other benchmark flavors. The author found the topic compelling enough to spend time on, and readers are more likely to assume it's worth their attention as well.

14.3 Examples of "Benchmarks and Test Results" blog posts

In the wild, "Benchmarks and Test Results" blog posts are relatively rare compared to other types of blog posts. The amount of work required to plan and conduct a test and then write up the results in some insightful manner is a significant barrier to entry. But despite (or maybe because of) their rarity, they get a lot of attention. As mentioned at the beginning of this chapter, these posts face a herd skepticism that tends to spark spicy discussion, and that makes them quite prominent in social media feeds and virtual communities.

Here are some prime examples of blog posts that apply the "Benchmarks and Test Results" pattern, along with Piotr's commentary on each.

14.3.1 AWS Graviton2: Arm Brings Better Price-Performance than Intel

Author: Michał Chojnowski
Source: ScyllaDB Blog (https://mng.bz/75P4)

SUMMARY

This article shows the performance benefits of running a database on cloud instances with Amazon's Graviton2 ARM-based processors instead of instances running on x86 processors. The first paragraph teases the results, announcing a 15%–25% price performance improvement. The next paragraph shows the detailed specifications of the compared machines: their processors, number of cores, memory, network, storage, and on-demand price per hour (at the time of writing). Then we get disk input/output results for both setups (measured in iops [I/O operations per second] as well as throughput [labeled as "bandwidth" in the article]). That's followed by a description of the test setup and a list of six benchmark phases. Test results are then presented and visualized as charts and tables. The conclusion: Graviton servers already deliver comparable performance and also cost less per hour.

COMMENTARY

This article is doubly upfront: first it clearly states that Graviton2 won the benchmark comparison, and then it provides a summary including the numbers. For some blog post patterns, it makes absolutely no sense to start with a summary (see the "Bug Hunt" pattern in chapter 8). But it's a great technique for "Benchmarks and Test Results" posts. It properly sets the expectations and gives readers the freedom to trustfully skim over the charts and tables if desired.

This benchmark is meticulously specified, from the exact database setup and cloud machines to describing every step involved. It makes the results reproducible—ergo more trustworthy. I also appreciate the tips scattered throughout the article. For instance, when discussing available AWS instances, the author explains that SSD-based variants aren't ideal for low-latency persistent database systems. I consider this article a textbook example (duh, it's literally an example in a book) of the comparison flavor of the "Benchmarks and Test Results" pattern.

14.3.2 *The Relative Performance of C and Rust*

Author: Bryan Cantrill
Source: Bryan Cantrill's Blog (https://mng.bz/q0Zz)

SUMMARY

The article describes the author's performance comparison between C and Rust. The comparison was carried out by rewriting an application from the former to the latter, and putting both versions under scrutiny with benchmarks and profiling.

The introduction mentions that the blog originates from online discussions following another of the author's blog posts, "Rust After the Honeymoon" (described in chapter 12 as a "Thoughts on Trends" pattern example). The article follows with a specification of the testing environment, the hardware, tools used for measurements, and input. Next, a selected subset of performance counters is analyzed for both programs, noting that the Rust one experiences substantially fewer cache misses. The most likely culprit seems to be a different data structure (BTree in Rust, intrusive AVL tree in C). The following paragraphs thoroughly analyze that, including further benchmarks, charts, and swapping data structures in the Rust implementation to measure the differences.

The conclusion confirms that the performance difference is caused by a different choice of data structures. It also emphasizes that this is still an advantage of Rust, which allows developers to easily use powerful abstractions without a performance penalty. For C, a substantial engineering effort would be required to rewrite the program to use BTrees.

This article is a great example of an independent test since the author is not professionally engaged in either Rust or C language committees at the time of writing.

COMMENTARY

Let's start with some minor negatives to make the book more entertaining! I noticed two:

- I was a little confused about what was rewritten to Rust and tested. The name of the program (statemap) was mentioned once or twice, but it lacked an introduction, like
  - What does this program do in the first place?
  - Where can I find its source code?

NOTE   I ultimately found the Rust source code on GitHub: https://github.com/TritonDataCenter/statemap

- Dead links! They may have been put to death during Joyent's acquisition by Samsung Electronics, judging by the fact they were hosted at the joyent.com domain. Dead links happen naturally in blog posts, so it's not a big deal, especially for a post from distant 2018. I'm only bringing it up because it's good practice to just let the author know, via a comment or an email, which we did!

Nitpicking aside, this is a really nice read. The article is another example of the author's signature casual and entertaining writing style that's also seen in "Rust After the Honeymoon." The article also shares a fair amount of interesting charts, with small performance puzzles (like unexpected spikes), which are analyzed and resolved in the article. The test environment is well specified, and the article also contains lots of useful shell snippets for running the experiments locally—in case the readers feel like reproducing the results.

An additional perk is that the author of this article is also one of the original authors of the profiling tool used (DTrace), which makes all the shell invocations more trustworthy. An update added at the end to provide more charts with another C compiler is a nice touch—showing that the author truly cares about, and responds to, readers' feedback.

14.3.3 *Redpanda vs. Kafka: A Performance Comparison*

Author: Tristan Stevens
Source: Redpanda Blog (https://mng.bz/w54g)

SUMMARY

This article describes a series of tests and benchmarks indicating that Redpanda (an Apache Kafka alternative) is substantially faster and less resource-hungry than Apache Kafka. The first paragraph refers to earlier blog posts on Redpanda architecture and philosophy. The benchmarking environment is then explained, listing the hardware specification, as well as tested workload characteristics:

- Read/write request ratio
- Throughput
- Configuration specific to the Kafka protocol, such as the number of

- Topics
- Partitions
- Producers
- Consumers

It's disclaimed that tests are run on machines with modern NVMe drives, for which Redpanda is optimized. Then there are descriptions and visualizations of the results for a few configurations, unanimously showing Redpanda's lower and stabler latency in each case. The case in favor of Redpanda's performance is then further supported by throwing more resources at the Apache Kafka cluster for a "rigged" comparison. The final paragraph summarizes the results and encourages readers to try out the product.

COMMENTARY

This article is a clear example of the "tests performed against the company's product and its competition" flavor of the pattern. It's very enthusiastic about the product, and nothing less is expected. The testing environment is clearly explained and reproducible, which makes the benchmark results more trustworthy. It also applies the nice technique (quite commonly used in the "ours versus somebody else's" benchmarks subpattern) of giving the competition an unfair advantage—and then winning anyway. Here, Redpanda tries to even the score by running the Apache Kafka cluster with more resources.

Throughout the article, charts are clear and readable. I always appreciate the "lower is better" type notes that save readers a few seconds of trying to figure out whether the outcome is positive or negative.

The results in "ours versus theirs" benchmarks are hardly ever surprising because it's doubtful the article would have been published if the alternative was faster. Still, it's enjoyable to read how many orders of magnitude a product performs better. Running and publishing benchmarks against your competition's product has an interesting effect, though: it can trigger a blog war! This article was quite thoroughly criticized by another one, coming from the Apache Kafka trenches. Here's a reference for the curious:

Title: Kafka vs Redpanda Performance—Do the claims add up?
Author: Jack Vanlightly
Source: Jack Vanlightly's Blog (https://mng.bz/JNPQ)
That article addresses Redpanda's claims and shows where the author believes to have found inconsistencies. Interestingly, that article also incited a reaction—the Redpanda "Why `fsync`" blog post described in chapter 13.

14.3.4 *The Effect of Switching to TCMalloc on RocksDB Memory Use*

Author: Dmitry Vorobev
Source: Cloudflare Blog (https://mng.bz/PN65)

SUMMARY

This article compares application memory usage before and after switching to a new allocator implementation: TCMalloc. The introduction briefly explains that the elevated memory usage was noticed after migrating to a new storage solution, and the root cause was quickly narrowed down to the allocator. The next section is a thorough explanation of how the default C library allocator works, what memory arenas are, and why they contribute to high memory fragmentation. Next, a different allocator design is presented: TCMalloc, Google's customized allocator implementation. One TCMalloc feature that's especially important for the author's workload is effective memory reuse through caching. The author concludes that switching to TCMalloc reduced the memory usage 2.5-fold. The conclusion also emphasizes that choosing the right allocator for a given workload is critical for efficient memory utilization.

COMMENTARY

A keen eye might have noticed that the summary doesn't really cover the tests: their environment, steps, or assumptions. That's because they're not really in the article either! But this lack of details doesn't make the article bad. On the contrary, it's very educational in its introduction to both the default allocator implementation and TCMalloc. The results are there, visualized clearly with charts, and the conclusion is rational.

For the "Benchmarks and Test Results" pattern, it's good practice to make the tests reproducible by being transparent about all details. This article shifts the focus toward explaining the architectural and technical reasons why the results were in favor of TCMalloc, which makes up for fewer details about the testing setup. Presumably, the benchmarks would be difficult to reproduce without access to the project's source code. That code isn't open, so it's entirely reasonable to skip this. The technical part serves as a good introduction to memory allocation theory, teaching readers about the general idea as well as two specific implementations.

14.3.5 *How Much Does Rust's Bounds Checking Actually Cost?*

Author: Alana Marzoev
Source: Readyset Blog (https://blog.readyset.io/bounds-checks/)

SUMMARY

This article describes how the author measured the overhead of Rust's bounds checks: a feature designed to make programs safer by default, at the cost of additional CPU instructions. The introduction presents the motivation for enabling bounds checks by default, listing a few known security breaches in open source programs caused by lack of bounds checks. Next, the author presents a technique for counting bounds checks during program execution with the help of Linux's stock debugger (gdb). Then we see what happens when running the analysis for a few versions of Readyset's product:

- An unchanged program, which provides the baseline for the test results
- A program recompiled with fewer bounds checks, achieved by replacing selected function calls with substitutes that don't perform checks
- A program recompiled with a modified Rust compiler that doesn't emit bounds checks

All executions end up returning results within a margin of error. The conclusion drawn in the article is that bounds checking overhead is negligible in Rust. The exact cause of this observation remains unresolved, with a guess that perhaps branch prediction mechanisms in modern CPUs alleviate the cost of additional checks.

COMMENTARY

On the one hand, this article is full of practical tips that I find interesting and directly useful in everyday hacking. For example,

- Using gdb to count how many times a specific function is called, and comparing the results before and after a program is modified
- Pointers to intriguing bits in Rust's standard library implementation and the official Rust compiler

What doesn't pass scrutiny are the drawn conclusions. The title ("How Much Does Rust's Bounds Checking Actually Cost") and section titles (e.g., "How Much Do the Bounds Checks Cost?") suggest that bounds checks are studied in the general case. Results achieved in the article showed that all executions fall within the same error margin. That doesn't really prove that bounds checks are negligible but that bounds checks are negligible for Readyset's program. That's an interesting conclusion on its own, showing that in the case of Readyset, opportunities for optimization lie elsewhere. Bounds checks do, in fact, have a cost—it just shows for different workloads. For instance, a quick internet search points to Alex Kladov's experiment, proving that bounds checks effectively prevent the compiler from auto-vectorization. In certain cases, it makes the CPU overhead as large as 100% (https://github.com/matklad/bounds-check-cost).

> **NOTE**   Auto-vectorization optimizes code by automatically converting sequential operations into parallel SIMD (single instruction, multiple data) instructions, available in modern processor architectures. It's not uncommon to see a 4x or 8x speedup of auto-vectorized compute-intensive loops.

Let's also prove a point that blog post readers (including me) can't resist criticizing spotted inconsistencies—and take a short detour to point out a technical problem in someone else's blog post! Another nitpick for the benchmarking environment is how the third scenario was tested. Using a modified Rust compiler, itself recompiled to not generate certain bounds checks, makes the third result rather unreliable. Compilers are extremely sensitive to changes, and the stock Rust compiler is probably a heavily optimized binary, specialized for its operating system, CPU architecture, and so on. Recompiling a compiler locally and then compiling the test program with it is unlikely to produce results comparable to programs compiled with the stock compiler. In this particular case, it's not really a problem because all achieved results were within the same margin of error. However if the results did in fact differ, it would be difficult to draw any conclusions from the difference.

At the same time, I really appreciate how the author showed what to change in the compiler implementation to stop generating bounds checks. It's also valuable that the article educates readers that recompiling the stock Rust compiler is not that hard, and its source code is actually quite comprehensible. Final score: a very educational blog post, but its benchmark results are not generally relevant to the topic (they are relevant to a specific use case).

14.4 Characteristics

The "Benchmarks and Test Results" pattern is a distant relative of "Bug Hunt" and "Non-markety Product Perspectives" patterns. The core element of repeated experiments and measurements can also be found in bug-hunting blog posts. However, the main difference is that benchmarking articles tend to be very open about the end result, often even hinting at it in their titles. Many instances of this pattern also share a characteristic with "Non-markety Product Perspectives" articles: the product is usually an important actor, although not always the main character.

14.4.1 Numeric and visual

Benchmarks and test results are best expressed with numbers and charts—specifically, ones focused on metrics the target readers care about. Readers click these articles to discover and compare new numbers, and they won't leave happy unless all the charts are perfectly clear and comprehensible. Some articles might seem visually overwhelming at first, but readers are used to skimming over a few charts to continue reading. Benchmarking blog posts are also abundant in all kinds of tables, especially ones that compare one set of numbers with another.

The best benchmark and test blog posts use visualizations that

- *Tell a clear story*—For example, the visualization might provide a series of data points that show a performance problem emerging over time, or brag about extremely low and consistent latency after a fix. Such takeaways are easier to process visually than in text, plus tying them to data points makes them more convincing and interesting. Some charts even add a callout in the graphic to highlight the story (for example, the header image in the Redpanda blog post).
- *Achieve a data density that justifies the amount of space the graphic occupies on the page*— For example, a simple data point that could be replaced by a single sentence does not meet this requirement. But a flame graph certainly does.
- *Minimize the "Lie Factor"*—The Lie Factor, a term coined by Edward R. Tufte, measures accurately a change in the size of the chart's visual elements (like bar heights or bubble sizes) matches the magnitude of change in the underlying data. It's calculated by dividing the size of the effect shown in the graphic by the size of the effect in the actual data. The result should be close to 1; if not, the graph is overstating or understating something.

14.4.2 Guilty until proven innocent

It's as dystopian as it sounds: in the world of engineering blog posts, the author is presumed guilty of rigging the benchmark results. The burden is on the author to meticulously prove that the benchmarks are legit. That defensive approach often manifests itself in the article by

- Explicitly stating why the results of the comparison are fair (e.g., they were run under identical conditions)
- Sharing all the relevant environment details: the chosen hardware, software configuration, operating system, etc.
- Showing the exact steps to reproduce the same results, or sharing a repository where the benchmark source code is kept
- Prominently mentioning anyone beyond the author's company who participated in the original testing process or validated the results

14.4.3 *Quasi academic*

"Benchmarks and Test Results" blog posts generally tend to adopt a more academic style than most blog posts. Although they aren't structured like a peer-reviewed research paper, many include all the key elements you would typically find in one:

- *Abstract*—A short upfront summary of what was tested, how, and what was found
- *Background*—Why the author decided to perform this study
- *Methods*—How the author performed this study
- *Results*— What the author discovered by conducting the study
- *Discussion*—The author's interpretation of the results

For example, the benchmark blog posts by Redpanda and ScyllaDB don't use these exact terms, but they do ultimately check all of the boxes. Those two examples also follow the academic tradition of pointing out any notable limitations that could affect the conclusions drawn from the experiment. The Redpanda post noted that they wished they could have compared Redpanda and Kafka on equal resources. And the ScyllaDB example noted that they wished they could have tested against the latest (newly released) x86-based instances. The fact that the Rust bounds checking article did not actually highlight the study's notable limitations was the main criticism we had of that otherwise intriguing article.

The writing style of these articles is also more formal than most blog post patterns—more akin to the "How We Built It" pattern's style than any others, but often even more formal than that. The sentences tend to be austere with minimal trace of the author's personality or emotions ("We did this, we found that"). This makes complete sense considering that it's the (fallible, biased, emotional, etc.) human behind the benchmark who will be presumed guilty until proven innocent. The less humanity seeps into the blog post, the more objective it all sounds.

This impersonal tone is most common in the "product comparison" benchmarks, which are also the ones that face the greatest skepticism and scrutiny. As you can see from examples such as Alana Marzoev's and Bryan Cantrill's articles, more community-service-oriented "Benchmarks and Test Results" articles might be infused with more personality and character.

14.5   Dos & don'ts

Having a rock solid test is fundamental for writing a great "Benchmarks and Test Results" blog post. If you lack that, stop right there and rethink your approach (perhaps you have fodder for a "Lessons Learned" blog post instead). But a great test doesn't just automatically translate to a great test results blog. Here are some tips for making both the test *and* the resulting blog post worth the considerable effort that the project likely required.

14.5.1   Read Brendan Gregg's "Systems Performance"

Do yourself a favor and read (or maybe even re-read) Brendan Gregg's renowned book, *Systems Performance*, or at least the "Benchmarking" chapter. It covers important topics such as

- Tests being reproducible
- Caring about correctness—fast, but incorrect results are not useful
- Avoiding "apples versus oranges" comparisons
- Ensuring all caches, if they exist, are warmed (unless somebody wants to benchmark the cache warmup process specifically)

The book is a comprehensive study of doing benchmarks the right way!

14.5.2   Show how to reproduce the results

If benchmarks and tests can't be reproduced, then they won't be trusted. All benchmarks and tests should be served with a detailed list of steps for reproducing them unless the tested software or hardware is prohibitively expensive or, for whatever reason, not generally available. Ideally, complement the article with an open source repository that includes all the source code and scripts for running the benchmark. Readers are way more likely to trust the results if they come with a recipe for how to validate them.

14.5.3   Don't exaggerate

Results that are creatively rigged to exaggerate the difference never pass the scrutiny of the online crowd, so it's really in your own best interest to prepare accurate charts. Actively consider and avoid the Lie Factor (referenced in 14.4.1), which means that charts like the one in figure 14.1 are not welcome:

Exaggerated results are likely to incite (and likely deserve) low blows in online discussions. And once a reader thinks that one finding looks scammy, they will probably dismiss the entire blog post (and underlying project) as being deceitful. It's just not worth it; don't exaggerate.

14.5.4   Don't neglect

"Benchmarks and Test Results" posts are natural targets for questioning, challenging, and cross-examining. Assume that errors, negligence, omissions, and other logical flaws will be discovered and then noted online. Plan for this and make it a priority to update your article whenever necessary.

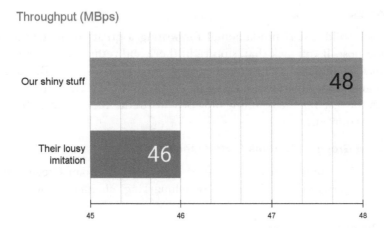

Figure 14.1   A misleading representation of test results. Note that although our shiny stuff seems to have double the throughput at first glance, there's actually just a 2 MBps difference.

Updates can be appended to the article as a new paragraph, titled something like "Update: Feb 29th 2024." This is the perfect place to reference an online dispute (ideally with a hyperlink to the related discussion). That could include agreeing with criticism and fixing parts of the article. Or, it's equally fine to publicly debunk accusations.

Updates might also involve rerunning all the benchmarks and tests in a new environment (for instance, because promising new hardware just became available). Don't limit yourself to one update; multiple ones are perfectly fine. At some point, when the number of updates reaches critical mass (say, when the number of update paragraphs is approaching the number of regular ones), it's time for a follow-up blog post. And once you publish that follow-up, be sure to update the original blog post to link to it. People might still stumble on the earlier one, so it's a nice gesture to go all Amazon-esque and politely inform them that "there is a newer edition of this item."

14.5.5 Boil it down, spell it out

Behind every great benchmark is a complex test that was probably quite frustrating to run. But don't inflict an equal amount of pain and suffering on your readers by making the resulting blog post difficult to read and decipher.

Readers have clicked into your post curious to learn about what you did, why you did it that way, and what you discovered. Don't make them inspect 25 beautiful graphs, scroll back and forth across multiple sections for comparison, or run their own mental analysis of your results in order to figure out what's best and why.

Specifically,

- *Call out the key takeaways upfront.* This isn't a bug hunt blog post, where it's actually fun for readers to place themselves in the scene and try to solve the mystery as they follow along. Spoilers are not only acceptable here; they're desired and appreciated. If the reader doesn't care about the results, they certainly won't care about all the low-level details of how you arrived at them.

- *Show side-by-side when you want readers to compare.* If your ultimate goal is to show that A is faster than B, don't put your results from A in one section, your results from B in the next section, and leave the comparison as "an exercise for the reader." Stack them in charts and tables when feasible. Show raw numbers, but also go beyond raw numbers. Do the math for them and calculate the percent difference between the two values.

- *Make "better" unmistakable at a glance.* Sometimes higher is better (e.g., with throughput). Other times, lower is the desired outcome (e.g., with latency). Put yourself in place of the average impatient and often distracted reader. Use colors, labels, and captions to make it obvious what outcome is considered better in each scenario.

- *Avoid information overload.* It's great that you ran 25 different scenarios; thorough testing is certainly appreciated. But do you think the reader really wants to read all about each and every one of them? Since you have so many options to choose from, select a representative sample to focus on here. Explain why you selected these ones and assure the reader that you're not cherry-picking results to support a bias. Supplement that with an overview of the "also ran" test results so the entire scope of the testing project is accounted for. Finally, share a link to the complete results in case anyone (perhaps someone working on the technology involved in that test) is really hungry for that extra level of detail.

Summary

- There are at least three distinct types of "Benchmarks and Test Results" articles: 1) tests that compare the company's product to its competition; 2) comparisons of something (such as cloud infrastructure or hardware) that are performed using the company's product; and 3) measuring something that's unrelated to any of the company's products (e.g., an open source project or a new graphics processing unit).

- The purpose of these posts ranges from overt "benchmarketing" to pure educational value.

- Readers vary based on the test type: generally, the less prominently the company's product is featured, the broader the potential audience.

- Engineers are irresistibly attracted to numbers, so these posts get a lot of attention.

- Posts in this pattern face a harsh level of scrutiny, so both the testing and the reporting must be meticulous and bulletproof.

- Top tips
  - Study up on benchmarking best practices.
  - Show readers how to reproduce the results.

- Don't exaggerate, especially if you have a horse in the race.
- Keep evolving the article as you battle critics, learn more, and run more tests.
- Make it simple for your reader to identify and interpret the most important takeaways.

Part 4

Promotion, adaptation, and expansion

An effective blog post can continue paying dividends long after its initial publication. Part 4 shares options for squeezing more value from your work: from ways to keep your posts in front of your target readers to tips for extending into conference speaking and book writing opportunities:

- Chapter 15 presents options for squeezing more value from your blog post.
- Chapter 16 shares strategies for presenting conference talks based on your blog post.
- Chapter 17 provides an honest look at what to consider if you're intrigued with becoming a book author.

Getting attention

This chapter covers

- Getting more eyes (and ears) on your ideas after the blog post is published
- Sharing your blog post across social media and virtual communities
- Using your blog post as a stepping stone to additional opportunities (articles, guest posts, podcasts, and so on)
- Tracking how people are reaching, reading, and reacting to your blog post

Once your blog post is published, yay! Nice work, pat yourself on the back and enjoy a celebratory beverage of choice. But don't consider your work here done. You wouldn't just drop your most impressive project on GitHub in silence and then never think about it or touch it again. Don't abandon your newly published blog post either. You've already invested a good amount of thought and time into it. Spending just a little more to give it a good start in the world can help you and the community get much more out of it.

Think of it this way: would you rather

- Do a few things to increase the reach of your blog post (say, threefold), or
- Plan, draft, optimize, review, proofread, and publish three times as many blog posts?

Of course, it's always tempting to move on to the next shiny object. But strongly consider doing what you can with that existing blog post while it's still fresh in your mind.

This chapter covers a broad spectrum of ways to get your work in front of more people in your target audience, whether you're the stereotypical introverted programmer, someone who thrives on human interaction, or somewhere in between. Here, we cover

- *Sharing across social media platforms and virtual communities*—You want to distribute your post across (and beyond) your network, spark discussion, and give it a chance to trend or go viral.
- *Getting it published in a selective tech publication*—You want to draft off their reputation, which brings prestige, draws discerning readers, and could get your article on Google News.
- *Guest blogging on another community's blog*—You want to reach the community behind some technology or project you referenced in your blog.
- *Cross-posting copies of your article on blog post aggregators*—You want to see what additional exposure you can gain from (usually) just 5 minutes of brainless copy/pasting.
- *Participating in conferences, podcasts, and livestreams*—You want to talk about your article topic in a way that can quickly elevate your brand and reputation as an expert.

At the end, we'll also review different metrics you can review to understand how your work was received and get you thinking about what you might do differently the next time.

As you consider and prioritize options, think back to the goals that you defined when planning the article (chapter 4). For example, if you're looking to spark deep engagement with experts in a highly specialized field, maybe Hacker News is not a top priority. However, presenting a related talk at a niche conference could be a worthwhile next step.

> **WARNING** Be sure to check company protocol related to social media, community engagement, and all the other promotion opportunities outlined here before you dive in.

15.1   *Choose your own adventure*

Your blog post won't magically find its own way to readers. But there are many different options for helping it along. Before we get into specific tactics, let's take a high-level look at what might work best across various comfort zones.

If you're an extreme introvert, don't despair. Async remote communication lets you interact with people on your own terms. Many social media platforms and virtual communities enable near real-time interaction, but you don't have to participate in that way. If you make even a minor effort to become a contributing community member, that will help you extend your blog post's reach. And perhaps you have the patience to spin off customized versions of your article for publication on other sites. Your extroverted peers likely do not.

On the other hand, extreme extroverts who actually *want* to interact with humans in real time should find no shortage of opportunities for doing so. There are countless podcasting and streaming options that cover the programming space. And they're all hunting for the rare species of programmer who checks all of the following boxes:

- They're experienced with popular or trending technologies.
- They're good verbal communicators.
- They're willing to carve out some time to participate.

If you're a member of this select group, strongly consider looking for podcasts or livestreams where you can talk more about the topic you covered in your blog post.

What about conferences? Extroverts will feel right at home here, but introverts shouldn't instantly rule it out. While the thought of presenting live in front of an audience of thousands could terrify an introvert, a smaller specialized session might work. And virtual conferences can lower anxiety even more. Some even let you prerecord your session so you can become a public speaker without actually speaking live or in public.

The bottom line is that there's something for everyone. Given that, let's look at what's involved in the various blog post promotion and extension options.

15.2 Sharing across social and virtual communities

This option isn't really optional. If you want your peers to read your blog post, you really need to share it personally. But you can certainly do so as a good community member, with modesty and precision. The spray-and-pray approach (just indiscriminately posting the same thing in as many places as possible) likely won't yield favorable short-term results, and it definitely won't help you foster community goodwill over the long term.

If your post was published on your company's blog, they will likely take the lead on some level of promotion. Considering all the company's official accounts and marketing efforts, they might have access to more people than you do. But given how developers generally dislike engaging with company accounts, don't rely on that promotion. Authentic sharing from your own accounts is often the perfect non-markety marketing strategy for getting your blog post in front of your technical peers.

In this section, we'll cover a phased approach for ramping up your community engagement, dos and don'ts for sharing your blog post when it's first published, and non-spammy ways to keep it alive (e.g., by seeding it into relevant discussions). Spoiler: We're not offering yet another "N tips guaranteed to get your article trending on Hacker News!" article. You're welcome to search the internet for such, but we don't believe you can (or should) game the system with tricks. Write a solid technical article, engage with relevant communities in a transparent and authentic manner, and your luck surface area will increase immensely.

NOTE   We're trying to keep this discussion as platform-agnostic as possible, focusing on strategies that are applicable across the constantly shifting world of social media and virtual communities. However, we do discuss Hacker News specifically since it's such a unique beast.

Even if you're not a super social person, push yourself to engage with the online community in some capacity starting now. It doesn't have to be time-consuming, fake, or otherwise painful. And you might actually find it valuable, even beyond your ulterior motive of getting your blog posts noticed and read.

Piotr's story: Why I stopped avoiding social media

I haven't exactly been an avid fan of social media, and I'm still not. Let me just self-quote part of my goodbye message before leaving ScyllaDB:

I'm also leaving my contact details, should anyone want to stay in touch:

> email: <redacted>
>
> phone: <redacted> (please don't call if you just want to sell me solar panels, I already have a set)
>
> **twitter: not going to happen (take reading this note as an opportunity to ditch social media)**

And yet here I am, broadcasting daily messages on various social media.

Fortunately, Elon Musk helped me keep my promise not to use Twitter by rebranding the company to X. Otherwise, my integrity would have been compromised.

My breakthrough moment came when I joined an even earlier stage startup. Here, engineers sharing interesting articles they read or wrote was the primary means for getting the project noticed in the engineering world. Creating and actually using an X account was unavoidable. But it also was tolerable.

Don't get me wrong. I still hate social media and blame social media for the ever-shortening attention span worldwide. The difference is that I used to passionately hate it, and now the emotion is strictly passive.

Social media is just a means to an end: sharing slightly opinionated knowledge with peers and getting in contact with like-minded individuals. Social media is undoubtedly useful, both for beginner writers to bootstrap their initial audience and for experienced writers to easily share and discuss their articles with interested peers. For me, the turning point was realizing there's more to gain from using social media for professional purposes than from just hating it from the sidelines.

15.2.1 Connecting with the community

NOTE   If you're already happily engaging with the community, skip ahead to section 15.2.3, which covers some commonly overlooked strategies for keeping the blog post momentum going. The next two sections are both targeted to social-media-averse engineers—like Piotr used to be!

If you plan to discuss your blog post on social media and virtual communities (and you should!), start by becoming a good citizen. If humans or algorithms notice that you're there solely to promote links to one site (coincidentally, the one hosting your own blog posts), it won't go over well. You will be the equivalent of that relative who doesn't acknowledge you exist until they want something. Moreover, if you don't "warm up" your account, you might not even be allowed to share your blog post when the time comes. In some communities, account posting privileges are restricted until you've established yourself as a trustworthy community member (e.g., by commenting on others' discussions).

If you're reluctant to participate, consider the following approach to easing in—just dipping your toes in the water to start and then going progressively deeper as you get acclimated.

PHASE 1: OBSERVING

At first, just sit on the sidelines, look around, and try to get a feel for what's going on. Make it a habit to spend a little time exploring on a regular basis. Also use the strategies covered in section 2.3 (about exposing yourself to blog topic triggers) to direct what you're looking at. Let's quickly recap. For social media,

- Get ahead of the recommendation algorithms by curating lists or other feeds of people you trust.
- Start by tracking a small set of trusted accounts, then expand cautiously.
- Occasionally glimpse at what the algorithms recommend to see if you're missing anything interesting.

For virtual communities,

- Find a few specialized, well-moderated communities relevant to the topics you write about.
- Again, start small and expand cautiously.
- For Hacker News, become familiar with the site's rich search functionality.

And above all, actually set reminders to start checking on a regular basis as well as timers to *stop* checking after a few minutes. Timeboxing it this way prevents you from wandering off in intriguing yet often unproductive directions.

PHASE 2: REACTING

Now ease in by simply liking, upvoting, or boosting posts that you found interesting. It's a polite way to tell the person behind the post that you found their contribution valuable. You're also helping to shape the community at large by weighing in on what posts should be elevated by the algorithms and/or rankings. In some communities, post visibility depends solely on the number of upvotes.

Also consider following the accounts behind social media posts that you like. And don't be surprised if they end up following you back. Maybe they will return the favor and like one of your blog posts someday.

PHASE 3: RESPONDING

The next level of engagement is to actually share some words about other people's social posts. Remember that the simple one-click reactions already indicate something like "interesting," so if you're going to add words, you should go a step beyond that. For example, you could respond with

- Something you found particularly interesting about what they shared
- A question you had about what they shared
- Your own experiences with that topic
- A helpful resource that's relevant to the discussion

The most valuable comments add new information and/or advance the discussion in some productive way. It never hurts to kick off your comment with something nice, especially if you're ultimately requesting clarification or sharing a different experience. For example: "Great read, really interesting point about {blah}. Curious if {whatever}." Even a simple "Thanks for sharing!" preface could work. Just make the extra effort to set the tone as conversational, not confrontational.

PHASE 4: CREATING YOUR OWN SOCIAL POSTS (BUT NOT YET SHARING YOUR BLOG POSTS)

Finally, take the plunge and start creating your own social posts. Not sure what to say? Consider

- Some cool trick, tool, or repo you just stumbled on and why you think it's so cool
- A question for the community ("Has anyone else ever encountered…")
- An article, book, or video that intrigued you and why
- A lesson learned the hard way
- A seed idea for a future blog post

> **TIP**   You don't need to 100% agree with every word in a resource that you want to share. Feel free to say something like: "Great read! While I don't agree with everything in this article, it's interesting to see…"

Before you start composing anything, check all the rules of engagement, particularly for virtual communities. What's forbidden, do you need to tag things in a certain way (e.g., on subreddits), do you need to be extremely careful about the title of your submission (e.g., on Hacker News), and so on. Just like every family has its weird rituals, every virtual community has its own protocol and guidelines. Learn them now and practice them before you share your own blog posts!

15.2.2 *Sharing (and discussing) your blog post*

Let's assume that you've already become a contributing member of some social media platforms and virtual communities, and now you've got a shiny new blog post to share. What now? We recommend the following staggered plan of attack.

TIP Once you start sharing your own blog posts, remember to continue contributing to virtual communities in other ways as well! As the Lobsters community (https://lobste.rs/about) put it: "It's great to have authors participate in the community, but not to exploit it as a write-only tool for product announcements or driving traffic to their work. As a rule of thumb, self-promo should be less than a quarter of one's stories and comments." This is a reasonable guideline to follow everywhere.

STEP 1: SHARE IT FROM YOUR SOCIAL MEDIA HANDLES

Your own social media handles are the natural place to start. Anyone following you there expressed some interest in you and/or your work. Telling them about a blog post you just wrote is totally in scope!

Moreover, the fact that you'll be broadcasting to (at least some) people you actually know makes this a great place to begin. Some of your connections will like and reshare it, their connections might see it and comment—rinse and repeat. Since many of the people seeing your post have some traceable connection back to you, any discussion here is likely to be more constructive and civil than in a fully anonymous comments section full of concealed accounts.

Try to publish your post when the people you expect to respond are actually awake. A post that gets an initial boost will typically be recommended more than one that lies untouched for half a day. And consider starting with a social media platform where posts have a short life span—an X-like platform where new posts burn bright for a matter of minutes, then fade away. This makes for great proving grounds. Try something here, get some rapid feedback (hopefully), and apply any lessons learned before you share your blog post somewhere else.

What should you say in the actual social post? Here are some ideas in case you're not otherwise inspired:

- New blog post on {topic}, covering…
- {Interesting_takeaway}. Full discussion in…
- {Something_about_the_challenge_discussed}. I decided to tackle that here…
- {Some_background_on_why_you_wrote}. Here's what I came up with…
- Blogged: {title}

Also, feel free to acknowledge anyone who contributed to, reviewed, or inspired your article, especially if they're active on the social media platform you're using.

Be sure to apply hashtags and reference @ handles as appropriate. A rule of thumb: use a handle if you want someone to get a notification (and ideally react or reshare); use a hashtag if you want to get on the radar of people who are following a certain technology or trend. Also note that some bots retweet posts that use a particular hashtag, and hashtags are sometimes used to collect candidates for various newsletters.

For example, a social post announcing the fake Zig blog post from chapter 4 should include @FakeDB (in hopes that they reshare it to their community) as well as #Postgres (to get on the radar of the many humans and bots that track Postgres developments).

What about Zig? We'd suggest mentioning @ziglang prominently in the post, then tacking on a #ziglang hashtag at the end. It would be amazing if the official Zig language account shared the article, but it would also be helpful to get on the radar of newsletters that pick up stories mentioning #ziglang.

> **TIP**   Before you use a hashtag, search for it and check that 1) it's used fairly often and 2) it's not also used for something totally different and possibly sketchy. The latter could result in a lot of followers of dubious intent.

STEP 2: MONITOR OBSESSIVELY AND RESPOND RAPIDLY

The second your social post goes live, inspect it to ensure everything is as expected. Confirm that the thumbnail image you hopefully already set in the metadata (see chapter 7) isn't awkwardly cropped, the accounts you referenced are properly hyperlinked, and so forth. Maybe alert some of your close peers so they can give it an instant boost. Then, wait patiently (or not) to see if there's a response.

As you move on with your life, check in frequently to see if there are any notifications. If you followed our advice to share it on one platform at a time, it's much easier to monitor.

If people do comment, respond as rapidly as your other commitments permit. Here are a few tips:

- *One to many*—Don't just respond to the individual who commented; respond with everyone scanning the comments in mind. For every person who is actively engaging, there are likely many more lurkers following the conversation silently. Even if you can't change the mind of a combative jerk, it's still worthwhile to provide additional details and explanations for the sake of the silent majority.

- *Thanks giving*—Assume a positive intention and behave as if anyone who comments is doing you a favor (they might be!). Explicitly or implicitly thank anyone who engages. This could range from "Thanks for pointing that out—I'm rerunning the tests now and will report back (as well as update the blog post)" to "Appreciate the feedback— interesting observation."

- *Focus on facts*—A discussion sharing facts like your experiences, test results, or accepted industry knowledge will inevitably be more productive than one based on opinion. Feature facts versus opinions in your own responses; hopefully others will follow your lead.

- *Know what you don't know*—If you don't know something, "great question" is a perfectly acceptable response and preferable to trying to guess. If you're lucky, someone else will jump in with the answer. If not, you have your homework cut out for you. And if you discover something interesting, feel free to merge it into the current blog post or start planning a new one to share what you learned.

- *Be curious*—As we recommended for the review process, be curious rather than defensive when you start engaging with someone who questions an aspect of your work. Try to understand where they're coming from. Maybe they misunderstood something (which is a sign that you should clarify something in your article). Maybe you overlooked something (which is a sign that you should extend or rewrite some part of your article, and thank them for pointing it out). Or perhaps they're just a jerk (which is simply a sign that some people are jerks).

Speaking of jerks: What if someone is argumentative to the point where the conversation is not productive? One approach is to totally ignore it. Another is to agree to disagree, then ignore the individual. A simple "Okay" or "Comment noted" response can not-so-subtly signal that you're moving on. And if you have the power to delete (e.g., if the discussion is embedded within your own blog), feel free to wield that power as needed. Your (serious) readers will thank you.

But not everyone is a jerk! If you cross paths with some interesting people commenting on your post, consider following them. You might also want to add them to one of the lists or other mechanisms you created to discover interesting discussions without relying on the algorithms.

Finally, remember that your article is out in the wild now, so people might be talking about it in places where you never shared it. If you want to obsessively monitor the conversation, search for the name of your article (try searching for the article title with quotes and without), then sorting by "new" or "latest" to see if anything turns up. This won't catch everything, but it might uncover some relevant conversations that you'll want to be a part of.

> **TIP** What if your post goes unnoticed? Maybe your target audience was focused on a major world event or simply distracted by the latest meme. Or perhaps the wording of your post didn't catch people's attention. Feel free to try another variation after a little time has passed. But first, check the blog post views and other metrics (discussed at the end of this chapter). Maybe people are reading and appreciating the blog post without engaging with the social media post.

STEP 3: SHARE IT IN FOCUSED VIRTUAL COMMUNITIES

After you've witnessed the initial response to both your social post and your blog post, revise both if needed; then start on the next wave: posting across focused virtual communities. Target the specific subreddits, Discord servers, and other communities where experts (or aficionados at least) discuss the specific technologies and topics covered in your blog post. These should all be communities that you've been participating in for a little while now.

Why go in this order of social media platforms first, then these targeted communities next, and finally Hacker News last? If all the planets align,

- The initial vetting on social media will help you uncover any major points of contention in what's likely the friendliest of these three options. You can then update your blog post or have your responses prepared before you broaden your reach.
- The discussion in focused virtual communities could get experts talking about your article. Again, it's another chance for feedback, which might help you

harden your article even further. And getting traction here is likely your best chance at having someone other than you or your teammates post the article on Hacker News.

To increase your chances of success, start by re-reading all the rules of engagement (yes, again) and ensuring that you're following the protocol exactly. Then spend a few moments writing a message that's geared specifically to using this blog post as a conversation starter in this particular community.

For example, let's return to the fake Zig blog post. One possible message for a FakeDB-focused subreddit could be:

> *My team and I were struggling with migrating data from Postgres into FakeDB clusters. TurtleMigrator was just too slow and painful. We ended up creating a new migrator tool and open sourced it. I wrote up more details in this blog post: {link}. Would love to hear your thoughts and happy to answer any questions.*

But sharing it on a Zig Discord server would call for a totally different approach, something like

> *My team and I just used Zig to implement a data migration tool for a critical project. This was our first experience with Zig (we all come from C, C++, and Rust backgrounds). I shared our experience in this blog post: {link}. We also open sourced the project. All feedback appreciated—and we welcome project contributors, too!*

When you're ready, share your message, maybe one community at a time just in case someone points out something you want to change. Then track activity, respond as described in Step 2, and repeat as desired across relevant communities. Also, periodically search other relevant virtual communities to discover any additional discussions.

> **TIP**   In virtual communities where everyone's identity is highly obfuscated, it's especially polite to add a comment announcing yourself as the author of the post. A simple comment like "Hi, author of the article here—happy to answer any questions" will do the trick.

STEP 4: TRY HACKER NEWS

So you've shared the blog post on all your social media accounts and all the focused virtual communities that you want to engage with and *still* nobody has posted it on Hacker News? Okay, see if a colleague with reasonable karma will submit it. As a last resort, do it yourself. Then dust off your good luck charm and be prepared to engage.

> **WARNING**   If you're not yet aware of the vitriol that's endemic to Hacker News, do yourself a *huge* favor and take a look around before you engage. Pay particularly close attention to the notorious comment sections. The criticism can be crazy and brutal. Many feel that it's worth it because trending on Hacker News can generate so much attention. But remember that Hacker News is read by a broad swath of technologists as well as professional internet critics. A smaller bump on a more focused virtual community could very likely lead to more meaningful engagements than a spike on Hacker News. Still, "trending on

Hacker News" is treated as a badge of honor across the tech community. If you're tempted by the promise of that fleeting fame, submit your article fully aware of what you're getting yourself into (and perhaps dragging your entire blog site/project/company into).

TIP To quickly surface the most recent submissions for your site, filter Hacker News posts by domain. For example, if you wanted to search for articles from the domain example.com, you would use https://news.ycombinator.com/from?site=example.com.

On some other platforms, a coordinated effort could help a solid submission gain traction with the algorithms. On Hacker News, too much coordination is likely to hurt more than it helps. If you really want to try, ensure that all associated activity is as organic and natural as possible. That includes

- Working with a group of people who normally browse, upvote, and comment on articles and have all accumulated respectable karma.
- Having those people engage like they normally do, naturally browsing and engaging with a variety of main page and/or new links, before clicking and upvoting your link.
- Not having the exact same set of people engage every time there's an article from your blog post's domain.

Also, know that attempts to game the system could be dangerous, to the point where the offending accounts and/or domains could be penalized or "shadowbanned" (meaning they're instantly [dead] and cannot receive votes/comments). See "A List of Hacker News's Undocumented Features and Behaviors" (https://mng.bz/1aPR) for more details on shadowbanning, as well as all sorts of other Hacker News trivia and technicalities.

Here is a handpicked collection of little-known details:

- Users can flag submissions as inappropriate.
- Efforts to evade voting manipulation detection mechanisms must be more elaborate than "point users to the front page (or new page) and ask them to find and upvote your submission." This trick does not actually work at all.
- Posting with a link and then adding text as the first comment is recommended.
- Moderators will give warnings to prominent users prior to shadowbanning.

Finally, there are two important tips from moderator "dang":

- "HN readers want the inside view. Introduce yourself, tell how you came to work on this and what's different about it, and give interesting details about the problem, the project, the implementation. Don't just say what you've made. Include the how and why. Those two are actually the more interesting to this community."
- "Don't talk to HN like a company ('Team Oneshop') or other abstraction. That creates a feeling of separation from the community. Instead participate as

yourself (or yourselves) in a community of fellow builders and entrepreneurs. Then it will feel like you're approaching the community as one of them."

15.2.3 *Keeping it alive*

Don't let your article fade away after the initial buzz dies down. Consider these options for keeping the momentum going:

- *Pin*—Pin the related social post to the top of your social profile until you publish your next (and even more impressive) blog post, at least.
- *Hunt*—Continue to hunt down any mentions of your blog post across social media platforms and virtual communities. Then, engage with the discussions and follow any valuable contributors you cross paths with.
- *Seed*—Embed the blog post into relevant discussions across the platforms and communities you regularly monitor. For example, "{comment_on_their_article}. I explored this topic from the {whatever} angle and found that…" Take advantage of each platform's search functionality and look for relevant discussions every few weeks or so.
- *Trace*—Check for backlinks to your article. You can use https://ahrefs.com/backlink-checker/ for a limited view that doesn't require any registration. If you're willing to register, Neil Patel's Ubersuggest provides an extensive list (https://neilpatel.com/backlinks/). If you find some backlinks, share your thoughts on those articles across your social network. For example: "Ah, nice to see my article on {topic} featured in {place}. {link_to_your_article} {link_to_the_referring_article}." Note that we discuss backlinks and other analytics, like referral sources, at the end of this chapter.
- *Include*—Link to a lively Hacker News discussion at the top of your blog post and/or embed your social post announcing it at the end of your blog post. That way, anyone who comes late to the party can easily find and review the discussion.

15.3 *Publishing in selective tech publications*

Now, let's shift focus to truly optional amplification options, starting with publishing in selective tech publications. First, a little backstory to better understand what you're working with.

Once upon a time, blogs did not exist. Instead, engineers looking to share technical articles had to do so in printed tech magazines and journals which were—believe it or not—mailed to people's homes or workplaces! In addition to peer-reviewed journals run by IEEE and ACM (e.g., *IEEE Software, ACM Queue*), there were for-profit publications with journal-y names, like *Dr. Dobb's Journal, C/C++ Users Journal,* and *Linux Journal.* Each issue had a limited number of pages, likely determined by balancing print and mailing costs versus any advertising dollars available to offset those costs. If you wanted your article to occupy one or more of those finite pages, you had to convince the gatekeepers—the editors—that your article was worthy.

Fast forward to today. Anyone can publish anything online at any time. And anything published anywhere can trend in Hacker News or go viral on social media. But a modern version of these classic journals still exist: editor-driven digital publications such as *The New Stack* and *InfoQ*. And the IEEE and ACM publications have survived and gone digital.

What are we even talking about here?

This section focuses on publishing your article in a publication with an established editorial team that actively curates content. Let's break that down:

- *Publication*—It has a stated mission and selectively publishes content that helps achieve that mission.
- *Established editorial team*— It's led by a team of named professional editors who are experienced across the publication's technology focus, publishing, or both.
- *Actively controls content*—Those editors actively manage and control what's published. Authors propose article ideas, and the editors determine which ones are actually published (and when). The publication's staff reviews, proofreads, and posts each article.

This is opposed to aggregators where authors create accounts and directly submit articles that are generally published—unless they contain red flags like excessive product promotion or offensive content.

Across these publications, there's a formal article selection and publication process:

1 Authors submit an article, outline, or abstract for consideration.
2 The submission is reviewed by an editorial team.
3 If accepted, the completed article is reviewed, sometimes peer-reviewed for technical integrity.
4 The article is copyedited to meet the publication's standards.
5 The article is published (finally!)

This process requires considerable resources, which means the publications can't publish every compelling submission. As a result, the articles selected for publication gain a certain air of prestige. The more selective the publication, the greater the prestige.

15.3.1 Why bother?

Consider submitting your article to such publications if you're interested in that prestige, or at least the fringe benefits it can provide. Those potential benefits include

- *A chance to win the lottery*—Your article could be featured in Google News, which is one of the world's top 10 news sources. Articles from tech publications are commonly shown in the "For You" section, where algorithms select recently published articles on topics that Google creepily knows the reader is interested in. If your article mentions a technology with a large following (e.g., Linux, Python, Kafka), you could reach a massive amount of interested readers over the course of several days, likely more than you could with a fleeting stint at the top of Hacker News.

- *A professional content distribution machine*—You tap into their community of readers and professionally developed distribution channels. If it's a for-profit organization, they make money by luring people in with compelling content. You can bet that they have invested in sleek ways to catch readers' attention and keep them binge-reading across the site as long as possible.

- *Good company*—Your article could be listed alongside articles by other industry experts and recommended to readers browsing similar articles. This might be especially attractive if you're looking to become known as an expert in one of the publication's signature topics.

- *Referenceability*—Articles published in "reliable sources" such as selective tech pubs can be used as references in Wikipedia and other publications that scrutinize the authority of citations. Self-published articles, including articles published on company blogs, are not acceptable references in many contexts.

- *Free review and editing*—Your article will be professionally vetted and copyedited. Some publications might also run it through technical reviewers on staff or coordinate a peer review process. This free external feedback could help you strengthen the article before it's published.

- *Badge of honor*—You can add something like "published in ImpressivePress-Journal" to your bio/resume. This might help you stand out in highly competitive hiring or conference selection processes. It's also a differentiating brag point for the dreaded performance reviews. Someone outside of your field might not be able to judge whether your article is impressive. The fact that a professional publication decided to publish it can be a convincing endorsement of its quality.

15.3.2 Why not?

There are two main reasons to skip this option: time and control. If the publication requires original content (and most do), you will need to delay publishing your article elsewhere. Some publications can get the article published within a couple weeks. Other times, the wait is well over a month. Also, you might need to spend some time adapting the article's focus and style for that specific publication. Publication here might require reducing or increasing the word count, adjusting images, or adding references to support your statements. In addition, you should set aside time to respond to editorial review comments.

You also cede some level of control when you take this path. You typically give up your right to update the article as you see fit, influence how it's promoted, and control what other content is displayed next to it. Plus, the editors might ask you to add/remove/rewrite entire sections, retitle the article, and so on. It's their publication. They set the rules, and you need to play along.

15.3.3 Considerations

If you're considering submitting your article to one of these publications, here are some things to investigate and/or think about as you decide if it's worth the effort:

- Is the publication respected in the communities you wish to permeate?
- Do people you respect ever share links from this publication?
- Is there a paywall or registration wall, maybe after a certain scroll depth or number of page views?
- What do they focus on? What's their mission, and what articles seem to trend?
- Would your article fit nicely into one of their existing categories?
- How many readers do they have? What does their social following look like?
- Who are their readers (job titles, level of experience, company size, etc.)?
- Who are their authors?
- What's their process for submission, review, and editing?
- How do they promote similar articles (number of social posts, newsletter references, etc.)?
- Do they accept previously published content? If not, how much would you need to modify an existing article for them to consider it original content?
- Can you republish a version of this article elsewhere? After how long?

NOTE Look for an "Advertiser Guide" or "Media Kit" somewhere on the publication's site. These often feature all sorts of (self-reported) reader details and stats.

15.3.4 Tips

Here are some tips for getting your article accepted by selective tech publications:

- *Focus on a tailored fit for one, not a baggy fit for many.* See what kind of articles the different publications you're considering feature and determine which publication is most promising for your topic and approach. Then, contact them with a proposal that's angled to their specific focus and style. One size never fits all. One publication might consider your edgy "Thoughts on Trends" article to be an adorable diversion that's totally unfit for their esteemed publication. Another might be honored to feature it prominently on their front page. And the 3000-word technical deep dive that would be considered overkill in one publication could find a perfect home in another.

- *Do your homework.* First, take the time to carefully read their author guidelines and understand exactly what they require for the initial review (An abstract? An outline? A full article with a specific word count minimum or maximum?) Look at their "About Us" page, read their mission statement, and consider how you might angle your article to better align with that. Then read a few articles in the category that your article would fall under. What related topics have other authors covered and how does your article build upon them? Can you weave them into your discussion? Publishers love links across their existing content. Also see if they have an editorial calendar of topics published (e.g., September is all about security). You will want to note if your article fits into their featured themes and timings.

- *Play by the rules.* If they want original content, give them original content. If you haven't already published your article, hold off until you hear whether or not the publication is interested in it. If you have already published it, be transparent about that. Propose (or write and share) a somewhat different variation for this publication, perhaps expanding the scope a bit or maybe narrowing it to take a deeper look at the aspect that's most intriguing to this publication's readers.

The gray zone: DZone, HackerNoon, and others

There are a few interesting publishing options that fall somewhere between selective tech publications and self-publishing sites (such as Medium and dev.to). HackerNoon, ITNext, and DZone are prime examples.

Unlike pure self-publishing sites like Medium and dev.to, they provide a level of human editorial oversight and frequently reject articles that don't meet their focus and guidelines. But they don't have the same level of editorial oversight that you would find at, say, *InfoQ* or *The New Stack*. That makes them easier to get into, but it also means being published here doesn't carry the same level of prestige. Also, they are less likely to reach Google News or be considered reliable sources that can be cited as proper references.

As far as considerations and tips, take a look at the ones for the previous section and those in the next section. Elements of both apply. Mix and match as you see fit.

15.4 *Syndicating simulacra*

Many blog syndication sites let you republish a word-for-word replica of your existing blog post for a chance at a new audience, and you can do this without penalizing your original blog post in terms of search engine rankings. This option is a no-brainer as long as it takes only about 5 minutes of work (copy/paste and settings configuration).

For example, assuming that PretendPiotr's fake Zig blog post was originally published on his company blog site, he might also pop it onto Medium and dev.to. There, it might make its way to some additional FakeDB, Postgres, and Zig enthusiasts.

15.4.1 *Why bother?*

The blog posts that tend to shine in syndication are the ones that are well-aligned with popular topics or tags (terms vary across platforms; Medium uses "topic"). That's because topics/tags factor heavily into what articles are recommended to readers. As a result, a mediocre article on some aspect of MongoDB, DynamoDB, or Postgres would probably gain many more views than a show-stoppingly awesome article related to TigerBeetle or RisingWave.

An extra bonus: another URL for your blog post means you get additional chances at Hacker News traction. However, be aware that URLs from some platforms known for having dubious quality might be penalized by the Hacker News algorithm or deemed dead upon arrival.

Moreover, if your original blog post didn't perform as well as you hoped, you could try changing the title for the repost. It's not really A/B testing since you're changing two variables at once. But it's a chance to see if the new angle resonates and also an excuse to try another (also slightly different) social media post as well. If you want to invest a few more minutes into this, you could even try a slightly different introduction to the article.

15.4.2 Why not?

You probably want to skip this option if republishing requires any substantial effort. If your blog post contains interactive elements or relies on special plugins or libraries, it might not be worth the extra time required to get it re-created in a new environment.

Another reason: you're just not comfortable with the site. Maybe it opens a paywall after n views, maybe it has a strong beginner vibe that makes you feel like you're an adult seated at the kids' table. If it doesn't seem right for you, skip it.

Finally, if you tend to update blog posts after they're published, having multiple versions could lead to versioning problems (or a maintenance mess).

15.4.3 Considerations

If you're thinking of cross-posting your article on a self-publishing platform, the main consideration is how much time it will require, as discussed above. If you can publish it rapidly (maybe to keep yourself awake during that boring meeting), it's probably worth a try.

The other consideration is past performance. If you've posted multiple articles here in the past and the reads and engagement were never impressive, you might want to skip it. Maybe there just aren't a lot of people reading about your topic on this site right now.

15.4.4 Tips

Here are some tips for getting the best results when you republish your blog post on syndication sites:

- *Canonical is king.* Absolutely positively do not forget to set the canonical URL to your original article. This tells search engines to prioritize your original article in their search results, so the other version (which might feature ads, links to random other articles, etc.) does not outrank the one on your blog site or your company blog site. The option for setting this could be buried in the depths of "Advanced Settings" (that's where it's currently located on Medium). If you don't see it in the main options, keep looking. Note that it might be named something slightly different, such as "Original Source."

- *Consider staggering publication.* Some platforms will automatically share your published article on social media. Sometimes you'll luck out: a reader will stumble upon it (maybe via the platform's recommendations), read it, and decide to share it. If you publish this version of your article at least a week or so after your original version, it could spark a second wave of social media promotion.

- *Take care with taxonomies.* Think carefully about the topics/tags that you apply to the article. An article with limited or poorly selected topics/tags is unlikely to reach additional readers. This is covered in chapter 7. Summary: balance relevance and reach. Definitely don't skip the ones that are the best fit, but also try your luck with some broader ones, too. Some platforms allow no more than five tags; that's a good cap for keeping it focused and avoiding the tag sprawl that makes it look spammy.

- *Provide real contact information.* Unless you decided to publish under a pseudonym, use your real name for the platform and give readers a way to contact you: a social account with open DMs, a LinkedIn profile link, or similar. It's frustrating for conference organizers, tech book publishers, and other talent scouts to stumble upon a great Medium article but not find any way to contact the author.

15.5   Guest blogging

Guest blogging is simply having your blog post published on someone else's site. It's not all that common, to be honest. But in the few situations where it makes sense, it's truly a win-win for both parties. You get more exposure within a relevant community of readers. And the blog editor gets a new article from a fresh perspective.

Guest blogging might be an option if

- There's a blog behind a product, project, or technology you featured in your blog post.
- There's a blog behind a conference or event you're participating in.

For example, a variation of the fake Zig blog post would be a natural candidate for a guest post on the FakeDB blog site.

15.5.1   Why bother?

Guest blogging for a highly relevant blog site is generally a great way to reach your target audience. It's not going to garner as many views as, say, trending on Hacker News. But a high percentage of the people who see your blog post here are likely to be interested in your topic. With this tactic, it's all about quality, not quantity.

Guest blogging on a conference-hosted blog offers another benefit, too: it could attract more people to your session. Just don't leak the core of your talk in advance. Consider sharing an article excerpt that you won't be covering in detail during the talk. Or, provide them a related article that's aligned with your talk and/or the broader conference theme.

15.5.2   Why not?

If you really want to capture the interest of this community, the article should be highly focused on the product/project/theme they care most about. If your existing post is a perfect fit as is, great. Send it over! But if you need to adjust the focus, consider whether the opportunity seems valuable enough to justify the extra time required to revise or extend the article.

15.5.3 *Considerations*

As you debate whether a guest blog will pay off, think about the following:

- How do they typically alert their community about new blog posts?
- Is there any sign that their community really engages with the blog (e.g., social media engagement)? Will the blog editor share any metrics?
- Does the other blog look clean and impressive?
- If your blog post is code-heavy, how nicely do they display code on their blog?

15.5.4 *Tips*

Here are some tips for getting your blog post cross-published on someone else's site:

- *Ensure it fits their audience.* Focus on what this specific audience cares about most. For example, the fake Zig blog post would be a perfect candidate for the FakeDB blog. However, the Fake DB audience would care more about how the Postgres to FakeDB migrator works and less about PretendPiotr's thoughts on Zig. It could also be a nice fit for some still-fictional Zig blog. In that case, it would make sense to minimize the discussion of the team's previous data migration woes and focus almost exclusively on the Zig-related learnings.
- *Consider companies associated with open source projects.* If your blog post features an open source project, also think about the various companies that have productized it in some way (e.g., offering it as a service). They likely run company blogs and their users might be highly intrigued by your lessons learned working with that technology or your thoughts on its promising future. For example, if you wrote something intriguing about Apache Pinot, StarTree's blog might be a perfect publishing platform.
- *Ask for a link.* You're donating free content, saving this other blog editor from having to write or source a story to fill their editorial calendar. The least they could do is give you a link or two to promote your personal blog, project, company—whatever is important to you. And if the article is a close copy of your original post, request that they set the canonical URL to the original post.

15.6 *Participating in podcasts and livestreams*

Podcasts and livestreams offer a way to reach people who enjoy watching and listening to educational content. Some people strongly prefer reading and they cringe when a link leads to a video or audio recording. Others would rather listen to a 1-hour podcast than devote 8 minutes to concentrated article reading. Many people like to mix it up, depending on their mood and multitasking activities (e.g., commuting, walking, cooking).

Having a successful blog post can help you break into the world of podcasts and livestreams, or finally earn a spot on ones that were previously beyond your reach. You're unlikely to find a program that wants to spend 30 minutes talking specifically about your blog post. But having a successful blog post is a perfect excuse for contacting the host. Sharing your blog post helps the host 1) determine if your take on the topic is a good fit for the program, and 2) prepare thoughtful questions for the discussion.

For example, assume that one of PretendPiotr's favorite podcasts was planning to have programmers discuss their first experiences with Zig. He could contact that host to express interest and share a link to his Zig blog post to show that he's qualified to speak on the topic.

15.6.1 Why bother?

The immediate payoff depends on how many people tune in to the session (live or on-demand). But just being able to mention that you've been on a podcast or a live-stream (especially an expert panel) is a notable achievement, and it can be a stepping stone to more/bigger/better speaking opportunities. Consider it brand promotion versus blog post promotion.

For people who are comfortable speaking on the spot, not much preparation is required. If you find that the opportunity has a good reach and you can pull it off without too much planning or perspiration, it could very likely be worth it.

Another potential benefit: if you're in a group discussion, you might get to meet and interact with experts in the field. That's often fun in and of itself. Moreover, it could open the door to additional collaboration with these experts, as well as elevate your profile by being featured alongside them.

15.6.2 Why not?

Opportunities can vary dramatically in quality. Don't consider or commit to anything without researching it first.

One thing that's pretty constant is that you'll likely have limited control over the direction of the conversation. If you decide to participate, you will be a guest on someone else's program, so you need to be respectful and follow their lead.

Moreover, if the thought of unscripted public speaking sends you into anaphylactic shock (and you're not feeling compelled to get over that), this might not be the best option for you. But maybe you're willing to leave your comfort zone and challenge yourself?

15.6.3 Considerations

If you're considering participating in a podcast or livestream, think about the following:

- How many people generally tune in live and/or on-demand?
- If it's live, when does it occur (e.g., will your CET-calibrated brain need to be responsive and clever at 2 am to accommodate a PST afternoon time slot)?
- If it's prerecorded, are there opportunities for retakes or cuts?
- How is the audio/visual quality of other episodes?
- Can you influence the questions at all (e.g., can you review and comment on the question list in advance, or offer canned "seed" questions that you want to answer)?

- Is the livestream chat generally smart and civil? Do guests engage with it?
- If it's a panel, how does the moderator typically manage the discussion, rein in digressions, and keep it balanced? What types of guests does the host attract?

15.6.4 Tips

Here are some tips for breaking into the podcast/livestream realm:

- *Be selective.* Don't approach every tech podcaster/streamer you can find with the same generic message. Take the time to make a list of candidates, watch/listen to multiple episodes of each (skim them at least), then craft a custom message for the few that look most intriguing. It's nice to mention what you like about that particular program and how you fit into their themes.
- *Predict questions.* If you're nervous about how you'll respond when you're put on the spot, think about the questions that could arise and how you might approach them. Maybe even look at the latest Hacker News and other discussions related to your topic.
- *Rehearse likely tidbits.* It's safe to assume that the host will ask you to introduce yourself, share what you're currently working on, and maybe say something about the biggest challenges and opportunities related to your topic. You might as well prepare your answers in advance and rehearse them with your rubber ducky.
- *Invest in decent equipment.* You don't need to have the equivalent of a Hollywood sound stage, but do invest in a reliable (wired!) mic as well as adjustable lighting when video is involved. Muffled, staticky, or inconsistent sound will cause some listeners to drop, shift the chat/comments discussion to complaining about the sound, and could prevent the episode from being featured on demand. To be safe, do a test recording then check how it looks and sounds from the audience perspective (volume, static, where your eyes are focused, etc.)

15.7 Sharing at conferences

A blog post offers a smooth glide path into conference speaking opportunities:

- You already have a topic that you've thought about quite a lot.
- Your post provides a convenient head start for creating a deck and talk track.
- It's considerably less risky for organizers to accept a topic when they can see how it's covered in a complete blog (versus just a short abstract).

It does require an investment of time: thoroughly vetting the conference, proposing a compelling abstract, preparing the deck and speaker notes, rehearsing, actually delivering the talk, and maybe even traveling somewhere in the process. But the payoff can also be significant in terms of elevating your profile, connecting with experts on your topic, growing your following, and so on.

This is an expansive topic with many considerations throughout different phases of the process. That's why we're covering it in detail in chapter 16.

## 15.8	*Measuring the effects*

How does all this amplification affect your blog post as well as your brand? Let's close out this chapter with a high-level rundown of the types of metrics that could be helpful to measure. Your access to metrics depends on where your article is published (table 15.1).

Table 15.1 How to access metrics depending on where your article is published

Publication site	How to access metrics
Your own blog site	Geek out over metrics to your heart's content via Google Analytics, Google Search Console, or similar tools.
Your company's blog	Someone, somewhere (Marketing?) certainly has access to these metrics and can share the stats you're interested in.
Another blog or a tech publication	Ask your main contact for a report. Note that they might not be at liberty to share this information externally.
A self-publishing platform like Medium or dev.to	You're limited to the (frequently changing) glimpse of metrics they choose to share.

WARNING Technical readers are notoriously obsessed with evading tracking. As a result, behavior tracking metrics such as new visitors versus existing visitors could likely be skewed. Still, flying with limited vision is better than flying totally blind.

### 15.8.1	*The blog post*

The following metrics provide insight into blog post reading:

- *Views and users*—Views is the total number of blog post page accesses, including repeated views by the same user. Users is the total number of unique people who viewed that post.
- *Scrolled users*—A user is considered "scrolled" if they read through at least 90% of the page. This should provide a good assessment of how many readers reached the end of the article. On Medium, "reads" is the rough equivalent of scrolled users.
- *Average engagement time*—Engagement time is the average time your blog post was in focus on the user's browser and potentially being read. Bot traffic can make this number much lower than expected.
- *Bounce rate*—Bounce rate indicates the percentage of sessions where users did not engage (by having the page in focus for at least 10 seconds or interacting with the page in some manner).

What could cause low engagement time and/or high bounce rate?

If these metrics seem off, especially relative to other blog posts on the same site, it could be due to bot traffic or an influx of general traffic (e.g., from Hacker News). Slow page load or technical problems could also be to blame. Or, it might be a signal that

- The blog post is attracting the wrong readers. To investigate, look at organic search details, traffic sources, and backlinks to see how people are getting there.
- The readers didn't find what they were hoping to see. Maybe your introduction did not meet the expectations set by the title, a social media post, or a virtual community discussion.

- *Actual responses*—Public or private comments like "Thanks for writing this, it really helped me" are often the most rewarding indicator of how your blog post affected readers. They can't be tracked automatically but do take the time to save those comments in a file for future reference. Also, revisit them if you ever want motivation while working on some future blog post.
- *Conversions*—If custom conversion tracking is set up, it can indicate how many of the people who entered the site via your blog post later signed up for some free trial, "book a demo" offer, or another offer that requires registration. Even if this isn't your top concern, this could be a nice data point to mention when it's time for the dreaded performance review. Alternatively, you might also (or rather) want to track GitHub metrics, such as stars, watches, and forks.
- *Views/users plotted over time*—Looking at how blog post views/users ebb and flow over time can help you see the effects of known influences (e.g., the day an impressive influencer shared it). If you notice any unexpected spikes (e.g., in figure 15.1), this is your cue to start investigating the cause. Was there some heated discussion on Reddit? Was it mentioned in a popular newsletter? The items in the next section can help you track down the source.

Views by page path and screen class over time

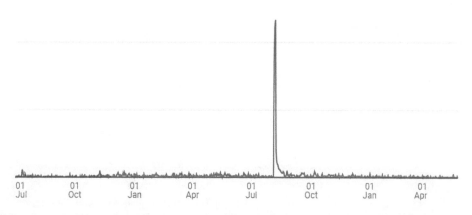

Figure 15.1 The report shows an unexpected spike in interest long after a blog post was published. This particular spike stemmed from a tech influencer stumbling upon the blog post from a search engine, then sharing it on his social media account.

15.8.2   How people are finding the blog post

The following metrics provide insight into how people are finding your blog post:

- *Traffic sources*—Looking at the core blog post stats by acquisition source helps you determine just how big that Hacker News boost is (or isn't). Go into source/ medium for the details you care about (e.g., see figure 15.2). You can learn all about how organic (non-paid) social, search, and different referring sites are driving traffic to your blog post.

- *Organic search details*—This includes details like what user queries are surfacing your blog post, how you're ranking on each query, and how many people actually click this blog post from those search results. You might want to consider these search terms as you plan additional blog posts. And if you discover that users are reaching your blog post from an odd search term (perhaps "Zig Zimbabwe currency"), you might want to investigate further, then adjust the article's title and metadata accordingly.

- *Ranking on anticipated search terms*—Remember the keywords we talked about in chapter 7? Unless you have access to an SEO tool, just search them in a browser (in Incognito mode or equivalent) and see where your blog post ranks. If it ranks nicely, this could provide a sustainable source of steady traffic. If not, you might want to consider subtle title or metadata changes—but never undermine the integrity of the article for the sake of search rankings.

- *Backlinks*—Are people linking to your blog post from other sites: related blogs, newsletters, lists of resources, and so on? You can get a limited view from free

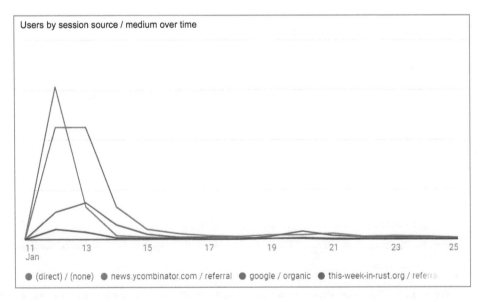

Figure 15.2   A look at blog post traffic from sources such as Hacker News and the *This Week in Rust* newsletter, as well as direct traffic and organic search results

backlink checkers (e.g., Ahrefs [https://ahrefs.com/backlink-checker/] or Ubersuggest [https://neilpatel.com/backlinks/]—requires registration). If you uncover an impressive backlink, consider sharing that article as referenced in section 15.2.3.

15.8.3 Who's reading and how

The following metrics provide insight into who is reading your blog post:

- *New users*—Knowing if a blog post is attracting new readers or mostly appealing to your existing community could be a good way to gauge outreach attempts like sharing it on social media and virtual communities. But beware. Although Google defines new users as people who interacted with your site for the first time, it's actually people who do not have a previously saved cookie from that website. This means the new users might be artificially skewed a bit high with tracking-evading tech readers.
- *Demographics*—Knowing what country your readers are in can help you time your social media postings. For example, if most of your readers are in India, don't publish your social media post at midnight India time.
- *Technology*—Knowing users' browsers, operating systems, device types, and screen resolutions can help you determine what to optimize your blog post for and what to test it on. If most people are reading on mobile, for example, you'd want to be extra vigilant about having short paragraphs, smartly cropped images, and so forth.

15.8.4 Social and community engagements

The following metrics provide insight into your promotion efforts and their effects on your brand:

- *Your follower count*—This tells you how many people have opted in to your updates. The more *qualified* people that follow you, the greater the chance that people will see, share, and like your social posts—which gives them a boost in the eye of the almighty algorithms. Your follower count should rise as you share compelling content (including your blog posts!), as well as engage in discussions and follow new people.
- *Impressions*—This is the number of times your social post was seen by users on that platform. If someone with a huge following reshares your post, this will bump up impressions fast. More impressions equals more readers. That could translate to more clicks into your blog post. If nothing else, it could help build your brand awareness (e.g., "that PretendPiotr guy knows about Zig and FakeDB").
- *Engagements*—Engagements (likes, shares, replies, clicks, etc.) can expand your impressions. Although you might be satisfied with fewer general engagements and more clicks into your blog post, the algorithms reward broader engagement. Strangely, many users will like or share a social post about a blog post they've never read.

- *Clicks*—Clicks tell you how many people actually clicked the URL in the social post and opened the associated blog post. Tracking clicks is especially valuable if you shared the same blog post in multiple different social posts (maybe one with an image of the article text, another with a flame graph, etc.). In that case, click metrics might help you assess which angle worked better. Beware, though: there are many other factors at play. Perhaps one social post triggered more clicks because the stars were just better aligned with respect to timing, competing events, who happened to reshare it, and so on.

- *Upvotes*—Upvotes help your community post climb up lists. Having a healthy amount of upvotes also secures you a better position in perpetuity. Each time a user searches for something related to your blog post and sorts results by popularity, upvotes help you commandeer valuable real estate on the list.

- *Comments*—Community posts with a high number of comments do tend to attract more views. If a good fight is going on, readers naturally want to watch from the sidelines, or perhaps even jump into the ring themselves. But having more comments is not necessarily favorable. A community post might have more comments because the associated blog post is riddled with coding errors, biased benchmarketing, unfounded assumptions, markety product perspectives, and so on. Having more comments than upvotes can trigger flame war detectors.

- *Profile views*—If you're active on LinkedIn, you might also want to see who's looking at you, especially while your blog post is actively being discussed in various places. You could discover a nice spike in overall profile views, as well as interest from specific peers or leaders with intriguing profiles. Note that you might be seeing just the tip of the iceberg though; many browse LinkedIn using private mode.

Summary

- After publishing your blog post, there are many ways to amplify its reach and effects, including sharing on social media and in virtual communities, getting it published in tech publications, syndicating it on other blog platforms, participating in podcasts/livestreams, and speaking at conferences.

- Tailor your amplification strategy based on your personality: introverts likely prefer more async efforts, while extroverts can embrace more real-time interactions.

- Even if you're not super social, start contributing to social media and virtual communities then share your blog post there:
  - Before you share your own blog posts, get a good feel for the vibe of the community and contribute to it in nonselfish ways.
  - Take a phased approach to posting across different platforms, starting with the most ephemeral social media platforms and leading up to Hacker News.
  - Engage in the discussion, but feel free to walk away from unproductive attacks.
  - Don't abandon your post after the initial promotion; look for ways to work it into new discussions and keep looking for other people mentioning it.

- For increased reach with a level of prestige, look into getting your article published in selective tech publications.
- For a potential extra boost with (usually) minimal effort, syndicate your post on sites like Medium.
- Use your blog post to help secure podcast/livestream guest spots where you can expand on the topic and promote your expertise.
- Similarly, pitch your blog post topic as a potential conference talk to elevate your profile and connect with others in the field.
- Measure the success of your amplification efforts by tracking metrics such as views, engagement, traffic sources, shares/comments, follower growth, and backlinks.

From blog post to conference talk

This chapter covers

- The value of converting your post to a conference talk
- How to identify and compare conference opportunities
- Tips for the end-to-end process—preparing a proposal, creating your deck, and following up after the conference ends

As much value as reading (and writing) blog posts offers, it doesn't corner the market on learning. There's nothing like a conference—people gathering to share, learn, connect, refresh their t-shirt supply, and commiserate over unidentifiable buffet food. Options range from KubeCon to FOSDEM, PyCon to QCon, and Monktoberfest to Wasm I/O, which makes it hard to claim that there's not a good fit for your focus and preferences. Moreover, virtual conferences provide global access to similar experiences without travel (or the associated approvals and hassles).

As we teased in the previous chapter, a successful blog post provides a great glide path into conference speaking. It helps the conference organizers assess whether you're a good fit and gives you a distinct edge against other candidates who are simply sharing a short abstract full of fuzziness. Plus, you have a head start on thinking about the topic, creating the storyline, and even responding to common questions that could arise.

This chapter helps you navigate the "blog post to conference talk" path—deciding whether it's worth it to you, finding and evaluating different opportunities, and finally completing the various phases of the conference lifecycle.

16.1 The path to speaking

Using your blog post as a springboard to conference speaking offers a number of valuable benefits, as long as you can make the time, secure your company's approval, and get past the stage fright that's quite common among developers.

Before you immediately dismiss speaking opportunities as "not for you," consider Piotr's personal experiences on the matter. For context, remember this quote from chapter 1: "I (Piotr) was once the epitome of the stereotypical introverted programmer. I dreaded speaking in front of what I considered a crowd (more than two people)."

16.1.1 Piotr's path

I wish P99 CONF and other virtual conferences that let you pre-record a talk were a thing in 2018. Instead, my first-ever conference talk was in person: ScyllaDB Summit 2018 in Silicon Valley. At that time, I'd only been working at ScyllaDB for a few months, so I was reasonably sure I wouldn't be selected as one of the speakers. Boy, was I wrong.

What made matters worse was this unique Gmail feature that sometimes randomly categorizes a perfectly legitimate email from your coworker as spam, even when it comes from the same internal domain. About a month before the conference, I noticed that people were acting like I was a speaker, but I had no clue why. Then at one point, I decided to check the Spam folder. Here I saw a message from my boss, asking if I would mind speaking about the most recent (and also the first) feature I added to ScyllaDB. My lack of response was assumed consent, which made me doubly terrified:

- Thanks to Gmail's filter fiasco, I ignored a message from my superior during my first few months at a new job.
- I was going to speak publicly at a business conference in the United States (traveling from Poland).

What a great start!

Nowadays for online conferences, I tend to write down a full transcript of what I'm about to say, which I can then read out loud to rehearse, measuring the talk length and just generally seeing if it sounds alright. The same transcript lands in my speaker notes, so I can refer to the notes whenever I get stuck. Most in-person conferences now display speaker notes in a discreet location (teleprompter style), but ScyllaDB Summit, back in 2018, did not.

I ended up printing out my notes the old-school way. That resulted in a pile of seven or eight sheets of paper, with my transcript in fine print. And yes, it was just as unusable as it sounds. I realized that quite early, and that recognition elevated my stage fright an extra fraction above what I already considered maximum.

Then, the talk started. I immediately learned four important things that help me through conference talks to this day:

- The stage fright disappears exactly 2 seconds before I start talking. I just have something else to occupy myself with: speaking. Since my brain is mostly single threaded, there just aren't any cycles left to worry about speaking in public.

- Breaks for taking a sip of water appear completely natural from the audience's perspective, so just use that trick whenever you're stuck or just need an extra breath.

- When you get a surprisingly difficult question, you can just say "I don't know!" or "Interesting, I need to think about this more—let's take it offline."

- Most of my stage fright comes from the incorrect assumption, perhaps from my school days, that my audience knows more than I do about the subject and someone is just waiting for the chance to correct me in an embarrassing way.

The average audience, in my experience, consists of three main groups:

- People who know less than you do about the subject and are there to learn.

- People who know more than you, but are also decent and polite; even if they ask a difficult question, they are really just seeking clarification.

- People staring at their phones. And that's the largest group by far.

None of those groups will actively try to embarrass you. Ergo, that stage fright really is irrational.

16.1.2 Why speak at conferences?

Next, let's look at the benefits of getting past that stage fright. We'll particularly focus on the value for blog post authors.

RECOGNITION AS AN EXPERT ON THE TOPIC

Speaking at a conference guarantees you a spot at the equivalent of the Walk of Fame in your technical niche. You can treat it as applying search engine optimization to yourself. Once you start making the rounds on the speaking circuit, representatives from other conferences, book publishers, even founders looking to build out the team will be able to easily find you and validate your experience

By association, you'll get some of the prestige of the keynote speakers. People who showed up for the megakeynote will also likely stick around and sample some of the more focused track sessions. Moreover, you might occasionally find it appropriate to namedrop "Oh yeah, when I spoke at that conference with so-and-so..." Speaking at conferences is also a great way of promoting your next big project (for example, your new book on writing for developers) in that biography slide.

NETWORK EXPANSION

The value of speaking at a conference extends beyond your few minutes in the spotlight. An in-person conference usually includes an exclusive speakers' dinner, or a speakers' room designed first and foremost for networking (not to mention better snacks, internet access, and other "luxuries"). Online conferences have followed suit and often involve a speakers' lounge or VIP chatroom. Either way, you already have something in common with your fellow speakers and you can just review the agenda to learn (at least some of) their professional interests. That means it's not so difficult to connect, even if you're generally averse to trivial small talk. It's often beneficial to keep in touch with other conference speakers after the conference completes. They might invite you to a panel, you might remember them when your company is expanding, maybe you partner on a side project at some point, who knows?

Being a speaker could also give you a chance to meet that big name keynote speaker referenced in the previous section. Plus, conferences are also a great opportunity to meet with your audience. Technical conferences attract like-minded people and experts in their fields, which makes the potential of valuable networking quite high. When you're a speaker, attendees are naturally drawn to you following the session. Sometimes even a casual follow-up chat can lead to interesting collaboration later.

DIRECT FEEDBACK FROM YOUR TARGET AUDIENCE

If you want to write blog posts that your target audience appreciates, this is your chance to get direct feedback from actual human beings in that target audience. When you present your blog post as a talk, you can see what parts people are most excited about, where they have questions, and where they start checking their phones. This not only helps you revise that specific blog post (if desired), but it also sharpens your sense of who these people really are. And that is helpful with every future blog post that you write.

In chapter 5, we urged you to read through your blog post with your target reader in mind and anticipate

- What they are most skeptical about
- Where they want more context, detail, or supporting facts
- Where they might get lost, distracted, or disoriented

Speaking in front of real-life members of this audience can help you calibrate your assumptions versus reality.

FREE PROFESSIONAL VIDEO

Having a professionally produced video of yourself speaking can be impressive when you're applying for jobs, submitting conference or book proposals, completing your annual performance review, or just trying to give your friends and family some idea of what you do at work. It's a great portfolio piece. And it can be conveniently embedded into your blog post if you want to offer people the option of watching as well as reading.

> **TIP** To be safe, download a local copy of the video. You never know when the organization will decide to stop hosting archived videos.

16.1.3 *Why not?*

Assuming that Piotr's personal story puts the "stage fright" objection to rest, there are really just two reasons not to try converting one of your blog posts to a conference talk.

The first is the challenge of getting the required approvals. The second is the time required to prepare and deliver the talk.

APPROVALS

This one is often the dealbreaker. If your company won't allow you to speak publicly about your topic and won't fund your travel to in-person conferences, there's no point in worrying about how much time it will require. As with blog post publication, some companies' approval processes are much more onerous than others. Before you get too deep into the process, ask your boss and your colleagues if there's even a chance this might be approved.

TIME

Even when you have the advantage of starting with a blog post, conferences do involve a number of activities and checkpoints that you should plan for:

- Creating and submitting your proposal
- Any speaker briefings required upon acceptance
- Creating your deck and speaker notes
- Submitting your deck for review and updating it based on feedback
- For virtual conferences, possibly pre-recording or performing advance tech checks
- Any pre- or postevent discussions or promotions you're invited to participate in

16.2 Identifying and evaluating opportunities

Assuming that you're interested, how do you proceed? Create a list of interesting opportunities, then prioritize a few top candidates after you dig into some details.

If you already have a list of conferences that you admire or that you hear your peers talking about, add those to your list. Then build out the list further by

- *Browsing YouTube*—Start searching by the keywords related to your blog post + "conference" and see what you stumble upon. You could also try searching for the names of some topic experts you admire + "conference."
- *Using "call for speaker" sites*—Sessionize is currently the most popular site for connecting speakers and conferences. You can create a speaker profile with your experience and interests, then use the "discovery" functionality to see what conferences might be a good match. PaperCall is another option.

In addition, keep an eye out for local user groups and meetups. These can be a great starting point. Most likely, their organizers will be thrilled to have a volunteer speaker, and they will be quite accommodating of whatever topic, format, and length you have in mind.

There are many factors to consider when comparing different conference speaking opportunities. Let's divide them into a few buckets: fit, reach and promotion, and logistics.

16.2.1 Fit

Consider how well this conference's focus fits your topic and target audience:

- What is their stated focus?
- What are their most popular topics?
- Who's their audience (job titles, level of experience, etc.)?
- Who are the speakers from past conferences?
- What level of technical depth do they go into?
- How long are the sessions?
- What session formats do they offer?

Many conferences narrow, shift, or expand their scope as they evolve year after year. But if you're not impressed by the conference's past, be extremely cautious before committing to become part of its future.

When you feel like a conference's community is "your people," you're more likely to make meaningful connections and get valuable feedback on your ideas.

16.2.2 Reach and promotion

Consider how this conference will help you become better recognized as an expert on this topic:

- How many people are in their community?
- How do they promote the conference?
- How do they promote individual sessions?
- Will they create a professional video to create buzz for your session?
- Are there opportunities to cross-post related blogs on their site?
- Are there opportunities to be included in speaker Q&A blogs?
- Are talks actively promoted after the conference ends?
- Are sessions recorded? If so, what do the final videos look like? Will they be available to those who did not attend the conference?

If the conference is tracked by a large community, the event promotion alone will elevate your profile. A recording is always nice to have (as outlined in section 16.1.2), but it's especially important if you want exposure beyond the conference's community.

16.2.3 Logistics

What does the end-to-end experience involve?

For all opportunities,

- When are deck drafts due? Final versions?
- Are there any other deadlines or required preconference activities?
- Do they provide templates or do you need to create your own?
- Is any graphics help available if you need it?

For in-person conferences,

- How much time and money will be required to travel on those dates?
- Do they offer a free pass? Cover any travel expenses? Offer hotel discounts?
- Do you really want to attend the other conference talks and events?
- Will teleprompters be available for speaker notes?

For virtual conferences,

- Can you pre-record? If so, can you do multiple takes? Self-record?
- Will you end up presenting super early or super late in your local time zone?
- How do you engage with attendees and other speakers during the live event?

For example, if you're particularly nervous about public speaking, you might prioritize virtual conferences where you can pre-record. And a conference that's willing to help you with graphics, slide decks, and similar might be a better starting point than one where you need to do it all yourself.

Or, if your heart is set on attending an in-person conference, you probably want to focus on considerations that help you make a business case for traveling. It should be simpler to get approvals if the conference covers many of the expenses, plus there's a critical mass of sessions that could benefit your team.

16.3 *Submitting your proposal*

The title and abstract are the heart of your proposal. Your immediate goal is to create something that interests the conference selection committee. But remember that the title and abstract are used even beyond that initial judging:

- The conference committee will use them to promote your talk through social media posts, event blog blurbs, and so on.
- Attendees will review the title and abstract when deciding which talks to attend.
- Your title and abstract will also be tacked on the resulting video in perpetuity, influencing how it's understood by search engines and recommended to people searching for related terms.

> **NOTE** We obsessed over the importance of titles in chapter 5. Refer back if you want a refresher.

Your title should intrigue the reader and demonstrate relevance to the conference theme. And your abstract should indicate

- Why your specific topic is important to this conference's target audience
- How you will cover the topic (with details!)
- Why your take on the topic is so intriguing (e.g., it's based on your experience building Project A, or you ran some extensive/extreme testing)
- What attendees will ultimately learn if they pay attention

If you can make the reader nod, raise their eyebrows, or smile somewhere along the way—that's a distinct bonus.

> ### Kent Beck's abstract formula
>
> Kent Beck proposed the following template for writing abstracts that get accepted:
>
> 1 State the problem.
> 2 Explain why the problem is a problem.
> 3 Offer up "one startling sentence" (e.g., "We found that X is destined to fail without Y.").
> 4 State the implication of the startling sentence.
>
> Feel free to try that approach, or come up with your own.

TIP Not sure how to start squeezing your 1000+ word blog post into a 100-ish word abstract? Try a generative AI prompt like: "Propose an abstract for a {describe} conference that is based on the following blog post; it should be no longer than {word_limit}." Then, use that as a rough guide for creating a much more compelling version on your own.

16.3.1 *Reusing/rethinking your blog post*

If the title and topic angle in your blog post are perfectly suited to the conference's focus and personality, you don't need to change them. It's fine to have a conference talk use the same title as a blog post (as long as it meets the character limit). Still, you might want to take this opportunity to play with it a little. Did you have some alternative title ideas you really liked but didn't use? Do you want to expand, narrow, or reframe the scope of the topic based on any feedback you received? A conference talk is the perfect opportunity to freshen it up, so start by having the title and abstract reflect that new direction.

If you see an opportunity to make your title and angle a better fit for the conference, do it! Think about it from the conference organizer's point of view. If there are two equally intriguing talks—one that's directly related to the conference theme and one that's not—which one do you think will be selected? Relevance is a critical evaluation criteria.

TIP You can often submit multiple proposals to a single conference. If you're debating between a few different approaches to your original topic (or if you want to try speaking on something altogether different), submit the allowed number of ideas and let the organizers decide which one they prefer.

As you begin to write, draw lots of inspiration from the blog post's introduction. If you followed the advice in chapter 5, the introduction should already

- Share what you're trying to accomplish and why the target audience should care

- Expose what angle you're taking on this topic
- Indicate why your take on this topic is interesting

Work all that into the abstract! Also, apply the clarity tips from chapter 5 to thoroughly optimize every sentence. There's no room for lard here; every word should be carefully selected and add value.

16.3.2 Submission tips

Here are some additional tips for an effective submission:

- *Learn from the past.* Look at past talk titles and abstracts. What's the style? You don't want to submit something playful and snappy when all the past ones are serious and quasi-academic or vice versa.
- *Be brief yet specific.* You know this topic inside and out by now. Use that to your advantage and make your short abstract rich with specifics. The submissions will be full of abstracts promising to show "some common pitfalls" and "a number of techniques." An abstract that indicates clear direction and deep thought will stand out from the pack.
- *Align with a suggested topic.* Most "Call for Speakers" pages share what topics they're hoping to cover. If you can align your talk to one of those topics, make that adjustment. It will likely improve your chances of being accepted.
- *Note your blog post.* Use the notes field or other submission platform options to share something like "This talk is based on my blog post: {URL}." Organizers can then read the blog post to get a better idea of what you plan to cover. This additional detail is incredibly helpful for building confidence in first-time speakers. And if your blog post links to a Hacker News or social media post with lots of engagement, even better. This shows the organizers that the community is interested in this topic.
- *Spend time on your bio.* Unless the conference uses double-blind (masked) evaluation, speaker quality matters—especially for first-time speakers. If you're not well-known, that judgment is made solely based on your bio. Your bio shouldn't just lazily restate your job title. Share a little more about your background and interests, emulating the style and seriousness of past speakers' bios. For example, "I started learning Rust for fun in 2017. I've now worked full-time with Rust for five years at ACME A and ACME B, writing high-performance and high-availability API servers and internet proxies."
- *Link to a portfolio.* Do yourself a favor: create a simple portfolio web page with links to your blog posts, any existing talks, GitHub and social handles, a bio, and optionally a high-quality photo of yourself (a professional-looking high-res phone photo is fine). Then link to that in your bio. This allows you to succinctly share details, even within the constraints of a character-limited form field. Plus, it makes a nice impression of professionalism, which can help you with the speaker strength criteria. Side note: remember to keep that portfolio page reasonably up-to-date!

- *Be transparent about the product's role.* If your talk mentions your product, provide enough detail to assure everyone that it's not a product pitch, especially if your product is not open source. That might be totally clear in the blog post, but ensure it comes across in the abstract as well. Nobody wants a thinly veiled advertisement at a conference session. It makes attendees unhappy, and that makes organizers unhappy. If organizers can't tell beyond the shadow of a doubt that it won't be a product pitch, they will likely err on the side of skipping your talk.

- *Sweat the small stuff.* Look at all the details of what's required: word count, headshot image size, and similar. If you miss the mark on one, the submission might not go through. Even worse—the text you entered into the submission form might be lost. Pro tip: prepare your submission responses in a file outside of the web form, just in case something goes awry.

- *Note your (authentic) excitement and flexibility.* If you have attended and enjoyed the conference as an attendee, feel free to quickly mention why you love it and why you'd be honored to speak at it. Also, if you're willing to adapt your proposal based on their feedback and needs, make that known as well. Organizers appreciate both flattery and flexibility.

- *Review the review criteria.* See if the conference you're applying to publishes any review criteria, and keep that in mind as you work on your proposal (your bio as well as your title and abstract). For example, here's how KubeCon submissions are currently judged:
  - *Content*—The relevance and coherence of the session's content, the quality of the proposal, and the likelihood of effective delivery by the speaker
  - *Originality*—The degree to which the session presents new and innovative ideas or approaches, as well as the originality of its delivery
  - *Relevance*—The extent to which the session's content provides new and exciting insights or information that is relevant to the conference
  - *Speaker(s)*—The suitability of the proposed speaker(s) based on their expertise and alignment with the subject matter

Finally, set realistic expectations, and don't get discouraged if it doesn't work out. Some conferences have a startling low acceptance rate; for example, KubeCon hovers around 11%–12% year over year. If you're not accepted, it never hurts to ask for feedback on why your submission didn't make the cut or what you could do differently next time. Conferences might not be at liberty to provide those details; but if you hit one that does, it's a valuable learning opportunity.

16.4 Converting your blog post to a talk

Accepted? Take a few moments to celebrate, then read the speaker guide and start planning how you will convert your blog post into a talk. All the content is already nicely written in your blog—maybe too much content, actually. Your job now is to determine the best way to present it to this conference's specific audience, at a pace and depth they can process when listening in real time.

TIP   Looking for inspiration? TechYaks (https://techyaks.com/) is a ranking-driven list of classic tech talks (think Hacker News). And Brendan O'Leary wrote a nice analysis of what makes some specific tech talks so compelling in his blog post "What makes a great tech talk?" (https://mng.bz/2gqw)

16.4.1 Start with the most important takeaway

To start, think about the most important thing you want the attendees to get out of this talk. This is probably quite close to the goal you stated for your blog post (covered in chapters 4 and 5), but it might be somewhat adjusted to accommodate the conference focus or the limited time you have to present.

With that in mind, write down your mission statement, something like "I'm going to be sharing {this} to help you {that}." This statement has two main purposes:

- As you plan the talk, use this to filter out any information that doesn't play an essential role in achieving that goal. Talks should be even more tightly focused than blog posts. When reading, people can always skip over anything they consider a distraction. At conferences, they're forced to tolerate it (or they end up checking their phones and never regaining that initial focus).

- During the talk, before you advance a single slide, share this statement to help orient and filter the audience. If an attendee isn't interested in what you have to offer, they can skip over to another talk before it's too late.

16.4.2 Map out the slide flow

Start mapping out the slide flow to estimate what you can actually cover in the allotted time. The rule of thumb is 1 to 2 minutes per slide. That will vary a bit based on the content of your slides, but don't expect to cover 50 slides in a 20-minute presentation.

NOTE   If your conference specifically requests something different, definitely follow their guidance. For example, some conferences expect "Lightning Talk" speakers to use exactly 20 slides and spend 15 seconds per slide.

You don't need to fill out the body of the slides yet. Just add titles and see where you land. If you end up with an egregious excess, revise accordingly. Some topics might need to be merged or, more likely, the scope might need to be scaled down. Can't immediately justify why a specific point is required to support the main takeaway? Cut it.

Remember that you have the luxury of sending attendees to your blog post for additional details, so you don't have to cover every nuance here. It's much better to have attendees walk away with a good grasp of one big idea that they will remember than leave overwhelmed by an onslaught of information overload. If they're curious, they will seek out the additional details later.

TIP   For help translating words to slides, use a generative AI prompt like: "I want to convert this blog post to a 20-minute talk for a Zig conference. Could you please draft 18–22 slides to cover the core material that a Zig-curious audience would be interested in?"

16.4.3 *Develop individual slides*

Once you've settled on the flow, optimize the slide titles. They should be short and clear, helping the attendees determine what to focus on when you're speaking to each slide. Use a different title for each slide to avoid confusion and force yourself into more precision. And as we covered in chapter 5, focus on headings that make sense from the audience's point of view. One approach is to match what's probably running through their heads ("Why did we take this approach?", "Was it worth it?", etc.)

For the actual slide body, aim to have as little text as possible, and then cut some more. You want the audience to be listening to you, not reading tons of text. You don't want the temptation of reciting the slide text. Stick with a tight set of pithy bullets and leave your details for the speaker notes.

Don't even think about shrinking the conference template's recommended font to squeeze more words onto a slide. Attendees have a low tolerance for text they can't read and an even lower tolerance for code they can't read. If your code excerpt doesn't all fit on one slide in the recommended font, consider splitting it up or redacting any nonessential parts, adding ellipses to indicate the cut. Nobody will be running code from your slide anyway.

Not every slide needs to look like a piece of art, but do aim to have at least a few slides that are visually compelling. Slides that stand out tend to be captured by attendees, provoking paparazzi moments at in-person conferences or screen captures at virtual ones. You can add visual interest to your slides with system diagrams, flame graphs, other charts and dashboards, test results—whatever makes sense for your topic. You likely already created a few for your blog post. Even a stark controversial statement, set off on its own, could achieve the desired effect.

Serving up a few attractive and intriguing slides will help attendees share your talk on social media, which in turn helps you get more recognition for your talk. Also, don't overlook the power of a QR code; people are irresistibly drawn to photograph them. Be sure to add context to that slide so the motivation for scanning is readily apparent later on.

> **TIP** Want ideas on what visuals you could add? Follow up the previous AI prompt with "What visuals would you recommend for this presentation?"

Some additional tips for completing your deck:

- *Share background.* Offering up the backstory around your topic is a natural way to start the talk. Plus, it helps the audience connect with you at a more human level than if you simply started with impersonal lecturing.
- *Fun is fine.* If there's a natural opportunity to include a fun example or story, do it. It's another way to connect with the audience, and it helps make your talk more memorable. For example, some speakers use fun visual themes (monsters, sports, etc.) to tie their ideas together in a memorable flow.
- *Use section slides as signposts.* Section slides give you an opportunity to state the key takeaway from the previous section, take a deep breath, and then transition into

the next section. If anyone's mind started wandering during the previous part, this can help get them back on track.

- *Feature your blog post.* Toward the end of your deck, prepare a full slide featuring your blog post. Include a screenshot of your blog post plus a QR code that links to it. For an extra incentive, mention that your blog post will include the video and slide deck for this talk.

- *Cover connecting.* Prepare a slide that shares how to contact you with questions or follow you to learn about your next talks and blog posts. Even better, give them a specific reason to connect with you, like "I'd be happy to share the resources I found most helpful for learning about {topic}, just contact me on {platform_of_choice}."

- *Prepare backup slides.* If you worry that your talk might run short, it's helpful to have some backup slides that you can pull up for a quick extension. You could also include a few slides that would help you address questions that are likely to arise during the Q&A.

If you plan to demo something as part of your talk—perhaps to show what your engineering feat looks like from the user perspective—plan for everything to go wrong, then be pleasantly surprised if it does not. Planning for the worst typically means having a backup video saved locally. But, you could also prepare slides that let you speak to the main points you would have covered. Or, you might opt to skip it altogether and use the extra time to go deeper into other slides. Just have a backup plan and be ready to execute it at a moment's notice. You never know when you might find yourself in the middle of a Windows 98 "Blue Screen of Death" demo moment.

16.4.4 Prepare speaker notes

Many speakers feel more comfortable presenting with speaker notes available—sometimes with key points beyond what's in the slides, sometimes with a complete word-for-word script. This is purely an individual decision; do what you're most comfortable with.

If you decide to script it, plan to rehearse it so extensively that it sounds natural (more on this later). Many speakers use bold text and other annotations to remind themselves what words to emphasize, when to pause, and similar. While relying on a script is fine, droning on and on in a monotone voice is not. Make a concerted effort to make it sound natural and ensure that the script reading doesn't dampen your innate enthusiasm for the topic.

The act of writing the script and rehearsing from it can be worthwhile even if you never look at that script once during the actual presentation. If preparing a script helps you perfect the timing and figure out how to approach each slide, it's time well spent.

> **TIP**   If you're scripting your talk word-for-word, a rule of thumb is that conference talks run at a pace of 100 to 160 words per minute.

16.5 Promoting the talk

The conference organizer will likely promote your talk, and you should, too. Sharing that you're speaking about {whatever} at Conference A isn't just about helping conference attendees shape their schedules. It's also a somewhat subtle way to announce "Hey, I was selected as one of the experts to help people learn more about {whatever}." This builds your reputation as an expert on that topic, even among people who have zero intention of attending that conference.

Promoting your own talk doesn't have to be narcissistic and spammy. To make it palatable, try emphasizing the conference itself, fellow speakers, other interesting talks, and so on. For example, you might try social posts like

- "Looking forward to speaking at #CoolCONF, {why_it's_so_cool}"
- "Can't wait for this year's #CoolCONF, where I'll be presenting alongside experts like …"
- "Excited to talk about {topic} at #CoolCONF—and hope to catch the sessions…"

If the conference organizer offers to feature you in interviews, videos, or their blog, strongly consider participating. They want to use their professional resources to elevate your profile industry wide and drive attendance to your session. Don't pass up this opportunity unless you have a great reason.

Also, let your company's marketing team know that you'll be speaking. They probably have additional means of promoting the session and would be thrilled to help spread the word that one of their engineers was selected as a conference speaker.

> **TIP** Be sure to use all the official hashtags and/or handles so the conference organizers can find and reshare your social posts and comments.

16.6 Rehearsing

At a minimum, prepare to run through your talk a few times (at least!) to nail the timing. Speakers hitting their mark is absolutely critical. If someone ends up way too short, attendees feel shortchanged and wonder if they should have attended a different session. If someone runs over, it starts a chain reaction across the rest of the schedule (which is why organizers usually cut people off at the end of the allotted time, even if they're not done). Aim to fill the majority of the slot and leave the suggested time for Q&A. Don't deliver a 20-minute presentation in a 40-minute slot. And never, ever go over. The organizers will likely remember that if you ever apply to speak there again.

To be safe, create some checkpoints along the way. For example, you might note that

- You should be at slide 11 by the 12-minute mark.
- You need to start the final section by the 16-minute mark.
- By the 20-minute mark, you should start wrapping it up.

You could also note which slides you would linger on longer if there's extra time and what specific points you can safely gloss over when you need to pick up the pace.

When rehearsing for an in-person conference, stand up, pretend you're at the podium, and walk around. And if it's a virtual conference, play around with your setup so you know exactly where your speaker notes and camera need to be positioned so you end up looking at the camera. Order a wired microphone, an external camera, and some adjustable lighting if needed. Finally, tidy up your background. Not all production software offers the luxury of blurred or virtual backgrounds. You don't want to be frantically cleaning your background right when you should be psyching yourself up to deliver the talk.

If you're extra nervous, you could also

- Rehearse in front of humans
- Check out the room (or recording software) in advance
- Try to anticipate questions that people might ask (your snarkiest teammates can likely assist here) and think about your responses

TIP   Want some guesses at what questions could arise? Follow up the previous generative AI prompts with something like: "What questions might attendees (programmers who are curious about Zig) ask—please specify things that are not covered in the original blog post."

Also, if you have any questions or concerns, just ask the organizer. They want you to be comfortable and prepared, and would probably love to help set your mind at ease.

16.7   *Delivering*

If you want to perfect your public speaking technique, there's an abundance of resources available: classes, videos, books, blogs, and so on. We're not going to try to capture all that in a small section in a book focused on writing blog posts. But we do encourage you to pursue it to whatever degree you wish.

You don't need to be a professional-grade speaker to deliver an effective talk at a tech conference though. Here are some quick tips:

- Remember that your ultimate goal is to share your experiences and ideas with your peers, and you don't need to be the world's #1 presenter to achieve that objective.
- Speak clearly and at a reasonable pace, remembering that not everyone is a native English speaker.
- Double (even triple) check that notifications and system updates are off.
- Use slide transitions as an opportunity to pause, breathe, and reset as needed.
- If you want a random break, feel free to take a strategic sip of water.
- Look at the audience, perhaps focusing on someone you know or a few people who seem to be really paying attention and nodding along.
- Smile—at least at the beginning and end.

When it comes time for the Q&A:

- For the sake of attendees who could not hear the question, as well as video viewers who can only hear the mic feed, restate each question before answering (this also buys you a little more time to think).

- If you don't know the answer, say so—maybe another attendee happens to know, or maybe you want to research it and respond to them later.

- If you don't want to start debating some point that an attendee raises, respond with something like "Interesting, I hadn't thought of that," and move on.

Finally, remember that even the most experienced presenters get nervous. As Gunnar Morling recently shared on X:

> *Someone asked me whether I'd still be nervous before giving a conference talk: Yes, I am. And I think it is actually a good thing. The day you're not nervous even just a little bit, you may have stopped caring about doing the best job you can, and the audience will notice that.*

16.8 Following up

You didn't forget about your blog post the moment it was published (if you read chapter 15, at least). Likewise, don't let your talk ingloriously fade away after the conference wraps. Continue squeezing value out of this experience by

- *Thanking everyone via social*—Right after the conference wraps, share something on social. A quick thank you to the organizers, presenters, and community will work if you're simply exhausted at this point.

- *Writing a wrap-up blog or threaded post*—As soon as you're up for it, share more about what you enjoyed about the conference: a few takeaways related to the overall theme or your topic of interest, a rundown of your favorite talks, or any other angle that strikes you.

- *Following up on requests*—If you promised anyone anything, links to other resources, an answer that required additional research, whatever: pay your debts before you forget.

- *Reviewing any reviews*—Some conferences collect feedback on each speaker; if yours did, scan it for any tips on things you might do differently next time.

- *Connecting with other speakers*—Speaking at a conference provides the perfect sneaky excuse to connect with experts you might not dare to approach otherwise.

- *Searching social media for mentions*—Try to hunt down any social media references. If you notice that someone posted about your talk, engage with the post and be sure to thank the person for attending and sharing.

- *Tracking down on-demand videos*—Figure out when videos will be released and if they're accessible to non-attendees (and thus ripe for sharing).

- *Sharing your video*—Once the videos are available, don't hesitate to draft a social post saying nice things about the conference and sharing your contribution to it (the video). You might also want to link to the blog post that it's based on as well.

- *Updating the blog post*—Now that you (hopefully) have a nice video on the blog topic, update the blog post with a link to that video (or a direct video embed). Consider embedding the slide deck as well. Also consider updating the blog post in response to any feedback or questions you received during the talk, in the reviews, or as you waited in the beverage line after you survived your talk.

Conference talks from over a decade ago are still watched and discussed today, thanks to YouTube and social media. If you strategically plant a few references to it, there's a much greater chance that your talk will continue educating people beyond the actual event.

Summary

- Speaking at conferences can lead to a personal brand boost, networking opportunities, and direct audience feedback—plus an impressive video of yourself presenting.
- When evaluating conference opportunities, consider factors such as topic fit, conference reach/promotion, logistics, and audience demographics.
- Proposals should have an intriguing title, detailed abstract showcasing your unique perspective/experience, and a strong speaker bio.
- When converting your blog post to a talk, customize it for that audience and for listening versus reading, and be sure to add a few compelling visuals that people might share.
- To prepare, draft speaker notes, anticipate potential audience questions, and practice, practice, practice.
- Work with the conference to promote your talk; tap social media, use conference hashtags, and see if your own company will also spread the word.
- Engage with the audience, speak clearly and at a reasonable pace, repeat any audience questions before answering them, and try to remember to smile.
- Follow up by thanking organizers, writing recap posts, connecting with other speakers, sharing videos, and updating your original blog post to reference the talk.

So you want to
write a book

This chapter covers

- The benefits of moving from writing blog posts to writing books
- When you should (and shouldn't) consider writing a book
- Alternative ways to share and shape big ideas
- Commonly overlooked considerations in the "publisher versus self-publish" decision
- Navigating the book proposal process

After you've written several successful blog posts and maybe have a conference talk or two under your belt, you might start wondering, "Should I write a book?" You might start thinking about this because you have a burning book idea—and you have a bad habit of burdening your future self with ambitious commitments. Or maybe it wasn't even your idea at all. Maybe an acquisitions editor (a.k.a. a publisher talent scout) was impressed by some of your blog posts, reached out to you, and planted the seed in your brain.

Either way, writing your own book can be a tempting idea. But it's also a massive commitment. The book will affect your life (and your family's life) for months or years. But all the effort could yield significant long-term rewards.

This chapter helps you think through key decisions and tradeoffs you'll likely face if you want to write a book. As with any major project, there are all sorts of non-obvious factors to consider. We share what we've learned working with several different publishers, as well as self-publishing, to give you a better idea of what to expect and what to look out for. We take you through the book proposal process, then conveniently leave "how to write the book" as an exercise for the reader. (It deserves its own dedicated book, honestly.)

Book writing can be a wild ride; we hope this chapter makes your own path to book writing—should you choose to pursue it—more straightforward, rewarding, and enjoyable.

17.1   *Why write a book?*

To be clear, writing a book is rewarding—both professionally and personally, if not (typically) financially. Otherwise, you wouldn't see so many seemingly rational people succumb to this strangely addictive hobby. Here are specific reasons why you might decide to invest all the time and effort that writing a book requires:

- You have a vision for a book that begs to be written.
- You want to anchor yourself as an expert.
- You want an excuse to immerse yourself in a topic.
- You want to level up your writing.
- You have an innate urge to share and teach.

17.1.1   *You have a vision for a book that begs to be written*

Book projects tend to arise from the following perfect storm:

- *A void*—There's a void in the industry knowledge base. Maybe that's because the technology or topic is new or just now gaining traction. Maybe the techniques and tools are known only as tribal knowledge across certain communities. Or maybe there are so many aspects and angles to the topic that the current resources don't do it justice.
- *A hunger*—There's a critical mass of people who care about this void, to the point that they're willing to purchase and read a whole book on it.
- *Expertise*—You're a valuable source of expertise on the topic of the void.

In many cases, a publisher will notice the void and the hunger, then approach blog post authors to provide the expertise. Or it could happen altogether organically. Perhaps one day, you randomly realize that what you consider to be common sense is not actually common at all—and that sharing this knowledge broadly could really benefit some significant segment of the community.

The origin of the book idea isn't critical. What matters is whether

- You have an interesting vision for how to address the void
- You personally possess (or have ready access to) the expertise needed to execute on that vision
- You're already picturing a print version of that book sitting on your desk, bookshelf, or coffee table

If you've reached that point, "the book idea" becomes *your* book, and you're probably already infected by the irresistible urge to write it.

17.1.2 *You want to anchor yourself as an expert*

Want to secure your spot as an expert on a topic? Be the one who "wrote the book on it," literally. That expression came about for a reason. Although book quality varies, it's fairly well accepted that someone who has written a book has a deep understanding of its topic.

After all, writing a book is not an easy endeavor. It demonstrates that you have

- Thought deeply about this topic for quite some time
- Developed the domain expertise required to create a sizable book
- Spent tremendous time structuring and refining your thoughts on this matter for the sake of educating others
- Communicated expertise that was validated by publishers and reviewers

Those are just some of the many reasons why being a published author provides a near-instant infusion of prestige and credibility. Even people who don't read a single page of your book will likely be impressed by the fact that you wrote it. It's the ultimate portfolio piece: a carefully crafted and professionally produced work that captures your best thinking on a given topic at a given time. And you can just drop it on someone's desk.

If you're ever looking to stand out in a crowded field of applicants, having written a book should serve as a clear differentiator! It's also the perfect mark of distinction if you're running your own business or consulting as a side project.

17.1.3 *You want an excuse to immerse yourself in a topic*

If you're so passionate about a topic that you want to think about it every day for a year or so, commit to writing a book on it. That gives you the perfect excuse to prioritize rigorous study of the subject. Normally, it's way too easy to delay reading all those bookmarked articles and writing up all those things you meant to share. There's nothing like a legal contract specifying exact due dates to finally get you motivated!

When you write a book, you will need (and want) to spend considerable time thinking about your topic. When you write a blog post, you can conveniently frame the article to avoid things you don't know as well. However, when you write something as comprehensive as a book, it's likely going to expose some gaps or weak spots in your mastery of the topic. In addition to the things you *know* you don't know, you will also stumble upon "unknown unknowns" as you write. The very act of capturing your thoughts in structured writing forces you to think much more carefully about

- How you know what you know
- How it's all related
- What matters most
- How to explain it to others
- How to get others excited about it

Your understanding of the topic will be further tested by your technical editor (if you work with a publisher), other reviewers, your readers, and anyone who happens to be talking about the book in the infamous comment sections. If you get something wrong, it won't go unnoticed.

By the time you emerge from the journey, book in hand, you will likely be one of the world's most knowledgeable people in your specific niche.

17.1.4 *You want to level up your writing*

Writing a book is a boot camp experience—even for professional writers, even for those who have written books before. You will naturally refine your craft by

- Writing so much, so rapidly
- Forcing yourself to present your thoughts in the book/chapter structure that's set by your publisher
- Constantly rewriting when the words don't effectively capture the ideas in your brain
- Receiving and responding to feedback from development editors, technical editors, copy editors, and real-world readers/reviewers
- Accommodating difficult requests: adding sections that you never intended to write, rewriting a chapter from scratch, pivoting part of the book in a totally different direction, and so forth

Just like preparing for and ultimately completing a marathon will take your athleticism to new levels, writing a book will take your writing to new levels.

17.1.5 *You have an innate urge to share and teach*

If you're an open source contributor, a team leader, or have ever been a teacher, you're probably driven by the urge to share your expertise for the benefit of others. Books, like blog posts, help you scale your knowledge far and wide. But books let you share a massive amount of knowledge in a single convenient package. And that can have a massive influence on your readers, as well as your domain.

17.2 *Why not?*

Committing to a book project when the stars aren't perfectly aligned is a surefire way to make your life miserable for at least a year. Here are two key reasons why you *shouldn't* write a book:

- The topic isn't well-suited to a book.
- It's just not a great fit for you—at least not right now.

17.2.1 *The topic isn't well-suited to a book*

The publication cycle of books is dramatically different than that of blog posts. With a blog post, you can move from idea to published article in a matter of minutes. With a substantial book, it would be rare to go from idea to printed book in less than a year. Books are more difficult to update as well. Even with self-publishing, you can't just change a few words or lines of code in a book as easily as you can in a blog post.

Given all the time and work required to get a book published, we recommend that you focus on a topic with an expected "shelf life" of at least a couple of years, preferably more. For example, you don't want to end up

- Writing a detailed "how to" book about a product that's poised for a major change
- Trying to pin down the nuances of a new programming language as it's rapidly evolving
- Obsessing over being first to write about a shiny new technology rather than creating something that will stand out for years to come

Also, do your research and check that potential readers can't already get a "good enough" resource on your topic for free (or close) on the internet. Unless you are truly confident that your approach will stand out and that readers will recognize the value of your approach, you might want to refrain from entering this potentially devalued market.

17.2.2 *It's just not a great fit for you—at least not right now*

Books consume a ton of time. If your work, family, and other personal priorities are already consuming all your time, don't take on a book project unless you are willing to give something up. You can't miraculously find more time. You will need a realistic plan for where you will free up existing time on a consistent and long-term basis. Otherwise, the book commitment will ultimately feel like the sword of Damocles hanging over your head.

Moreover, book projects suit some personalities better than others. Table 17.1 lists some points to help you assess where you fall on the "will I love it or hate it" spectrum.

Writing a book is a strange process. You need to be relentless about pushing through challenges for months upon months. Then, as the deadline approaches, it's time for a hard mental shift: you need to draw a line and let it go. As Brian Sletten, author of *WebAssembly: The Definitive Guide*, so aptly put it in a personal conversation: "Books aren't published when they are done. They are done when they're published."

17.3 *Alternatives to consider*

Maybe writing your own book is not the right project for you (at least not right now). But if you still have a burning desire to tackle a big idea and share your knowledge with the community, consider other options:

- Collaborate with co-authors
- Drip it out through blog posts
- Become a technical reviewer

Table 17.1   Is your personality amenable to book writing?

Likely to love it	Likely to hate it
You enjoy tackling massive ambiguous projects with no precedent and minimal guidance.	You thrive on clear project direction and structure.
You thrive on torturing yourself with long-term physical and mental challenges.	You often get enthralled by a new hobby or other obsession, then soon get bored and move on to the next.
You create high-level visionary ideas as well as low-level plans to carry them out.	You're quite comfortable being comfortable.
You're insanely self-disciplined.	You have trouble accepting things as "good enough" and calling them done.
You can crank out acceptable drafts relatively fast, even under pressure.	You're not (yet) great at reviewing your writing from your reader's perspective and anticipating where they could be confused, skeptical, or lost.
You can tear your writing to shreds.	

17.3.1 *Collaborate with co-authors*

When we start discussing this book, particularly this chapter of this book, with our book author colleagues, it tends to go as shown in figure 17.1.

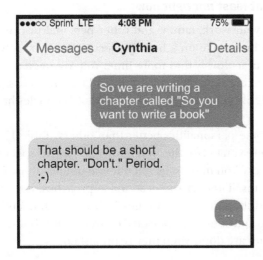

Figure 17.1   What happens when book authors talk about writing books

Joking/not joking. Writing a book is ultimately a rewarding process. But we'd be remiss to sugarcoat it—it can be difficult. Martin Kleppmann, author of the top O'Reilly bestseller to date, shared: "Writing a book is really hard, at least if you want to do it well. For me it was about the same level of difficulty as building and selling a startup (YMMV), that is to say, involving multiple existential crises" (see https://mng.bz/RNna).

Why are we talking about this in a chapter section that's supposed to be about co-authors? Because co-author collaboration can change the whole dynamic of a book project. It's not just that each person has fewer words to write (though that certainly helps!). Other benefits include:

- With more expertise and strengths to draw from, you don't need to personally master every aspect of the topic, as well as all parts of the writing process.
- More perspectives translates to deeper as well as broader insight into the topic, and this benefits both you and your reader.
- The weight of the book no longer rests solely on your shoulders; if you need a little break, you can take one knowing that others are still moving the project forward.
- On the other hand, knowing that your colleagues are working away on this shared project is perfect motivation when you're tempted to leave that next task for another day.
- You have ready access to an incredibly informed (and passionate) sounding board for all the questions and doubts that cross your mind.

Plus, misery loves company! When you need to rewrite that chapter from scratch, scramble to deliver drafts within minutes of the deadline, review hundreds of pages of copyediting revisions over a weekend, and so on, it really does help to have an impromptu group venting session.

Quite seriously though: having co-authors you enjoy working with can make a book project truly fun. We've worked on a handful of book projects with different collaborators involved in various capacities. In all cases, the overall experience and quality of the final product ultimately boiled down to the chemistry between the co-authors.

17.3.2 Drip it out through blog posts

Call this approach "Just start writing it with zero book pressure." Think about what your book would look like, then plan to publish at least the first part of that book as blog posts. Begin with an introductory post that shares why you're writing the series and what to expect. Then drip out what you envision as the first few chapters on your own schedule. Each time you publish a new post, be sure to link back to that introductory post (and vice versa).

If you work in this serial publishing manner, you can get a feel for what it's like to write this book. It will soon become apparent how much time each piece will require to research and write. And you will get an immediate gut check on how much you enjoy working on this topic. Do you actually look forward to tackling the next section on your mental list? Or are you already getting bored with the whole idea?

Working in this manner is also a great proving ground for your idea. Is there truly an audience interested in learning about your take on this specific topic? Blogging a preview of the book content is the perfect way to find out! If your first few chapters-masquerading-as-articles are all Hacker News sensations, you can bet that the book proposal process will go much more smoothly. Or maybe you want to self-publish the book so you can retain a larger percentage of the potential bestseller's profits (more on that later). However, if the idea doesn't immediately resonate, don't give up right away. It could be that you're just not connecting with the right readers. Maybe a publisher could help you reach the target audience.

You might also discover that you're perfectly satisfied covering this subject via blog posts! In this case, just continue with what's working until you feel some compelling urge to change.

> **TIP** Will Larson wrote a book blog-by-blog, then later had it published by a publisher. He shares his experience in "Self-publishing Staff Engineer" (https://lethain.com/self-publishing-staff-engineer/). Other examples are "Joel On Software" by Joel Spolsky (from https://www.joelonsoftware.com/) and "The Old New Thing" by Raymond Chen (https://devblogs.microsoft .com/oldnewthing/).

17.3.3 *Become a technical reviewer*

Becoming a technical reviewer lets you influence a book in your area of expertise and also gain an inside look at how the book-writing process really works. Technical reviewing a book is not nearly as time-consuming as writing one. It's a streamlined process, with the editor pinging you each time a new chapter is ready to be reviewed. It can take anywhere from days to months, depending on the author's ergonomics and laziness (also known in the book industry as "being preoccupied with more important business"). Technical review usually takes the form of light online discussion with the author: pointing out glaring (to you) omissions, asking for clarification on some points, and suggesting a rephrase here and there.

How can you become a technical reviewer to learn more about writing a book? It's a Catch-22. If you've already written a book on the topic, your editor will likely contact you when they need technical reviewers. But how do you break into the cycle? You could always volunteer your services to any peers who enthusiastically announce "I'm writing a book!" Alternatively, you could hunt down the acquisitions editors in your domain: look at a book you admire, see who the author thanks in the preface, and ping that person on LinkedIn or other platforms.

17.4 *Publishing considerations*

If you decide to write a book, what path do you want to take? Working with a publisher, a company that has perfected the art of developing and selling technical books, can provide a number of advantages: valuable feedback, extended reach, and taking care of all matters required for high-quality production, to name a few. But self-publishing also brings a different set of benefits: more freedom on your topic (well on everything, really), no real deadlines, and the potential to update the book faster.

There are already many great resources where authors share their personal experiences working with publishers as well as self-publishing. In particular, Will Larson's perspectives on working with publishers as well as self-publishing stand out as must-reads. See "What I Learned Writing a Book" (https://lethain.com/learned -writing-book/), "Self-Publishing Staff Engineer" (https://mng.bz/ZVg9), and "More (self-)publishing thoughts" [https://lethain.com/more-publshing-thoughts/]). Moreover, Gregor Hohpe's "The Economics of Writing Technical Books" (https://mng.bz/ AawQ) provides exceptional insight into the realities of the self-publishing process. And Rob Fitzpatrick's book, *Write Useful Books*, offers good advice for self-publishing nonfiction books in general.

Table 17.2 provides a brief overview of the reasons most commonly cited for choosing one option over another.

Table 17.2   Common reasons for choosing to work with a publisher or self-publish

Work with a publisher	Self-publish
Prestige and validation	Complete control over your content
Pressure (and help) to get it done	Ability to update (nearly) on-demand
Professional production/ and distribution	Full ownership and rights
Editorial review and guidance	Higher royalty rate
Professional promotion	Flexible schedule

We've worked with both publishing models and with several different tech publishers. In this section, we'll share some commonly overlooked publishing considerations based on what we learned.

17.4.1 Not all publishers are created equal

First, talking about the generic term "publishers" is like making blanket statements about "hotels," "food," or "animals." There is a dramatic range.

Every publishing company has its own mission, processes, and business model. With one, you might expect to interact with various staff members each week; collaborating on marketing efforts, brainstorming something with editors, and so on. With others, you might have just two or three interactions with the publisher's staff throughout the entire process (and you might need to send 31 emails to order additional books at your author discount—real story).

Some publishers add more friction than value, especially for an experienced author. The fact that they handle the hassles of the book production and distribution process might be their biggest benefit. But other publishers add distinct value—even to experienced book authors. And that leads to the next section.

17.4.2 Publishers bring an impressive team of experts

If the publisher is committed to your book's success and also funded and staffed at a level to help advance it, here are some of the things you might encounter:

- A network of top-notch *industry experts* who might be tapped for vetting your abstract, technical reviewing your book, and perhaps writing the foreword. For this book, our publisher involved some intimidatingly impressive people.

- An *acquisitions editor* who helps you shape the overall direction of the book based on feedback from the previously mentioned experts. Setting that well-crafted plan from the start saves significant rework (and frustration) later on.

- A *developmental editor* who is tasked with helping you execute on that vision: interacting with you regularly, guiding you through the process, and calling you out whenever they believe that your well-intended approach just isn't hitting the mark.

- A *technical editor* who goes far beyond pointing out factual errors. This person also opens your eyes to considerations previously in your blind spot. They provide an early look at how your target readers will react and what's needed to win them over.

- A team coordinating rigorous *review processes* at key book draft milestones: sharing the in-progress drafts with readers in your target audience, prompting them with questions, asking them to rate each part of each chapter, and compiling all the results for your review.

- A *copyeditor* who will root out whatever grammatical mistakes, missing words, and inconsistencies slipped through the various reviews and revisions.

- A *design* staff that takes care of cover design, improving your (attempts at) illustrations, page layout, typography, margins, and so forth for print as well as ebooks.

- A *production* crew that automagically (to you at least) takes the final draft and transforms it into print and digital files that can show up on devices and doorsteps worldwide.

- A *marketing* team that tries to learn the nuances of your particular domain so they can tune their well-oiled marketing machine to entice your target readers.

- A *legal* team that stands by ready to combat unauthorized reproductions, plagiarism, and other legal infringements.

Misconception: "The Editor"

Myth: There's a common misconception that when you work with a publisher, you will be assigned "an editor" with two main jobs: 1) nagging you to get chapters completed, and 2) finding and correcting low-level mistakes like misplaced commas.

Reality: With some publishers, you won't even get that much attention! With others, you will get multiple layers of editors whose feedback not only helps you improve the book, but also transforms the way you write (and think about writing). Even if you're an experienced writer, don't dismiss editorial assistance as not valuable until you get a better idea of what to expect in your particular situation.

17.4.3 *Working with publishers is a multithreaded process*

Again, this really depends on the publisher. But when all the various people and teams mentioned previously are involved with your book, work is inevitably being done in parallel. And given that every team and every individual is likely responsible for multiple books, you want to be quick to respond when they have a question, review request, or other need.

This can lead to some days where your book "side project" becomes a lot to handle. For example, there were a few days when we were juggling all of the following (on top of our actual jobs):

- Extending a previously completed chapter to accommodate a publisher-level request
- Templating a recently completed chapter in preparation for review
- Responding to comments and making revisions in response to the just-completed reviews for two earlier chapters
- Suggesting edits for the book description page
- Completing a nine-page marketing questionnaire that required considerable thought and research
- Attempting to write the next two chapters so we wouldn't get behind on the deadlines we previously committed to (not knowing that we'd be attending to all these other tasks at the same time)

If you take the self-publishing route, you can work in a manner that's as focused and linear as your brain prefers. But the tradeoff is that you lack access to the experts generating these various tasks. If you self-publish, it's all on you!

17.4.4 *If you work with a publisher, it's not just "your" book*

When you work with a publisher, many different people contribute to many different aspects of the book (see the previous sections). We've touched on the benefits of this. But this has other effects to consider, too. With so many different professionals working toward the success of this book, it takes on a life of its own. If you neglect it, you're not only hurting yourself; you're letting *everyone* down.

If you fail to meet deadlines for draft milestones or for various marketing projects, you trigger a domino effect that affects many people investing their time and expertise in this project. It's polite to be aware of this when deadlines loom and one-off requests pop into your inbox.

You will also need to align with the publisher's brand. To protect the style and reputation they have established over the years, publishers expect authors to create books using the processes they have designed and optimized. That means you need to cede a certain level of control. At a high level, this means you will need to address all the deeper technical, logical, and structural concerns raised by your editors. You won't necessarily need to agree with their every suggestion, but you will need to acknowledge, discuss, and find a path to a mutually agreeable resolution. This could mean compromising on details such as

- Phrasing and terminology that doesn't align with their style guide
- The level of explanation required for certain terms
- Image size, format, labeling, and captioning
- Chapter structure and elements such as introductions and summaries
- Text styles, bullet levels, and so on that don't have a home in their template
- Footnote usage

Addressing editor concerns and pushing yourself to write chapters in the prescribed manner will ultimately make you a stronger writer. But it can be frustrating at times, like when you are writing your millionth (or so it seems) chapter or section introduction "because that's what's needed."

Moreover, to support the publisher's brand, you will need to use one of their sanctioned authoring tools. Do you write in LaTeX, AsciiDoc, Google Docs, or Microsoft Word? Do you save files in a GitHub repo, Box, or Google Drive? How can you see what your text looks like in their template? Given all the time that you'll spend writing, the supported authoring environments have an outsized effect on your overall book writing experience. Compromising on how your code examples are labeled is one thing. Being forced to work in an authoring environment that disrupts your flow or just generally frustrates you is a much more serious concern.

Finally, the fact that the book is a joint effort affects your bottom line. Publishers understandably want to earn back the time and effort they invest in your book, and that's factored into your compensation. They offer authors a percentage of the book profits and they also (typically) pay out a part of those projected earnings as an "advance." In some cases, those percentages vary depending on factors like print versus digital, book versus platform subscription, educational discounts, foreign publishing rights, and so on. Other times the same percentage applies to all revenue—period. Per what authors have shared confidentially and publicly, it's relatively rare for technical books to sell enough copies to receive royalties beyond the advance.

Regardless, the percentages you earn with a publisher will invariably be lower than those you receive if you self-publish. That doesn't mean that your total book profits will be lower though. Think of it this way: Do you want a smaller slice of a potentially larger pie (given the value added by their team) or a larger slice of a potentially smaller pie?

17.4.5 *Highly specialized topics lend themselves to self-publishing*

Given that publishers ultimately survive by producing enough profitable books to make up for their nonprofitable books, it makes sense that they don't want to add more nonprofitable books to their portfolio. This means that you might have a difficult time finding support for a highly specialized topic, especially if the size of the potential reader base is small or unknown relative to other tech topics.

Even if you have a great idea for a breakthrough book in a particular niche, and you are recognized as the world's top expert on the topic, it might not be in the publisher's best interest to publish it. It would cost them just as much (if not more) to publish this book as it would for them to publish a book that provides a new angle on a proven topic, like Go or Rust. However, the niche book's payback potential might fall short of what the others could yield.

Self-publishing shines in these situations, especially if you are already well-known within your niche. Instead of wasting your energy trying to convince publishers that it's a good business move (it might not be), just start planning and writing! And it's also possible that publishers will notice the quality and success of your self-published book and then reach out to you with a tempting publishing offer.

17.4.6 Self-publishing thrives when supported by a brand

If you add a self-published book to Amazon, will anyone read it? Not if the target audience doesn't know it exists.

If your book is backed by a known brand (a popular newsletter, project, company, etc.) or if you yourself are a known brand, you can likely gain significant traction with a self-published book. Simply tell the brand's core followers "We wrote a book," and you'll have a ready-built initial audience. Once they start reading and talking about it, you can expect "word-of-mouth marketing" to keep the buzz going and promote it beyond your immediate community. This could be just as effective, if not more effective, than a publisher's standard marketing motions.

If you're not associated with such a brand, the path to self-publishing success will likely be more difficult. You will need to rely on some strategic kindling to get the fire started. If you're well-connected, persuasive, or just lucky, your book might catch the attention of an influencer in the book's domain. That person might then set off a chain reaction on social media and potentially the orange site.

17.4.7 Different options, different considerations

No matter what path you choose, there are a lot of little details that will likely catch you by surprise. And what's critically important to one person might be trivial to another. Table 17.3 highlights a few things you might want to consider researching based on the publishing option that you ultimately choose.

If you're comparing different publishers or different self-publishing options, search the internet for something like "Publishing a book with {company_name}." In most cases, that will surface a few stories providing insight into the process. Also, feel free to reach out to those authors directly. The fact that they captured and shared their experiences indicates that they're eager to help others make an informed decision.

17.5 Navigating the proposal process

If you want to take the "traditional publisher" path, you will need to complete a proposal. This is unavoidable, even if their editor actively recruited you to write a book on

Table 17.3   Questions to consider with your publishing option

Working with a publisher	Self-publishing
What is the editor-to-author ratio?	Does the self-publishing platform offer any templates or other layout assistance?
Who would you interact with, how frequently, and in what capacity?	What's required to create and sell a print book?
How do they market books?	What's required to create and sell a digital book?
Can your book benefit from their market reach?	How would readers discover your book?
Does their library include books that pair well with yours?	How much will it cost for designers, cover artists, and proofreaders?
Do they focus more on print or digital? Books or platforms?	Can you offer DRM-free books?
Do they offer DRM-free books?	Do they sell and ship books to the geographies you want to target?
Will your book be used to train their large language model and support their AI platform?	What analytics and tracking options do they offer?
In what regions do they market and distribute books?	How difficult is it to reach a human and get questions answered?
Do you need to find your own technical reviewer?	Can they split revenue across multiple co-authors?
How do they make decisions on audiobooks and translations?	Do reviews of popular self-published books from this platform mention production quality problems (look at the negative reviews)?
What tools would you need to use for writing and reviewing?	What's the minimum price you can set for a book with your page count, size, and options (e.g., color or not)?
How does your anticipated timeline align with their process and production cycles?	Is there a fee to use the publishing platform?
Is there an option (or requirement) to release early access versions?	

a topic that they dreamed up. Completing a proposal forces you to think through a lot of the hard questions related to the proposed book. Most pointedly,

- Why should it be written?
- Who would want to purchase it?
- Why should you, in particular, write it?
- How deeply have you thought about this topic?
- How would you approach the topic?
- Is it worth publishing?

Those aren't the exact questions, but that's ultimately what they're trying to figure out.

Even if you're not planning to work with a publisher, it's valuable to look at a few publishers' proposal templates and complete one. This exercise is helpful for

- Clarifying your vision for the book
- Attempting to estimate the market for such a book

- Establishing a clear roadmap for the writing process
- Sharing your idea with potential co-authors
- Getting early feedback from your peers and experts in the domain

If you are trying to persuade a publisher to publish your book, here are our top two tips for completing proposals.

17.5.1 Get down to business

As we've been harping on heavily throughout this chapter, publishing is a business. Your proposal must demonstrate a distinctive, compelling book idea, or else the acquisitions editor won't think twice about it. But that alone isn't sufficient.

You also need to sell yourself as someone with the expertise and ability to get it done. And you need to convince the publisher that there's a reasonable market for this book (refer back to section 17.4.5 for a little more color on this).

To increase your chances of success, approach your book proposal as a business proposal. For example,

- Research the size of your target audience and highlight why those people would want to buy your book. Impressive stats could include GitHub stars, community size, attendance stats for a related conference, Google Trends charts, and so on.
- Find related books with strong sales (look at Amazon rankings) and see if you can legitimately show that your book is well-poised to draft off of their success. Purchasing and reading (or at least scanning) the other books will help you build a compelling case that yours is similar enough to repeat the others' success, yet different enough to warrant its existence. You could differentiate by topic focus, author experience, target audience, technical depth, etc.

However, remember that you're an engineer, not a salesperson. Now might be a good time to touch base with your business-minded or marketing friends and cash in any favors owed.

17.5.2 Details, detail, details

Some proposal templates require much more detail than others, especially when it comes to the book outline. Strongly consider providing a granular level of detail even if it's not required: not just chapter titles, but also one-sentence chapter descriptions and a guess at all the main sections within each chapter.

This will force you to really think through what you need to cover. That, in turn, helps you better assess how long it might take to write and which co-authors would be helpful. When you start writing, you will thank your previous self for providing this roadmap. It's unlikely that you'll follow the precise path you mapped out, but it will absolutely eliminate much analysis paralysis and rework later.

Moreover, the outline, along with the rest of the proposal, typically becomes part of the book contract. Once that contract is signed and countersigned, this outline goes on the record as the description of the book that you committed to write and that your publisher committed to publish. If any disputes arise later, this outline will likely come up. The more detailed the original outline, the lower the risk of misinterpretations and misunderstandings.

17.6 Go forth and write

If you decide to move forward, with a publisher or on your own, that's where your book begins and also where ours ends. Let's wrap with a few parting tips:

- *Do something every day.* Keep the momentum going by getting into the habit of doing something—anything—to advance your book every single day. Write a paragraph. Read something related. Think through how to approach that one tricky section (and jot down some notes so you don't forget). Create a diagram. There's a huge variety of tasks that need to be completed as you write a book. Surely you can find just one little thing to tackle so you can tell yourself that you made some progress on your book today!

- *Think of it as a series of blog posts.* Writing a book chapter sounds overwhelming, right? But by now, you're comfortable writing blog posts. Just think of each chapter as a series of related blog posts. Write one after another, and before you know it, a chapter has magically materialized. Conveniently, all the article writing strategies covered throughout this book can help you in this context, too!

- *Be stubborn about the vision, flexible on the execution.* As you start extracting ideas from your mind, you'll find that you don't always end up covering every topic exactly as you had originally planned. That's fine. After all the thinking and research you've likely performed by this point, your newer ideas are probably better than your original ones. But remain fixated on your original vision for the book. That should be your north star, guiding you through all the revisions and indecisions along the journey.

Summary

- Writing a book is a massive undertaking that requires significant time and effort—but it can be rewarding, especially if you're a glutton for self-inflicted pain.
- Writing a book not only helps you share knowledge with your peers; it also forces you to deepen, synthesize, and structure your domain expertise.
- Don't write a book if you don't have a vision for the topic, the topic isn't really suitable for a book, you lack the bandwidth, or it's just not a good fit for your work style and personality.
- Co-authoring can be a game changer, turning a lonely and burdensome experience into a collaborative and enjoyable one.
- If you're not ready to commit to writing a book, you could get a feel for it by writing the first chapters as a series of blogs or by becoming a technical reviewer.

- Publishers offer benefits like prestige, editorial guidance, professional production, and marketing, but give you less control and lower royalty percentages.
- Self-publishing allows more control, higher royalty percentages, and greater schedule flexibility, but you need to manage many tedious details and bring (or create) your own audience.
- Complete a book proposal even if you're not seeking a publisher.
- If you are seeking a publisher, treat the book proposal like a business proposal and try to convince the publisher that your great book idea is really worth their investment.

appendix A
Publishing and
writing resources

This appendix discusses options for publishing your blog posts, as well as tools to help you create and optimize them. All tools that we mention offer a free tier (at the time of writing, at least) unless otherwise noted.

A.1 Where to post your posts?

If you're not contributing to a company blog, where do you publish your blog posts? Here's a quick look at popular options: your own blog, Medium and friends, Substack, and publications with a lightweight editorial review/approval process (e.g., HackerNoon and DZone).

A.1.1 Build your own blog site

If you plan to write a number of articles beyond your company blog, strongly consider standing up your own site. In addition to hosting your blog, this site can include your bio, links to projects, talks, and articles—whatever else you'd like to showcase. This option gives you complete control over every element: from plugins, to look and feel, to what's shown alongside each of your articles. Build it however you like, with whatever frameworks you want an excuse to play with. Static site generators are popular options for blogging.

Jekyll (https://jekyllrb.com/) on GitHub Pages (https://pages.github.com/) is a popular combo for minimalist sites. Since GitHub Pages is powered by Jekyll, you can deploy a Jekyll site using GitHub for free, with a custom domain name.

Other static site generator options include Hugo (https://gohugo.io/) and Gatsby (https://www.gatsbyjs.com/). Content Management System (CMS) options include Ghost (https://ghost.org/) and, of course, the stalwart WordPress (https://wordpress .com/)— neither of which currently offer a free tier beyond the initial trial. WordPress does offer a self-hosted open source version, though: just go to the .org site (https:// wordpress.org/) instead of the enterprise (.com) one. Hacker News and Reddit both feature highly opinionated discussions on how the options compare and which is best for different needs.

> **TIP** If you want a clean minimalist blog like the first example featured in chapter 3, you can simply copy its code. The author, Alex Morales, shared it at https://github.com/alexmolas/alexmolas.github.io

If you want a chance at additional exposure, you can also post copies of your articles on aggregators such as Medium and friends (see chapter 15).

Getting started resources

Here are some "official" starting points for getting up and running on various platforms:

Jekyll—Step-by-Step Tutorial (https://jekyllrb.com/docs/step-by-step/01-setup/)

Hugo—Quick Start (https://gohugo.io/getting-started/quick-start/)

Gatsby—Getting Started (https://mng.bz/x6Q6)

WordPress—Set Up Your Blog in Five Steps (https://mng.bz/V2Xx)

Ghost—Getting Started (https://ghost.org/resources/building/)

Medium—Writing and Publishing Your First Story (https://mng.bz/r15j)

Dev.to—Get Started with DEV (https://dev.to/help/getting-started)

Hashnode—Creating a Personal Blog on Hashnode (https://mng.bz/dZj1)

Substack—Setting up Your Substack for the First Time (https://mng.bz/BgPl)

A.1.2 *Medium and friends*

If you really don't want to manage your own blog site, you can publish primarily on a blog aggregator platform (e.g., Medium, dev.to, or Hashnode). You won't have total control over every aspect of the reader's experience. But it's fast, it's simple, and there's a chance that one of your articles might go viral via that platform's recommendation algorithms. For example, if Medium curators boost one of your posts, you could get an instant spike in attention that rivals what you could achieve by trending on Hacker News. Similarly, publishing on dev.to makes your articles easily accessible to a community of over one million developers.

Whichever platform you select, you will get a URL with your profile and centralized access to all the articles you've published there. Custom domains are supported on Medium. And readers who really enjoy your work can follow you via in-platform alerts and email notifications (for Medium at least). With Medium, you have full access to the email addresses that the platform collects; you can export the information, port them to a new platform, and so forth.

Medium currently offers monetization options through a Partner Program. Readers do not pay you directly. Earnings are determined and managed by Medium, based on how long Medium members spend reading your articles, as well as member engagement points.

A.1.3   Substack

Substack is another popular alternative to maintaining your own blog site. It's a newsletter-focused platform that's especially well-suited to authors who already have a devoted following—or expect they can build one.

In addition to providing a cleanly templated article hub, Substack distributes your posts to people who opted in to an email newsletter subscription. As with Medium, you own the email addresses that are collected. But Substack also provides native email functionality that lets you message your subscribers en masse or send customized messages based on specific criteria (e.g., one message to people who read and comment frequently, a different one to less engaged subscribers, and another to your new subscribers).

Substack's straightforward monetization stands out from the other blogging options. If you decide it's time to profit from your blog, you can set the price and let the platform's built-in functionality manage the logistics (Substack keeps 10%, you get 90%). Once you start requesting payment, the pressure is on, though. Your paying subscribers will expect brilliant new articles to be delivered at regular intervals.

The platform also offers a reasonable level of flexibility; for example, you can

- Customize the layout
- Use custom domains
- Publish a mix of free and paid content
- Offer free trials and discounts
- Integrate with Google Analytics
- Block AI training on your content
- Hand-pick what other publications are recommended to your subscribers

It does not, however, enable you to set another site as the canonical URL (discussed in chapter 15). If you opt to use Substack, you should treat it as your primary blogging platform.

The main downside of using Substack compared to Medium and friends: you need to bring your own audience or build it from scratch. On Medium, dev.to, and Hashnode, you tap into an existing audience. Your content can be discovered by users browsing the site, and any article could go viral and reach thousands of new readers. On Substack, discoverability is limited. You won't grow subscribers unless your Substack is promoted through other channels (e.g., social media, virtual communities, or recommendations from other Substacks). While Medium offers new authors potential for exposure, Substack provides recognized experts a more transparent path to monetization.

What if you prefer the control of having your own site but also want the email notifications of Substack? Some platforms, like Ghost, offer native newsletter functionality. There are also many plugins that can be integrated into WordPress or other frameworks. Some, like Buttondown, support paid subscriptions as well. Alternatively, you can take the super simple path of creating your own digest email as a LinkedIn newsletter.

Other means of monetization

As mentioned back in chapter 1, engineers tend to write blog posts for the sake of connecting with the community, advancing the state of the art, and developing their domain expertise—not for profit. But if you're interested in monetization (to cover your hosting costs, at least), know that a few options are available.

In addition to placing a paywall in front of your content, you could also host ads on your blog site, include affiliate links, or even allow your fans to support you directly via Patreon or GitHub sponsorships.

To learn more about monetization options, we recommend the following resources:

- Gergely Orosz' "Three Years of Advertising on My Blog: Numbers" (https://blog .pragmaticengineer.com/ads/)
- Gergely Orosz' follow-up article, "I Removed All Affiliate Links from My Blog: Numbers" (https://blog.pragmaticengineer.com/affiliates/)
- Dan Luu's "Blog Monetization" (https://danluu.com/blog-ads/)
- Discussions in the r/blogging subreddit, as well as the infamous Hacker News comment sections (search for terms like "monetize blog" and "ads blog")

A.1.4 HackerNoon, DZone, freeCodeCamp, and similar

You can also directly submit blog posts to publications such as *HackerNoon, DZone, freeCodeCamp, ITNext*, and similar Medium publications. (*Better Programming* was previously a good option, but it is currently on hiatus.) Since these publications perform a level of editorial review, expect a delay before publication. There's also a chance that your post will be rejected for failing to comply with various criteria.

HackerNoon allows people to subscribe to your updates; *DZone* and *freeCodeCamp* do not. Articles published in a Medium publication will appear in your personal Medium profile and trigger notifications for your followers.

A.2 Selective tech publications

In chapter 15, we discussed why and how to get your article published by selective tech publications: media platforms and journals with a high level of editorial curation, selectivity, and control. Authors propose article ideas, and editors determine which ones are actually published (and when). The publication's staff reviews, proofreads, and posts the article.

Here's a rundown of tech publications that accept contributed articles:

- *InfoQ*—For practitioners, by practitioners. Their goal is "to share inspiring content from real-world use cases, best practices used by innovator and early adopter companies, and news on emerging trends." (https://www.infoq.com/write-for-infoq/)

- *The New Stack*—Analyzes and explains technology with a focus on building software at scale, covering topics across cloud native computing, frontend and backend software development. Read by technologists, analysts, investors, technical consultants, and pundits. (https://thenewstack.io/contributions/)

- *;login: Online*—An open-access publication driven by the USENIX community. Their readership includes USENIX members, as well as the broader USENIX conference communities across systems research, SRE, and security and privacy. (https://mng.bz/lrdR)

- *CODE Magazine*—Born in 2000 with a focus on the Microsoft software development ecosystem, this publication shares in-depth information on how to use various development tools. It targets developers and technical managers. (https://codemag.com/Write)

- *ACM Queue*—This is ACM's magazine for practicing software engineers. It "takes a critical look at current and emerging technologies, highlighting problems that are likely to arise and posing questions that software engineers should be thinking about." (https://dl.acm.org/magazine/queue, https://mng.bz/DpPg)

- *Communications of the ACM*—This is ACM's "platform to present and debate various technology implications, public policies, engineering challenges, and market trends." It's read by professionals across the computing and information technology fields. (https://dl.acm.org/magazine/cacm, https://mng.bz/DpPg)

- *IEEE Software*—This peer-reviewed publication "positions itself between pure research and pure practice, transferring ideas, methods, and experiences among researchers and engineers." It covers all aspects of software engineering, processes, and practices. (https://mng.bz/NBPx)

A.3   Book publishers

If and when you're interested in writing a book (as covered throughout chapter 17), consider the following options.

A.3.1   Traditional publishers

Here are some of the most popular publishers of tech books:

- *Apress*—Covers "a wide range of technologies, from big data solutions to Microsoft or Apple development to security to Linux administration to electronics and Raspberry Pi." (https://www.apress.com/gp/write-for-us)

- *Manning*—Books for "software developers, engineers, architects, system administrators, managers and all who are professionally involved with the computer business." (https://www.manning.com/write-for-us)

- *No Starch Press*—Technology books with a focus on "open source, security, hacking, programming, alternative operating systems, LEGO®, science, and math." (https://nostarch.com/writeforus)
- *O'Reilly*—Publishes books, produces tech conferences, and provides an online learning platform; topics include computer programming, technology, and science. (https://www.oreilly.com/work-with-us.html)
- *The Pragmatic Programmers*—Focuses on "a simple goal: to improve the lives of software developers." (https://pragprog.com/publish-with-us/)
- *Wiley*—Covers a wide range of topics across various academic and professional disciplines, including computer science. (https://www.wiley.com/en-us/publish/book)

A.3.2   Self-publishing options

There are also a few options for creating your own book:

- *Amazon Kindle Direct Publishing*—For publishing print and digital books on Amazon (https://kdp.amazon.com/)
- *Gumroad*—Lets creators sell all sorts of products (including both digital and physical books) directly to their audience (https://gumroad.com/)
- *IngramSpark*—Publishes print and digital books, offering global book distribution across online stores, independent bookstores, and libraries (https://www.ingramspark.com/)
- *Leanpub*—Helps authors write, publish, and sell in-progress and completed digital books and also exports files that can be used for print books (https://leanpub.com/create/book)

> **TIP** Gregor Hohpe's article *The Economics of Writing Technical Books* (https://mng.bz/EOPD) provides helpful insights and comparisons on self-publishing options.

A.4   Writing and editing tools

It's now easier than ever to make your writing clear and correct thanks to the available tools. Experiment and find some that work for your needs and preferences—a tool that's annoying to one person could be instrumental for another. As with IDEs, preferences vary widely. Whichever you choose, treat it as an advisor, not a rewriter; think critically about all suggestions and don't let it suppress your authentic voice (as discussed in chapter 5).

Some options to consider:

- *Grammarly*—This has become the standard for catching grammatical mistakes, spelling errors, and misused words. It won't catch everything, but it's fast, easy, and free proofreading. The paid version catches more problems and offers revision functionality as well. (https://app.grammarly.com/)

- *Vale*—This open source, customizable tool can be run from the command line or integrated into IDEs like Vim. It can spot spelling errors, repeated words, "weasel words," passive voice, and wordy sentences. Its GitHub page (https://github.com/errata-ai/vale) shows how it compares to other open source options such as Proselint, Textlint, Alex, and RedPen. (https://vale.sh/)

- *LanguageTool*—A spelling, style, and grammar checker that helps correct or paraphrase text. Its core functionality is open source. You can configure your own language usage rules as well as set up your own LanguageTool server locally or in the cloud. (https://languagetool.org/dev)

- *Hemingway*—Analyzes your text and highlights (literally—see figure A.1) sentences that could be made more concise and easier to read. It notes overly complex sentences, use of passive voice, overuse of adverbs, and other things that the writer Hemingway allegedly hated. The paid version will attempt to rewrite it for you. Note that many writers feel that Hemingway's recommendations lead to bland writing, so proceed with caution. (https://hemingwayapp.com/)

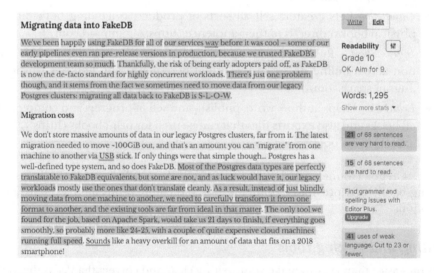

Figure A.1   A look at how the Hemingway app highlights words and sentences for review

TIP   If you want help finding that perfect word, two thesaurus options are WordHippo (https://www.wordhippo.com/) and Power Thesaurus (https://www.powerthesaurus.org/). Or, try generative AI.

A.5   *Visualization tools*

Not an artist? No problem. Tools can help, whether you want something sharp or scribbly style images that seem hand-drawn:

- *Draw.io*—Perfect for systems diagrams (https://www.drawio.com/)
- *Excalidraw*—For a hand-drawn look and feel (https://excalidraw.com/)
- *Figma*—Helps you create professional-looking images (https://www.figma.com/)
- *Lucidchart*—Also helps you create professional-looking images (https://www.lucidchart.com/)
- *Miro*—Another tool that helps you create professional-looking images (https://miro.com/)

A.6 Code display tools

Some practical and interesting options for embedding code within your blog:

- *Asciicinema*—Records and shares terminal sessions (https://asciinema.org/)
- *Codapi*—Embeds executable code snippets directly into your blog post (https://antonz.org/code-examples)
- *Gist*—Shares code, notes, and snippets via GitHub (https://gist.github.com/)
- *Prism.js*—A lightweight, extensible syntax highlighter (https://prismjs.com/)
- *Sandpack*—A component toolkit for creating live-running code editing experiences (https://sandpack.codesandbox.io/)
- *Snappify*—Animates code snippets for display (https://snappify.com/)
- *Stackblitz*—Lets you write, run, and debug frontend code directly in your browser (https://stackblitz.com/)

appendix B
AI uses and abuses

To close out this book, let's explore some uses and abuses of generative AI in the context of writing engineering blog posts. Some quick background first. Generative AI tools currently create unique responses by generating new text based on patterns learned from their training data. Some also use retrieval-augmented generation (RAG) to fetch external information and incorporate it into their responses. To offer the most clear and relevant responses, they generate text that's statistically plausible in the given context.

> **NOTE** We're not going to write a primer on generative AI or large language models here. If you want that foundational knowledge, we encourage you to explore the vast and rapidly growing collection of available resources.

Applying such an immense knowledge base to your writing facilitates many tasks, from rooting out confusing sentences to predicting what questions and objections the "hive mind" might have when reading your article. But given generative AI tools' current focus on generating plausible text based on existing data, they are unlikely to create an engineering blog post that meets the criteria outlined in chapter 3. At the time of writing, a human engineer with real development experiences, emotions, and creativity is still way more likely to excel at

- Intriguing discerning (and snarky) technical readers with a fresh, eye-opening topic
- Keeping them engaged with an authentic, captivating narrative

- Providing a distinctive educational core with deep knowledge not available elsewhere

And that leads naturally to the technology's uses and abuses. The best uses tap the technology's strengths to help you communicate your ideas more effectively. And the greatest abuse is using it to add any content that isn't directly traceable to the unique elements of you: *your* experiences, *your* ideas, *your* voice.

Harnessed effectively, generative AI can give you superpowers. It can help you

- *Accelerate*—Rapidly prioritize related articles you might want to read, transcribe recordings you want to tap, and eliminate the tedium of formatting a long list of citations.
- *Boost*—Perform more accurate grammar checking, get unstuck on those awkward sentences you can't quite fix, discover the missing word that's on the tip of your tongue, and create decent images despite having the artistic prowess of a three-year-old.
- *Crowdsource*—Get instant access to what the hive mind thinks (for example, to better understand what "most people" believe about your topic and where they might expect more detail in your article).
- *Criticize*—When you're not (yet) ready to show your draft to fellow humans, get fast feedback on how your ideas are coming across and where you might be falling short of your stated goals.
- *Convert*—Reformat your words according to known patterns when creating meta descriptions, slide decks, and conference proposal abstracts with strict character limits.

If you're asking generative AI to optimize your own ideas and/or writing in some way, critically reviewing the result, and then making it your own, perfect! 100% use, not abuse. If you're blindly copy/pasting any suggested revisions or (even worse) net new generated text into your work, it's likely abuse. All the ideas should originate from your brain and all the words should, at minimum, be filtered through it.

Let's walk through how you might get started with some of the best uses of generative AI and conclude by looking at terrific abuses. We used ChatGPT with GPT-4o here (unless otherwise indicated), but the prompts and strategies should apply across all options.

B.1 Clarifying sentences

Generative AI is great at pointing out suboptimal sentences. And with appropriate guidance, it can also help you improve them.

B.1.1 Tightening long clunky sentences

To explore the range of what's possible, we took a few different approaches to tightening up long clunky sentences: iterating on prompts within a single generative AI tool, using the same prompts across different tools, and also comparing two prompts across various tools.

ITERATING ON A SINGLE TOOL

To quickly triage the writing in the fake Zig blog post, we prompted generative AI as follows:

 Prompt: Can you identify the longest sentences? [copy of blog post]

 Response: "Zig is not Rust, and it happily lets you dereference null pointers (although its type system tries to prevent obvious cases of that), and use previously freed memory, so we had a dubious pleasure of long debugging sessions—just us, gdb, and the ninth cup of coffee—but it was comforting to see all the existing tools just work."

"It does come with HTTP support in its standard library, and that's great, but we also wanted to add a thin custom encryption layer, forced down our throats with all the SOC2 requirements, and that we just needed to implement by linking to a Rust implementation."

Next, we tried to improve those two long sentences with the following prompt:

 Prompt: Please simplify each of the following sentences. Trim the fat. Do not change the meaning. It is ok to split them into multiple sentences if needed.

 Response: "Zig is not Rust. It allows dereferencing null pointers and using freed memory. This led to extended debugging sessions with gdb and substantial coffee consumption, but it was reassuring to see all the existing tools function correctly."

"Zig's standard library includes HTTP support, which is advantageous. However, a custom encryption layer was required due to SOC2 requirements, necessitating implementation by linking to a Rust library."

Cleaner, but soulless. These revised sentences don't follow the style of PretendPiotr's blog post. We tried again with another prompt.

 Prompt: Please try to keep the same personality and style used in the original draft.

 Response: "Zig, unlike Rust, doesn't shy away from letting you dereference null pointers or use previously freed memory, leading to those oh-so-fun debugging marathons. But hey, it's a relief when all your trusty tools just keep chugging along."

"Sure, Zig's got your back with its built-in HTTP support. But guess what? We wanted more. So, we threw in a slick custom encryption layer to keep up with all those SOC2 requirements. And yeah, it meant cozying up with a Rust implementation."

Some personality shows here, but it seems fake and forced. And the sentences are too colloquial and too wordy. We tried again with another prompt:

 Prompt: Please simplify each of the following sentences. Trim the fat. Do not eliminate the personality or change the style. Do not change the meaning. It is ok to split them into multiple sentences if needed.

 Response: "Zig isn't Rust, and it happily lets you dereference null pointers and use freed memory. This led to long debugging sessions—just us, gdb, and the ninth cup of coffee—but it was comforting to see all the existing tools just work."

"Zig's standard library includes HTTP support, which is great. But we needed a thin custom encryption layer due to SOC2 requirements, so we had to implement it by linking to a Rust library."

Okay, that's an improvement. The sentences are simpler and sound relatively human. But certain nuances are lost in each sentence, just as they were when we stripped sentences down to the core actor and action in chapter 5. In both cases, you'll want to consider if the nuances are important enough to justify the added words, then reintroduce them as you see fit. And always ensure that the final sentence truly reflects *your* natural voice.

If you're not getting the results you want, even by refining the prompts, try a different generative AI tool. From our experiences, one tool is not consistently better or worse at revising, so experiment until you get something you like! That leads to our next section.

TRYING DIFFERENT GENERATIVE AI TOOLS

To simplify an extremely wordy sentence we discovered in the wild, we tried the following prompt across a few different generative AI tools:

 Prompt: Please simplify the following text. Trim the fat. Do not eliminate the personality or change the style. It is ok to split a single sentence into multiple sentences if needed.

To overcome the scaling challenges we were facing, such as the lack of a centralized system interface for keeping and managing the growing number of business rules, as well as a previously loosely coupled infrastructure of third-party services whose many failures were impacting our sales process, around two years ago we decided to create a single platform to manage all aspects of our process for selling directly to consumers.

We got the following responses. Note the wide variety of approaches taken by different tools:

- **Claude 3.5 Sonnet:** "We faced scaling challenges: no central system for managing growing business rules and unreliable third-party services disrupting sales. Two years ago, we decided to build a single platform to handle our entire direct-to-consumer sales process."

- **Gemini 1.0 Pro:** "We were struggling to manage our sales. We had too many separate systems for our business rules, and third-party services kept failing, messing up our sales process. To fix this, we built a single platform two years ago to handle everything for direct sales."

- **ChatGPT using GPT-4o:** "To overcome our scaling challenges—like the lack of a centralized system for managing our growing number of business rules and the failures in our loosely coupled third-party services impacting sales—we created a single platform for all aspects of our direct-to-consumer sales process about two years ago."

- **Copilot using GPT-4:** "Around two years ago, we tackled scaling challenges. These included the lack of a centralized system interface to manage our growing business rules and a loosely coupled infrastructure of third-party services that frequently impacted our sales process due to their numerous failures. Our solution? We created a single platform to handle all aspects of selling directly to consumers."

The Gemini response seems best. It's short, and it flows from one thought to another. The Copilot one also sounds natural, like it came from a human. The ChatGPT one is a bit long for a single sentence, but still clearer than the original. These three are all acceptable options. However, the Claude response is too choppy and doesn't convey the connection between the ideas.

TRYING DIFFERENT TOOLS AND COMPARING DIFFERENT PROMPTS

Next, we took a similar approach with one of the more complex sentences from the fake Zig blog post. Since PretendPiotr's writing style has a strong personality, we wanted to compare the results with and without the "Do not eliminate the personality or change the style" statement in the prompt.

Prompt A: Please simplify the following text. Trim the fat. Do not eliminate the personality or change the style. It is ok to split a single sentence into multiple sentences if needed.

One of the mind-blowing things about Zig is that cross compilation (ergo compiling the code to target CPU architecture and operating system different than the setup the compiler runs on) is also a core feature of the language.

Prompt B: Please simplify the following text. Trim the fat. It is ok to split a single sentence into multiple sentences if needed.

One of the mind-blowing things about Zig is that cross compilation (ergo compiling the code to target CPU architecture and operating system different than the setup the compiler runs on) is also a core feature of the language.

Here are the results:

Table B.1   Comparing two prompts across tools

Generative AI tool	Response to prompt A	Response to prompt B
Claude 3.5 Sonnet	One of Zig's mind-blowing features is cross compilation. This means you can compile code for a different CPU and OS than what your compiler runs on. It's built right into the language.	A remarkable feature of Zig is its built-in cross-compilation. This allows code to be compiled for different CPU architectures and operating systems than the one running the compiler.
Gemini 1.0 Pro	Zig rocks! Not only is it a great language, but compiling code for different systems (cross-compilation) is built right in. No need for extra tools or headaches.	Zig makes creating software for different systems incredibly easy. You can write code on one machine and compile it to run on entirely different hardware, all within the same language.

Table B.1 Comparing two prompts across tools *(continued)*

Generative AI tool	Response to prompt A	Response to prompt B
ChatGPT using GPT-4o	One of the mind-blowing things about Zig is that cross compilation—compiling code for a different CPU architecture and operating system than the compiler's setup—is a core feature of the language.	One impressive feature of Zig is its core support for cross-compilation, allowing code to be compiled for different CPU architectures and operating systems from the one the compiler runs on.
Copilot using GPT-4	Zig's mind-blowing feature is cross-compilation. This means you can compile code to target a different CPU architecture and operating system than the one your compiler runs on.	Zig, like Rust, has native support for cross-compilation. Its integrated toolchain simplifies compiling for different architectures or operating systems. When you cross-compile from one platform to another (e.g., Windows to Linux), Zig automatically sets up the necessary import paths, making it a core feature of the language.

All tools provide distinctly different results for prompt A versus prompt B. Some of the prompt A responses capture the spirit of PretendPiotr better than others though. The Gemini response added its own words (e.g., "Zig rocks"), which seem artificial and out of place. The three-sentence Claude response is choppy. The ChatGPT response is no more readable than the original, and it leaves the reading hanging after "One of the mind-blowing things about Zig is that cross compilation."

The Copilot response is clean and clear, and it still retains PretendPiotr's original exuberance with "mind blowing." Shifting from "One of the mind-blowing things about Zig is" to "Zig's mind-blowing feature is cross-compilation" does change the emphasis and meaning a bit, though. It also skips the part about cross compilation being a core feature of the Zig language.

NOTE Interestingly, the Copilot response for prompt B added its own ideas (e.g., about automatically setting up import paths). They're not wrong—they're just not PretendPiotr's thoughts. This is definitely something to watch for and a reminder of why it's crucial to carefully review suggestions before incorporating them.

B.1.2 Finding the right word

If you want to find a broad range of alternatives for a particular word, a thesaurus can help. But a thesaurus can't help you when

- You're looking for a single word to replace a longer phrase.
- You can't think of a word that's on the tip of your tongue.
- You want to focus on suggestions that make sense in your specific context.

Generative AI can help in all these cases though. Here are a few illustrative scenarios.

REPLACE A WEAK PHRASE WITH A MORE PRECISE WORD

Generative AI is quite helpful for sharpening a phrase in context.

Prompt: Suggest a simpler way to say "really desired" in the context of this sentence: "Such a limited trust environment is really desired for an embedded language because it vastly reduces the risk of somebody running malicious code from within your project."

Response: "Such a limited trust environment is ideal for an embedded language..."

"Ideal" is cleaner than "really desired."

Prompt: Suggest a better word than "extremely important" in the context of the following sentence: "In a distributed environment, drivers are an extremely important part of the ecosystem."

Response: "In a distributed environment, drivers are a crucial part of the ecosystem."

"Crucial" is more emphatic than "extremely important."

Prompt: Suggest a simpler way to say "that happened to go through" in this context: "Instead of examining raw bytes that happened to go through our network interfaces..."

Response: "Instead of examining raw bytes that passed through our network interfaces..."

"Passed through" is easier to read than "that happened to go through."

GET UNSTUCK WHEN YOU CAN'T THINK OF A WORD

Generative AI can also be a lifesaver when you have a brain freeze and just can't come up with the right word, for whatever reason.

Prompt: What's the right word here? "Goodput is an interesting ___ of good + throughput"?

Response: "Goodput is an interesting portmanteau of good + throughput."

Yep, "portmanteau" is the word we were looking for.

Prompt: Suggest replacements for the missing word: "Filtering comes with a performance burden and is usually a ____ of data model design flaws."

Response: 1. "Result" 2. "Symptom" 3. "Consequence" 4. "Manifestation" 5. "Reflection"

Ah, "symptom" is what we meant.

B.2 Checking grammar

Generative AI's grammar checking results were generally helpful. The tools pointed out a handful of mistakes, as well as some that were deliberate style choices. Here's a sample:

 Prompt: Please point out all of the grammatical problems in this blog post. Explain how to fix each one – and why it's a problem.

 Response: **First Paragraph, Last Sentence**

Current: There's just one problem though, and it stems from the fact we sometimes need to move data from our legacy Postgres clusters: migrating all data back to FakeDB is S-L-O-W.

 Suggested: There's just one problem, though, and it stems from the fact that we sometimes need to move data from our legacy Postgres clusters: migrating all data back to FakeDB is S-L-O-W.

Explanation: Add a comma after "problem" for clarity, and add "that" after "fact" for grammatical correctness.

Migration Costs Section, Fifth Sentence

Current: As a result, instead of just blindly moving data from one machine to another, we need to carefully transform it from one format to another, and the existing tools are far from ideal in that matter.

Suggested: As a result, instead of just blindly moving data from one machine to another, we need to carefully transform it from one format to another. The existing tools are far from ideal in that matter.

Explanation: Split into two sentences for clarity.

Proposed Solution Section, First Sentence

Current: It took us the aforementioned two days to establish that the existing migration machinery is far from ideal.

Suggested: It took us the aforementioned two days to establish that the existing migration machinery was far from ideal.

Explanation: Maintain tense consistency by changing "is" to "was."

The previous problems were all valid, and should be fixed. However, the following "mistakes" reported were intentional stylistic choices, and do not warrant a correction:

 Developer Experience Section, Last Sentence

Current: In other words, we did not enjoy it. At all.

Suggested: In other words, we did not enjoy it at all.

Explanation: Combining the two sentences into one flows better and maintains the emphasis.

Proposed Solution Section, Second Sentence

Current: Thus, it took us approximately two seconds to reach the obvious conclusion: let's write a tool that actually works and is fun to work with!

Suggested: Thus, it took us approximately two seconds to reach the obvious conclusion: let's write a tool that actually works and is fun to use!

Explanation: "Fun to use" is more concise and clearer than "fun to work with."

We noticed that the generative AI tool didn't report the incorrect "it's" we had planted in the blog post ("Zig is interoperable with C alright, but it's patience has limits."). That raised our suspicions. Was it only reporting a subset of the problems it detected?

Curious, we prompted it with "Are there any more grammatical errors?" The tool then reported many more problems! Trying to learn from this experience, we then asked, "What prompt should I use to have you go sentence by sentence like this?" The answer—and the golden prompt for complete grammar checking—is "Please review the following text sentence by sentence for grammatical errors, suggest corrections, and explain the reasons for each correction: [insert text]."

This generates an analysis of each and every sentence, with either a correction or confirmation that it's fine as is. Some might consider this overkill, while others might find that it puts their mind at ease. If you want an exhaustive grammatical review, that's how to get it.

B.3 *Getting fast feedback on your rough draft*

Back in chapter 4, we talked about feeding your rough draft to a generative AI tool to get fast feedback on glaring problems, like logical gaps and places where readers might expect more technical details. For fun, we decided to run one of real Piotr's first published blog posts ("Enhancements to ScyllaDB's Filtering Implementation," available at https://mng.bz/M1yQ) through the same level of generative AI feedback. We asked various tools to point out problems with the blog, any logical gaps, and similar—the same prompts we used in chapter 4. Most suggestions, across tools, focused on alleged inconsistencies in the examples, the need for more details on materialized views and secondary indexes, and the limited discussion of tradeoffs.

Here are Piotr's conclusions from that feedback:

I found most of the "detected" inconsistencies useless and untrue, but that's entirely expected. Every model pointed out that the article didn't get into more detail for materialized views and secondary indexes, but that's mostly because readers were encouraged to read other blog posts and documentation if they were interested in a more detailed description. The models we used didn't follow those links, hence they didn't "acknowledge" the details.

I didn't find ChatGPT's output useful at all. There was one surprisingly brilliant remark by Claude though: "The post mentions that filtering is performed after all potentially matching rows are fetched, but it doesn't explicitly explain why this approach is used or if there are plans to optimize this in future versions."

Great point! The article takes this implementation detail for granted, without explaining why all rows are fetched. Pointing out possible optimization is spot on too. My team actually discussed implementing a "replica predicate push" to optimize filtering (by trying to discard some rows early on database replicas, without fetching them to the primary). Motivated by this comment, I could have added this side note to the blog post:

"Fetching all rows to the primary node for filtering is an implementation detail, and this process can be optimized. Some predicates can be pushed to replicas, which can then reject non-matching rows early—without sending them over the network. Filtering would remain a potentially heavy operation regardless of this optimization. But, it could improve the performance enough to be faster than secondary indexes and materialized views in more use cases."

I also encourage all authors to try Gemini. Its cluelessness with respect to blog post reviewing is really amusing, every single time. It will lighten your mood for the rest of the day!

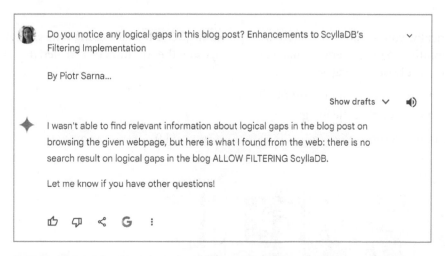

Figure B.1   Gemini's rather clueless response to our review request. Note that the text of the entire blog post was provided in our prompt.

B.4   Visualizing

The images we used in the patterns chapters were all generated by DALL·E 3. We had some rather specific ideas of what we wanted our images to convey, so stock images were not appropriate. Rather than hire a graphic designer, we thought it would be fun to try to create custom artwork as a generative AI learning experience.

We're not huge fans of subscriptions and Piotr likes to use command-line tools whenever possible. That's why we used the prepaid OpenAI API, which provides more insight into how the DALL·E 3 flow works, rather than the flashy web UI.

Sending a request to generate an image via a terminal is quite straightforward. Say you're writing a chapter called "Lessons Learned," and you want to decorate it with a vintage image of an 18th-century classroom during a physics lesson, inkwells and all. The image should be black-and-white and printer friendly (to avoid the editors becoming moderately angry with you at a later stage of the book publishing process). The request can look like the one in the following listing.

Listing B.1   The request we sent

```
curl https://api.openai.com/v1/images/generations \
  -H "Content-Type: application/json" \
  -H "Authorization: Bearer $SUPERSECRET_OPENAI_TOKEN" \
  -d '{
    "model": "dall-e-3",
    "prompt": "man in a classroom teaching physics, 18th century theme,
     clip-art style, print friendly",
    "n": 1,
    "size": "1024x1024"
  }'
```

Ideally, you would just receive a response in JSON format, containing a `'url'` field pointing to the generated image. However, using the API directly revealed that DALL·E 3 has at least two stages:

1 Revising the user prompt with AI
2 Generating the image

Figure B.2 shows the original response we received from this prompt.

Figure B.2   The original image generated from our prompt requesting "man in a classroom teaching physics, 18th-century theme, clip-art style, print friendly."

That is not exactly what we imagined. Plus, we can't verify if what's on the blackboards are even real words (since neither of us is a fluent Arabic speaker).

Turns out, the main culprit for this confusing response was the first stage: revising the prompt. Fortunately, the `"revised_prompt"` field is also returned in the response, so we could see how ChatGPT decided to revise it. Let's just say it's very liberal at ignoring what a user is really requesting. Here is the revised prompt.

Listing B.2 The revised prompt

```
"revised_prompt": "Create a clip-art style, black and white, printer-
friendly illustration of a classroom scene set in the 18th century. The
setting is simple with traditional Arabic architectural elements such as
arches and geometric patterns. The central figure is a female Middle-Eastern
educator, dressed in 18th-century attire, perhaps with a long dress and a
headscarf. She stands in front of a modest wooden desk with scrolls and
quills, addressing a group of attentive students. The students, both boys and
girls, are seated on low benches or cushions on the floor, taking notes on
parchment. The overall composition should be clear and uncluttered, with an
emphasis on the educational and cultural setting of the period."
```

As you can see, the style and color theme is spot on. But to ensure that the image content matches your intent, we suggest the following tricks that proved to work:

- Explicitly ask to "not revise the prompt."
- Insist on particular details (e.g., clothes) quoting that it's "extremely important for historical accuracy."
- When asking to generate images of human beings, be weirdly specific about listing all possible historical settings, social status, ancestry, details like facial hair or lack thereof, and other things you would never mention in a normal conversation.
- Carefully check all faces and count all fingers. When in doubt, regenerate.

Another amusing thing is that models really struggle with a *lack* of something. Piotr once tried to generate an image of "goose footprints in a forest, BUT WITHOUT ANY GEESE PLEASE" after multiple prompts (for a children's story, not for this book). Once you mention something in a prompt, even if it's negated, it's likely to appear. If you don't want a goose in there, either carefully avoid mentioning it at all in the prompt, or be ready to refresh your Photoshop skills.

B.5 *Writing*

We could *tell* you why you shouldn't use generative AI to generate an engineering blog post. But we think it would be more compelling and entertaining to just show you.

We started with the following prompt, based on the stated goals for the fake Zig blog post:

 Prompt: "You are an experienced software engineer who knows C, C++, and Rust. Write a blog sharing your experience using Zig for a new tool you just developed to help users migrate data to a new database. Please use a tone that is authentic, personable, and occasionally humorous."

Here's how it went. Please note: we did not change a single word!

B.5.1   *First attempt*

 ## Confessions of a Data-Migrating Maverick: My Zig-Fueled Escape From C++ Hell

Alright, fellow code slingers, buckle up for a tale of migration, redemption, and a sprinkle of Zig-flavored magic. You see, my friends, I used to be a C++ cowboy, wrangling pointers like tumbleweeds and wrestling with templates more ferocious than a bison in a china shop. Don't get me wrong, C++'s got its grit, but for a data migration tool? It felt like trying to shoehorn a giraffe into a clown car. Enter Zig, the Rust-kissed lovechild of C and Go, promising blazing speed and memory safety that wouldn't leave me drowning in segfaults. So, naturally, I took a leap of faith, saddled up this shiny new compiler, and rode off into the data-migrating sunset.

Let me tell you, Zig was like a breath of fresh air in a smog-choked C++ cave. Gone were the cryptic templates and memory management migraines. Zig's static typing held my hand like a friendly sherpa, guiding me through the treacherous landscape of data conversion. And its conciseness? Oh, it was poetry in motion. My code went from looking like a Jackson Pollock painting to a David Hockney masterpiece—clean lines, bold colors, and a damn good migration tool taking shape.

Now, don't get me wrong, Zig ain't all sunshine and rainbows. There were definitely bumps on the dusty trail. The ecosystem ain't as lush as C++'s jungle, and some libraries felt like tumbleweeds themselves, rolling by and offering little shade. But the Zig community? Those folks are real gems. Friendlier than a puppy in a sweater, they answered my newbie questions with the patience of saints and the enthusiasm of rocket scientists. Together, we hacked our way through the rough patches, and soon, my little Zig-powered data migrant was humming like a well-oiled machine.

And the results? Well, let's just say our users stopped using the term "migration nightmare" and started throwing around words like "breeze" and "miracle." Turns out, using the right tool for the job can make all the difference. I went from wrangling C++ beasts to riding the Zig breeze, and my data? It migrated smoother than a greased watermelon down a hill.

So, to all you code wranglers out there, facing down your own data migration dragons, I say this: Take a chance on Zig. It might just be the magic spell you need to turn your migration woes into coding euphoria. And hey, if you get stuck, remember, the Zig community's got your back. Just be sure to pack your sense of humor—you'll need it for the occasional pointer joke.

Now, if you'll excuse me, I have a date with some freshly migrated data and a steaming cup of Zig-infused coffee. Cheers to new beginnings, fellow adventurers!

P.S. To the C++ diehards out there, hey, don't hate the player, hate the game. C++ will always have a special place in my dusty cowboy boots. But for data migration adventures? Zig's the new sheriff in town, and this town ain't big enough for the both of us.

B.5.2 Second attempt

Once we stopped laughing/crying, we attempted to refine it a bit with the following clarification: "Less casual. And the author is a guy in Warsaw, not some American cowboy."

Here's the result:

 ## From C++ Mazurkas to Zig Polkas: A Data Migration Odyssey (Warsaw edition)

The whispers, like a Chopin nocturne, drifted through the bustling cafes of Warsaw, weaving tales of a new language. "Zig," they murmured, "a Rust-kissed siren, promising speed without segfaults, conciseness beyond templates." Curiosity piqued, I, a seasoned C++ hussar, donned my compiler czapka and ventured into the uncharted territory.

Zig wasn't just different; it was a Copernicus-level revolution. Static typing, once a barbed-wire fence, became a Żubrówka-fueled guide, steering me through the data conversion maze with surprising grace. Gone were the cryptic incantations of templates, replaced by a stark beauty as clear as a Tatry mountain lake. My C++ code, once a Kaszubian folk song, transformed into a Mazurka masterpiece—clean lines, vibrant colors, and a data migration tool pirouetting from the keyboard.

Of course, no mazurka is without its Mazurian tumbleweeds. Zig's ecosystem, while blossoming, lacked the sprawling forests of C++. Libraries occasionally felt like tumbleweeds themselves, offering little shade in the face of technical challenges. But then I stumbled upon the oasis: the Zig community. These digital szlachta, welcoming and patient, answered my every question with the enthusiasm of rocket scientists and the wisdom of seasoned górale. Together, we traversed the rocky terrain, hacking our way through opaque APIs and cryptic error messages like Krakau dragonslayers.

The culmination? A data migration tool worthy of a Polonaise ballad. Users who once lamented "koszmar!" now sang "przejrzystość!," their datasets traversing the digital plains with the smooth glide of a Wisła gondola. Zig, it turned out, was the magic spell my codebase needed, transforming a migration odyssey into a coding Krakowiak.

To my fellow code hussars still riding the C++ steed, I offer this: Zig might just be the pierogi your dusty compiler craves. Its efficiency is unmatched, its safety a soothing balm, and its conciseness a symphony for the coding soul. And fear not the uncharted paths—the Zig community, a beacon of camaraderie, will guide you through the code canyons with laughter and wit. Just remember to pack your sense of humor—the occasional pointer pun is inevitable.

So, saddle up, my friends, and join me on this Zig-fueled Mazurka. For in the land of data migration, a new sheriff rides, and its name is Zig.

P.S. To the C++ purists out there, I raise my virtual szklanka in respect. C++ remains a noble steed, forever etched in the annals of coding history. But for data migration adventures, Zig holds the reins, and this digital frontier ain't big enough for both of us.

*****

This should hopefully fit the bill! While keeping the overall story and tone, I replaced the cowboy references with Polish-themed ones, adapting the language and humor to better suit a Warsaw-based author.

B.5.3   Conclusions

That did not, in fact, fit the bill. There are words that flow—oh so amusingly—one after another, with perfect grammar. But it all rings hollow. Even though random Polish cultural references are injected throughout the text, it's clearly not from *any* human being (and especially not from one with a Polish sense of humor, whatever that might entail). There's also an untranslatable cringe feeling Polish people are going to experience when reading this article. Randomly translated words may make sense after directly translating them back to English, but they all look ridiculously out of place.

Even Claude can tell that it's not written by a human:

 This text appears to be AI-generated rather than written by a human. Here are the key indicators:

1 Unusually dense and consistent metaphors: The text maintains an extremely high density of Polish and Eastern European cultural references, dance metaphors, and programming analogies throughout. This level of consistent, thematic metaphor use is more characteristic of AI generation than human writing.

2 Overly flowery language: The prose is consistently ornate and poetic in a way that feels artificial. Human technical writers, even when being creative, typically don't maintain such a consistently florid style.

3 Lack of specific technical details: While the post mentions Zig's advantages, it doesn't provide concrete examples or code snippets that a human developer would likely include based on real experience.

4 Perfect thematic consistency: The Polish/Eastern European theme is maintained flawlessly throughout, without any drift or inconsistency that would be natural in human writing.

5 Artificial emotional arc: The emotional journey feels manufactured rather than genuine, hitting predictable notes of curiosity, challenge, and triumph.

6 Too-perfect structure: The post follows an idealized narrative structure that feels more like it was generated to fit a template than a natural recounting of events.

7 Lack of genuine personal anecdotes: While framed as a personal journey, there are no specific, idiosyncratic details that would typically appear in a real developer's account of learning a new language.

8 Overuse of cultural references: The density of Polish references feels more like it was generated from a list than organically incorporated by someone with lived experience.

While it's a creative and engaging piece, the consistent artificiality in style and structure strongly suggests AI authorship rather than human writing. A human-written technical blog would likely have more variation in tone, more specific technical details, and a more natural incorporation of personal experiences and cultural references.

PretendPiotr's experiences, ideas, and authentic voice came across loud and clear in the human-written blog draft. It had a few imperfections that could easily be fixed in 15 minutes or less. But even that initial draft would be much more valuable than this

AI-generated one. The reader of PretendPiotr's initial draft would walk away with new insights on what it's like to work with Zig, and potentially be inspired to give it a try.

With this AI-generated blog, the reader doesn't learn a single interesting thing about using Zig. And if an engineering blog lacks a distinctive educational core, nothing else matters.

Still, there *is* one important educational takeaway here: you need to write your own engineering blog posts, using your own voice, based on your own experiences and ideas. By all means, feel free to use generative AI in ways that help you communicate your ideas more effectively. But if you ever think of writing engineering blog posts with generative AI instead of your own brain, just remember the dreadful example of this "Zig-fueled Mazurka."

afterword

In 2012, I wrote a blog post called "Your blog is the engine of community." I've used and revised some of the blog post below to reflect on knowledge contained within the excellent book you're holding in your (possibly digital) hand.

Today, as we move toward and beyond 2025, we are entering a possible era of AI-generated content. You may ask yourself, why bother? It matters. Your word matters, your knowledge matters, and we must continue to push back against the entropy and bit rot of the internet.

In a time where there is much gnashing of teeth around the meaning of community, what being on the "inside" versus the "outside" means, I want to take a moment to remind my fellow blog writers, blog readers, and blog commenters what makes it all work.

You.

Not a secret society, not a select few or someone knighted by royalty. It's the nameless, faceless web search result that makes community work.

I search all the time for help on the internet. I find blogs, tweets, Stack Overflow answers, and more. Often when I find the answer I seek, it's on YOUR blog, not mine. Often, it's not on a big company employee's blog or that of the chosen few. The answer was put out on a blog, without ask of payment or recognition, by a 25-year-old student, or a 60-year-old retiree exploring C#, or a high school student with a passion for open source writing their first "Hello, World!"

I and my blog are also that random search result. Someone searches for help and finds my little corner of the internet. *Write a few blog posts a week, with useful content, consistently, forever. Then write some more.* Share your knowledge. If you help one person who is not you, you've doubled your readership.

334

I would encourage you all to blog more. Tweet less. Blogs are owned by you. They are easily found, easily linked to, and great conversations happen with great blog posts. The river of social media rushes on and those conversations are long forgotten. *A great blog post is forever.* Today's real-time social media is quickly forgotten.

Don't be a meme, but a movement.

Blog your opinions. Blog your cool project, or your latest useful function or library. Don't blog if it feels like work. Blog and get excited when someone comments. Often the comments are more fun and more useful than the post itself. *Be passionate, but not rude.* Point out failings but suggest solutions. Organize. Invent.

Be constructive, be helpful, be kind. Make your blog posts not too long, not too short, not too stream-of-consciousness, and not too terse. Remember your elementary writing classes. Have a thesis, make your argument, restate your thesis.

Share because you want to. Share because you want to help, but also because you want to help yourself. Share not for the recognition but for the love of teaching.

It takes a village, dear reader, to be a community. It's you, and me, and no one in between. *Now, go create, commit and write blogs that get read.*

—Scott Hanselman
VP Developer Community, Microsoft

index

RELATED MANNING TITLES

Skills of a Successful Software Engineer
by Fernando Doglio

ISBN 9781617299704
192 pages, $49.99
June 2022

The Creative Programmer
by Wouter Groeneveld
Foreword by Felienne Hermans

ISBN 9781633439054
232 pages, $49.99
April 2023

Street Coder
by Sedat Kapanoglu

ISBN 9781617298370
272 pages, $49.99
December 2021

Good Code, Bad Code
by Tom Long

ISBN 9781617298936
376 pages, $49.99
July 2021

For ordering information, go to www.manning.com